Alternative Dispute Resolution

ALTERNATIVE DISPUTE RESOLUTION

Melting the Lances and Dismounting the Steeds

Thomas E. Carbonneau

UNIVERSITY OF ILLINOIS PRESS
Urbana and Chicago

© 1989 by the Board of Trustees of the University of Illinois
Manufactured in the United States of America
C 5 4 3 2 1

This book is printed on acid-free paper.

Library of Congress Cataloging-in-Publication Data

Carbonneau, Thomas E.
   Alternative dispute resolution: Melting the lances and dismounting
the steeds / Thomas E. Carbonneau.
      p.   cm.
   Bibliography: p.
   Includes index.
   ISBN 0-252-01640-8 (alk. paper)
   1. Arbitration and award.   2. Mediation.   3. Dispute resolution
(Law).   I. Title.
K2400.C37   1989
347′.09—dc19
[342.79]   89-4703
                                                            CIP

This book is dedicated to the memory of my mother, Lucille C. Carbonneau.

Contents

Preface

This book is a product of the contemporary debate surrounding the modification of existing litigious practices and the revision of adjudicatory values. Much of its content is inspired by an intellectual dissatisfaction with the jesuitical methodology of law, the artificality of its concepts, and with the myopic orientation of American legal education. This book seeks to contribute to the formulation of a discipline surrounding the emerging field of alternative dispute resolution (ADR). To my knowledge, no other writing insists as emphatically upon a thorough analysis of the character of disputes and of the attendant and anticipated remedies. Nor do other writings look to long-term educational goals or draw upon the comparative and transnational experience to sustain a philosophy of nonadversarial dispute resolution in the domestic context. The distance achieved through a consideration of foreign law and legal systems and the unruly character of international conflicts generates new perspectives and builds a better bridge to the understanding of national problems and their solution.

The considerations that follow apply exclusively to civil proceedings and disputes. Although alternative mechanisms may be useful in the resolution of domestic public law conflicts, the value structure of that field requires a separate treatment of possible remedies and an independent evaluation of their potential. The essential thesis of the book is that individuals should look primarily within themselves and to their own human resources to confront and resolve private law conflicts. Legal adjudicatory institutions are paralyzed by the intricacies and sophistication of their own processes. The analytical rigor of legal reasoning and the complex formalism of legal procedure are inadequate substitutes for individual rationality, personal understanding, and mutual cooperation in the quest to gain the civil resolution of conflictual circumstances. Antihumanistic both in its principle and in its practice, the adversarial ethic works a subterfuge on society. It is deceitful not only as to its concern for individual interests, but also in its regard for legality and the integrity of substantive law. To establish a more truthful and humane societal dispute resolution ethic, remedial mechanisms should transcend the simple containment of the destructive human feelings that accompany conflict and avoid their exploitation. The adjudicatory framework should respond to and develop the full range of feelings and perceptions experienced by people in conflict. The goals of social order and stability must be achieved through educational programs and the cultivation of humanistic priorities in adjudication.

Too much of the current literature on ADR is constrained by limited objectives and by a narrow focus upon professional conduct and attitudes. In terms both of its practical design and of its revisionist theories, ADR needs to penetrate all levels of society if it is to compete effectively with the pervasive ideology of adversarial convictions. Simply touting the benefits of arbitration or mediation to a professional audience with vested economic interests is not enough—nor is the episodic use of summary jury trials or special masters in the federal judiciary. Advocates need to agree upon objectives and methods; the observations of critics and proponents must be heard throughout society. The social contract for adjudication must be founded upon a collective consensus about the true potential and disposition of the human personality when it confronts disagreement.

The vigorous pursuit of ADR goals, however, should not cloud the analyses of the alternative remedies and solutions. Substitute mechanisms must be understood on their own merits and in full view of their possibilities and limitations. Modifying the role of the courts and the social function of lawyering should not be lightly undertaken. Placing great expectations upon nonjudicial mechanisms and altered processes is unwise if not accompanied by a rekindling of values and a refashioning of the human spirit in the circumstances of dispute. This book further argues for the utility of interdisciplinary studies in assessing adjudicatory procedures and constructing substitute processes. It is only by understanding the function of legality from a wider perspective that a generic dispute resolution methodology and a viable societal dispute resolution ethic can be created.

Accordingly, recommendations are made for revising public and legal education and for informing remedial frameworks with a variety of professional expertise. The possibility of humanistic dispute resolution is explored with specific reference to the controversial adjudicatory circumstances of divorce and personal injury litigation. In both instances, adapted alternatives can remedy many of the deficiencies of the present process by guiding individuals to the use of their own rational abilities. Self-determination and an informed evaluation of personal needs and dispositions are the central features of privately instituted justice. External coercive judicial authority should be resorted to only when all else has failed, and then with reasonable dispatch in abbreviated proceedings.

This book owes much to a number of people and institutions. Time for research and writing was made available by Tulane University through a sabbatic leave. Additional financial support for research was provided by Dean John R. Kramer (Tulane Law School) and the Canadian Studies Faculty Grant Program. Dean Kinvin L. Wroth (University of Maine Law School) provided an invaluable opportunity to experiment with ideas and exchange views with colleagues. The general topic of the 1987 meeting of the Henri Capitant Association, "Truth and Law," provided much of the initial inspiration for the underlying theme of the book. I owe much to Richard B. Lillich, the late Henry P. de Vries, and Lillian Robinson for their mentorial direction. I am also indebted to Allison Burbank for her research assistance and to Helen Carbonneau, Stephanie Mitchell, and Armond McClain for the typing of the manuscript. Finally, Terry A. O'Neill made a substantial contribution to the written and conceptual quality of the work. I, of course, remain exclusively responsible for any errors, omissions, and other over- and undersights.

1 | From Malady to Truth in Legal Adjudication

The Current Pathology

The age-old complaints lodged against lawyers and the legal process have gained an amplified resonance in contemporary American society.[1] The common perception is that judges and lawyers, the procedural rigor of justice and substantive incantations of legality, lay juries and technical experts hurt more than they help. The recourse to legal actors and proceedings is costly, emotionally debilitating, and potentially counterproductive. In many respects, justice has become an empty facade; the august wisdom and high-minded discipline of the law merely create an appearance of dispensing what is right and just among parties in dispute. Although adjudication provides coercive finality to conflicts, the pathway to justice is dehumanizing and riddled with abusive interpretations of the truth.

A plaintive chorus of voices now inveighs against the deception of adversarial posturing and advocacy, the callous greed that seems to motivate legal representation, and the generally nightmarish quality of legal proceedings.[2] Integrity, truth, and the public good are dysfunctional concepts — whimpering truisms — in the framework for achieving justice. Succinctly stated, the legal means for protecting rights have become barriers to the most fundamental of legal rights — the effective redress of grievances. In operation, legal adjudication defeats its own underlying gravamen.[3]

Without referring to statistical appraisals, a number of telling examples illustrate the seriousness of the current discontent. With former Chief Justice Warren Burger, the United States Supreme Court criticized the professional ability and competence of attorneys.[4] This criticism also indicated an acute concern for the threat that the volume of litigation poses to the general availability of justice in American society.[5] Moreover, the Court impliedly questioned whether adversarial litigation remains a viable mechanism for resolving disputes. Using the

1925 and 1970 Federal Arbitration Acts as a foundation for its authority, the Court, for example, has become the champion of arbitration as a preferred remedial alternative to judicial adjudication in both domestic and international commercial and other matters.[6] The Court's most recent pronouncements in matters of arbitration, involving considerations of domestic federalism[7] and the public policy stature of antitrust laws,[8] reveal a reinforcement, rather than retrenchment or moderation, of its espousal of a larger, nonjudicial and nonlitigious dispute resolution ethic.

Divorce and personal injury litigation provide accounts that further demonstrate the deficiencies of judicial adjudication as a response to the societal need for dispute resolution. The outcome of contested divorce and child custody battles has promoted the view among family law lawyers, mental health professionals, and the lay public that the submission of such disputes to the warring ways of adversarial litigation is irrational.[9] An important number of states[10] have enacted legislation advancing mediation as a more salutary mechanism by which to deal with the allocation of parenting responsibilities and rights following a dissolution of marriage. In personal injury litigation, judicial activism combined with the availability of a civil jury trial have destabilized the decision-making calculus, introducing an untoward level of unpredictability and potential bias in determinations.[11] The use of prejudicial trial tactics and histrionic influences upon the jury are especially marked in medical malpractice and corporate enterprise liability cases. As a consequence, public confidence in the integrity of the legal adjudicatory framework is undermined, liability insurance—the glue that once bound the system together—is either unavailable or excessively expensive, and the commercialization of products and the rendition of professional services in society are imperilled.[12]

However impressionistic, the general criticism and supporting illustrations compel the consideration of dramatic, unsettling questions. Does the democratic ethos, as symbolized by the presence of a jury in civil proceedings, have any real place in the process for resolving private law disputes? Would the exclusive reference to legal expertise, knowledge, and experience, despite their elitist political connotations, provide for more predictable and principled adjudicatory results? Are the concepts of procedural due process and adversarial justice unworkable in contemporary American society? Do they represent an inappropriate integration of public law values and safeguards into the adjudication of private law rights? Should these concepts apply exclusively in the adjudication of constitutional and civil liberty claims?

The statement of these questions, however, implies another litany of queries advocating a contrary perception of the matter. For example, should considerations of mere efficiency, cost, and time prohibit the use of consecrated legal procedures to resolve private law grievances? Are private rights any less fundamental constitutionally than basic political freedoms? The facile compromise of ideals and convictions can be more dangerous than tolerating what appears to be a bottom-line, finality-oriented process for dispute resolution. The undoing of democratic and juridical values may be a costly cure for the perceived pathology in legal adjudicatory procedures. Given the extent of envisaged reforms, a healthy level of skepticism should inform the evaluation of accounts that describe, in both statistical and normative terms, the disabling of American society through litigation.

Moreover, if a problematic and litigious America does exist, lawyers and legal proceedings may not be to blame. They may, in fact, be victims of the displaced frustrations that arise inexorably from human conflict and controversy. In contested divorce or child custody actions, for instance, party dissatisfaction with the legal management of claims could be attributed to factors other than the operation of the legal system, such as disappointment over the failure of the marriage or over the inability to achieve a fantasized absolute victory in court. To complicate the causative analysis further, these factors, separable from the legal process, may act concurrently or may have a variegated impact in different cases. Moreover, in the ostensibly nonpolitical setting of judicial adjudication, activist judges and lay juries may give expression to a tacit mandate of general corporate accountability and social insurance in personal injury cases. It may be that such a stance has wide currency in society and cannot be given legislative endorsement because of the influence of special interest groups upon legislatures. Although judicial adjudication may appear far removed from the fulfillment of humanistic ideals, it has long functioned in the pragmatic universe of social reality, serving as the primary means of civilizing the clash of competing social and individual interests.[13]

Tempered by the statement of opposing perceptions, the disparagement of the legal process takes on a more ambiguous form. Still, the need to examine legal adjudication and its viability as a framework for dispute resolution remains. The current complaints at least warrant investigation of other mechanisms and experimentation with different modes and ethics of dispute resolution. What are the significant drawbacks of the legal approach to conflict resolution? Do they surface in all areas of dispute resolution? Can an amended adjudicatory framework, supplemented or replaced by other devices, generate a more effective, responsive, and fairer process?

The consideration of alternative dispute resolution (ADR) mechanisms has in fact become extremely popular in legal and other professional literatures.[14] Inspired to some extent by the success of labor and commercial arbitration,[15] ADR proponents espouse a larger and less traditional view of lawyering skills, criticize the physical and financial barriers to justice, and focus attention upon the drawbacks of the judicial process—the seemingly needless complication of issues, the unidimensional character of adversarial representation, the excessive cost and interminable delays.[16] In its most ambitious form, the ADR vision is of a complete restructuring of the adjudicatory framework and a reeducation not only of lawyers and other professionals, but also of the general public about the significance of and solution to private law disputes.

Predictably, the stated objectives and scope of the ADR initiative have generated distrust and criticism from a number of sectors. Questions have been raised regarding the qualifications and licensure of mediators;[17] according to some, arbitral awards constitute objectionable "pie-splitting" results;[18] also, allowing the arbitrability of such claims as those involving securities brokers or personal injury disputes may jeopardize the objectives of consumer protection legislation.[19] Immixing lawyers into the process of arbitral adjudication can seriously compromise the flexible adjudicatory mission of the arbitral framework, and having lawyers participate in mediation efforts raises complex, perhaps intractable, ethical questions.[20] In addition, the critics of alternative dispute resolution mechanisms have expressed concern regarding the fate of substantive law, the public adjudicatory mandate of the courts, and the integrity of legal rights in nonjudicial settings.[21] What types of alternative remedies are available? Which professional or lay groups will service them? What relationship, if any, should be instituted among these mechanisms and legislative and judicial institutions? How are both individual and social interests to be represented and accounted for in such proceedings?

Finally, recent experimentation with arbitration in medical malpractice matters[22] teaches that alternative adjudicatory techniques cannot be indiscriminately transposed into areas of dispute without a keen sense of the specialty of the particular disputes and of the remedies. Although mediation and court-annexed arbitration have an evident remedial potential for some disputes, the reach of these mechanisms and the exact extent of their implementation warrant further refinement.[23]

The questions that ADR raises about legal adjudication and those that are raised about ADR can be elucidated, at least initially, by arriving at an operative account of the social purpose and objectives of adjudication. What are the ends of adjudication? Which values does it seek to foster and achieve? How does the legal approach to and legal method of dispute resolution promote the social mission of adjudication?

A Theory of Adjudicatory Truth

The provision of a mechanism for redressing grievances in society is, from a Hobbesian perspective, a means of guaranteeing the minimal order and stability necessary to viable social organization. From a more normative but equally compelling vantage point, the legitimacy of adjudicatory determinations is not only a factor of coercion and necessity, but also a product of the view that such resolutions, although coercively imposed and necessary, are fair. The societal consensus that the adjudicatory process achieves fairness of result proceeds from a sense that equal treatment is at the heart of the administration of justice. Whatever their imperfections, procedures are universally applicable to plaintiffs and defendants, individuals and corporate entities. Unwarranted discriminatory treatment would undermine society's acceptance of—and support for—the process, signalling its potential downfall. Procedural neutrality and impartiality are indispensable to adjudicatory legitimacy; without them, the process would be unable to exercise coercive dispute resolution authority for the public good.

The process of legal adjudication, however, has both a procedural and a substantive component. Fairness of administrative implementation, so vital to the viability of the legal process, must be accompanied by similar even-handedness about the application of substantive rules of law. Having ascertained the facts, the legal process resolves the dispute at hand in accordance with the patterns of decision that applied in prior cases. As in previous litigation, the merits are adjudged ac-

| 5

cording to received standards established by legal experts, the community, or both. Moreover, these standards will continue to prevail in subsequent proceedings. Society demands and wants to believe that the legal adjudication of disputes is done on the basis of a reasonably accurate knowledge of the litigious circumstances and of the applicable rules of law.

A form of truth-seeking, therefore, enters into the rationale for—and operation of—adjudicatory mechanisms. Truth and fairness work hand in hand;[24] they are the founding elements of a socially valid and morally acceptable process of legal adjudication. As a purveyor of truth in human relations and social institutions, the legal process bears a special, albeit ambivalent, kinship to the literary quest for truth.[25] Like novelists and poets, legal theorists yearn to infuse reality with enlightened principles, a transcendent idea of the truth of legality that yields a social order in which the values of justice, moral goodness, and equity are triumphant.[26] Like poems, short stories, and novels, laws, legislation, and court decisions can be seen as vehicles for having what is right and just, the Absolutely True, triumph over the iniquity and infamy of evil.

Although nourishing to the soul, speculative metaphysical visions of the Just Truth are, however, too subjective and volatile to act as a generalized basis for establishing legal veracity in society. They present too broad a ground for disagreement and debate. Looking for The Truth could only hinder the practical and collective functioning of the process. Legal adjudication does not strive to achieve Absolute Truth, but rather a version of humanly ascertainable truth that promotes social order. Within the constraints of the political dynamics of society, legality can only achieve a process version of truth; legal truthfulness is a factor of the system's objective to be socially effective and workable. Finally, the material interests that are the usual subject matter of private law litigation support the requirement that adjudicatory truth be comprised of basic factual accuracy combined with reasonable substantive predictability and fair and equal treatment.

No matter how mundane, truth, then, has intrinsic value for the process of legal adjudication. It is also a goal of that process because substantive and factual accuracy promote and maintain the collective impression of fairness. Analytically sound decisions engender professional adherence, thereby avoiding a basis for generating public disfavor. Factually and substantively accurate, like procedurally neutral, determinations foster individual and public compliance. Indeed, it might be argued, albeit by extremists, that the adjudicatory process need only yield an appearance or support a collective impression of accuracy, objectivity, and neutrality to remain functionally viable. Adherence and recourse to the adjudicatory process merely because it appears to be fair, however, might eventually imperil the legitimacy of the process. The truth propounded would be at the outer boundary of moral acceptability. The current use of discovery techniques in legal adjudication illustrates the point.

Evidence-gathering devices are fair in the sense that they are available to both parties in a lawsuit.[27] These procedures are intended to enable disputing parties to develop a factual record that is sufficiently complete to allow for the application of legal rules. In this sense, discovery procedures promote legal truthfulness. An accurate knowledge of the material elements of the controversy is a prerequisite for establishing the legal truth of the matter. Nevertheless, experience with actual litigation—for example, the history of the lawsuits brought against cigarette manufacturers[28]—shows that, in practice, discovery techniques do not function as truth-seeking instruments. Rather, they are used as tactical devices to wear down the opposition and to make it simply too expensive to arrive at a ruling on the merits. Protracted evidence-gathering, deployed ostensibly in the name of juridical due process, becomes—in the context of adversarial adjudication—a means by which the financially advantaged party can force a settlement or withdrawal of a lawsuit. Evidence-gathering then is a means of avoiding a determination of what is legally truthful in the circumstances. Ultimately, the truth of legality is reduced to, or rather eliminated by, purely process considerations that have no anchor whatsoever in an epistemological mission.

Although legal adjudication cannot provide society with an absolute form of truthfulness, the procedures for integrating the principles of legality into the social fabric should not forsake all reference to the content of substantive legal rules (no matter how analytically deficient some of those rules may be). Allowing the implementing framework to develop an independent operation, motivated by an opposite dynamic, subverts the essential truth of law. At the very least, the adjudicatory process should not be duplicitous in its design, allowing the proffer of a merits resolution and of parity among litigating parties to be foiled by so-called practical procedural realities. In effect, this dichotomy between theory and practice can amount to a breach of adjudication's systemic promise and undo its social legitimacy.

A Larger Vision of Adjudication

A fully functional adjudicatory process should, moreover, strive to accomplish ends that go beyond achieving finality in dispute resolution and that transcend the rendering of adjudicatory outcomes that have sufficient legal truthfulness to gain general societal acceptance. Adjudication's greater truth and the legal system's core responsibility as a social process reside in an essential pedagogical mission. The adjudicatory process should impart upon disputing parties an understanding of the origin and development of their conflict and provide them with an opportunity to find how to achieve both a collectively and individually satisfying resolution. It should also give participants a sense of how to avoid those and other conflicts in the future.

Individuals involved in private law controversies would then cease to feel powerless in the face of disputes. They would no longer see the legal process as a quasi-magical structure invested with far-reaching, nearly deified authority. By teaching reliance upon individual initiative and accountability, the adjudicatory process could develop a new dispute resolution ethic in society as a whole, one founded upon a sense of individual self-confidence and personal responsibility. Assisted by legal and nonlegal actors, the disputing parties could define their own dispute resolution priorities, set their own goals, and bring their own creativity and imagination to bear upon the fashioning of a solution to their controversy. Such a dispute resolution framework should not only enhance the level and quality of compliance with outcomes, but also foster a generalized commitment to a belief in self-empowering rationality. The primary design of the adjudicatory process then would be to house, channel, and guide the dispute resolution initiative of disputing parties. It would invoke its coercive authority and reference to external truth only when the recourse to a personal inner truth fails.

Certainly, the utopian overtones of this more comprehensive vision of the adjudicatory process may make its realization difficult. To some extent, the vision is founded upon a perhaps wishful desire to have the general objectives of society defined by initial reference not to collective interests, but to individual needs that thereafter inform the collective disposition. Although an opposite procedure tends — in varying degrees—to typify most forms of social and political organization, the notion that the quality of the whole is never better than that of its parts should support redirecting the orientation of the adjudicatory process to individuals and developing its educative potential.

Given the dimensions of the possible change, a gradual form of experimentation should be undertaken to test the viability of the new dispute resolution ethic in private law controversies. However limited initially, the incorporation of a self-empowering ethic into the adjudicatory framework should improve the quality of outcomes and generate greater satisfaction with adjudicatory procedures. One of the major drawbacks of the current system is that litigants have only a peripheral involvement in the process. They are nearly totally dependent upon legal professionals for both a statement and the resolution of their conflict. Moreover, the adjudicatory framework's coercive imposition of an external solution not only ignores the parties' inward upheaval and the emotions generated by the conflict, but also leads the parties to misperceive and misunderstand the goals of dispute resolution.[29] The operation of the adjudicatory process can create expectations in the parties that are unrealistic and unworkable.

For instance, lacing the emotional turmoil to which disputes give rise with the firm resolve of affording legal protection to rights sometimes creates the erroneous impression that all wrongs can and should be righted. It induces the view that the legal system and its actors contain, somewhere in mystical procedural meanderings and the maze of legal doctrine, a resolution for the dispute that is so truthful that it corresponds perfectly to the individual's perception of justice in the circumstances. When lives are disrupted by personal injury or divorce, the call to litigation is, to some extent, a means of vindicating objective rights, but it is also an instrument for expressing anger and frustration for the intrusion upon one's person and life. In emotional terms, the call to litigation represents a cry for vengeance and vindication; it satisfies, at least partially, the desire for an immediate rectification of the situation. Bringing a legal action symbolizes a stance that the wrong done should be righted by public exposure and acknowledgment of the misdeed and the grievances redressed by a declaration of the full truth from a higher, specially annointed source.

Although the reality of litigation often attenuates such expectations, its tempering effect takes hold progressively over the course of the trial procedures and usually comes too late to rectify fully the misimpressions. More important, the experience of litigation still fails to teach the ultimate lessons of dispute resolution. Not all of life's injustices and misfortunes can or should be righted through coercive adjudicatory means. Accidents do happen; individual lives sometimes are afflicted with unavoidable difficulties and loss. As a consequence, the call to litigation should not always be heeded, nor absolute emotions always indulged. The legal truth and resolution of a particular situation may well be impossible or too costly to discover. Rather than project the possibility of absolute vindication, the legal system should enable individuals to exercise their judgment in circumstances of dispute, encouraging them to initiate and participate in a process that can lead to effective compromise. An acceptable statement of the truth of a given situation might be established through other than legal action. Currently, in some areas of litigation (most notably in personal injury cases),[30] the legal process itself avoids the recourse to adjudicatory determinations to achieve finality. In the vast majority of actions that are brought, after greater or lesser episodes of litigious posturing, out-of-court settlement is the preferred remedy. The duty of a fully functional, all-encompassing adjudicatory process should be to acquaint disputing parties with the variety of available remedial options and the consequences of pursuing a single pathway to justice and truth in their particular circumstances.

In its most advanced form, adjudication should teach the parties that a cooperative form of self-reliance provides the best access to justice, and that the veracity of a disputed situation is best established through the individual inward truth that can be developed by a rational approach to interpersonal conflict. In a responsible society, reliance upon the mystery and coercion of legal procedures should yield to a participatory and self-directed form of justice in private law controversies. For example, the dilemma that currently afflicts personal injury litigation cannot be effectively resolved simply by imposing a legislative solution from on high. Although the adjudicatory determinations of the existing process threaten to prejudice or undermine the rendition of necessary social services,[31] the enactment of ceilings on recovery, statutes of repose, and privity requirements for some malpractice suits[32] can substantially impair the interests of justice by creating a new, equally pathological imbalance among the competing interests. The essential problem does not so much reside in the process and its structures as in the attitudes and assumptions that underlie them.

Casting the dialogue of litigation in terms of a battle for victory between diametrically opposed interests only enhances the irrational emotional expectations associated with adjudication;[33] the dynamics of the process inevitably lead to results that are only half-truths. The more effective solution to the present dilemma is to redefine the social role of adjudication and the responsibility of disputing parties within that process. Institutional truth will always be dissatisfying, whether voluntarily accepted or coercively imposed, so long as litigants are not made to rely and act upon their understanding of the conflict and the concept of truth that emerges from their participation in achieving a solution.

The basic perimeters of the debate having been demarcated, and a concept of both a workable and a more ideal form of truth in adjudication advanced, the inquiry now turns to an analysis of the truth-seeking methodologies that are practiced in various legal traditions and systems. Comparing the American legal system's processing of private law claims with its counterpart in other national legal systems may generate ideas about appropriate borrowings or may provide insights into how current or longstanding deficiencies might be remedied or, yet again, may establish the essential rectitude of the current system within existing realities. The principal concern of the next chapter centers upon the question of how effectively various legal methodologies achieve a comprehensive sense of truthfulness in dispute resolution settings and upon the question that logically follows of whether they should remain the primary or exclusive instruments by which to address private law claims.

NOTES

1. "We are all suffering a progressively debilitating disease—the disease of hyperlexis, too much litigation." (Sen. McConnell, 132 Cong. Rec. S1009, daily ed. Feb. 5, 1986). "Across the country, people are suing one another with abandon; courts are clogged with litigation; lawyers are burdening the populace with legal bills." Anderson, *U.S. Has Become a*

Nation of Lawsuits, Wash. Post, Jan. 25, 1985, at B8, col. 5. "Everybody in the USA suddenly seems to want to sue anybody with liability coverage. The explosion of litigation has choked court dockets. And too-few lawyers tell potential clients that some cases are a waste of time." *Hold Down Awards to Ease the Crisis,* USA Today, June 6, 1986, at 12A, col. 1. Foregoing sources cited in: Galanter, *The Day After the Litigation Explosion,* 46 MARYLAND L. REV. 3, 3-4 (1986).

According to a recent Lou Harris poll sponsored by the Aetna Life and Casualty Insurance Co., "about half of the American public believes either that the civil justice system needs to be rebuilt completely because so much is wrong with it (14%) or that it has some major problems which can only be corrected through fundamental changes (34%)." The other half (43%), however, believes that the tort system could be corrected with only minor changes. The poll also showed that a majority of Americans support tort reform measures: 71% favor a repeal of joint and several liability, 78% favor limits on punitive damages, and 67% favor the elimination of the collateral source rule. See 1 MEALEY'S LITIG. REPS. NAT'L TORT REF. 1647 (Mar. 1987).

For an earlier view of the deficiencies of adversarial litigation, see Pound, *The Causes of Popular Dissatisfaction with the Administration of Justice,* 40 AM. L. REV. 729 (1906). Pound described common law litigation involving contentious procedure as a game whose effect "is not only to irritate parties, witnesses and jurors, in particular cases, but to give to the whole community a false notion of the purpose and end of law" (Id. at 738-39).

See also Miller, *The Adversary System: Dinosaur or Phoenix,* 69 MINN. L. REV. 1 (1984):

> Having survived the preliminary motions, it is just a hop-skip-and-a-jump into the quicksand of discovery, a debilitating and often interminable process. This pretrial structure permits artful attorneys to hide the ball and keep alive hopeless claims, as well as defenses, for a much longer time than was possible under the more arduous, discarded procedural systems of the past. In many ways, contemporary federal litigation is analogous to the dance marathon contests of yesteryear. The object of the exercise is to select a partner from across the "v," get out on the dance floor, hang on to one's client, and then drift aimlessly and endlessly to the litigation music for as long as possible, hoping that everyone else will collapse from exhaustion.

Id. at 9.

On litigation practices in America and the need to consider alternatives to the present process:

> Important and as effective as the adversary system can be, it is not without a deliterious side. It can be a hugely inefficient means

of uncovering facts; its relentless formalities and ceaseless opportunities for splitting hairs are time consuming and expensive. It is not available therefore to everyone, and if it is the only system for obtaining redress then justice cannot be done. For that reason, it may mislead us as a society into supposing that its availability is a guarantee of safety. Litigation is not a panacea; social policies are not necessarily carried out merely because there is an avenue open to some. . . .

Moreover, like every other human system, litigation is subject to regular abuse. The limitations of semantics, the fallibility of memory, the will to prevaricate, all contribute to unpredictability. The outcome is never certain, and litigation is therefore frequently an exercise in anguish and futility. As a mechanism to instill in people a fiduciary regard for others, it can be effective. But for all that it does not often treat well those who are ensnared in it. Litigation, and especially the trial itself, can be unremittingly harsh. Lawyers are often adversaries not only of each other but of their clients; some kinds of litigation are prolonged (and even initiated) solely to ensure the lawyers sufficient billable hours to earn a decent or even a handsome living. The process can be psychologically harmful, hurting self-esteem as well as pocketbook. Other modes of resolving disputes and solving problems bear scrutiny.

J. LIEBERMAN, THE LITIGIOUS SOCIETY 171 (1983). See also Appendix A (ch. 1) infra.

2. On the adversarial system of adjudication, see J. FRANK, COURTS ON TRIAL 80-142 (1949); S. LANDSMAN, THE ADVERSARY SYSTEM: A DESCRIPTION AND DEFENSE (1984) (reviewed in 21 CAL. W. L. REV. 239 [1984]; 20 TRIAL 84 [1984]; 84 MICH. L. REV. 1011 [1986]); A. STRICK, INJUSTICE FOR ALL (1977). See also Appendix B (ch. 1) infra.

3. See, for example, ch. 5, infra, text at note 19 and accompanying text (Coogler's description of the adversarial process of divorce). It is quite clear that the adversarial adjudication of divorce disputes is counterproductive and inappropriate:

If one were to set out to design a system poorly adapted to the resolution of family conflict or for safeguarding the children, one would, with a little luck, invent the adversarial system presided over by a perplexed, frustrated judge whose background in law and politics have no conceivable bearing on the issues before him — or her.

Keynote speech by Frank Sander, ABA National Conference on Alternative Means of Dispute Resolution (June 1982) (quoting J. Wallerstein) (American Bar Assoc. transcription at 22), reprinted in Comment, *The Best Interest of the Divorcing Family — Mediation not Litigation,* 29 LOY. L. REV. 55, 57 (1983).

Consumers also can face considerable frustration in pursuing their claims.

Upon discovery of a material defect, they can be faced with a recalcitrant (perhaps dishonest) seller who denies the veracity of the allegations, pursues discovery at a snail's pace, or engages in a dissembling posture of settlement. A claim of $10,000 to $60,000 is too much for small claims court and not really big enough to litigate. During this period, the consumer faces the costs of legal fees and the aggravation of legal proceedings. At the end of the process, the consumer is left (in all likelihood) with a meager settlement and the distinct impression that procedural justice can service and be significantly abused by dishonest motives. In this regard, Alschuler lucidly notes in a related vein that,

> judges, court administrators, rulemakers, and others should abandon their current emphasis on hammered settlements and other shortcuts and renew our society's commitment to the provision of basic adjudicative services.
>
> In a more civilized society, the extensive rationing of adjudication by price and queue would not assure wrongdoers that they always could "settle" and profit from their wrongs. In this society, a right would be something that one gets, not merely something that one has. People would know that they could take their disputes to the courts and that the courts would resolve them. With this assurance, people might be less likely to take their disputes to the streets or to the subways.

Alschuler, *Mediation with a Mugger,* Appendix A (ch. 1), at 1859.

4. See, for example, Burger, *Today's Challenge: Improving the Administration of Justice,* 55 N.Y. ST. B.J. 7 (1983); address by Chief Justice Burger, ABA Midyear Meeting (Jan. 24, 1982), reprinted in 68 A.B.A. J. 274 (1982). See also *Chief Justice Burger's State of the Judiciary Address,* 109 N.Y.L.J. at 1, col. 4 (Feb. 4, 1982); *Time to Review Our Reliance on Adversary System: Chief Justice Faults Lawyers for Frivolous Suits, Discovery Abuse* (address by Chief Justice Warren Burger at A.B.A. Midyear Meeting, Las Vagas, Feb. 1984), L.A. Daily J., Feb. 15, 1984, at 4, col. 3.

5. See *Time to Review Our Reliance on Adversary System,* note 4 supra.

6. See ch. 4 infra.

7. See id. (the trilogy cases: Byrd, Keating, and Moses Cone; McMahon v. Shearson/American Express, Inc.; and Perry v. Thomas).

8. See id. (the Mitsubishi case).

9. See ch. 5 infra.

10. The following table lists (as of 1987) the states that have endorsed alternative dispute resolution to some extent and the types of programs they either have instituted or are contemplating:

TABLE 1. State Statutes Providing for Alternative Dispute Resolution

	Mediation			Conciliation		
	Mandatory, Children Involved	Court's Disc.	Only Certain Counties	Under Investigation*	Mandatory	Disc.
Alaska		b				
Arizona			a			e
California	a					e
Colorado	a					f
Connecticut		b				f
Delaware	a					
Florida			a			e
Illinois						f
Indiana				x		f
Iowa						e
Kansas						e
Kentucky						f
Louisiana		a				
Maine	b					
Maryland		c				f
Michigan				x		e
Minnesota		a				
Montana						f
New Hampshire				x		f
New York			b			
N. Dakota						f
Ohio						f
Oregon			d			
Pennsylvania		b				
S. Carolina					f	
Texas				x		f
Utah				x		f
Vermont				x		
Washington			d			
Wisconsin						e

* = not a comprehensive list
a = child custody, support, visitation
b = all issues when children involved, including property
c = property only, no custody issues
d = county option, rules vary
e = statute generally observed
f = statute on books but largely ignored

11. See ch. 6 infra.
12. See id.

13. See, for example, S. LANDSMAN, THE ADVERSARY SYSTEM, note 2 supra.

14. The current literature on alternative dispute resolution has, quite literally, exploded to unmanageable proportions. "The search for alternative methods of resolving disputes has burgeoned to 'a movement.'" Davidson & Ray, *Preface,* ALTERNATIVE MEANS OF FAMILY DISPUTE RESOLUTION (H. Davidson, L. Ray, & R. Horowitz eds. 1982). See Appendix C (ch. 1) infra.

15. See my article *A Consideration of Alternatives to Divorce Litigation,* [1986] ILL. L. REV. 601, 606-07, n.7 (1986).

16. See id. at 606-07, 612-15.

17. For a discussion of professional responsibility issues in divorce mediation, see J. FOLBERG & A. TAYLOR, MEDIATION: A COMPREHENSIVE GUIDE TO RESOLVING CONFLICTS WITHOUT LITIGATION 244-50 (1984); Bishop, *The Standards of Practice for Family Mediators: An Individual Interpretation and Comments,* 17 FAM. L.Q. 461 (1984); Crouch, *The Dark Side Is Still Unexplored,* 4 FAMILY ADVOCATE 27 (1982); Gaughan, *Taking a Fresh Look at Divorce Mediation,* 17 TRIAL 39 (1981); J. LEMMON, ed., ETHICS, STANDARDS AND PROFESSIONAL CHALLENGES, 4 MEDIATION Q. 1-96 (1984); Riskin, *Toward New Standards for the Neutral Lawyer in Mediation,* 26 ARIZ. L. REV. 329 (1984); Silberman, *Professional Responsibility Problems of Divorce Mediation,* 16 FAM. L.Q. 107 (1982); *Standards of Practice for Family Mediators,* 17 FAM. L.Q. 455 (1984); Note, *Family Law — Attorney Mediation of Marital Disputes and Conflict of Interest Considerations,* 60 N.C. L. REV. 171 (1981); Note, *Protecting Confidentiality in Mediation,* 98 HARV. L. REV. 441 (1984).

18. Practicing attorneys often voice this criticism of arbitration. To some extent (probably a considerable one), this view reflects their adversarial training and experience. It implies that there always is a "right" answer to controversies and that one side should always triumph over the other. Brought to its logical conclusion, the criticism implies that the only true adjudicatory processes are those that do not reach compromissory results.

In this regard, it is also worth noting that adversarial adjudication is essentially a homeopathic process. When faced with the disease of conflict, the legal system proposes a treatment in the form of further conflict that takes place in the setting of organized rules. Although the treatment does achieve a desired result—the external finality of conflict, it can hardly be said to provide a cure for the underlying illness. This purely symptomatic approach to dispute resolution could itself become completely ineffective if the underlying disease is not addressed forthrightly.

Moreover, the more adversarial the posturing on one side, the more the other side will feel obliged to counter with its own attack. This phenomenon of mutual aggression is not limited to divorce litigation. According to Alberti and Emmons, in ordinary human relations, "direct aggressive attack provokes additional aggression, both in the attacker and in the subject." R. ALBERTI & M. EMMONS, YOUR PERFECT RIGHT 110 (6th ed. 1984) (citing Berkowitz, *The Concept of Aggressive Drive: Some Additional Considerations,* in 2 ADVANCES IN EXPERIMENTAL SOCIAL PSYCHOLOGY [L. Berkowitz ed. 1965]; L. BERKOWITZ, ROOTS OF AGGRESSION: A RE-EXAMINATION OF THE FRUSTRATION-AGGRESSION HYPOTHESIS [1969].

Merely expressing anger, releasing steam as it were, is insufficient to gain relief and begin a resolution of problems:

> Recent research has shown the popular concept of anger as a "steam kettle" to be false. Many people have believed that by *expressing* one's anger, the anger would go away and prevent the problems associated with "building up inside." We now know that anger expression is only the beginning.
>
> It has been discovered recently that *emotional relief from anger comes only when expression is accompanied by some resolution of the problem which caused the anger.* Getting the feelings out — even in appropriately assertive ways — only "sets the stage." Working out the conflict with the other person, or sometimes within oneself [*sic*], is the all-important, follow-up step which makes the difference.
>
> The evidence also shows us that the lack of such coping or resolution action may actually increase anger whether it has been expressed or not. . . .

R. ALBERTI & M. EMMONS, supra, at 112 (emphasis in the original). Inasmuch as litigants do not engage in "resolution action" when they leave it to a judge to resolve their disputes, it may be that a healing process occurs despite — and not as a result of — the court system.

19. See (personal injury claims) Terry, *The Technical and Conceptual Flaws of Medical Malpractice Arbitration,* 30 ST. LOUIS U. L. J. 561 (1986); (securities claims against brokers) McMahon v. Shearson/American Express, Inc., 788 F.2d 94 (1986), cert. granted 107 S.Ct. 60 (1986), ruling at 107 S.Ct. 2337 (1987). See also, *Plaintiffs Going for Broke(r),* ABA J. 18-19 (May 1, 1987).

20. See text at note 17 supra and accompanying text.

21. See Appendix A (ch. 1) infra (but see citations to Abel, Galanter, Delgado, and Fiss).

22. See, for example, Bassis, *Arbitration of Medical Malpractice Disputes,* [1979] INS. L.J. 260 (1979); DeGiacomo & Wyman, *Medical Malpractice Tribunals, Part I: Practice and Procedure,* [1977] MASS. L. REV. 101 (1977); Nocas, *Arbitration of Medical Malpractice Claims,* 13 FORUM 254 (1977-78); Sakayan, *Arbitration and Screening Panels: Recent Experience*

and Trends, 17 FORUM 682 (1981-82); Terry, *The Technical and Conceptual Flaws of Medical Malpractice Arbitration,* note 19 supra.

23. Although the criticism of the judicial process may be well-founded, the analysis must extend beyond an examination of the law and lawyers. Advancing alternative remedies as panaceas offers little guidance on essential questions such as gauging the expectations and needs of society and of individuals about dispute resolution and demarcating the boundaries of the public interest and individual accountability when conflicts arise.

Initially, the very utility of alternative mechanisms must be examined. Does society want to abandon court litigation as its principal dispute resolution process, especially where personal rights and family concerns are involved? What are the real shortcomings of the judicial adjudication of private law disputes? Why do these deficiencies exist? By what standards and according to what values should the court process be evaluated? Should speed, efficiency, alleged expertise, and financial economy be predominant factors of analysis? What about considerations of fairness? Can the would-be troublesome aspect of the adversarial process be identified readily and does it amount to a significant obstacle to effective dispute resolution? Will the alternative mechanisms respond appropriately to these deficiencies or merely act as barriers to litigation, either deterring or postponing recourse to the judicial process?

For example, with compulsory, nonbinding arbitration, the award cannot be enforced unless both parties acquiesce to it. Such an alternative mechanism is meant usually to act as a deterrent to judicial adjudication; its objective is to reduce the recourse to courts and to free court dockets by blocking access. With compulsory, binding arbitration, the award cannot be challenged except on narrow grounds. Both types of alternative mechanisms, where successful, can abridge normally applicable rights to have recourse to the courts without providing adequately for fairness and finality.

Although alternative mechanisms have fared well in specialized fields, for example, arbitration in the commercial and labor law areas, where they have succeeded they have been applied to well-defined, basically singular disputes. The evident limitations of this prior experience generate some gnawing questions about how comprehensively alternative processes can be administered. Will established alternative mechanisms respond to other disputes with similar effectiveness? If not, can the usual mechanisms be modified to create an appropriate remedial structure?

Contemplating alternative dispute resolution processes also touches upon larger systemic concerns. For example, when applied to new dispute areas, can traditional or adapted mechanisms properly safeguard the public interest and protect individual legal rights? What reach will be attributed to public policy considerations in terms of the submissibility of disputes to alternative procedures? Should alternative processes be binding or non-binding, compulsory or consensual? Would a mandatory and binding alternative mechanism raise constitutional due process and equal protection problems? What specific relationship should apply between the alternative mechanisms and the judicial system—should the courts be empowered to supervise the procedure, intervene on matters of substance, or review the outcome in de novo fashion?

A pragmatic identification of the failings of the judicial process can provide useful insight as to where and what remedial needs exist. Constructive proposals for change must appraise societal needs accurately and be vigilant of justice considerations. They must reflect a studied view of disputes (their origin and genesis, anatomy and content) and of the feasibility of alternative mechanisms in different contexts, and they must be mindful of the possible need to modify existing alternative mechanisms to accommodate the special character of disputes.

24. For a discussion of the concept of truth, see, for example, M. DEVITT, REALISM AND TRUTH (1984); Haecker, *A Theory of Historical Truth*, 13 PHIL. TOPICS 267 (1985); Laffey, *Faces of Truth and the Sociology of Knowledge: John Stuart Mill and Karl Mannheim*, 20 MILL NEWS 2 (1985); Price, *The Objectivity of Mystical Truth Claims*, 49 THOMIST 81 (1985); Rescher, *Truth as Ideal Coherence*, 38 REV. METAPHY. 795 (1985); Sadurski, *Social Justice and Legal Justice*, 3 LAW PHIL. 329 (1984); Stefanov, *Formal Truth and Objective Truth*, 13 BULL. SECT. LOG. 154 (1984); Tuomela, *Truth and Best Explanation*, 22 ERKENNTNIS 271 (1985); Webster, *Liberty and Justice for All: Keeping the Scales in Balance*, in THE SEARCH FOR JUSTICE 24 (W. Taitte ed. 1983).

On the concept of fairness, see, for example, Newman, *Rethinking Fairness: Perspectives on the Litigation Process*, 94 YALE L. J. 1643 (1985):

> For decades critics of the litigation system have bemoaned the delays and costs of courtroom encounters while working mightily to refine the system in ways that make it even slower and more expensive. This paradoxical approach reflects the strengths and weaknesses of legal training. Skillful in analysis and advocacy, lawyers have recognized those aspects of trial procedure that can be changed to increase the likelihood of achieving better results and then engrafted well-intentioned changes onto an already complex system. At the same time, lawyers' preoccupation with results and their inadequate appreciation of the need to evaluate the system in which they function cause them to ignore the adverse consequences of the litigation process they have constructed. They know that the system is slow and costly. But they fail to recognize that the solutions they have developed over the years are a large part of the problem.

The paradox will continue until we realize that constructive change requires not simply adjustments in what we do in the courtroom but fundamental rethinking about what we are trying to accomplish there. In my judgment such rethinking should begin with the concept that underlies so much of our procedural and substantive law—the concept of fairness. My premise is that the way we think about fairness, and not any specific result of our thinking, is a root cause of many of the undesirable aspects of our modern process of litigation. Our narrow emphasis on perfecting results in the case at hand stems directly from our narrow perception of fairness. A broadened concept of fairness—one that includes fairness not only toward litigants in an individual case but also to all who use or wish to use the litigation system and to all who are affected by it—can lead to changes that directly confront the challenges of delay and expense. Rethinking the concept of fairness can produce a litigation system that broadly achieves fairness.

Id. at 1643-44.

25. The poet's quest to transpose universal truths about human experience through poetry is a well-established part of literary theory. See *Les Correspondances* by Charles Baudelaire in LES FLEURS DU MAL (1857). For an extensive bibliography on Baudelaire, see N. JOUVE, BAUDELAIRE 323 (1980). On law and literature generally, see *Symposium: Law and Literature,* 32 RUTGERS L. REV. 603 (1979); *Symposium, Law and Literature,* 60 TEX. L. REV. 373 (1982). See also R. WEISBERG, THE FAILURE OF THE WORD: THE PROTAGONIST AS LAWYER IN MODERN FICTION (1984), reviewed in 84 MICH. L. REV. 974 (1986).

26. See, for example, O. BROWN, NATURAL RECTITUDE AND DIVINE LAW IN AQUINAS: AN APPROACH TO AN INTEGRAL INTERPRETATION OF THE THOMISTIC DOCTRINE OF LAWS (1981).

27. The use of interrogatories, depositions, and requests for production of evidence and documents occupies a massive amount of time in litigation practice. Attorneys need usually at least one day to prepare for depositions, and the actual deposition may take another day of professional time. It is not uncommon for a case to involve as many as twenty depositions, including witnesses and experts. Complex interrogatories, of a contentious nature, usually accompany such cases. Ordinarily, judges are reluctant to cut down upon burdensome discovery for reasons either of due process or settlement strategy—making burdensome discovery the rule rather than the exception. This practice, in conjunction with law firm economics, has the effect of pricing most disputes out of the range of the legal system. See generally, J. FRIEDENTHAL, M. KANE, & A. MILLER, CIVIL PROCEDURE (1985); M. GREEN, BASIC CIVIL PROCEDURE (1972); G. HAZARD, JR. & F. JAMES, CIVIL PROCEDURE (1985).

28. See, for example, Gardner, *Cigarette Dependency and Civil Liability: A Modest Proposal,* 53 S. CAL. L. REV. 1423 (1980); James, *The Untoward Effects of Cigarettes and Drugs: Some Reflections on Enterprise Liability,* 54 CALIF. L. REV. 1550 (1966); Note, *Federal Preemption of Cigarette Products Liability Claims Creates a Need for Congressional Action,* 6 REV. LITIGATION 339 (1987); Note, *Liability of Cigarette Manufacturers for Smoking Induced Illnesses and Deaths,* 18 RUTGERS L. J. 165 (1986); Siliciano, *Corporate Behavior and the Social Efficiency of Tort Law,* 85 U. MICH. L. REV. 1820 (1987). See also Albright v. R.J. Reynolds Tobacco Co., 350 F.Supp. 341 (W.D. Pa. 1972), aff'd mem., 485 F.2d 678 (3d Cir. 1973), cert. denied 416 U.S. 951 (1974) (court never reached merits because plaintiff received payment for lung cancer from municipality in settling a prior auto accident suit against municipality); Green v. American Tobacco, 304 F.2d 70 (5th Cir. 1962), question certified on rehearing 154 So.2d 169 (Fla.), rev'd and remanded 325 F.2d 673 (5th Cir. 1963), rev'd and remanded on rehearing 391 F.2d 97 (5th Cir. 1968), rev'd per curiam 409 F.2d 1166 (5th Cir. 1969) (en banc), cert. denied 397 U.S. 911 (1970) (after six appeals, two jury trials, and 12 years of litigation, American Tobacco won). See also Cipollone v. Liggett Group, Inc., Philip Morris, Inc., Lowes Corp., and Loew's Theatres, Civ. Act. No. 83-2864 (D.C.N.J. Sept. 20, 1984) (slip opinion), noted in 60 ST. JOHN'S L. REV. 754 (1986); Ann M. Palmer, Admin. Estate Joseph C. Palmer v. Liggett Group, Inc. and Liggett & Myers Tobacco, Civ. Act. No. 83-2445-MA (D.C. Mass. Feb. 1, 1984) (slip opinion). See generally Comment, *Strict Products Liability on the Move: Cigarette Manufacturers May Soon Feel the Heat,* 23 SAN DIEGO L. REV. 1137 (1986).

On June 13, 1988, in Cipollone v. Liggett Group, a federal jury held Liggett partly liable for the death of a smoker, awarding $400,000 in damages. The verdict represents the first time liability was ever imposed upon a cigarette manufacturer for the death of a smoker. The jury, however, specifically rejected charges relating to fraud and conspiracy against the manufacturer. It did determine that, through its advertising, the manufacturer created a contract between itself and the consumer containing an express warranty regarding the safety of the product. The latter determination resulted in the award of damages. The jury also found that the manufacturer had breached its duty to warn, but did not award the plaintiff compensation for the breach. The jury verdict, moreover, implies a finding of a legal causal link between cigarette smoking and lung cancer. Defense lawyers believe that the verdict is extremely limited and is inconsistent with prior determinations. They promise an appeal. Plaintiff lawyers see the verdict as a landmark determination likely to change the posture of litigation outcomes in the future.

The Cipollone result also illustrates that tort disputes are inextricably bound to the economics of litigation. Plaintiff lawyers admit spending in excess of $1 million to litigate the case, which involved a four-month trial. Given its previous posture in such cases, the cigarette industry must have spent even more on defense. Courts, therefore, appear accessible only to the wealthy, to plaintiffs who have suffered catastrophic injury, or to parties whose cases involve deep social divisions and are likely to have a wide-ranging financial impact. The cigarette litigation further points to the public law character of tort disputes. The debate underlying the litigation involves corporate accountability for the injurious consequences upon individuals of products that are introduced into the market for profit. It also pertains to the effect of individual choice and conduct upon that accountability. In effect, it is a profoundly political debate about the legitimacy of corporate practices and the viability of consumer protection.

29. See ch. 5, notes 1-29 infra.
30. See ch. 6, notes 76-77 infra.
31. See id. at notes 8-18.
32. See id. at notes 65-77.
33. See ch. 5, notes 1-29 infra.

2 | The Epistemology of Legal Systems

The Source of Law in Legal Systems

Without placing too great a strain upon the analogy between law and literature, one might say that, as there are different literary genres, there are various ways — in the form of traditions, systems, and methods — of expressing the truth of legality. There is a multiplicity of views on how world legal systems with their diverse juridical cultures should be classified.[1] The proposed grouping is based upon how each legal system goes about establishing its substantive epistemology of law: what the system identifies as the primary source of substantive legal rules. The four principal juridical traditions[2] that respond to this classification — the civil law, common law, soviet-socialist, and Scandinavian systems — represent divergent intellectual assumptions, methods, and processes about how the truth of legality should be integrated into society.

The distinction between the source of law in civil-law and common-law systems[3] can be illustrated by the way in which lawyers in each system approach the discovery of governing legal principles. For example, in a legal action brought by divorcing parents over the custody of children, a civilian lawyer would typically refer to the codified law for guidance. By training and disposition, the civil-law lawyer is inclined to believe in and be persuaded by general rules that proceed from an organic, intellectually cohesive text of law. Accordingly, the Civil Code articulates the governing rule — be it a regime of sole custody, maternal preference, joint custody, or the caretaker parent standard[4] — and the courts simply read the specific facts of each case and reach a determination in light of the Code's general answer to the problem. The civil-law lawyer is guided by the belief that the Code's general directives are sufficiently universal to provide answers to the resolution of particular controversies.

A lawyer trained in the common-law tradition has a much different evaluation of the legal significance and meaning of a general statutory statement of applicable law.[5] The controlling directive on child custody matters would be of dubious adjudicatory merit until it had been implemented and refined in the context of specific cases. Succinctly stated, common-law lawyers view legislative answers, the "solemn expression of the legislative will"[6] in civil-law systems, with considerable skepticism. Common-law systems do not fashion governing legal rules by initial and final reference to a codified text of law, but rather through the progressive elaboration of legal principles in judicial decisions.[7] The heart of the common-law enterprise resides in a vision of the law as emerging in an evolutive context in which factually similar cases gradually yield a controlling rule of law, a precedent applying in subsequent, factually analogous litigation.

This basic difference between the two systems is operative primarily at the general level of systemic abstraction. It separates the systems and the actors within those systems on intellectual grounds and in terms of general disposition to ascertaining the truth of law. Yet, despite the divergence in conceptual methodology, courts in each system tend to reach similar, sometimes identical, adjudicatory results.[8] Moreover, civil-law systems, to some extent, do recognize the binding force of prior decisional law; in any event, they do not ignore the importance of facts and the specificity of factual patterns in reaching adjudicatory determinations.[9] By the same token, the accumulation of precedent in common-law systems, especially in England, in conjunction with the growing enactment of and reference to statutes, does yield controlling and generalized principles of law, tending to moderate the skepticism about codified law.[10]

Despite their affinity to the civil-law pattern, socialist legal systems[11] espouse a unique epistemology of law—one that differs from its counterparts in all other juridical cultures. Under socialist organization, law is relegated to the status of an ancillary social force. Its content and scope are dominated by the political and historical dynamic that propels the evolution of the state. Laws are mere instruments for the expression of a higher political truth embodied in the tenets of Marxist-Leninist ideology. Accordingly, legal rules and principles are temporary vehicles in the quest toward a perfected communist society. Once the collective and individual consciousness have united in the ultimate socialist ideal, law will no longer be necessary.[12] The truth of socialist law, therefore, is inextricably bound to the convictions of a political ideology that seeks to redeem humanity from its alleged historical and social corruption. Grounded upon absolute beliefs about humanity and the purpose of social organization, and bent upon transposing that creed into a social order, socialist legal systems and their truth resemble legal orders and systems founded upon religious teachings and beliefs.[13]

Like socialist legal regimes, Scandinavian legal systems also are an offshoot of the civil-law paradigm.[14] Although these systems have some form of codified law, continuous legislative enactments are the primary source of law. Legislative revision provides the social organization with the legal truthfulness necessary to its viability. With some national variations on the basic pattern,[15] the intellectual disposition of Scandinavian lawyers is to look to the specificity and responsiveness of contemporary legislation for the content of their substantive legal epistemology. It has been said that "Swedish lawyers tend to think and argue in terms of legislative rulings and to regard statute law as the most important source of law."[16]

The identification of a primary source of substantive law is, however, only part of the epistemology of legal systems. While the various systemic approaches reflect a diversity of intellectual foundations for establishing core legal principles and the truth of legality, civil codes, case law, political ideology, or statutes, by themselves, provide little guidance in evaluating how justice is finally achieved in a particular system. The sources of law also fail to proffer an adequate basis for appraising whether and how greater truthfulness might be introduced into legal systems. A comparison of the approaches merely indicates that the systems adopt a variable knowledge predicate for their eventual assertion of what is legally truthful.

In order to fulfill their social function, legal systems must implement the truth of legality, whatever its source and however ascertained, incorporating it into and having it govern the specific factual fabric of individual disputes. The adjudicatory procedures and mechanisms for implementing the substance of legal rules into the resolution of private law disputes provide the truth of legality with its final content and ultimate expression.

The Adjudicatory Process and Legal Truth

The received wisdom of the comparative study of law is that the various legal systems can be further classified according to their adjudicatory methodologies.[17] Moreover, this further basis for distinction corresponds to, and reinforces the classification of, legal systems according to their technique for discovering substantive law.

There are two basic methods of adjudicatory truth-seeking among legal systems: the inquisitorial and the adversarial models of adjudication.[18] Typically, civil-law systems are reputed to espouse the inquisitorial method of adjudication because it better accommodates their central concern for the primacy of codified law and their general tendency to attribute subordinate importance to procedural law.[19] Accordingly, adjudication through inquisition is an attempt to ascertain legal truth in disputes through oligarchical judicial control that places foremost value on the integrity of the substantive law.[20] Discounting confrontational debate as a means of discovering the truth of disputed circumstances, it attributes significant weight to written evidence, an active role to the judge in the discovery of facts, and a central authority to the court in the conduct of the proceedings. The characterizing element of the process is that professionally trained judges, not the advocates or the parties, are invested with public adjudicatory authority and responsibility. Concomitantly, the truth of adjudication and legality should arise from the knowledge of law that proceeds from judicial expertise and experience.

The adversarial ethic is said to epitomize the common-law approach to the adjudication of civil disputes.[21] At first blush at least, the adversarial methodology to legal truth-seeking appears to contrast sharply with the characteristics of inquisitorial justice. In adversarial adjudication, the parties do combat and are the prime movers of the proceedings. Judges assume an "umpireal" role,[22] and juries—at least according to the general theory—perform a vital decision-making function in the civil trial process. The adversarial methodology, therefore, attributes predominant responsibility to the parties, in their confrontation, for the discovery of facts and for the evolution of the proceeding. It also places significant importance upon the intricacies of procedure. Finally, it democraticizes determinations by making the jury, the voice of community standards, the essential means of arriving at legally truthful results.

It might be argued that the development of the adversarial method of adjudication and its insistence upon procedural considerations in common-law systems must have been prepared by the preference of these systems for the ad hoc epistemology of precedents rather than the universalism of codified law. A specific rule of law, embedded in the precise circumstances of a case, emerges from the clash of antagonistic positions and the community's sense of right and wrong—not from the judicial implementation of the organic text of written law.

Righting the Misimpressions About Adjudication in Common-Law Systems

The received wisdom on the basic procedural orientation of legal systems is flawed in a number of important respects.[23] In fact, the received wisdom is so erroneous that its primary distinctions cease to have any meaningful analytical value. The common-law procedural tradition, as represented by Anglo-American legal systems, is significantly more complex than the general grouping of these systems under the epithet of adversarial adjudication indicates. There are, moreover, fundamental differences between the English and American mechanisms for adjudicating private law claims.

In England,[24] there appears to have been a gradual evolution toward a judge-centered, albeit adversarial, trial process, accompanied by a decline in the importance of procedural requirements in judicial proceedings. Reliance upon legal expertise and specialized skills seems to characterize most stages of the English civil adjudicatory process. Under the bifurcated structure of the English legal profession, solicitors undertake to establish the evidence relevant to a client's case, including a summary of the client's statements and documents as well as interviews with other parties who have information pertaining to the matter. Barristers traditionally are distant from, and have little authority in, the fact-finding phase of the process, and limit their involvement to consultations with the solicitor.[25]

Masters, who are either former barristers or former solicitors, perform another specialized pretrial function, called "the summons for directions" procedure, which is roughly equivalent to the American pretrial conference.[26] The summons procedure is the interlocutory phase of the eventual proceeding; there, amendments to pleadings, the discovery of documents, the obtainment of expert opinions, and other similar matters are addressed. The purpose of the procedure is to apprise the parties "as to the future course of the action as appear[s] best adapted to secure the just, expeditious and economical disposal"[27] of the case. The masters may dispose of the case by encouraging either settlement or withdrawal; failing such attempts, they refine the case for trial by eliminating procedural conflicts and reducing the controversy to its essential substantive issues.

As in the United States, the trial in England is an event, a dramatization of the parties' controversy, their opposing interests, and their positions on the law.[28] Intended to be an uninterrupted, single occurrence, the trial proceeding is a highly concentrated, predominantly oral process that emphasizes the barrister's advocacy skills. That most, if not all, of the relevent documentation, including judicial precedent and statutes, are read aloud in court underscores the fundamentally oral character of the trial proceeding. Working from the documents supplied by the solicitor, the barristers call and examine witnesses (whose testimony may sometimes diverge from documentary accounts), debate the probative value of evidence, and argue pertinent points of law. The relatively rigid demarcation of professional duties among barristers and solicitors prevents staging the proceeding with prepared witnesses or with a stock presentation of the case. The oral, spontaneous discourse with its attendant element of surprise places a premium upon quick understanding and response in the dialogue among the barristers, the court, and the witnesses.[29]

By comparison to their American analogue, the English rules of evidence, especially when the judge is sitting on the case alone, are quite relaxed. Judges usually take an active part in the questioning of witnesses and in developing their testimony. "Evidence precluded in the United States often is admitted unchallenged in an English proceeding, and a barrister is more hesitant in objecting to a line of inquiry presented by the judge than by opposing counsel."[30] English judges, who are probably more revered than their American counterparts, also rule upon evidentiary and other procedural matters that arise during the trial and generally have the responsibility of supervising the proceedings to maintain fairness and efficiency.[31]

To an American common-law lawyer, there are a number of striking points of contrast between the English and American administration of civil justice. From the vantage point of an American attorney, the English system places more significant reliance upon a professional division of labor. Each phase of the process is informed by specialized skills and expert knowledge—a characteristic designed to promote the general efficiency of the entire process. The American concept of the "all-purpose lawyer" is unknown in England. The central role of the solicitor in gathering relevant evidence and the general exclusion of barristers from that phase of litigation (but for consultations with the solicitor) differ quite considerably from the American attorney's trial preparation. The nearly exclusive oral character of the trial, necessary to maintain its concentrated character, considerably elevates the importance of the barrister's advocacy skills and ability for quick verbal response. While American proceedings are imbued with the features of adversarial dialogue, the American trial is not so heavily anchored in a pattern of spontaneous orality.[32]

The most significant differences, however, lie in the role of the court and of the jury within the trial process. In contradistinction to American practice, the institution of civil trial by jury has all but disappeared in England.[33] Except for defamation and a few other civil actions in which a plaintiff has a right to demand a jury trial, most civil litigation in England is conducted before a trial judge sitting without a jury. Masters rarely allow the recourse to juries even in cases in which the provision for a jury is discretionary. Juries are very infrequent in personal injury cases. The view in England is that juries would not award uniform recoveries in similar cases; the desired uniformity in damage awards is much more likely to be achieved through judicial rulings.[34] The decline of the civil trial by jury may account for, or at least correspond to, the central role that specialized legal expertise plays in the adjudication of private law disputes. It also provides a partial explanation for other features of the process: the less stringent evidentiary rules and the English judge's generally greater participation in the adjudicatory proceedings. Therefore, although English civil procedure is attentive to fairness, it is not unmindful of the requirement of efficiency and the need to have the civil adjudicatory process yield reasonably accurate and predictable results on the law.

In the United States, the civil trial by jury is firmly embedded in the juridical consciousness of the nation and its founding political values.[35] The Seventh Amendment to the United States Constitution provides that "in suits at common law, when the value in controversy shall exceed twenty dollars, the right of trial by jury shall be preserved." Most state constitutions contain similar language, thereby extending the right to a jury trial to civil adjudication in state court.[36] This right is perceived as a fundamental constitutional guarantee. Studies indicate that it is invoked with some frequency by plaintiffs, although it appears that few cases progress to finality by way of jury verdicts.[37] To some extent, the availability of, and recourse to, civil jury trials account for current court congestion in the United States and for the unpredictability of litigation outcomes. Moreover, the use of juries in civil trials requires complex procedural and evidentiary rules, and gives greater play to the dramatic effect of adversarial confrontation. Finally, the jury's vital decision-making role in American civil litigation may privilege a more procedural view of justice and lessen the significance of the substantive epistemology of legal truth.

Another major difference between the English and American processes resides in the role of the courts. English judges tend to view their judicial function in more conservative terms than their American analogues. In civil litigation, English judges, although they participate actively in the proceeding, generally adhere strictly to the applicable legal precedents in reaching their determinations. As a rule, English judges do not see themselves as creators of, or innovators in, legal doctrine.[38] In the modern practice of English common law, the view of justice as obtaining from rigorous conformity to the procedural strictures has been replaced by a relatively strict judicial adherence to a system of substantive precedent. The procedural rule of law reigned at an earlier time when precedent either had yet to evolve or was evolving.[39] The eventual rise of a substantively oriented epistemology of legal truth entailed the deflation of procedural requisites. By way of rough comparison, the historical evolution of the English common-law system has given the use of precedent a status similar to that of codes in civil-law countries.

American judges, especially federal judges, have a more expansive view of their potential law-making authority.[40] Otherwise-applicable precedent is often distinguished from the question in the instant matter, allowing the court to create law from cases that in England would be controlled by precedent. Despite its advantage as a means of making law adaptable, the active and independent participation of judges in formulating law can undermine the predictability of the substantive legal regime. It can also tend to force the legal system to look to more neutral and objective procedural considerations as the essential rule of law in a majority of cases.

In light of these basic differences, grouping Anglo-American common-law systems under the general rubric of adversarial adjudicatory systems is a misleading oversimplification of the reality. English and American civil procedure do share a number of core traits. Both involve a trial proceeding that is a single, concentrated, and oral episode. Their affinity lapses, however, by their eventual adoption and implementation of different epistemologies for ascertaining the truth of legality. Contemporary civil litigation in England places foremost reliance upon the knowledge that arises from legal expertise and experience to discover how disputes can be truthfully resolved. Adversarial debate and jousting appear simply to be other parts of the process, limited to the dialogue that takes place among the barristers and the court. The institution of the civil jury—which arose as an element of civilization in early common law, replacing the trial by ordeal as the means of ascertaining the factual truth of controversies[41]—has a very limited significance in defining the truth of legality in the resolution of current private law controversies in England.

In the United States, the right to a civil trial by jury, an integral part of constitutional guarantees, gives the adversarial ethic a much greater imprint upon the process of civil adjudication. The presence of a civil jury in American proceedings attributes a much wider scope to the drama and possible distortion that can accompany adversarial legal dialogue. It makes complex procedural evidentiary rules necessary. Perhaps most significantly, civil trial by jury in the United States by comparison to England dislodges the expert reference to substantive law in the resolution of private law disputes, allowing in many instances procedural considerations and tactical maneuvering to dictate the rule of law. With the jury as the central decision-maker, mere adversarial posturing can sometimes be mistaken for the truth of a particular situation. The lack of a strict system of binding precedent among courts further encourages the recourse to this essentially ad hoc epistemology and emphasis upon procedural regularity as the central ingredient of justice.

The virtual elimination of the civil jury trial and the concomitant integration of a judge-centered feature to the trial proceeding brings the English process closer to some of the principal characteristics of the so-called inquisitorial prototype, in which substantive, expert determinations appear to have a greater hold. The English and American systems of civil adjudication, therefore, seek and achieve a markedly different form of legal truth.

Civil-Law Adjudicatory Mechanisms as Adversarial Processes

The commonly held perception that civil adjudicatory procedures in civil-law systems are inquisitorial in character is also mistaken. Although an inquisitorial procedural framework — referring to the judge's active part and controlling authority in the conduct of the proceedings and in the discovery of facts — does govern criminal law procedures, civil proceedings in most romanist legal systems contain distinctly adversarial elements despite their judge-centered characteristics.[42] The parties' right to be heard, known in French law as *le contradictoire*,[43] attributes an essential adversarial aspect to the trial and is an indispensable element of the civilian concept of procedural due process. According to article 16 of the French Code of Civil Procedure, "the judge must in all situations ensure that the principle that both sides must be heard be observed and must himself observe it."[44]

In civil trials, civil-law judges — like their English counterparts — take an active role in questioning witnesses and developing the evidence and testimony presented by counsel. In both the English and French systems, the parties initiate the litigation and define its content through their statements of facts, allegations, and contentions.[45] The court generally supervises and participates in these aspects of the process and is responsible for evaluating the issues generated by the dispute in reference to the controlling law. In England, the court decides the controversy in keeping with binding precedent and rules on the weight of the evidence according to flexible exclusionary rules. Similarly, in civil-law systems like France, the probative value of submitted evidence is subject to the court's free evaluation.[46] Moreover, according to article 12 of the French Code of Civil Procedure, the court has the ultimate authority to provide a legal ruling on the matter, provided the principle of *le contradictoire* (basically, adversarial representation) has been observed: "The judge decides the dispute in accordance with the applicable rules of law. He must give or restore their correct classification to the facts and acts in dispute, not accepting the characterizations proposed by the parties. He may not raise pure points of law on his own motion without having previously invited the parties to submit their views."[47]

Of all the procedural systems, the socialist model probably comes closest to minimizing adversarial dialogue and approximating the inquisitorial ideal in civil adjudication.[48] Because of the need to maintain the integrity of political dogma, socialist legal systems have a less mixed form of civil procedure. As with the substantive law, the procedural pursuit of legal truth in socialist systems is not divorced from, and is actually controlled by, a larger ideological vision of social and political truth. Their reliance upon the civil-law model is purely historical; unlike civil proceedings in contemporary civil-law systems, socialist civil trial judges possess substantial procedural authority, characteristic of the pure inquisitorial framework.

In one form or another, all socialist countries have a code of civil procedure; in variegated fashion, these codes attempt to achieve the systematic judicial implementation of the law and the efficient administration of justice.[49] Reflecting the influence of the classical civil-law model, two major attributes of socialist civil procedure are: (1) the wide discretion afforded to judges in the conduct of the proceeding; and (2) the relative insignificance in litigation of procedural technicalities. Although most socialist codes recognize the principle of party control of proceedings, they give courts very wide discretion in pretrial and trial matters. Judges appear to perform an essentially inquisitorial function in civil adjudicatory proceedings; they wield the type of inquisitorial authority that, in Western civil-law systems, would normally apply exclusively to criminal proceedings.

The extensive authority of the socialist trial judge illustrates the judge-centered character of civil proceedings. In socialist systems,[50] judges are responsible for the proper legal administration of the proceeding and for ensuring that the adjudication of the parties' rights and obligations is based upon a complete and objective examination of the facts. In the typical procedure, the court examines the complaint to determine whether it satisfies formal requirements. After summarizing the issues, the court calls upon the parties to present their case. Then, the court usually attempts to have the parties reach a settlement. If the effort at settlement is unavailing, the court decides whether the public procurator[51] should participate in the proceedings, questions the parties to clarify their earlier statements, and decides what and how much evidence is necessary—which witnesses should be called or excused, whether experts are necessary, and whether an inspection *in loco* should be conducted. Once the evidence is gathered, the parties make their closing statements. The court may, however, determine that additional evidence is required to clarify issues and reopen the proceeding after the parties' closing statements.

Other judicial powers demonstrate not only the extent of judicial discretion, but also the interface between court procedures and the socialist concept of social justice and truth. Courts, for example, can invite organizations and individuals to attend trials to foster the educational value of adjudicatory procedures. In some socialist systems, the court has express authority to render a ruling that goes beyond the plaintiff's complaint when the court deems that such a ruling is necessary for the protection of the rights and interests of other private individuals, state institutions, collective enterprises, and other public organizations. Moreover, although a defendant may stipulate to, or acknowledge the legitimacy of, the plaintiff's claim, the court can disregard the defendant's acknowledgment. The court may continue to investigate the plaintiff's claim and even dismiss the action. According to socialist procedural principles, the court must examine whether the circumstances of the case (the objective truth) justifies the defendant's action, further verifying whether the defendant's acknowledgment infringes upon the rules of law and socialist morality.[52]

Socialist civil procedure also exhibits a degree of procedural permissiveness and flexibility characteristic of civilian procedure and that permits the exercise of wide-ranging judicial discretion. The underlying policy of the procedural system is to minimize the effect of a party's failure to abide by procedural requirements.[53] Generally, technical deficiencies are remedied by the court; once reformulated according to appropriate legal standards through judicial assistance, disputes are decided on the merits. In fact, pretrial procedures contain liberal rules of amendment and afford the parties an opportunity to cure defects in the pleadings. Moreover, the courts assist the parties, proffering guidance on how to eliminate deficiencies and allowing the necessary time for amendment. The duty of the pretrial judge in socialist systems is to work out the procedural ramifications of a party-initiated cause of action and to make the pleadings legally sound.

Despite their tendency to encourage settlement at the trial level, socialist systems appear to have progressively restricted the availability of specialized courts and of nonlitigious mechanisms. Underlying this trend is the objective of developing and refining socialist law and legal processes.[54] Even the classical civilian tendency to espouse procedural flexibility must be understood in the context of the socialist principles of justice. All elements of the legal system are at the service of a preordained concept of social and political truth. Civil proceedings or their alternatives are intended to affirm the veracity of the socialist vision of justice, not to promote the self-discovery of truth by the parties.

Given appropriate variations to accommodate the particularities of the various national systems, Scandinavian civil procedure is also generally based upon the civil-law paradigm. It is perhaps more accurate, however, to characterize modern Scandinavian civil procedure as a product of eclectic borrowings from a variety of sources that includes the common-law English influence, civil-law contributions from the French, German, and Austrian systems, and some reference to the socialist legal systems.[55] For example, the concentration of the main hearing, the trial, into a single session generally corresponds to the English procedural model, while the requirement that the complaint set out all material facts is akin to the German "theory of substantiation."[56] The absence of a civil jury generally aligns Scandinavian civil proceedings with its counterpart in most other legal systems, reinforcing the civil-law tendency toward a judge-centered adjudicatory process. As with both the English common-law and French civil-law models, however, this feature of Scandinavian civil procedure does not mean that proceedings are devoid of adversarial content. Attorneys do juxtapose their views of the law and evidence in making the case for their clients.

The Scandinavian trial process exhibits a sharing of control over the conduct of the proceeding between the court and the parties, with the judge having a preponderant degree of authority.[57] The process consists of both a preparatory stage, where the complaint is examined and issues are refined, and a main hearing, where oral evidence is adduced, arguments made, and judgment rendered. The preparatory phase of litigation is roughly equivalent to the pretrial work done by the English masters and the judge in civil-law countries like France; to some but a lesser extent, it also parallels the pretrial conference in American litigation.

The Scandinavian judge does take an active role in assisting the parties to frame the issues on matters of fact and law, thereby assuring adequate preparation for the forthcoming trial.[58] At this intermediate stage, the parties must submit their written evidence (stating what each element is intended to establish—its theme) and indicate which witnesses they will call at the hearing. Because oral evidence is ordinarily not considered at the preliminary hearing, depositions usually are not taken; the principle of evidential immediacy[59] requires witnesses to be heard at the main hearing. Moreover, although counsel submit briefs, arguments on the facts and law are usually not heard at the preparatory stage. The objective is to prepare the matter for trial by refining issues and gathering material evidence in a timely fashion to avoid surprise at trial.[60]

The main hearing consists of opening statements, the production of evidence, and closing arguments. As in English practice, the principle of orality dominates the proceeding; there is generally very limited use of written materials or reference to documentary evidence (although documents can be admitted as evidence during the trial). Although witnesses are examined, they are not subject to the thoroughgoing examination and cross-examination of fundamentally contentious proceedings. In effect, witnesses testify without much interruption from counsel. In theory, the lack of exchange between witnesses and the parties' attorneys avoids influencing the witnesses during the process. The court, like the attorneys, can generally question witnesses. According to the principle of immediacy, the court must render its judgment only upon the basis of what has transpired at trial. Moreover, the judgment must be based only on the material facts alleged by the parties. The court, however, is free to apply rules of law other than those invoked by the parties and to evaluate the evidence freely regardless of the parties' recommendations. The principal adversarial element of the proceeding appears in closing arguments where counsel emphasize the evidentiary points that sustain their allegations and attempt to discredit the opposing party's case.[61]

Summary Observations

No matter what orientation legal systems espouse about the source of substantive law, then, most judicial adjudicatory processes involve some degree of adversarial dialogue in the litigation of civil disputes. Moreover, the character of legal representation in these various systems does not radically differ. The lawyer's professional duty is to advocate on behalf of the client and to have the client's version of the truth of the matter prevail. The traditional labels for classification—adversarial and inquisitorial—are, therefore, not very useful in establishing meaningful distinctions between civil procedure systems. Adjudicatory frameworks in various legal systems can be more meaningfully distinguished by reference to whether juries are involved in the resolution of civil controversies, the extent to which the court and the parties share responsibility in achieving the legal resolution of disputes, and how the trial process is structured and organized. For example, the framework for civil adjudication in common-law systems is meant to lead to a single, culminating confrontation between the parties in the trial. The adjudication of private law disputes in civil-law countries consists of a series of meetings between the parties and the judge, leading to a less climactic finalization of the dispute.

The Impact of Divergent Adjudicatory Approaches upon Legal Truth

The refinement of the commonplace assumptions about the role of inquisitorial and adversarial adjudicatory models in major Western legal traditions illustrates a clear tendency among most contemporary legal systems to ascertain the truth of legality through a judge-and-law-centered framework. Despite the divergence in their juridical cultures and contrasting views of the trial proceeding, English and French civil procedure share a propensity to have adjudicatory determinations founded upon the knowledge of law that arises from legal expertise. Also, while adjudicatory frameworks in both countries contain a component of adversarial legal representation in the trial process, the confrontation takes place between equally knowledgeable parties. By contrast, the adversarial ethic's pervasive presence in the American adjudicatory mechanism is an isolated occurrence among legal systems. It is also a special feature of American civil litigation that adversarial representation is made to function in a context of a democratized adjudicatory framework in which the jury, in theory at least, performs a major decision-making role. The firm hold of the civil jury trial in the American juridical and political consciousness and the diminution of the rule of strict binding precedent through judicial activism attribute predominant weight to procedural matters and to an inexpert sense of legality in reaching determinations about civil controversies.

These features of civil litigation in the United States combined with an extensive, party-dominated discovery process and other pretrial procedures[62] (including interviewing and preparing witnesses and rehearsing arguments and patterns of examination before mock juries) give the content of legal truthfulness a much different acceptation in the American adjudicatory process and legal system. The "staging" of a legal controversy by skilled advocates before the lay members of the jury can create such an imbalance between the law and its process of implementation that only an implausible appearance of legal truth remains once the determination is rendered. The rule of law can become subrogated to the influence of theatrical oratory and tactical consid-erations.

As practiced in the United States, the adversarial framework for legal adjudication is founded upon an illogical and mythical premise: that an impressionable lay jury, by its rough sense of justice, will eventually validate the parties' intricate procedural jousting and so-phisticated legal arguments. This view of the epistemology of legal truth holds, in effect, that the law is devoid of truthful substance; its truth-seeking responsibility must devolve to nonsubstantive procedural de-vices and a diffuse sense of lay justice. Zealous, unyielding advocacy is entertaining; it has a dramatic bravado that is the stuff of theatrical representations. In real life, however, discord is not feigned. Adopting adversarialism as the exclusive mode of dialogue in adjudication can become a costly and irrational choice. Gaming with people's interests by playing upon sympathetic emotions is a dehumanizing and cynical bottom-line approach to dispute resolution. A process of adjudication dominated by single-minded, intransigent arguments, shrewd (albeit unintelligent) procedural tactics, and the competition for the jury's favor can never generate the type of mutual cooperation and under-standing necessary for lucid, resourceful, and humanistic dispute res-olution. It may be that the chief benefit of an adjudicatory process dominated by the adversarial ethic is that, like conventional warfare, it takes place in accordance with elaborate procedural rules.

Judge-and-law-centered processes avoid the pitfalls of the Amer-ican adversarial framework.[63] Many of their features have a logical appeal and bear intrinsic value to the goal of achieving legally truthful results. The exercise of judicial control and the rule of judicial expertise, the minimization of procedural considerations and entanglements, and the general sway that is given to a coherent system of substantive law are naturally appropriate elements for constituting a foundation for legal truth. By definition, the civil jury trial, conjoined to a dominant adversarial ethic and a passive judge, are less conducive to the accom-plishment of legally truthful results. Here, the would-be protection of rights is often achieved by attrition or settlement. The vital decision-making role of lay jury members makes the appearance of being right a cardinal objective. The presence of the jury—often impressionable, possibly partial to the injured party, and usually baffled by obtusely worded legal standards and instructions or technical evidence—not only foils the essential expertise of the process, but also imperils even its modest truth-seeking design.

While judge-and-law-centered adjudicatory frameworks provide, in a way that rigorously adversarial and jury-oriented processes simply cannot, the accuracy and stability of knowledge that are indispensable to truth-seeking, a final question remains concerning the viability of any legal methodology to achieve a truth that is consonant with the full objectives of justice. Despite the superiority of judge-and-law-centered frameworks in truth-seeking, the ultimate value of dispute resolution through legal adjudication remains its coercive imposition of finality upon conflicts. Whatever the advantages or disadvantages of the various procedural schemes, none of them have the stated objective of educating the disputing parties or of having them participate in a direct and principal fashion in the resolution of their conflict. In effect, present dispute resolution frameworks suffer from a problem of "over-civilization." Having made certain assumptions about human beings and their behavior in circumstances of dispute, legal adjudicatory mechanisms have created their own dynamics that prohibit them from responding to a higher and more challenging dispute resolution mission.

The Principle of Adjudication and "Under-Civilization"

Having examined the results of "over-civilization" with domestic legal systems, the aim of discovering the essential principles of a suitably humanistic adjudicatory methodology and mechanism might be furthered by considering the example of long-standing and more recent efforts to develop dispute resolution norms in a basically lawless setting. The following section will introduce the problems associated with rule-making and adjudication in the international legal community.

The eternal debate among international law lawyers and scholars is whether a rule of law exists in the sphere of international activity.[64] In this setting, the phenomenon of sovereignty and the absence of an effective adjudicatory process, in addition to the diversity of national interests, culture, and ideology, have created a situation of adjudicatory "under-civilization." Supplementing the comparative analysis of legal systems with a study of international processes should provide a complete picture of the foreign experience in dispute resolution and should, therefore, inform the subsequent consideration of possible domestic reforms and test the mettle of creativity and humanistic values in adjudication.

International Politics: Its Sovereign Necessities

Notwithstanding a continuing history of attempts at harmonization through treaty relations and state participation in multilateral organizations, the international arena is a composite of unsettled and unsettling structures, beset by volatile political relations.[65] In such circumstances, the role of legality — as that term is understood within the internal operation of domestic legal systems — is precarious. Some academic and diplomatic accounts of the international legal order, however, abound with visionary statements of a worldwide rule of law.[66] According to such statements, in state-to-state relations, impartial and well-reasoned legal principles should predominate over the dictates of the realpolitik; moreover, in the conduct of governments toward individuals, acknowledged international human rights standards ought to govern the domestic behavior of political regimes.

The inability to integrate some of the basic elements of domestic juridical civilization into world community structures — for instance, agreement upon the source and content of law,[67] and the enforceability of judicial judgments[68] — fosters the suspicion that the idealistic aspirations are themselves the most concrete expression that can be given to the envisioned legal order. The irreducible principle of national sovereignty has always made an international rule of law elusive, and it has consecrated the fragmented truth of national self-interest as the primary source of legality in the international community.

Strident ideological divisions separate nations and groups of nations, frustrating the aim of achieving global peace and harmony. National and regional economic policies are often at variance. As a result, the clash of sovereign interests amidst the fragile balance of political alignments, economic interdependencies, and geographical configurations creates special dispute resolution needs. Temporizing imprecision, diplomatic latitude, and the indeterminacy of equivocal dialogue are better suited than adjudication or its analogues to deal with political confrontation among the Titans. Finality, as practiced in the domestic setting, is not the exclusive, or even primary, objective of international dispute resolution because coercive enforcement is available only through military means and can be dangerously unavailing or disruptive.

The recourse to legality is only one of the many means in a

panoply of remedies to approaching international conflict resolution, and its principal role is to act as an indirect instrument of persuasion. Unlike a domestic judicial tribunal, the World Court[69] is but a symbol of what binding legal adjudication might yield in the determination of state-to-state conflicts. By its composition, jurisdictional mandate, and authorizing foundation, the court and its pronouncements are merely part of a complex, essentially diplomatic calculus for resolving disputes. The legality of expropriations,[70] boundaries and fisheries claims,[71] acts of alleged political reprisal,[72] and the use of self-help devices[73] cannot be separated from the sovereign political interests of the concerned states.

International conflicts also arise in more mixed circumstances that involve both public and private interests. In addition to the diplomatic espousal of claims by governments, the activity of global, stateless enterprises[74] can give rise to controversies among the host and other countries, the commercial entity, and citizens of various nations. The litigation activity that followed the Bhopal tragedy[75] is a particularly illustrative example of the complex dispute resolution problems that can emerge in a public-private transnational setting. The alleged commission of an industrial toxic tort that affected thousands of people in India by a company with a worldwide corporate organization complicated the most elemental issues of adjudication. The incident gave rise to a question of (among others) jurisdiction to adjudicate: given its United States corporate headquarters, could Union Carbide be sued in a New York court for the calamities that took place in India?[76]

The objective in bringing suit in the United States—to have plaintiffs gain the advantage of a distinctly favorable procedure and law—was perfectly transparent from the outset. An American court's assertion of jurisdiction would not only have been foolhardy from the perspective of judicial administration, but could also have impinged upon the dictates of comity and compromised the integrity of the diplomatic relationship between the United States and India. Fortunately, the doctrine of forum non conveniens held sway.[77] Moreover, subsequent judicial rulings and legislation in India demonstrated the adaptability of the Indian legal system to the complex proportions of this type of litigation.[78]

From a dispute resolution perspective, Bhopal teaches that transnational corporate activity harbors the potential for confounding the usual scope of national political agendas and the regulatory capability of national legal processes. Depending upon the attitude of the national political and legal institutions involved, these hybrid public and private disputes can be as resistant to juridical solutions and as paralyzing to world community interests as state-to-state political conflicts. Finally, despite the likely political obstacles, Bhopal demonstrates the need to elaborate international standards regulating the legal obligations and liabilities of multinational corporate enterprises[79] and, concomitantly, the need to create some type of transnational organization to process claims and implement the regulatory standards.

Transnational Commerce: Needs and Emerging Norms

International commercial activity can also engender transnational disputes of a purely contractual nature either between private parties or between such individuals and states that engage in transnational commercial ventures. Indeed, in addition to striving for ideals of universal peace and harmony, the international legal order should seek similarly vital objectives anchored in the sobering realities of commercial needs. The world community is increasingly dominated by an international economic interdependence that has resulted in the internationalization of domestic economies.[80] A comprehensive global system of law should, therefore, include the development of a uniform commercial law and a workable procedural framework for resolving disputes that arise from international commercial activity.[81] International contracting presents considerable risks for commercial parties. Commercial activity in the world marketplace is subject to the politics of sovereign discretion (both territorial and contractual), to the absence of law and of a cohesive regulatory structure that is specifically transnational in character, and to the variegated rulings of national courts.[82]

The character of the parties and the nature of the transactions themselves are sources of potential difficulties. The differences between the parties, including those of nationality, language, and culture, can breed distrust and misunderstanding. Communicating the essential details of a business transaction through the veil of intermediaries can be both difficult and dangerous. Even astute parties may not know what to look for in an unfamiliar setting. Problems are compounded when national economic regulatory patterns conflict with respect to the imposition of custom duties, tariffs, and other trade constraints on imports.[83] Having lawyers from a plurality of legal backgrounds adds another level of complexity to business negotiations and the drafting of commercial agreements. International contracts are themselves special legal creatures,[84] requiring provisions that respond to the unique risks that attend transnational deals: for example, clauses pertaining to the controlling language of the contract, currency stabilization, gap-filling in long-term contracts, sovereign immunity, and force majeure.[85]

The risks that inhere in, and the special character of, international business dealings make an effective dispute resolution framework vital to the viability of transactions. In public law matters where politics demands the recourse to a panoply of nonjuridical remedies in the event of dispute, the use of alternative mechanisms can range from informal and formal efforts at negotiation and conciliation to establishing claims commissions, and can end with the use of force. Although its current operation is painstaking and its ultimate success remains to be gauged, the Iran–United States claims tribunal in the Hague,[86] established by the Algiers Accord,[87] stands as one of the more innovative attempts in the public law area to respond to private grievances in a political context with a modified form of adjudicatory procedures.

Traditional court adjudication is no more felicitous in transnational litigation involving purely private interests. The viability of international commercial ventures requires a reliable dispute resolution framework founded upon adjudicatory neutrality, expertise, and confidentiality.[88] Because of their predominant domestic orientation, national courts often lack the ability to decide international contract disputes knowledgeably and are usually unable to fashion determinations that respond to the unique contours and dynamics of international business relations. Typically, domestic court judges approach such litigation exclusively from a legalistic choice-of-law perspective, focusing upon whether a particular domestic law should govern the merits of the dispute.[89] Little, if any, consideration is ever given to whether the would-be applicable law provides an appropriate decisional basis in the transnational setting. As a consequence, domestic laws sometimes gain an extraterritorial reach.[90] Although they may have considerable domestic currency, some jurisdictional and procedural concepts—for example, long-arm jurisdiction, due process of law, and discovery—do not necessarily have universal recognition or, even if they are recognized by most legal systems, may be interpreted or applied differently in different countries. Also, courts may be partial, even unwittingly, to the interests of their nationals; in any event, they are likely to share their nationals' perception of commercial practice and of the nature of contractual breach. Finally, the public and confrontational character of court proceedings can do considerable, perhaps irreparable, damage to the parties' commercial status and relationship.

Given the magnitude of the uncertainty with domestic judicial adjudication, it is not surprising that international merchants have had recourse to alternative means for settling their disputes. One such means is based upon the principle of party autonomy in contract (also known as the freedom of contract)[91] and its self-empowering consequences. Rather than leave the selection of an appropriate forum and governing law to national court interpretation, commercial parties can provide for either or both in their agreement. The use of choice-of-forum-and-law clauses[92] as a remedy to the salient problems of international contracting, however, has a number of drawbacks. It assumes that the contracting parties will be aware or be made aware of, and want to address, these prospective legal problems and will be able to reach agreement on suitable contract language. It also assumes that national courts will give effect to the self-empowering contractual provisions without modifying, reinterpreting, or objecting to them. Also, perhaps most important, such contractual provisions can mitigate or resolve only some of the problems that accompany national court adjudication of transnational commercial disputes. They do not make courts any more sensitive to the particularities of these transactions or give them any better basis to act as international commercial tribunals. Inexpert, possibly biased domestic judicial forums, acting in public proceedings, could continue to dominate the available remedial process.

In light of these continuing difficulties, parties to international contracts could forego entirely the recourse to national judicial adjudication and rely upon self-help techniques or other third-party agencies to resolve their contract disputes. Either at the contracting stage or when a dispute arises, they could agree to negotiate their differences and arrive at a mutually acceptable consensus about what should be done. Agreeing that negotiated settlement is the sole remedy, however, may lock the parties into a scheme of dispute resolution that is eventually unwanted. A binding provision for the exclusive remedy of negotiation could, by its time and cost, imperil the viability of the transaction. In the midst of conflict, unless the parties' representatives are particularly skilled, it may not result in the desired resolution of the dispute. Moreover, the circumstances of dispute may make the process of negotiation of only limited value, addressing minor conflicts or acting as a precursor to litigation that determines what aspects of the dispute are intractable. Failing a negotiated accommodation of differences, the parties could provide for recourse to nonadjudicatory but third-party-assisted alternatives such as conciliation or mediation. Although such processes may be useful in resolving some differences, more substantial conflicts often require a process akin to judicial determinations, providing for adjudicated and binding results.

Arbitral adjudication fulfills many of the dispute resolution needs of international merchants.[93] It represents the use of the party autonomy principle of contract law to create an adjudicatory framework that yields binding results that reflect the realities of commercial practice. Although arbitration is usually touted for its economical and expeditious character, its primary contribution to the adjudication of transnational commercial disputes resides in its provision of neutrality, privacy, and expertise in the rendering of rulings. In the context of the pragmatic dictates of commerce, international commercial arbitration symbolizes the full use of a self-empowering ethic in dispute resolution. The creative use and experience with arbitration in the resolution of transnational commercial disputes may contain the seeds for transformations in the international legal order generally and in the adjudicatory principle and process of domestic legal frameworks.

The chapter that follows considers the exemplary value of the dispute resolution ethic symbolized by international commercial arbitration. Aligning itself to the substantive contours of the foregoing prefatory discussion, the analysis first focuses upon state efforts to establish a viable transnational regulatory framework to deal with the liability of air carriers for corporeal and property damages that result from maloccurrences in air transportation. The consideration of the topic illustrates the difficulty, if not the impossibility, of achieving a formal rule of law through direct state-to-state dialogue. The experience with the Warsaw Convention then is contrasted with the universal consensus that underlies the 1958 New York Arbitration Convention, including a comprehensive statement of the current status of arbitral adjudication in various countries in the international community. Finally, in another chapter and in an attempt to draw final lessons, the concept of an organic private international law will be examined in reference to recent United States Supreme Court opinions in cases involving transnational litigation.

NOTES

1. The use of a comparative law methodology is, in many respects, indispensable to the assessment of the legal method for ascertaining truth in adjudication. Although there is debate about the character and goals of the comparative study of law, a complete comparative consideration should consist of a description and classification of legal systems accompanied by an analytical evaluation of the operation of legal institutions and concepts in diverse legal cultures. The comparative inquiry needs to straddle a number of differing considerations (e.g., the sociological, historical, and anthropological perspectives), while retaining a basic focus upon the systemic and juridical implications of phenomenon. In some measure, the comparative law inquiry attempts a form of observation akin to a literary writer's goal of capturing and reconciling the tensions of external reality in an esthetic fabric that holds universal insight about human experience and existence.

One of the principal aims of the comparative endeavor, therefore, should be to preserve a balance between the ideosyncratic tendencies of individual legal systems and their more generalizable properties. The cultural and national variations on the implementation of a legal idea should yield a core, albeit not overly generalized, sense of its juridical meaning and value—and of its place in the attempt to construct a cosmology of regulation that adequately balances societal and individual interests. The appeal of the comparative law method lies only in part in its academic orientation and quasi-scientific disposition; its primary attraction resides in its search for synthetic bridges between various legal worlds and for a transnational vision of law. See generally Symposium, *Comparative Law in the Late Twentieth Century*, [1987] B.Y.U. L. REV. 325 (1987).

For a discussion of the classification of legal systems, the design of comparative law, and the issues that surround the implementation of the comparatist methodology, see H. DE VRIES, CIVIL LAW AND THE ANGLO-AMERICAN LAWYER (1976); R. DAVID & J. BRIERLEY, MAJOR LEGAL SYSTEMS IN THE WORLD TODAY (3d ed. 1985); M. GLENDON, M. GORDON, & C. OSAKWE, COMPARATIVE LEGAL TRADITIONS (1983); J. MERRYMAN & D. CLARK, COMPARATIVE LAW: WESTERN EUROPEAN AND LATIN AMERICAN LEGAL SYSTEMS (1978); R. SCHLESINGER, H. BAADE, M. DAMASKA, & P. HERZOG, COMPARATIVE LAW (5th ed. 1988); A. VON MEHREN & J. GORDLEY, THE CIVIL LAW SYSTEM (2d ed. 1977); J. WHIGMORE, A PANORAMA OF THE WORLD'S LEGAL SYSTEMS (1928); 1 & 2 K. ZWEIGERT & H. KOTZ, AN INTRODUCTION TO COMPARATIVE LAW (T. Weir trans. 1977). See also Pound, *A Comparison of Systems of Law*, 10 U. PITT. L. REV. 271 (1948); Pound, *Philosophy of Law and Comparative Law*, 100 U. PA. L. REV. 1 (1951); Rheinstein, *Com-*

parative Law: Its Functions, Methods and Usages, 22 ARK. L. REV. 415 (1968).

2. In regard to the views advanced in the foregoing sources, the classification adopted in the text is both under- and overinclusive. Traditionally, legal systems have been classified according to whether they adhered to one of two major legal traditions: the common-law and civil-law traditions. The establishment of such distinctions is at the core of the comparative law enterprise and is premised upon the legal systems' concept of the primary source of, or method for, ascertaining law. The traditional classification, however, ignores the fundamentally different soviet-socialist variations on the civil-law model. In these systems, state ideology plays a central part in defining the function of law and of the legal system. See, for example, H. BERMAN, JUSTICE IN THE USSR: AN INTERPRETATION OF SOVIET LAW (1966); J. HAZARD, COMMUNISTS AND THEIR LAW: A SEARCH FOR THE COMMON CORE OF THE LEGAL SYSTEMS OF THE MARXIAN SOCIALIST STATES (1969); O. IOFFE & P. MAGGS, SOVIET LAW IN THEORY AND PRACTICE (1983); A. MAKHNENKO, THE STATE LAW OF THE SOCIALIST COUNTRIES (1976); I. SZABO & Z. PETERI, A SOCIALIST APPROACH TO COMPARATIVE LAW (1977). See also, Chloros, *Common Law, Civil Law and Socialist Law: Three Leading Systems of the World, Three Kinds of Legal Thought,* 9 CAMBRIAN L. REV. 11 (1978).

The classical civil law–common law dichotomy also does not recognize that the Scandinavian legal system's reliance on statutory law as the primary source of law may constitute a fourth major grouping of legal systems. See, for example, L. ORFIELD, THE GROWTH OF SCANDINAVIAN LAW (1953); F. SCHMIDT & S. STROMHOLM, LEGAL VALUES IN MODERN SWEDEN (1964); 1 & 2 S. STROMHOLM, AN INTRODUCTION TO SWEDISH LAW (1981); Mulder, *Judge-Made Law in the Netherlands,* 4 LIVERPOOL L. REV. 105 (1982). According to Hellner, a noted Swedish authority on contracts and sales,

> Swedish lawyers tend to think and argue in terms of legislative rulings and to regard statute law as the most important source of law. Precedents are not abundant and are not considered to be binding, though they are clearly influential. When a Swedish lawyer meets a question which cannot readily be answered by simple subsumption under a statutory rule, his first impulse will generally be to look for a statutory rule in some other field, which can be used as the basis for an analogy and thus provide guidance for the solution of his problem.

Hellner, *Contracts and Sales,* in S. STROMHOLM, ed., AN INTRODUCTION TO SWEDISH LAW ch. 7, at 201 (1981). Accord Mulder, *Judge-Made Law in the Netherlands,* supra.

For a discussion of major religious and non-Western legal traditions, see J. MERRYMAN & D. CLARK, COMPARATIVE LAW: WESTERN EUROPEAN

AND LATIN AMERICAN LEGAL SYSTEMS, supra note 1, at 6-11. For a discussion of the concept of mixed jurisdictions, see M. GLENDON, M. GORDON, & C. OSAKWE, COMPARATIVE LEGAL TRADITIONS, supra note 1, at 43-44. See also Lawson, *Family Affinities of Common-Law and Civil-Law Legal Systems,* 6 HASTINGS INT'L & COMP. L. REV. 85 (1982).

3. For a discussion of this point, see R. DAVID, FRENCH LAW (1972); F. LAWSON, A COMMON LAWYER LOOKS AT THE CIVIL LAW (1955); J. MERRYMAN, THE CIVIL LAW TRADITION (2d ed. 1985); K. RYAN, AN INTRODUCTION TO THE CIVIL LAW (1962); S. SCOTT, THE CIVIL LAW (1932); A. WATSON, LEGAL TRANSPLANTS (1974); Aldisert, *Rambling Through Continental Legal Systems,* 43 U. PITT. L. REV. 935 (1982); Bessette, *French Civil Law System Since 1804,* 73 L. LIB. J. 336 (1980); Carrio, *Judge Made Law Under a Civil Code,* 41 LA. L. REV. 993 (1981); Damaske, *A Continental Lawyer in an American Law School: Trials and Tribulations of Adjustment,* 116 U. PA. L. REV. 1363 (1968); Dainow, *The Civil Law and the Common Law: Some Points of Comparison,* 15 AM. J. COMP. L. 419 (1967); Fernandez, *Custom and the Common Law: Judicial Restraint and Lawmaking by Courts,* 11 S.W. U. L. REV. 1237 (1979); Lawson, *Comparative Judicial Style,* 25 AM. J. COMP. L. 364 (1977); Lucke, *Common Law as Arbitral Law: A Defense of Judicial Law-Making,* 8 ADEL. L. REV. 229 (1983); MacLean, *Judicial Discretion in the Civil Law,* 43 LA. L. REV. 45 (1982); Markesinis, *Conceptualism, Pragmatism and Courage: A Common Lawyer Looks at Some Judgments of the German Federal Court,* 34 AM. J. COMP. L. 349 (1986); Peters, *Common Law Judging in a Statutory World: An Address,* 43 U. PITT. L. REV. 995 (1982); Stein, *Judge and Jurist in the Civil Law: A Historical Interpretation,* 46 LA. L. REV. 241 (1985).

4. See, for example, T. CARBONNEAU, THE FAMILY AND THE CIVIL CODE 459-520 (1983); Garska v. McCoy, 278 S.E. 2d 357, 363 (W. Va. 1981). See also Minnesota Developments, *A Step Backward: The Minnesota Supreme Court Adopts a "Primary Caretaker" Presumption in Child Custody Cases: Pikula v. Pikula,* 70 MINN. L. REV. 1344 (1986).

5. See text at note 3 supra and accompanying text (sources cited).

6. See La. Civ. Code Ann., art. 1 (West 1986).

7. See text at note 3 supra and accompanying text (sources cited).

The accepted theory of sources of law in the civil law tradition recognizes only statutes, regulations, and custom as sources of law. This listing is exclusive. It is also arranged in descending order of authority. A statute prevails over a contrary regulation. Both a statute and a regulation prevail over an inconsistent custom. This may all seem very technical and of dubious importance, but in fact it is basic to our understanding of the civil law tradition, since the function of the judge within that tradition is to interpret and to apply "the law" as it is technically defined in his jurisdiction. Both state positivism and the dogma of separation of powers require that the judge resort only to "the law" in deciding cases. It is assumed that whatever the problem that may come before him, the judge will be able to find some form of law to apply—whether a statute, a regulation, or an applicable custom. He cannot turn to books and articles by legal scholars or to prior judicial decisions for the law.

. . .

To the average judge, lawyer, or law student in France or Argentina, the traditional theory of sources of law represents the basic truth. It is a part of his ideology.

In the common law world, on the other hand, a world less compelled by the peculiar history and the rationalist dogmas of the French Revolution, quite different attitudes prevail. The common law of England, an unsystematic accretion of statutes, judicial decisions, and customary practices, is thought of as the major source of law. It has deep historic dimensions and is not the product of a conscious revolutionary attempt to make or to restate the applicable law at a moment in history. There is no systematic, hierarchical theory of sources of law: legislation, of course, is law, but so are other things, including judicial decisions. In formal terms the relative authority of statutes, regulations, and judicial decisions might run in roughly that order, but in practice such formulations tend to lose their neatness and their importance. Common lawyers tend to be much less rigorous about such matters than civil lawyers. The attitudes that led France to adopt the metric system, decimal currency, legal codes, and a rigid theory of sources of law, all in the space of a few years, are still basically alien to the common law tradition.

J. MERRYMAN, THE CIVIL LAW TRADITION, supra note 3, at 23-25.

8. See H. DE VRIES, CIVIL LAW FOR THE ANGLO-AMERICAN LAWYER, supra note 1, at 1-6. See generally, Franklin, *A Study of Interpretation in the Civil Law*, 3 VAND. L. REV. 557 (1950); Lawson, *The Approach to French Law*, 34 IND. L. J. 531 (1959); Letourneur & Drago, *The Rule of Law as Understood in France*, 7 AM. J. COMP. L. 147 (1958); Loussouarn, *The Relative Importance of Legislation, Custom, Doctrine, and Precedent in French Law*, 18 LA. L. REV. 235 (1958); Sweigert & Puttfarken, *Statutory Interpretation—Civilian Style*, 44 TUL. L. REV. 704 (1970).

9. See H. DE VRIES, CIVIL LAW FOR THE ANGLO-AMERICAN LAWYER, supra note 1, at 243-49. See also Milsom, *Law and Fact in Legal Development*, 17 TORONTO L. J. 1 (1967).

10. See generally T. PLUCKNETT, A CONCISE HISTORY OF THE COMMON LAW (5th ed. 1956).

11. For a list of sources on soviet-socialist legal systems, see note 2 supra and accompanying text (sources cited).

12. See, for example, M. GLENDON, M. GORDON, & C. OSAKWE, COMPARATIVE LEGAL TRADITIONS, supra note 1, at 270-82.

13. See id. at 274-77.

14. For a list of sources on Scandinavian legal systems, see text at note 2 supra and accompanying text (sources cited).

15. See id.

16. Hellner, *Contract and Sales,* in S. STROMHOLM, ed., AN INTRODUCTION TO SWEDISH LAW, supra note 2, at 201.

17. See generally Cappelletti, *Social and Political Aspects of Civil Procedure: Reforms and Trends in Western and Eastern Europe,* 69 MICH. L. REV. 847 (1971); Goldstein & Marcus, *The Myth of Judicial Supervision in Three "Inquisitorial" Systems: France, Italy and Germany,* 87 YALE L. J. 240 (1977); Kaplan, *Civil Procedure: Reflections on the Comparison of Systems,* 9 BUFFALO L. REV. 409 (1960); Tomlinson, *Nonadversarial Justice: The French Experience,* 42 MD. L. REV. 131 (1983).

18. In discussing American civil procedure, Jolowicz provides the following definition of the "adversary system":

> The essence of the adversary system of trial is that the case that is heard by the judge is presented to him by the lawyers for the parties. Each lawyer will present his client's case in its most favourable light; it is the lawyers who decide what witnesses should be called, when they will be called and what questions they will be asked, and each lawyer has the opportunity, which he will normally take, to cross-examine the witnesses called by his opponent. The presentation of the case is thus entirely the function of the lawyers; the examination of witnesses by the judge is exceptional and, when it does occur, is almost always resented by at least one of the parties. It is the judge's function, as representative of the sovereignty of the state, to maintain decorum and order in the court room, to rule on motions and objections raised during the trial, to instruct the jury, if there is one, concerning the principles of law applicable to their decision, and, of course, to deliver the judgment of the court. Save as required by these functions the judge can and will do nothing which might indicate a lack of impartiality; the actuality and the appearance of impartiality are both preserved by the judge's "passive" role.

M. CAPPELLETTI & J. JOLOWICZ, PUBLIC INTEREST PARTIES AND THE ACTIVE ROLE OF THE JUDGE IN CIVIL LITIGATION 239-40 (1975). For a definition of the concept of inquisitorial justice, see, for example, Goldstein & Marcus, *The Myth of Judicial Supervision in Three "Inquisitorial" Systems,* note 17 supra. For a further discussion of comparisons between the two adjudicatory models, see generally Bisbane, *The Adversary System: Is It Any Longer Appropriate?,* 49 AUSTRL. L. J. 439 (1975); Zeidler, *Evaluation of the Adversary System: As Comparison, Some Remarks on the Investigatory System of Procedure,* 55 AUSTRL. L. J. 390 (1981). See also F. LAWSON, A COMMON LAWYER LOOKS AT THE CIVIL LAW, note 3 supra; Pound, *The*

Development of American Law and Its Deviation from English Law, 67 L.
Q. REV. 49 (1951); sources cited in note 17 supra.

19. See H. DE VRIES, CIVIL LAW FOR THE ANGLO-AMERICAN LAWYER,
supra note 1, at 250-64. See also LA. CODE CIV. PROC., art. 5051 (Supp.
1986), infra, at Appendix A (ch. 2).

20. See text at note 18 supra and accompanying text (sources cited).

21. See text at note 18 supra and accompanying text (sources cited).

22. The word and concept are borrowed from: Frankel, *The Search
for Truth: An Umpireal View,* 123 U. PA. L. REV. 1031 (1975) ("My theme . . . is
that our adversary system rates truth too low among the values that
institutions of justice are meant to serve." Id. at 1032. "The fact is that
our system does not allow much room for effective or just intervention
by the trial judge in the adversary fight about the facts." Id. at 1042).

For a set of dissenting responses to Frankel's article articulated primarily
from the perspective of criminal law, see Freedman, *Judge Frankel's Search
for Truth,* 123 U. PA. L. REV. 1060 (1975); Uviller, *The Advocate, the Truth,
and Judicial Hackles: A Reaction to Judge Frankel's Idea,* id. at 1067. For
a more dispassionate reaction to and appraisal of the general topic, see
Damaska, *Presentation of Evidence and Factfinding Precision,* id. at 1083.

Frankel's other writings on this subject include: PARTISAN JUSTICE (1980);
The Adversary Judge, 54 TEX. L. REV. 465 (1976); *From Private Fights
Toward Public Justice,* 51 N.Y.U. L. REV. 516 (1976). Most of the criticism
and commentary on Frankel's writing has focused upon the criminal law
implications of the recommended judicial and process changes. See, for
example, Patouris, *Partisan Justice and Party-Dominated Justice,* 57 N.Y.U.
L. REV. 203 (1982) (book review of M. FRANKEL, PARTISAN JUSTICE); Pizzi,
Judge Frankel and the Adversary System, 52 U. COLO. L. REV. 357 (1981).

23. See A. VON MEHREN & J. GORDLEY, THE CIVIL LAW SYSTEM, supra
note 1, at 150-203, 203-08; Von Mehren, *The Significance for Procedural
Practice and Theory of the Concentrated Trial: Comparative Remarks,* in
2 EUROPAISCHES RECHTSDENKEN IN GESCHICHTE UND GEGENWART:
FESTSCHRIFT FUR HELMUT COING 361, n.3 (N. Horn ed. 1982), cited in
Langbein, *The German Advantage in Civil Procedure,* 52 CHICAGO L. REV.
823, 824, n.4 (1985). For further discussion of Langbein's thesis, see Allen,
Köck, Riechenberg, & Rosen, *The German Advantage in Civil Procedure:
A Plea for More Details and Fewer Generalities in Comparative Scholarship,*
82 N.W. U. L. REV. 705 (1988); Langbein, *Trashing the German Advantage,*
82 N.W. L. REV. 763 (1988).

24. As Jolowicz aptly suggests, the American variation on civil procedure and the use of the adversarial ethic are probably sui generis: "the
extreme form of fishing . . . [in the American] discovery process . . . , viz,
bringing a lawsuit in order to discover whether you might actually have

one, is unknown not only in Continental procedures, but in English procedures as well." Jolowicz, *Some Twentieth Century Developments in Anglo-American Civil Procedure,* in 1 STUDI IN ONORE DI ENRICO TULLIO LIEBMAN 217, 241 (1979).

See Kaplan & Clermont, *England and the United States,* in XVI-6 INT'L ENCY. COMP. L. 3 (M. Cappelletti ed. 1984). For an extensive bibliography, see id. at 607.

For the following discussion on comparative civil procedure (text at notes 24-61 infra), I have relied principally upon the comprehensive treatments contained in volume XVI-6 of the INTERNATIONAL ENCYCLOPEDIA OF COMPARATIVE LAW. There is a paucity of available sources on this subject. For example, Professor Herzog's excellent CIVIL PROCEDURE IN FRANCE (1967) is unfortunately a relatively isolated example of thorough research in this area. Also, the few comparative references that exist generally do not focus upon the adversarial-inquisitorial dichotomy. The textual discussion also makes reference to the general sources cited in notes 1, 3, 7, 8, 17, 18, and to general knowledge information. Extensive bibliographical references are contained in the principal source and are, therefore, not reproduced in the following footnotes.

25. See Kaplan & Clermont, *England and the United States,* supra note 24, at 20-23.

26. See id. at 21.

27. Id. at 20.

28. See id. at 29-34.

29. See id. at 32 & 34.

30. Id. at 33-36.

31. Id. at 32-33.

32. Id. at 34-37.

33. Id. at 29-30. See also Jolowicz, *The Jury in the Law of Tort,* XI-13 INT'L ENCY. COMP. L. § 142-48 (1972).

34. See Kaplan & Clermont, *England and the United States,* supra note 24, at 30.

35. Id. at 34-35.

36. Id. at 35. In their constitutions, forty-eight of the fifty states — Colorado and Louisiana being the exceptions — provide a constitutional right to a jury trial in most civil actions. The right to a jury trial in civil cases guaranteed by the federal constitution has never been incorporated into due process requirements applicable to states — hence the need for state constitutional provisions. This differs from the right to a jury trial in criminal matters.

37. Id.

38. Id. at 34, 39.

39. See J. BAKER, AN INTRODUCTION TO ENGLISH LEGAL HISTORY 62-83 (2d ed. 1979).

40. See Kaplan & Clermont, *England and the United States,* supra note 24, at 35.

41. See J. BAKER, AN INTRODUCTION TO ENGLISH LEGAL HISTORY, note 39 supra.

42. See Kohl, *Romanist Legal Systems,* in XVI-6 INT'L ENCY. COMP. L. 57, 61 (M. Cappelletti ed. 1984). For an extensive bibliography, see id. at 100. For a discussion of the differences between common-law and civil-law civil procedure, see also M. CAPPELLETTI & J. JOLOWICZ, PUBLIC IN-TEREST PARTIES AND THE ACTIVE ROLE OF THE JUDGE IN CIVIL LITIGATION, supra note 18, at 246-48, 259-61.

43. See Kohl, *Romanist Legal Systems,* supra note 42, at 61.

44. Id.

45. Id. at 61-62.

46. Id. at 74-77.

47. Id. at 65.

48. See Wengerek, *Socialist Countries,* in XVI-6 INT'L ENCY. COMP. L. 141 (M. Cappelletti ed. 1984). For an extensive bibliography, see id. at 188. For a discussion of the concept of "objective" truth in socialist ideology and its influence upon civil procedure, see M. CAPPELLETTI & J. JOLOWICZ, PUBLIC INTEREST PARTIES AND THE ACTIVE ROLE OF THE JUDGE IN CIVIL LITIGATION, supra note 18, at 175-77, 262-63.

49. See Wengerek, *Socialist Countries,* supra note 48, at 141-46.

50. See id. at 168-71.

51. Id. at 166-65.

52. Id. at 171.

53. Id. at 149, 147-49, 153-62.

54. Id. at 182-84.

55. See Ekelof, *Scandinavian Countries,* in XVI-6 INT'L ENCY. COMP. L. 189 (M. Cappelletti ed. 1984). For bibliographic references, see id. at 210.

56. See id. at 190, 194, 195, 199.

57. Id. at 191-92.

58. Id. at 191-92, 196-97, 199-200.

59. Id. at 192-93.

60. Id. at 192-93, 196-201.

61. Id. at 201-05.

62. See Kaplan & Clermont, *England and the United States,* supra note 24, at 17-23.

63. See Appendix B (ch. 2) infra.

64. Proceedings, *Does International Law Exist?* (Debate between John

Norton Moore and Alona Evans; John Bassett Moore Soc. Int'l Law, University of Virginia School of Law, March 1977). See also R. JENNINGS, WHAT IS INTERNATIONAL LAW AND HOW DO WE TELL IT WHEN WE SEE IT? (1983). See generally Dinstein, *International Law as a Primitive Legal System,* 19 N.Y.U. J. INT'L L. & POL. 1 (1986).

65. The principal divisions include ideological differences between the East and West and economic development conflicts between the North (developed countries) and the South (developing countries). Religious conflicts continue to plague a number of countries. The Iran-Iraq War, for example, threatened to destabilize an already volatile yet strategic part of the world.

66. See, for example, G. MISCHE & P. MISCHE, TOWARD A HUMAN WORLD ORDER (1977); T. NARDIN, LAW, MORALITY, AND THE RELATIONS OF STATES (1983). See also W. MCKEAN, EQUALITY AND DISCRIMINATION UNDER INTERNATIONAL LAW (1983).

67. See, for example, the problem of terrorism and the political offense exception, the Warsaw Convention, and the Vienna Convention on the Law of Sales—discussed in ch. 3, infra, at notes 1-2, 14-39, and 13.

68. See, for example, Von Mehren & Patterson, *Recognition and Enforcement of Foreign-Country Judgments in the United States,* 6 L. & POL'Y INT'L BUS. 37 (1974); Carbonneau, *The French Exequatur Proceeding: The Exorbitant Jurisdictional Rules of Articles 14 and 15 (Code Civil) as Obstacles to the Enforcement of Foreign Judgments in France,* 2 HASTINGS INT'L & COMP. L. REV. 307 (1979). See also Comment, *The Reciprocity Rule and Enforcement of Foreign Judgments,* 16 COLUM. J. TRANS. L. 327 (1977).

69. STATUTE OF THE INTERNATIONAL COURT OF JUSTICE, done at San Francisco, June 26, 1945, entered into force for the United States, Oct. 14, 1945, 59 Stat. 1055, T.S. No. 993, 3 BEVANS 1153, [1976] Y.B. U.N. 1052.

70. See generally B. WESTON, R. FALK, & A. D'AMATO, INTERNATIONAL LAW AND WORLD ORDER 674-86 (1980). For a discussion of expropriations in state-to-state relations and the role of national courts, see Banco Nacional de Cuba v. Sabbatino, 193 F.Supp. 375 (S.D.N.Y. 1961), 307 F.2d 845 (2d Cir. 1962), 376 U.S. 398 (1964) (act of state doctrine held to prevent challenge of Cuban expropriation decree). See also H. STEINER & D. VAGTS, TRANSNATIONAL LEGAL PROBLEMS 691-728 (2d ed. 1976); Delson, *The Act of State Doctrine: Judicial Deference or Abstention?,* 66 AM. J. INT'L L. 82 (1972); Falk, *Toward a Theory of the Participation of Domestic Courts in the International Legal Order: A Critique of Banco Nacional de Cuba v. Sabbatino,* 16 RUTGERS L. REV. 1 (1961); Henkin, *The Foreign Affairs Power of the Federal Courts: Sabbatino,* 64 COLUM. L. REV. 805 (1964); Lowenfeld, *Act of State and Department of State: First National*

City Bank v. Banco Nacional de Cuba, 66 AM. J. INT'L L. 795 (1972). See generally Note, *International Arbitration and the Inapplicability of the Act of State Doctrine,* 14 N.Y.U. J. INT'L L. & POL. 65 (1981).

71. See generally M. MCDOUGAL & W. BURKE, THE PUBLIC ORDER OF THE OCEANS: A CONTEMPORARY INTERNATIONAL LAW OF THE SEA (1962); Burton, *Freedom of the Seas: International Law Applicable to Deep Seabed Mining Claims,* 29 STAN. L. REV. 1135 (1977); Nelson, *The Emerging New Law of the Sea,* 42 MOD. L. REV. 42 (1979).

72. See United States Diplomatic and Consular Staff in Teheran (U.S. v. Iran), [1980] I.C.J. 3. See also Note, *International Adjudication: Embassy Seizure: United States v. Iran,* [1980] I.C.J. 3, 21 HARV. INT'L L.J. 748 (1980).

73. See the Entebbe raid where Israel arguably resorted to self-help in order to recover its nationals. For a discussion of the Entebbe raid, see Y. BEN-PORAT, E. HABER, & Z. SCHIFF, ENTEBBE RESCUE (1977); F. BOYLE, WORLD POLITICS AND INTERNATIONAL LAW 77-121 (1985); H. KYEMBA, A STATE OF BLOOD 166-78 (1977); Y. RABIN, THE RABIN MEMOIRS 282-89 (1979); W. STEVENSON, 90 MINUTES AT ENTEBBE (1976).

74. See generally S. RUBIN & G. HUFBAUER, EMERGING STANDARDS OF INTERNATIONAL TRADE AND INVESTMENT (1984); Kronstein, *The Nationality of International Enterprises,* 52 COLUM. L. REV. 983 (1952); Vagts, *The Corporate Alien: Definitional Questions in Federal Restraints on Foreign Enterprises,* 74 HARV. L. REV. 1489 (1961). See also OECD Declaration, 75 DEP'T STATE BULL. 83 (1976); A. SAFARIAN, GOVERNMENTS AND MULTINATIONALS: POLICIES IN THE DEVELOPED COUNTRIES (1984); Note, *Multinational Business Enterprises in Lesser Developed Countries: The Role of the United States Legal System,* 2 FLA. INT'L L.J. 69 (1986).

75. See *Bhopal Symposium,* 20 TEX. INT'L L.J. 267 (1985).

76. See, for example, Westbrook, *Theories of Parent Company Liability and the Prospects for an International Settlement,* 20 TEX. INT'L L.J. 321 (1985). See also Maynard, *A Code of Conduct for Transnational Corporations,* 4 THE COM. LAW. 103 (1985); Note, *United States-Based Multinational Corporations Should Be Tried in the United States for Their Extraterritorial Toxic Torts,* 19 VAND. J. TRANS. 651 (1986); Tzouganatos, *Private International Law as a Means to Control the Multinational Enterprise,* 19 VAND. J. TRANS. L. 478 (1986).

77. In re Union Carbide Corp. Gas Plant Disaster at Bhopal India, No. 21-38 (S.D.N.Y. May 12, 1986):

This Court is firmly convinced that the Indian legal system is in a far better position than the American courts to determine the cause of the tragic event and thereby fix liability. Further, the Indian courts have greater access to all the information needed to arrive at the amount of the compensation to be awarded the victims. The presence in India of the overwhelming majority of the witnesses and evidence, both documentary and real, would by itself suggest that India is the most convenient forum for this consolidated case. The additional presence in India of all but the less than handful of claimants underscores the convenience of holding trial in India.

. . .

The administrative burden of this immense litigation would unfairly tax this or any American tribunal. The cost to American taxpayers of supporting the litigation in the United States would be excessive. When another, adequate and more convenient forum so clearly exists, there is no reason to press the United States judiciary to the limits of its capacity. No American interest in the outcome of this litigation outweighs the interest of India in applying Indian law and Indian values to that of resolving this case.

. . .

Plaintiffs, including the Union of India, have argued that the courts of India are not up to the task of conducting the Bhopal litigation. They assert that the Indian judiciary has yet to reach full maturity due to the restraints placed upon it by British colonial rulers who shaped the Indian legal system to meet their own ends. Plaintiffs allege that the Indian justice system has not yet cast off the burden of colonialism to meet the emerging needs of a democratic people.

The Court thus finds itself faced with a paradox. In the Court's view, to retain the litigation in this forum, as plaintiffs request, would be yet another example of imperialism, another situation in which an established sovereign inflicted its rules, its standards and values on a developing nation. This Court declines to play such a role. The Union of India is a world power in 1986, and its courts have the proven capacity to mete out fair and equal justice. To deprive the Indian judiciary of this opportunity to stand tall before the world and to pass judgment on behalf of its own people would be to revive a history of subservience and subjugation from which India has emerged. India and its people can and must vindicate their claims before the independent and legitimate judiciary created there since the Independence of 1947.

. . .

Therefore, the consolidated case is dismissed on the grounds of forum non conveniens . . .
Id. at 53-56.
See also Janis, *The Doctrine of Forum Non Conveniens and the Bhopal Case,* 34 NETHERLANDS INT'L L. REV. 192 (1987); Olejniczak, *Bhopal Disaster Litigation: A Jurisdictional Odyssey,* 2 EMORY J. INT'L DISP. RES. 205 (1987).

78. See M. C. Mehta & Anr. v. Union of India & Ors., Civil Writ Petition No. 12739 of 1985 (Sup. Ct. India) (decided Dec. 20, 1986):

Law has to grow in order to satisfy the needs of the fast changing society and keep abreast with the economic developments taking place in the country. As new situations arise the law has to be evolved in order to meet the challenge of such new situations. Law cannot afford to remain static. We have to evolve new principles and lay down new norms which would adequately deal with the new problems which arise in a highly industrialised economy. We cannot allow our judicial thinking to be constricted by reference to the law as it prevails in England or for the matter of that in any other foreign country. We no longer need the crutches of a foreign legal order. We are certainly prepared to receive light from whatever source it comes but we have to build up our own jurisprudence and we cannot countenance an argument that merely because the new law does not recognise the rule of strict and absolute liability in cases of hazardous or dangerous liability or the rule as laid down in Rylands v. Fletcher as is developed in England recognises certain limitations and responsibilities. We in India cannot hold our hands back and I venture to evolve a new principle of liability which English courts have not done. We have to develop our own law and if we find that it is necessary to construct a new principle of liability to deal with an unusual situation which has arisen and which is likely to arise in the future on account of hazardous or inherently dangerous industries which are concomitant to an industrial economy, there is no reason why we should hesitate to evolve such principle of liability merely because it has not been so done in England. We are of the view that an enterprise which is engaged in a hazardous or inherently dangerous industry which poses a potential threat to the health and safety of the persons working in the factory and residing in the surrounding areas owes an absolute and non-delegable duty to the community to ensure that no harm results to anyone on account of hazardous or inherently dangerous nature of the activity which it has undertaken. The enterprises must be held to be under an obligation to provide that the hazardous or inherently dangerous activity in which it is engaged must be conducted with the highest standards of safety and if any harm results on account of such activity, the enterprise must be absolutely liable to compensate for such harm and it should be no answer to the enterprise to say that it had taken all reasonable care and that the harm occurred without any negligence on its part. Id. at 29-30.

79. See, for example, Westbrook, *Theories of Parent Company Liability and the Prospects for an International Settlement,* note 76 supra.

80. See generally J. BARTON & B. FISHER, INTERNATIONAL TRADE AND INVESTMENT (1986); J. JACKSON & W. DAVEY, INTERNATIONAL ECONOMIC RELATIONS (2d ed. 1986); Symposium, *Contemporary Issues of International Trade Law,* 19 INT'L LAW. 725 (1985).

81. See discussion in ch. 3 infra.

82. See generally D. WILSON, INTERNATIONAL BUSINESS TRANSACTIONS (2d ed. 1984); Symposium, *Transnational Litigation,* 18 INT'L LAW. 522 (1984); Von Mehren, *Transnational Litigation in American Courts: An Overview of Problems and Issues,* in PRIVATE INVESTORS ABROAD: PROBLEMS AND SOLUTIONS IN INTERNATIONAL BUSINESS IN 1984 1 (J. Moss ed. 1985).

83. See generally text accompanying note 80 supra (sources cited).

84. See generally G. DELAUME, TRANSNATIONAL CONTRACTS, APPLICABLE LAW AND SETTLEMENT OF DISPUTES (A STUDY IN CONFLICT AVOIDANCE) (multi-volume series); G. DELAUME, LAW AND PRACTICE OF TRANSNATIONAL CONTRACTS (1988).

85. See id. See also Delaume, *What Is an International Contract? An American and a Gallic Dilemma,* 28 INT'L & COMP. L.Q. 258 (1979).

86. See, for example, THE IRAN–UNITED STATES CLAIM TRIBUNAL 1981-1983 [Seventh Sokol Colloquium] (R. Lillich ed. 1984); Belland, *The Iran–United States Claims Tribunal: Some Reflections on Trying a Claim,* 1 J. INT'L ARB. 237 (1984); McCabe, *Arbitral Discovery and the Iran–United States Claims Tribunal Experience,* 20 INT'L LAW. 499 (1986); Stein, *Jurisprudence and Jurists' Prudence: The Iranian-Forum Clause Decisions of the Iran-U.S. Claims Tribunal,* 78 AM. J. INT'L L. 1 (1984); Swanson, *Iran-U.S. Claims Tribunal: A Policy Analysis of the Expropriation Cases,* 18 CASE W. RES. J. INT'L L. 307 (1986); *Symposium on the Iran–United States Claims Tribunal,* 16 L. & POL'Y INT'L BUS. 667 (1984).

87. See 81 DEP'T STATE BULL. 1 (1981), reprinted in 20 INT'L. LEG. MAT'LS 223 (1981). See also Audit, *Les "Accords" d'Alger du 19 janvier 1981 tendant au réglement des différends entre les Etats-Unis et l'Iran,* 108 J. DR. INT'L-CLUNET 713 (1981).

88. See Carbonneau, *Arbitral Adjudication,* 19 TEX. INT'L L.J. 33, 33-39 (1984).

89. See discussion in ch. 3, infra, at notes 11-12; ch. 4, infra, at note 107.

90. See discussion in ch. 4, infra, at notes 78-87.

91. See *Arbitral Adjudication,* supra note 88, at 56-57, 77-78.

92. See The Bremen v. Zapata Off-Shore Co., 407 U.S. 1 (1977). See also Farquharson, *Choice of Forum Clauses: A Brief Survey of Anglo-American Law,* 8 INT'L LAW. 83 (1974).

93. See *Arbitral Adjudication,* supra note 88, at 33-39.

3 | Arbitration and the Creation of Transnational Adjudicatory Norms

Transnational Law-Making

While maintaining pluralism in the community of nations, international legal organization—in an effort to facilitate the resolution of disputes arising from international government relations and private transnational activity—seeks to unify substantive law. Effective harmonization of substantive standards can reduce the conflict among, and attenuate the impact of national variations in, juridical methodology, economic interest, and political belief. Although often accompanied by elaborate theoretical constructs, such attempts at transnational law-making rarely achieve their most ambitious, and sometimes even their more modest, goals.

In public law matters, for example, the world community has endeavored periodically to arrive at an agreed-upon definition of terrorism in extradition practice.[1] Ideological and other differences between nations, however, have prevented the articulation of a universal standard; the lack of consensus eliminates any possible foundation for a comprehensive rule of international criminal law that could effectively distinguish acts of terrorism from exempt political conduct.[2] In private law matters, the development of international travel, transportation, and communication has made transnational litigation commonplace in domestic adjudicatory processes. Consequently, national courts engage more frequently in evidence-gathering and other judicial functions across national boundaries. States, through a variety of international instruments,[3] have attempted to accommodate contemporary adjudicatory needs and ease the burdens of transnational litigation upon domestic forums by establishing a universal framework for international judicial cooperation. Here as elsewhere, the diversity of approaches—for example, to the classification and evaluation of evidence—impedes the creation of a set of meaningful worldwide standards.[4]

Contrasting social and political organization among countries also makes the unification of private law a difficult task. For instance, a transnationally uniform product liability law is, in all likelihood, an impossible objective to attain.[5] Issues of tort law generally implicate political and economic interests, and bring ideological considerations to bear in the assessment of the controlling legal regime.[6] In the United States, the judicial espousal of the compensatory objective of tort law makes that area of law function, in effect, as a legislatively unauthorized social insurance program. In the setting of the American legal system, therefore, the adoption of a strict rule of product liability fits into the existing demeanor of the system.[7] By contrast, in England, premising manufacturer liability for injuries done by products upon a negligence standard may be a sufficient juridical standard in light of the extensive English welfare system.[8] In any event, because of their commitment to social welfare goals, European democracies generally may need no more than a diluted rule of product liability that merges principles of legal fault with a no-fault premise.[9] However, given its impact upon the industrial sector, a strict rule of product liability would certainly be inapposite in developing countries where industrial growth and economic investment need to be encouraged.[10]

The national dichotomies in political and economic organization, therefore, make a universally applicable substantive legal framework for products a virtual impossibility. In fact, from an international perspective, the very diversity of substantive standards defeats the viability of a strict rule of liability. A consumer-oriented, absolute form of liability could always be undermined by the transnational distribution of allegedly questionable products from developed countries to developing countries.[11]

As a consequence, in private law litigation involving transnational interests, domestic courts generally do not anchor determinations in a universal rule of decision applied uniformly by all other national courts. Ordinarily, these courts invoke choice-of-law of principles and designate a particular set of national legal provisions as the law governing the merits of the litigation. Perhaps sensing that they lack the requisite jurisdictional basis, domestic forums, therefore, make no meaningful attempt to fashion a transnational rule of law that corresponds to the essential nature of the dispute under consideration. Whatever uniformity exists is achieved in a decentralized, ad hoc, and indirect fashion. Simpy stated, in a given jurisdiction, national legal provisions serve provisionally as international rules of law in the particular litigation.[12]

In other circumstances, an international instrument, ratified by the political branches of government, may be controlling. The theoretical uniformity of the convention framework, however, usually does not survive the multifarious judicial interpretations that can be given to synthetic, supposedly agreed-upon legal provisions. Stated differently, in most instances, the attempt to legislate transnational substantive uniformity fails because the national differences in juridical approach and interest are likely to appear, not at the level of the general statement of doctrine in the international instrument, but rather in the judicial implementation of the convention in cases brought before domestic tribunals.[13]

The Warsaw Convention

The history of the Warsaw Convention illustrates the potential ineffectiveness of transnational rule-making by convention.[14] The Warsaw Convention, signed in 1929 and ratified by the United States in 1934, represents a multistate attempt to establish an international rule of law to regulate the liability of air carriers for the corporeal and material damages that result from the risks of air travel and transportation.[15] As the international air industry was becoming a reality in the mid-1920s, government attention focused upon the need to protect the nascent enterprise from the prospect of unlimited tort liability. The apprehension was that a single aircraft disaster or a series of such disasters could completely paralyze the industry's commercial viability, depriving all nations of the benefits of the new technology.[16]

The convention's objective was to create a uniform regime of predictable legal rules—specifically, to limit prospective liability by establishing ceilings on the amount of recoverable damages.[17] In particular, the convention's liability scheme applies "to all international transportation of persons, baggage, or goods performed by aircraft for hire."[18] The convention adopted a two-pronged approach to the imposition of legal liability, reflecting an attempt to strike a somewhat precarious balance between protecting the air industry (the convention's foremost objective) and recognizing the consumer interest of passengers.

First, the convention provided for a presumptive, ostensibly non-absolute, form of legal liability against air carriers.[19] A presumption of liability arises against the carrier when a passenger suffers bodily injury or death "if the accident which caused the damage sustained took place on board the aircraft or in the course of any of the operations of embarking or disembarking."[20] The presumption of carrier liability appears to sound in negligence; however, it places a higher than reasonable duty of care upon the air carriers, a standard of conduct akin to the utmost care to which domestic common carriers are held in common-law jurisdictions.[21] Air carriers can avail themselves of three defenses. They can rebut the presumption of liability by establishing that (1) "all necessary measures" were taken to avoid the damage; or (2), in the circumstances, such measures were impossible to undertake; or (3) the passenger was contributorily negligent.[22] The provision for carrier exculpation through victim fault supports the view that, despite its strict liability formulation, the form of liability contemplated by the convention is based upon negligence.

Second, the convention contains limitation of liability provisions.[23] These provisions are the means by which the convention achieves its protective objective and balances the weighting of the liability scheme in favor of injured passengers. In the event of death or injury to a passenger, the carrier can be held liable only for a maximum amount of 125,000 francs (approximately $8,300)—provided, of course, that the event takes place under the conditions specified in the convention and defenses are unavailing.[24] Similar liability provisions apply to damage done to physical property (checked baggage, carry-on baggage, and cargo) transported by air carriers.[25] The convention sets maximum carrier liability for checked baggage and cargo at 250 francs per kilogram, and for carry-on articles at a global figure of 5,000 francs. These limitation-of-liability provisions are inapplicable to the circumstances of a maloccurrence when the carrier fails to give proper notice of the convention's applicability to the transportation in question, or when the carrier causes damage through willful misconduct.[26]

In terms of transnational law-making, the convention's methodological aim is of particular interest. In addressing the issues of legal doctrine likely to arise in a soon-to-be complex area of international activity, the convention endeavored to elaborate synthetic legal answers to questions of transnational liability within a cohesive, unitary, and comprehensive regulatory framework. In this sense, the convention's methodological scope was universal in character. While maintaining a basic respect for the distinctiveness of national legal systems, it attempted to overcome the potential diversity of legal regimes by creating a viable transnational framework for dealing with an activity essential to the organization of the world community. The convention's attempt to establish a uniform juridical approach to the question of air carrier liability, however, eventually became an ill-fated venture. Rather than act as a juridical instrument responding to an emerging, or codifying an already existing, international consensus, the Warsaw convention attempted to generate such a consensus.

The convention's focused practical design—to protect air carriers from potentially unlimited tort liability—rapidly became anachronistic, eventually conflicting directly with the development of tort and consumer protection law in most developed countries.[27] The provision for carrier protection at the expense of the consumer interest and in opposition to domestic liability regimes generated significant opposition and provoked both express and implied refusals to comply.[28] The attempt to elaborate a framework for private law adjudication among countries, in effect, fell short of the desired uniformity.

A number of technical problems of interpretation, ordinarily associated with legislation, also hindered the implementation of the convention. First, the convention's scope of application is difficult to ascertain. The text of the convention is ambiguous about what it means by "international transportation"; its general language has made the concept subject to a number of varying definitions by national courts.[29] Second, it is not entirely clear what conditions must be satisfied in order to trigger the convention's liability regime. For example, national courts have yet to provide a uniform definition for the physical operations envisaged by the phrase "operations of embarking or disembarking."[30] Moreover, questions exist concerning the exact meaning of the centrally important concept of adequate notice and delivery.[31] The concept refers to the air carriers' obligation to notify passengers of the convention's applicability and its limitation of liability provisions. According to the theory of the convention, delivery of adequate notice allows the passengers to make informed choices about assumption of risk—to take out personal insurance against the possibility of greater loss or injury.[32] How is adequacy to be defined in both typical and uncharacteristic circumstances? What type of print will be deemed sufficient? Finally, debate exists over what is intended by the presumption of negligence as a rule of liability and how that presumption might be rebutted in reference to specific circumstances.[33]

In addition to the usual problems of construction, the Warsaw Convention is beset by difficulties that arise specifically from its transnational character. The official text of the convention is in French; the convention's basic structure, its wording and concepts, are all embedded in an unmistakably civilian legal approach.[34] Confining the convention to one legal tradition and language raises the problem of appropriately translating the technical language of the convention, along with the civil-law tonality of its substance, for use by domestic courts in common-law jurisdictions. The difficulty of finding a suitable linguistic transposition of the French text of the convention exacerbates the difficulty of achieving a uniform national court interpretation of the convention's provisions.[35] For example, some national, primarily civil-law, courts hold that the basis for liability under the convention is a contractual one, whereas courts in other jurisdictions—primarily common-law countries—maintain that the liability contemplated by the convention is essentially one that sounds in tort.[36] This type of fundamental disagreement imperils the convention's status as an instrument providing for a comprehensive system of governing law.

The regulatory effectiveness of the Warsaw Convention is also undermined by the continued efforts of some governments—most notably the United States—to modify its content, especially its limitation of liability provisions.[37] The most critical obstacle to the convention's effective implementation is, in fact, national government and court dissatisfaction with the ceilings on liability. Indeed, there appears to be a mounting consensus, centering upon discontent with maximum recovery amounts, that the convention is no longer necessary or useful. The airline industry, it is argued, has matured considerably since 1929. The evolution of the law of tort has taken a direction at odds with the convention's policy imperative. Finally, the insurance industry is now sufficiently developed to enable it to provide coverage at economically feasible rates.[38]

Attempts have been made to modify the convention and adapt it to evolving juridical attitudes. Since 1929, international meetings in the Hague, Guadalajara, Guatemala, and Montreal have given rise to amending documents;[39] the vicissitudes of international politics, however, have prevented any of these texts from gaining universal ratification. As a result, the current regime for the transnational regulation of air carrier liability is in a state of chaos, with the United States government and courts acting as the principal sources of dissent.

The New York Arbitration Convention

The history and current status of the Warsaw Convention contrast vividly with the genesis, evolution, and contemporary stature of the 1958 New York Arbitration Convention.[40] The latter reflects a much more successful experiment in transnational law-making; it symbolizes a productive attempt to achieve a viable transnational rule of law through the unification of private law.

Like the Warsaw Convention, the New York Arbitration Convention was intended to act as a universal charter;[41] its provisions were meant to articulate a workable, agreed-upon juridical framework for regulating national legal conduct in an area of international activity. Unlike the Warsaw Convention, however, the New York Arbitration Convention embodied the tenets of an already existing and still emerging international consensus. Although the New York Convention undoubtedly contributed to expanding the recognition of the utility of international commercial arbitration, the force of its essential authority is based upon its codification of an already established international attitude toward arbitration. Also, rather than attempt to regulate all aspects of the process, the New York Convention focused directly upon two vital elements of arbitral procedure (the validity of arbitration agreements and the enforcement of arbitral awards),[42] leaving a more comprehensive regulatory scheme to be implied from its express principles.

It is clear from the face of the New York Convention that its express objective is to unify national law in regard to the enforcement of foreign arbitral awards and, more impliedly, to establish a transnational rule of law that favors the recourse to arbitral adjudication.[43] For example, article II(1) provides that the contracting states shall recognize an agreement to submit disputes to arbitration. The purpose of this article is to eradicate systemic hostility to arbitration — hostility stemming from the view that arbitration amounts to a usurpation of judicial authority to adjudicate disputes. Consequently, by adhering to the convention, contracting states agree to recognize the arbitral process as a legitimate means of resolving disputes.[44] Under paragraph 3 of article II, a request to compel arbitration can be defeated only by establishing that the arbitration agreement was null and void, inoperative, or incapable of being performed.[45] The legislative history of the convention demonstrates that these defenses were meant to function as ordinary contract defenses to the enforcement of an agreement.[46] Arbitration agreements, therefore, are valid contractual arrangements and do not, per se, violate principles of public policy. They symbolize party recourse to contractual prerogatives—a recourse that can be defeated only by a deficiency in contractual intent, capacity, or language. Accordingly, courts in the contracting states are under a legal imperative to enforce arbitration agreements, provided the latter meet the usual requirements of contractual validity.

The text of the convention proposes a unified transnational rule of law not only in regard to the validity of arbitration agreements, but also concerning the enforcement of foreign arbitral awards.[47] The institutional autonomy and systemic viability of any nonjudicial adjudicatory process are dependent upon both the legal system's recognition of the validity of agreements to enter into such processes and its willingness to give binding effect to the determinations of such parallel adjudicatory processes. The seven grounds in article V under which national courts may review arbitral awards for purposes of recognition and enforcement can be grouped into two broad categories. First, the technical grounds for a denial of recognition and enforcement refer to essential contractual and procedural due process requirements. The parties must have had the contractual capacity to enter into an arbitration agreement; they must have been afforded proper notice of the proceeding; the arbitrators must not have exceeded the jurisdictional authority conferred upon them by the agreement; the composition and appointment of arbitrators must have been in conformity with the provisions of the agreement; and the award must have been binding in the jurisdiction in which it was rendered.[48]

Second, national courts can deny recognition and enforcement to a foreign arbitral award upon the basis of two broad public-policy-oriented grounds.[49] The dispute that the award settles must have been arbitrable under the law of the requested jurisdiction; moreover, recognition and enforcement of the award must not be contrary to the requested jurisdiction's public policy. To some extent, the inarbitrability and public policy defenses to the recognition and enforcement of foreign arbitral awards overlap. As a general rule, disputes relating to the status and capacity of persons are not submissible to arbitration but rather fall exclusively within the scope of the state's jurisdictional competence. Accordingly, an award relating to an inarbitrable subject matter would also be, if recognized and enforced, contrary to the public policy of the requested jurisdiction.

As with any other legislative document, the broad general language of these fundamental and other provisions of the New York Convention could be subject to forms of judicial construction in specific cases that undermine the convention's underlying intent. As noted previously,[50] in the case of the Warsaw Convention, some American courts have rigorously interpreted the adequate notice requirement to defeat the application of the convention's limitation of liability provisions. Similarly, despite the content of its second paragraph, national courts could have given a stringent interpretation to the New York Convention's article II requirement that arbitration agreements be in writing. Courts could also have given wide effect to the article II contractual defenses to the validity of arbitration agreements, finding a plethora of circumstances for invalidating agreements. Moreover, as to the grounds for denying recognition and enforcement in article V, national courts could have given a highly legalistic content to the due process requirement or advanced an uncompromisingly rigorous view of their jurisdiction's public policy.

Actual decisional law outcomes[51] in signatory states reveal, however, that the vast majority of national courts interpret the convention uniquely by reference to its underlying intent. The contrast with the various national domestic cases relating to the Warsaw Convention is marked, and evidences that the New York Convention has successfully developed a transnational juridical framework relating to arbitration — a framework characterized by the reference to emerging international commercial realities and the dynamic interplay between the content of an international instrument and the interpretive and enforcement powers of national courts.[52] The convention's truly international stature and law-making capacity are built upon two factors: its passive and largely symbolic function of codifying an existing and emerging international consensus on arbitration, and its endorsement by national legal processes that seek to affirm and integrate the convention's content and underlying intent and, thereby, entrench the transnational recognition of and support for arbitration. The transnational law-making impact of the convention is reflected, to varying degrees, in the domestic arbitration law of a number of jurisdictions.

The French Law of Arbitration

Compared with other countries, France was especially quick to ratify the New York Convention. The longstanding French domestic court support for international commercial arbitration[53] probably contributed significantly to the alacrity of the French espousal of the convention. At the time of the French ratification[54] in 1959, the French law of arbitration, although progressing toward consolidation, was in need of revision.[55] In particular, French law was characterized by outmoded provisions on domestic arbitration and an absence of any statutory regulation pertaining to international arbitration, although a body of judicial opinions attempted to remedy statutory deficiencies and uphold the validity of arbitral dispute resolution.

Until 1980, the French law of arbitration consisted of articles 1005 through 1026 and article 1028 of the Code of Civil Procedure (originally promulgated in 1806 and subsequently modified in 1975) and article 631 of the Code of Commerce. The law of December 31, 1925, had modified article 631, legalizing the arbitral clause in certain specified commercial cases.[56] Because arbitration agreements were especially common in commercial cases, the amended content of article 631 eliminated much of the domestic judicial hostility toward arbitration. Given their early enactment, the provisions in the Code of Civil Procedure were ill-suited to the regulatory needs of modern arbitration practice. They contained gaps and referred to antiquated procedures that, in most cases, were supplemented or remedied by judicially created rules.[57] Moreover, the domestic legislation did not directly regulate international commercial arbitration. Despite the judicial adaptation of these provisions in domestic arbitration litigation, their application by analogy to international arbitration cases could have impaired severely the viability of the international process. Rather than use domestic law as a servile foundation for articulating legal rules pertaining to international matters, the French courts undertook to identify the special needs of international commercial arbitration and fashion an accommodating decisional law.[58]

For example, rather than merely transpose into international litigation the domestic provision prohibiting the French state from engaging in arbitration,[59] the courts held that the French state was bound by arbitration agreements included in private international contracts to which the state or its instrumentalities were parties.[60] Moreover, the courts confined considerably the reach of domestic public policy imperatives in matters of international commercial arbitration. In a number of significant rulings, the courts concluded that, for purposes of international adjudication, French public policy required only that arbitral proceedings guarantee the parties a fair opportunity to be heard and to present their case.[61] In addition, unlike domestic awards, international or foreign arbitral awards did not have to be accompanied by a reasoned opinion to be enforceable.[62] The courts further held that arbitral awards, unlike court judgments, were subject only to a limited form of review for purposes of recognition and enforcement and that a valid arbitration agreement constituted a waiver of the French rules of exorbitant jurisdiction.[63] These court opinions and others like them demonstrated that the French courts had a keen perception of the systemic needs of international commercial arbitration, did not neglect opportunities to foster its growth, and afforded it a privileged status in the French legal order.

Some years following its ratification of the New York Arbitration Convention, France enacted twin legislative provisions regulating both the domestic and international arbitral processes. This legislation reflects a formal statutory consolidation of the French law of arbitration. The Decree of May 14, 1980, repealed the antiquated provisions of the Code of Civil Procedure and replaced them with some fifty new articles.[64] The 1980 decree restructured the body of applicable law into a more coherent and intelligible whole. Its content responds to a number of critical questions left unanswered by the former legislation, most notably, whether arbitral tribunals could themselves rule upon jurisdictional challenges, and how great a role court supervision should play in arbitral proceedings. The decree also implicitly confers a new legal status upon the arbitral clause and reorganizes the recourse that can be had against arbitral awards.

As a general rule, the new legislative text remedied many of the uncertainties that attended the application or interpretation of the previous legislation. It gave the regulation of arbitration clarity of direction and the arbitral process official systemic autonomy. It aligned the arbitral proceeding with court actions — for example, giving arbitral awards *res judicata* effect once rendered. The principal originality of the decree lies in the relationship that it established between the arbitral and judicial processes. Under the new French law, the courts are perceived as a complement to the arbitral process, providing the public force of law to a private contractual process where such intervention is necessary to the successful implementation of the process. The decree's basic intent is unmistakable: it is designed to promote arbitration as a viable alternative dispute resolution process.

The legislation on domestic arbitration was followed by the Decree of May 12, 1981, dealing with matters of international arbitration.[65] The 1981 decree represents the first French legislative enactment on international arbitration. The content of the decree is in full accord with the express provisions and underlying intent of the 1958 New York Arbitration Convention; in fact, it is perhaps the most forceful national statement upholding the convention's transnational law-making objective. For example, in article 1492, the 1981 decree espouses a comprehensive definition of the concept of international arbitration, providing that an international arbitration is one that "implicates the interests of international commerce."[66] The absence of a choice-of-law reference to a nationality factor in establishing the definition, combined with the exclusive reference to the economic substance and impact of the transaction, impliedly recognizes a sphere of lawful transnational activity not anchored in the domestic statutory or decisional law base of any national legal system.[67]

Furthering this "anational" design, the 1981 decree contemplates imposing only essential national law restraints upon the arbitral process and gives predominant importance to the principle of party autonomy. For instance, parties to an international arbitration agreement may choose whatever procedural and substantive law they wish to govern the arbitral proceeding. While the arbitral tribunal must render its ruling in accordance with the rules of law, the parties can modify the content of the rules they have designated as applicable. Tracking the realities of international practice, the decree further provides that the tribunal must take commercial usages into account in its ruling. Finally, the parties can authorize the arbitral tribunal to rule *ex aequo et bono,* outside the boundaries of legal rules when a sense of equity so dictates. Thus, in the vital area of designating a law to govern the merits and the procedure, the decree, as it does in its other provisions, maintains the contractual principle of party autonomy essentially unfettered.[68]

The courts can intervene in the proceeding exclusively to assist the process, and judicial assistance can be provided only in fairly limited circumstances. For example, when the arbitration takes place in France or is governed by French procedural law, the district court in Paris can appoint arbitrators upon a party's request, unless the agreement provides to the contrary. The decree does not contemplate any other form of judicial assistance. If the agreement fails to provide for applicable procedural or substantive law, for instance, the arbitral tribunal has the authority to make the determination. Generally, the provision for limited judicial assistance attests to the French legislation's intent to give full recognition to the special characteristics of international commercial arbitration and provide regulations for a process that is "anational" in character.[69]

The decree then sets forth a set of rules pertaining to the recognition and enforcement of foreign and international arbitral awards. These rules apply independently of the provisions of the New York Arbitration Convention, either when a party designates them as applicable or when the award falls outside the scope of the convention. The rules are basically identical to their counterparts in the convention, but for their even less restrictive character. Recognition or enforcement may be denied only for technical violations of the arbitral tribunal's jurisdictional mandate and infringements of basic due process rights.[70]

The reception of the New York Arbitration Convention in the French legal order and the French legal system's evolving response to matters of domestic and international arbitration reveal that French law not only supports, but also fosters the transnational rule of law embodied in the convention. In addition, the French experience illustrates the basic procedure by which the international legal order can elaborate workable legal rules with authoritative content. The lawmaking authority of such rules arises initially because they codify and develop an existing (perhaps tacit) consensus among a majority of nations. Progressively, they acquire more formal legitimating sources (integration in an international convention, in national statutory and decisional laws, and in the modus vivendi of the affected communities). This multiple domestic adhesion is necessary to establish the international scope of the legal rule. Once such domestic recognition is achieved and consolidated, the internationally recognized rule — using the support gained from national legal processes — develops a dynamism of its own and begins to operate in an independent fashion, transcending the jurisdictional perimeters of national legal processes and acquiring a truly transnational regulatory character. Having established this foundation, they eventually supersede the bounds of municipal law by their continued presence and development, and acquire an autonomous transnational stature.

Not all countries, however, have embraced the rule of the New York Convention as quickly and as unqualifiedly as did France. Although the convention can boast of an overwhelming number of adherents, its acceptance and impact were more gradual in other jurisdictions. The reluctance was in evidence even among nations that, in theory, should have been drawn to the essentially western and northern underpinnings of the international commercial arbitration process.

The English Law

Even in its contemporary form, the English position on arbitration remains a less enthusiastic endorsement than its French counterpart. The United Kingdom acceded to the New York Convention in 1975.[71] In all likelihood, the belated accession reflected considerable doubts about the convention's purpose and principle.

The development of the English law of arbitration[72] has been impeded by the longstanding English tradition of supervising arbitral awards through judicial merits review and, generally, the persistence of judicial and legislative distrust of arbitration.[73] While the ostensible purpose of the Arbitration Act of 1950 was to institute a more liberal view of arbitration, recognizing it as a legitimate alternative adjudicatory procedure, the act nonetheless provided for fairly extensive judicial intervention both in the arbitral proceeding and in regard to the award.[74] The act adopted the "stated case" procedure, the principal mechanism for effecting judicial review of the legal content of arbitral awards.[75] The statutory procedure for review included both a "consultative case," applying to requests for judicial guidance on legal questions made during the arbitral proceeding, and "alternative final awards," applying to the arbitrator's statement of legal questions at the end of the proceeding.[76]

In effect, despite its stated intent, the Arbitration Act of 1950 embodied a continuing systemic distrust of arbitral adjudication, relegating it essentially to a fact-finding function in the process of adjudication. Although an arbitral tribunal could effectively rule pursuant to a binding agreement, it was required to apply legal rules in much the same way a court of competent jurisdiction would have done. The English concept of adjudicatory public policy seemed to require determinations based upon "correct" legal reasoning and results. Questions of law were to be referred to the High Court to guarantee basic substantive uniformity between court rulings and arbitral awards. Because the award, upon review, was tantamount to a judicial determination, the parties' initial intent to refer the dispute to arbitration was, in effect, defeated. The parties' contractual stipulation providing for arbitration allowed them to gain only procedural flexibility in a perhaps less costly and more expeditious proceeding. Therefore, before 1979, the stated case procedure, which the parties could not waive by contract, provided for mandatory judicial review and appeal of arbitral proceedings on questions of law at either party's request and, thus, negated some of the primary benefits of arbitration.

The Arbitration Act of 1979 redefined judicial supervision of arbitral proceedings and awards in England and Wales.[77] The 1979 act generally lessened the courts' supervisory authority. It repealed an entire section of the 1950 act and, subject to certain exceptions and qualifications, abolished the common-law jurisdiction of the High Court to set aside an award for a manifest error of fact or law. More significantly, the 1979 act abolished the stated case procedure, replacing it with "a more limited right of appeal to the High Court."[78] With respect to international arbitration, the act authorized exclusion agreements in nondomestic arbitrations, allowing the parties to limit judicial intervention by eliminating some of the High Court's supervisory powers. Under the act, parties to an international or, more precisely, a nondomestic contract, have the right to eliminate judicial review of future disputes by inserting a stipulation into the principal contract precluding the courts from hearing appeals, requiring reasoned awards, or providing interlocutory clarification of questions of law. The exclusion agreement is applicable only to nondomestic arbitrations and is void in so-called "special category" contracts (involving shipping, insurance, and commodity contracts) that are governed by English law. Finally, exclusion agreements cannot be used to eliminate "the benefits of English lex loci arbitri," namely, the judicial assistance of the arbitral proceeding.[79]

Chronologically, the liberalization of the English law on arbitration follows relatively closely the English adherence to the New York Arbitration Convention. Although the 1979 act represents an attenuation of judicial supervision, its content is not free of ambiguity or lingering skepticism. The act contains a rather narrow and formalistic definition of international arbitration, referring to such arbitrations as "non-domestic" arbitrations. Rather than define the concept of international arbitration (as does the French legislation) by reference to the economic content and impact of the transaction, this standard takes into account only the parties' nationalities and places of residence. Although it is quite conceivable that parties residing in England or of English nationality could enter into a contract that has all the trappings of an international economic transaction, the 1979 act denies to such parties the benefit of entering into a pre-arbitration exclusion agreement.

Moreover, the invalidity of exclusion agreements in "special category" contracts, despite the evident international character of many of these transactions even under the English definition, is a source of serious concern. Presumably, these types of transactions constitute a major part of the international business that goes through England. Even when English law governs these agreements, one wonders why, given their international commercial character, they should be singled out for possible substantive judicial supervision. Surely, the objective of achieving uniform interpretation of English law is relevant only in the setting of domestic adjudication. Once English legal rules are applied outside the boundaries of the English legal system, they cease to have their special relevance to the domestic English legal order and assume an entirely different status. This provision for judicial review diminishes severely the achievements of the other, more liberal sections of the 1979 act.

Unlike their French analogue, English legal developments pertaining to arbitration lend only qualified support to the transnational rule of law embodied in the provisions of the New York Arbitration Convention. The view that arbitral proceedings and rulings should conform to judicial standards still lingers in the domestic English statutory framework and taints the legitimacy of the arbitral process. It is a view that continues to express fundamental distrust of the arbitral process, refuses to recognize its coming-of-age, and ultimately can rob international commerce of an effective and necessary dispute resolution mechanism.[80]

Although a balance needs to be struck among the judicial and arbitral processes and their competing needs and interests, primary recognition should be given to the international consensus that surrounds the private dispute resolution process. As the provisions of the New York Arbitration Convention illustrate, court supervision should be limited to the fundamental concerns of procedural fairness: the need to thwart the abusive exercise of arbitral authority and to protect the rights of third parties in the private proceeding between the contracting parties. Although the provisions of the 1979 act attempt to inaugurate a new age of arbitration in England, the success of that effort ultimately depends upon how the English courts implement and interpret the underlying conditions and restrictions of the new legislation, and also what meaning they ascribe to the status and content of the New York Convention.

Some cases indicate that, as a result of the 1979 act, the English decisional law has shifted away from its former insistence on legal certainty to an emphasis upon promoting the finality of arbitral awards.[81] The prior attitude of allowing judicial review in virtually every case has been eliminated. In comparative terms, however, there is still a fairly large degree of judicial supervision in England. The purpose of the 1979 act was not to create full arbitral autonomy, but rather to redress the imbalance between the institutional independence of arbitration and the would-be benefits derived from the legally accurate application of English commercial law.

The Revised Canadian Law

Due in part to its juridical affinity with England, the position of the Canadian legal system on arbitration was, until recently, characterized by substantial misgivings about the legitimacy and utility of arbitration as an adjudicatory mechanism.[82] Canada's ratification in 1986 of the New York Arbitration Convention,[83] accompanied by the national and provincial adoption of the United Nations Commission on International Trade Law (UNCITRAL) model law on arbitration,[84] however, constituted a radical departure from that long-standing skepticism. These events indicate that the Canadian attitude toward arbitration is now substantially distanced from the historical and, to some extent, even from the contemporary English influence. Canada's willingness to participate in the overriding world consensus on arbitration appears to be unconditional.

Canada's previously reserved, almost apathetic, posture on arbitration arose from systemic, constitutional, and other factors. In terms of geopolitical organization,[85] Canada is—like the United States—a federal system; it became a confederated union with the adoption of the British North American Act of 1867. Canada is comprised of thirteen jurisdictions: two territories, ten provinces, and the federal government. With the exception of Quebec, which is a civil-law jurisdiction, the provinces and territories adhere to the principles of common-law juridical organization and procedures.[86]

Prior to the 1986 ratification of the New York Convention, there was no federal Canadian law of arbitration; each province and territory had its own arbitration act.[87] In the nine common-law provinces and two territories, the statutory law on arbitration was based upon the English concept of arbitration, dating back to the English Arbitration Act of 1899. This provincial legislation was relatively uniform and its salient provisions basically fostered the autonomy of arbitral adjudication—for example, the provincial statutes recognized the validity, irrevocability, and enforceability of arbitration agreements and their divesting impact upon judicial jurisdiction; they provided for judicial assistance of the arbitral proceeding; and they generally allowed for the enforceability of arbitral awards. The provincial statutes on arbitration, however, also incorporated the English practice of the stated case (also known as the special case) procedure.[88] As noted earlier,[89] by requiring arbitrators to refer questions of law to the courts, this procedure substantially undermined the incentive to have recourse to arbitration, reducing arbitration to a form of adjudicatory fact-finding.

Despite basic regulatory agreement among the common-law provinces, the Quebec law on arbitration,[90] relying upon the French Code of Civil Procedure as a model, deviated in some significant respects from the statutes in the other provinces. For example, under Quebec law, the agreement to arbitrate future disputes (the arbitral clause) was still of questionable legal validity, notwithstanding modern legislative reforms pertaining to arbitration. As a consequence, parties to an arbitral clause could be required to execute a submission once a dispute arose. Also, in conformity with French (pre-decree) provisions on arbitration, the Quebec Code of Civil Procedure authorized arbitrators to rule as *amiables compositeurs*—a form of equitable jurisdictional authority that allows arbitrators to disregard the rules of law in reaching a determination. With this French influence on the Quebec provisions on arbitration, they could not logically contain a procedure comparable to the special case proceeding that applied in the common-law provinces. Unlike English practice, the civil law concept of adjudicatory imperatives and arbitration did not require arbitral tribunals to reach outcomes that necessarily were legally correct. In somewhat contradictory fashion, however, the Quebec code did mandate that arbitrators, regardless of whether they ruled in equity or law, issue reasons with their awards. A feature of the French domestic law on arbitration, the requirement of reasoned awards had no equivalent in the common-law provincial legislation.[91]

Accordingly, not only did the Quebec law on arbitration differ from its counterpart in other provinces, but it was not entirely consistent in articulating a basic position on arbitration. While questioning the validity of the arbitral clause and mandating reasoned awards cast doubt upon the legitimacy of the process, the recognition of a flexible jurisdictional authority for arbitrators sounding in equity gave arbitration systemic autonomy. Finally, Quebec law (although it did not permit a review on the merits) was generally unclear about the role of judicial scrutiny in the enforcement of awards, did not distinguish effectively between foreign (or international) and domestic awards, and required judicial sanction of awards for purposes of enforcement.[92]

The provinces' general reliance upon rather antiquated statutory models from parent legal systems and the classical dichotomy between common-law and civil-law legal regulation (as it related to arbitration) made the adoption of a uniform national Canadian law on arbitration, basically required by the adoption of the New York Convention,[93] difficult. These difficulties were accompanied by—and perhaps partly generated—apathetic responses to arbitration from both government and business sectors.[94] The lack of interest gave little reason to expect that the basic Canadian juridical concept of arbitration would be revised and provincial differences reconciled.

Beginning with the Geneva convention and Protocol,[95] Canada failed to participate in four major multilateral conventions on arbitration.[96] Moreover, domestic experimentation with arbitration had resulted in failure.[97] For example, the Canadian-American Commercial Arbitration Commission (CACAC) was created in 1943 to lay the groundwork for Canadian-American business arbitration. Efforts under the CACAC to establish a form of institutional arbitration were unavailing. Moreover, the design of creating an arbitration program between the Vancouver Board of Trade and the Japanese Commercial Arbitration Association was never realized. These failed experiences, the business community's lack of interest in and demand for arbitration, and the seeming indifference of the federal government were supplemented by the legal community's skepticism about whether there was any need to deviate from traditional adjudicatory mechanisms and procedures, whether arbitrators could effectively dispense adjudicatory functions, and, ultimately, whether courts would enforce arbitral awards.[98]

The cardinal difficulty confronting the elaboration of a uniform Canadian national law on arbitration, however, resided in a much larger systemic consideration that reinforced these other barriers. In systemic terms, the absence of a Canadian law on arbitration was attributable to the dictates of Canadian federalism that made provincial agreement to a uniform law constitutionally indispensable yet difficult of practical achievement.[99] The Canadian Constitution allocates power between the federal parliament and the provincial legislatures. As in the United States, this doctrine of separation of powers is fundamental to the Canadian concept of constitutional federalism:

> The vital core of a federal constitution is the division of legislative powers between the central authority and the component states or provinces. This division represents the compromise between the forces which make a union and those which inhibit the formation of a closer union. It marks the limits of what can be done by common agreement and the extent to which the separate states must be permitted to differ and work out their own destinies.[100]

The constitution gives the federal parliament power over the regulation of trade and commerce, transportation and communication, banking, currency, and customs; the provincial legislatures have authority over other areas, like property and civil rights in the province, the administration of justice, and procedure.[101] According to this enumeration and insofar as arbitration relates to interprovincial and international commercial and trading activities, arbitration could be deemed to be within the powers delegated to the federal parliament. Unlike their American analogues, however, Canadian courts generally have restricted the scope of the federal parliament's authority over interprovincial commerce by defining the latter term narrowly.[102] As a result, the accepted view in Canada is that the constitutional allocation of powers implies that the regulation of arbitration is a matter of contract and procedure, and therefore comes within the legislative competence of the provinces.[103] Arguments to the contrary are likely to be unavailing:

> The case for constitutional validity of a federal arbitration law under the trade and commerce rubric could therefore only rest on the proposition that the subject matter of arbitration transcends the

bounds of provincial competence; that, in other words, the arbitration contract and award, and their enforcement, as adjuncts to trade and commerce both interprovincial and international, constitute regulation of trade and commerce rather than an invasion of an exclusive provincial field. To rest the argument on this ground is to affirm that the subject of commercial arbitration goes beyond the subjects of contract and/or procedure and touches upon commerce, such that federal authority can be seen to begin. This is a mode of reasoning that is unlikely to be followed. . . .[104]

Moreover, although the federal government has treaty-making power, it would lack essential constitutional authority over the subject matter of an international treaty on arbitration:

While the federal government is the sovereign authority constitutionally empowered to participate in the creation of a treaty with another state, and the only Canadian authority able to issue international obligations thereunder, it does not thereupon acquire the constitutional competence to execute that obligation if its subject matter is provincial. . . . The only obligation that the Canadian federal authorities can assume and effectively discharge under a multi-lateral or bilateral convention on arbitration is, therefore, that of bringing to the attention of the appropriate provincial authorities that which is within their own competence with a view to the several provinces implementing the real substance thereof.[105]

Lacking constitutional authority, the federal government's only recourse—other than excluding Canada by default from participation in international commercial arbitration and impairing Canadian interests in international trade—was to undertake efforts to persuade the provincial legislatures of the need for and benefits of Canadian recognition of the New York Arbitration Convention. After the English accession in 1975, Canada was the only major Western country not to have ratified the convention, which by then had nearly fifty adherents.[106] Without a knowledge of the Canadian federalism issue and its implications, it was difficult to understand why Canada, for all these years, had failed to undertake action that would have been in its best national self-interest. The English Arbitration Act of 1979, despite its guarded acceptance of arbitration, may have had some impact in coalescing forces at the various levels of Canadian government. Recent United States statutory and decisional law developments may also have had some bearing on the change of attitude.[107] Given the views of provincial autonomy in Canada and the intensity of political debate, achieving a consensus among all provinces may have been particularly arduous and painstaking, requiring years and the appropriate circumstances to initiate and complete. Or, more simply, the level of transnational acceptance of and developments in arbitration law may have been, finally, too overwhelming to disregard any longer. In any event, one or a combination of these factors dictated a sudden and dramatic reversal of the Canadian law on domestic and international arbitration.

On May 12, 1986, the Canadian government acceded to the New York Arbitration Convention, and, subsequently, all the Canadian provinces and territories enacted legislation implementing the convention.[108] What is even more remarkable and attests to the dramatic character of the reversal is that, along with the ratification of the convention, both the federal government and the provinces (with the exception of Saskatchewan) adopted the UNCITRAL model law on arbitration, making it, in effect, the Canadian national law on arbitration.[109] The model law's provisions are designed to provide a comprehensive regulatory framework for arbitration, one that reflects a liberal and supportive attitude toward arbitration and that fosters the uniform interpretation of the New York Convention.[110] The model law seeks to give arbitrating parties "maximum freedom to conduct the arbitration in accordance with their stated expectation. . . ."[111] According to a distinguished commentator, "for countries without any settled and explicit law of arbitration, the adoption of the model without adaptation should provide a valuable legislative 'package' which will convert them into suitable venues for international arbitrations."[112] Nearly thirty years after the New York Convention was first opened for signature, Canada not only had ratified the convention, but also transformed itself, nearly overnight, into a receptive forum for arbitration.

A number of commentators have already singled out those national characteristics that recommend Canada as a venue for arbitration.[113] For example, Canada's geographic proximity to the United States might enable it to act as a forum for arbitrations between United States business interests and those from other nations. Canada is also midway between the East and the West. The ethnic diversity of its minority population and its distinctive life-style, it is argued, could make Canada a neutral forum for accommodating arbitrating parties from opposing social, economic, and political backgrounds. Too, Canada is familiar with international trade and commerce. Canada ranks among the top ten manufacturing countries of the world and is also a world leader in the volume of foreign trade.[114] Finally, movement is under way to establish arbitration centers in British Columbia and Quebec, and there is some talk about a possible third Canadian arbitration center.[115]

It is true that Canada's political, economic, and cultural distinctiveness may allow it to become a major arbitration forum, especially in regard to the Pacific Rim and developing countries. The more permanent domestic consequences of the Canadian ratification, however, remain difficult to gauge. Federal and provincial courts have yet to interpret the new statutory law; experience in other countries demonstrates that the judicial response to enabling legislation on arbitration is always of critical importance in evaluating that legislation's long-term effectiveness. The general disposition of the legal profession, still undetermined, will also be of significant importance. There does appear to be a revitalization of the business community's interest in arbitration; that interest may be rather fragile and short-lived, however, and could be directed exclusively to matters of international commercial arbitration where lucrative possibilities exist. The export of arbitration services (to remedy trade imbalances and invigorate sluggish national economies) has become an exceedingly competitive international business, in which a number of countries have a clear head-start.

The vital significance of the Canadian ratification lies elsewhere than in conjecture about the practical ramifications of its adoption of a developed statutory framework for arbitration. Canada's accession to the New York Convention not only represents a departure from dependence upon European arbitral models, but it is also an important indication of the continuing strength and development of the transnational consensus on arbitration as an extrajudicial means of resolving disputes. Given Canada's cultural and political diversity—its affinity to both developing and developed countries—its ratification of the New York Convention is a forceful symbol of the truly comprehensive appeal of the convention in the divisive pluralism of the international community. The gradual reconsideration by Latin American countries of their attitude toward arbitration,[116] the increased participation of African countries in International Chamber of Commerce (ICC) arbitration,[117] the ratification of the New York Convention by the People's Republic of China[118] in 1987, conjoined with the Canadian action on arbitration, indicate that the provisions of the New York Convention are approaching the ideal of universal adherence and have genuine law-making authority.

The further consolidation of the New York Arbitration Convention in national laws indicates that the recourse to arbitral adjudication is firmly entrenched in the emerging transnational commercial process. In fact, the recognition of arbitration as a legitimate adjudicatory process is a de facto condition precedent to effective national participation in international trade. Moreover, this recognition, along with the development of advanced national arbitration laws, could have an impact upon purely internal concerns. The growing familiarity with and acceptance of arbitration as a viable and vital adjudicatory process might make national legal systems generally more receptive to the consideration and adoption of alternative dispute resolution mechanisms. The experience with international commercial arbitration could become a foundation upon which to begin the domestic transformation of adjudicatory values and processes: devising a variety of remedial frameworks that respond to the diversity and the actual needs of disputes.

The next chapter examines the American law of arbitration that reveals precisely this sort of relationship between domestic processes and the international experience. Also, the internal systemic aspects of the Canadian experience have particular relevance to the United States law. Although the specific character of the federalism problem differs, Canada's struggle with federalism questions associated with arbitration is germane to the most recent United States Supreme Court decisions on arbitration. In those cases, the Court—relying upon an expansive interpretation of interstate commerce under the Commerce Clause, invoking the Supremacy Clause, and emphasizing the congressional intent underlying the Federal Arbitration Act —appears to be engaged in a process of federalizing the American law of arbitration. Given the disruptive systemic consequences, a legislative approach, reflecting the Canadian experience, might be more a feasible way to achieve the same ends.

NOTES

1. See R. LILLICH, ed., TRANSNATIONAL TERRORISM: CONVENTIONS AND COMMENTARY (1982), reviewed in 19 TEX. INT'L L.J. 250 (1984); J. MURPHY,

THE UNITED NATIONS AND THE CONTROL OF INTERNATIONAL VIOLENCE: A LEGAL AND POLITICAL ANALYSIS (1982); *Symposium on International Terrorism,* 8 WHITTIER L. REV. 681 (1986); W. WAUGH, INTERNATIONAL TERRORISM (1982). See also Baker, *The Western European Legal Response to Terrorism,* 13 BROOKLYN J. INT'L L. 1 (1987). For additional references, see Appendix A (ch. 3) infra.

2. The application of the political offense exception to extradition in the context of terrorism has given rise to a growing body of commentary, the volume of which follows the ebb and flow of the phenomenon itself. For a comprehensive list of sources, see Appendix B (ch. 3) infra.

3. On the topic of international judicial assistance and cooperation, see generally *A Bibliography of Transnational Litigation in Socialist Countries: Discovery, Evidence, and Enforcement of Foreign Judgments,* 21 TEX. INT'L L.J. 383 (1986); Gaw, *Bibliography: International Judicial Assistance,* 18 INT'L LAW. 555 (1984); Gerber, *Extraterritorial Discovery and the Conflict of Procedural Systems: Germany and the United States,* 34 AM. J. COMP. L. 745 (1986); O'Kane, *Obtaining Evidence Abroad,* 17 VAND. J. TRANS. L. 69 (1984); McKay, *Compelling Discovery and Disclosure in Transnational Litigation: A Selected Bibliography,* 16 N.Y.U. J. INT'L L. & POL. 1217 (1984); Note, *Judicial Assistance: Obtaining Evidence in the United States under 28 U.S.C. § 1782 for Use in a Foreign or International Tribunal,* 5 B.C. INT'L & COMP. L. REV. 175 (1982); Note, *Reexamining the American Response to Judicial Assistance Among Nations: Suggestions for Improvement,* 7 ASILS INT'L L.J. 41 (1983); Platto, *Taking Evidence Abroad for Use in Civil Cases in the United States: A Practical Guide,* 16 INT'L LAW. 575 (1982); Ristau, *Overview of International Judicial Assistance,* 18 INT'L LAW. 525 (1984); Smith, *Letters Rogatory: Compelling the Evidence of Witnesses in Canada,* 31 FED'N. INS. COUNS. Q. 333 (1981); Sutherland, *The Use of the Letter of Request (or Letter Rogatory) for the Purpose of Obtaining Evidence for Proceedings in England and Abroad,* 31 INT'L & COMP. L.Q. 784 (1982); Von Mehren, *Discovery of Documentary and Other Evidence in a Foreign Country,* 77 AM. J. INT'L L. 896 (1983). For a discussion of the Hague Evidence Convention, see Appendix C (ch. 3) infra.

4. As Maier notes, the Hague Evidence Convention's objective of achieving international cooperation sometimes conflicts and needs to be coordinated with the full disclosure principles of the Federal Rules of Civil Procedure (FRCP). "Courts in the United States have reached three different conclusions about the relationship between the Hague Evidence Convention and the . . . [FRCP]." Maier, *Extraterritorial Discovery: Cooperation, Coercion and The Hague Evidence Convention,* 19 VAND. J. TRANS. L. 239, 240 n. 3 (1986). See also Oxman, *The Choice Between Direct Discovery and Other Means of Obtaining Evidence Abroad: The Impact of the Hague*

Evidence Convention, 37 U. MIAMI L. REV. 733 (1983). The United States Supreme Court ruling in the Aérospatiale case, however, significantly compromises the Hague Convention's status as a transnational framework. See Société Nationale Industrielle Aérospatiale v. U.S. District Court, 482 U.S. 522, 107 Sup. Ct. 2542, 96 L.Ed.2d 461 (1987) (holding, inter alia, that the Convention does not provide an exclusive and mandatory procedure for obtaining documents and information in transnational litigation). See Bermann, *The Hague Evidence Convention in the Supreme Court: A Critique of the Aérospatiale Decision,* 63 TUL. L. REV. 525 (1989); Note, *A Look Behind the Aérospatiale Curtain, Or Why the Hague Evidence Convention Had to Be Effectively Nullified,* 23 TEX. INT'L L. J. 269 (1988); Recent Developments, *The Hague Evidence Convention in United States Courts: Aérospatiale and the Path Not Taken,* 17 GA. J. INT'L & COMP. L. 591 (1987); Youngblood & Welsh, *Obtaining Evidence Abroad: A Model for Defining and Resolving the Choice of Law Between the Federal Rules of Civil Procedure and the Hague Evidence Convention,* 10 U. PA. J. INT'L BUS. L. 1 (1988). See also Note, 22 LOY. (L.A.) L. REV. 217 (1988)

The goal of the Hague Evidence Convention is to achieve transnational uniformity in the critical areas of litigation, but disruptive political and juridical factors—although they can be balanced in some circumstances—are ever present and remain difficult to reconcile:

> The Hague Evidence Convention was designed to permit cooperation among legal systems that in many situations reflect fundamentally different views about the role of courts in achieving justice and applying law. A principal goal was to ease the burden on litigants in common-law countries in procuring evidence located abroad. The Convention sought to establish a system for transnational evidence-gathering which was acceptable to the states parties and which would harmonize conflicting views about sovereignty and jurisdiction reflected in differing systems of civil procedure used by the members. The problems which the Convention addresses often flow from fundamentally different assumptions about the role of courts in the legal systems of many of its signatories.

Maier, *Extraterritorial Discovery,* supra note 4, at 242 (footnote omitted).

5. See, for example, H. DUINTJER TEBBENS, INTERNATIONAL PRODUCT LIABILITY (1979); Cooper, *Product Liability: The Problem of the Unknown Defendant,* 130 SOLICT. J. 621 (1986); Dielmann, *The EEC's Council Directive on Product Liability,* 20 INT'L LAW. 1391 (1986); Hulsen, *Design Liability and State of the Art: The U.S. and Europe at a Crossroads,* 55 ST. JOHN'S L. REV. 450 (1981); Note, *The EEC's Proposed Directive On Products Liability: A Call for Reappraisal in Light of the Model Uniform Product Liability Act,* 6 B.C. INT'L & COMP. L. REV. 315 (1983); Note, *Products Liability: A Comparison of U.S. and EEC Approaches,* 13 SYR-

ACUSE J. INT'L L. & COM. 155 (1986); Note, *Recent Supranational Developments in European Products Liability Law: Defective and Unreasonably Dangerous?*, 6 SUFFOLK TRANS. L.J. 277 (1982); Stapleton, *Products Liability Reform: Real or Illusory?*, 6 OXFORD J. L. STUDIES 392 (1986); Van Wassenaer & Van Catwijck, *Products Liability in Europe*, 34 AMER. J. COMP. L. 789 (1986); Will, *Asides on the Nonharmonization of Products Liability Laws in Europe*, in HARMONIZATION OF LAWS IN THE EUROPEAN COMMUNITIES: PRODUCTS LIABILITY, CONFLICT OF LAWS, AND CORPORATION LAW, 28 [Fifth Sokol Colloquium] (P. Herzog ed. 1983). See also Orban, *Product Liability, A Comparative Legal Restatement—Foreign National Law and the EEC Directive*, 8 GA. J. INT'L & COMP. L. 342 (1978).

6. See discussion in ch. 6, infra, at notes 19-26.

7. For a discussion of product liability law in the United States, see, for example, D. NOEL & J. PHILLIPS, PRODUCTS LIABILITY IN A NUTSHELL (2d ed. 1981); D. OWLES, THE DEVELOPMENT OF PRODUCT LIABILITY IN THE UNITED STATES (1978).

8. See, for example, Gibson, *Products Liability in the United States and England: The Difference and Why*, 3 ANGLO-AMER. L. REV. 493 (1974); Plummer, *Products Liability in Britain*, 9 ANGLO-AMER. L. REV. 65 (1980).

9. For a discussion of product liability law in European countries, see sources cited in note 5 supra.

10. For a discussion of product liability law in developing countries, see Agege, *Products Liability: An Analysis of the Legal Position in Nigeria*, 7 J. PROD. LIAB. 297 (1984); Miller, *Products Liability in Argentina*, 33 AM. J. COMP. L. 611 (1985).

11. For example, when infant nightwear and milk products were deemed dangerous and unsuitable for sale in the United States, they were sold in foreign countries that had less stringent product regulations.

12. See generally DICEY AND MORRIS ON THE CONFLICT OF LAWS (J. Morris ed. 10th ed. 1980); A. EHRENZWEIG, A TREATISE ON THE CONFLICTS OF LAWS (1962); A. EHRENZWEIG, CONFLICTS IN A NUTSHELL (3d ed. 1974); P. NORTH, CHESHIRE'S PRIVATE INTERNATIONAL LAW (9th ed. 1974); Cook, *The Logical and Legal Bases of Conflict of Laws*, 33 YALE L.J. 457 (1924); Currie, *Notes on Methods and Objectives in the Conflicts of Laws*, in SELECTED ESSAYS ON THE CONFLICT OF LAWS 177 (B. Currie ed. 1963); Lorenzen, *Territoriality, Public Policy and the Conflict of Laws*, 33 YALE L.J. 736 (1924); Yutema, *Autonomy in Choice of Law*, 1 AM. J. COMP. L. 341 (1952).

13. The United Nations Convention on Contracts for the International Sale of Goods (Vienna Convention), Final Act of the United Nations Conference on Contracts for the International Sale of Goods, April 11, 1980, U.N. Doc. A/Conf. 96/18 (1980), stands as an example of an

international convention that is disunified in its substance, and that is unlikely to generate uniform interpretation by national courts. See Carbonneau & Firestone, *Transnational Law-Making: Assessing the Impact of the Vienna Convention and the Viability of Arbitral Adjudication,* 1 EMORY J. INT'L DISP. RES. 51 (1986); Rosett, *Critical Reflections on the United Nations Convention on Contracts for the International Sale of Goods,* 45 OHIO ST. L.J. 265 (1984). Accord Patterson, *United Nations Convention on Contracts for the International Sale of Goods: Unification and the Tension Between Compromise and Domination,* 22 STANFORD J. INT'L L. 263 (1986).

14. The Convention for the Unification of Certain Rules relating to International Carriage by Air [Warsaw Convention] resulted from international conferences held in Paris in 1925 and Warsaw in 1929 and the work of the interim Comité International Technique d'Experts Juridiques Aériens (CITEJA). The CITEJA resulted from the 1925 Paris Conference. The Warsaw Convention was signed on October 12, 1929, and is contained in 49 Stat. 3000 (1934), T.S. No. 876, 137 L.N.T.S. ll. Spain, Brazil, Yugoslavia, and Rumania were the first countries to ratify the convention; France, Poland, and Latvia later ratified it on November 15, 1932. Great Britain and Italy ratified it the next day. The Warsaw Convention became effective on February 13, 1933. By the end of 1933, there were 12 high contracting parties, including most European states. Today, the convention has more than one hundred signatories.

There are a number of secondary sources on the convention. Lowenfeld & Mendelsohn, *The United States and the Warsaw Convention,* 80 HARV. L. REV. 497 (1967) [Lowenfeld & Mendelsohn] contains a comprehensive discussion and analysis of the history of the Warsaw Convention from the 1929 Warsaw Conference until the Montreal Agreement of 1966. For a detailed account of the convention's provisions and the various amendments of it (especially the 1955 Hague amendments), see R. MANKIEWICZ, THE LIABILITY REGIME OF THE INTERNATIONAL AIR CARRIER: A COMMENTARY ON THE PRESENT WARSAW SYSTEM (1981) [MANKIEWICZ]. See also 1 & 2 L. KREINDLER, AVIATION ACCIDENT LAW (1986). For an extensive bibliographical listing on the Warsaw Convention, see Appendix D (ch. 3) infra.

15. See Lowenfeld & Mendelsohn, supra note 14, at 502. See also Matte, *The Warsaw System and the Hesitations of the United States Senate,* 8 ANN. AIR & SPACE L. 151, 153 (1983) (describing in detail the movement of the United States toward ratification). Briefly, after the State Department conveyed its approval to the president, the treaty was submitted to the Senate, which rendered its advice and consent by voice vote on June 15, 1934. The United States deposited an instrument of adherence on July 31, 1934, and the president proclaimed the treaty ninety days later. It is

significant — in view of the later dissatisfaction and controversies — that the Senate went ahead without debate and that the executive branch took no part in the treaty's negotiation and drafting. The United States only sent an observer to the Warsaw Conference.

16. This point was emphasized at the Warsaw Conference and is referred to in a number of works. See, for example, Lowenfeld & Mendelsohn, supra note 14, at 499. See generally, R. HORNER & D. LEGREZ, SECOND INTERNATIONAL CONFERENCE ON PRIVATE AERONAUTICAL LAW MINUTES WARSAW 1929 (1975) [WARSAW MINUTES].

17. This objective, often expressed at the Warsaw Conference, is noted by Sheinfield, *From Warsaw to Tenerife: A Chronological Analysis of the Liability Limitations Imposed Pursuant to the Warsaw Convention,* infra Appendix D (ch. 3), at 658; the Second Circuit Court of Appeals in Franklin Mint Corp. v. Trans World Airlines, Inc., 690 F.2d 303 (2d Cir. 1982) (rev'd on other grounds). See also WARSAW MINUTES, note 16 supra.

18. Warsaw Convention, art. 1(1). For determining the scope of the convention, the term *international transportation* in article 1(1) is defined in article 1(2) as,

> any transportation in which, according to the contract made by the parties, the place of departure and the place of destination, whether or not there would be a break in the transportation or a transshipment, are situated within the territories of two high contracting parties, or within the territory of a single high contracting party, if there is an agreed stopping place within the territory subject to the sovereignty, suzerainty, mandate or authority of another power, even though that power is not a party to this convention.

Transportation under an international postal convention is excluded by article 2 from the Warsaw system.

G. MILLER, LIABILITY IN INTERNATIONAL AIR TRANSPORT: THE WARSAW SYSTEM IN MUNICIPAL COURTS 18 (1977) [MILLER] notes that under article 1(1) the terms of the parties' contract are crucial. MANKIEWICZ, supra note 14, at 28, discusses the different countries' various interpretations of the term *high contracting party* in article 1(1). Transportation by several successive air carriers may be covered by the convention if it is deemed to be "one undivided operation" under article 1(3). See MILLER, supra at 20-23.

19. Articles 17 to 19 delineate the conditions for carrier liability under the convention. They are discussed in detail by MANKIEWICZ, supra note 14, at pt. IV; MILLER, supra note 18, at chs. 3, 6, 7, 8, 9, and 11.

20. Warsaw Convention, article 17. For a discussion of the courts' interpretation of "accident" (an important requirement in article 17), see, for example, Cahn, *Saks: A Clarification of the Warsaw Convention Passenger Liability Standards,* infra Appendix D (ch. 3), at 547; Reukema,

Article 17 of the Warsaw Convention: An Accident Is Required for Recovery, infra Appendix D (ch. 3), at 191. Generally, "accident" is defined in Warshaw v. Trans World Airlines, Inc., 442 F.Supp. 400 (E.D. Pa. 1977), as,

> an untoward event out of the ordinary triggered by some external event [not] triggered by normal operating conditions as a result of the passenger's own weakness or disability.

For a discussion of an unsuccessful attempt in Air France v. Saks, 105 S.Ct. 1338 (1985), to extend the term *accident* and almost create a travel insurance under the Convention, see Note, *The Applicability of the Warsaw Convention to a Passenger Injury Sustained During a Routine International Flight,* infra Appendix D (ch. 3), at 164-65.

21. See MANKIEWICZ, supra note 14, at 92. For a discussion of carrier liability at common law, see W. PROSSER, HANDBOOK OF THE LAW OF TORTS 180-81 (4th ed. 1971). Generally at common law, the carrier is under a high standard of care but is not an insurer. Although liability is based on negligence, *res ipsa loquitur* can lessen the plaintiff's burden of proof. With regard to property damages, the carrier is subject to a high duty and is generally considered an insurer (with certain exceptions). On the "conclusive presumption of negligence," which arises at common law once the plaintiff has established a prima facie case for damaged goods, see Albert, *Limitations on Air Carrier Liability: An Inadvertent Return to Common Law Principles,* infra Appendix D (ch. 3), at 129. For a comparison of that presumption to *res ipsa loquitur,* see Note, *Aviation: Liability Limitations for Wrongful Death or Personal Injury—A Contemporary Analysis of the Warsaw System,* infra Appendix D (ch. 3), at 395.

Davison & Solomon discuss the minimal advantage of the Warsaw Convention over the common-law system. See Davison & Solomon, *Air Carrier Liability Under Deregulation,* 49 J. AIR L. & COM. 31, 49-51 (1983).

22. For discussion of the rebuttal provisions (articles 20 and 21), see MANKIEWICZ, supra note 14, at 99-109. Under article 20(1),

> The carrier shall not be liable if he proves that he and his agents have taken all necessary measures to avoid the damage or that it was impossible for him or them to take such measures.

The defense is available only after the cause of the accident or damage has been established. For a discussion of the drafting history and the American courts' initial construction of article 20(1), see MILLER, supra note 18, at 66, 161-62. There is a trend toward requiring only reasonable measures to have been taken.

Article 20(2) establishes a defense, with regard to the "transportation of goods and registered baggage"; it provides that the carrier is exonerated,

> if he proves that the damage was occasioned by an error in piloting, in the handling of the aircraft, or in navigation and that, in all

other respects he and his agents have taken all necessary measures to avoid the damage.

The courts seem to be more stringent with regard to injury to the person than to goods and baggage. See Davison & Solomon, *Air Carrier Liability under Deregulation,* supra note 21, at 42.

Article 21 contains the contributory negligence provision. Under it, the carrier can be totally or partially exonerated by establishing that the injured victim caused or contributed to the injury. *Lex fori* determines the extent of the carrier's exoneration under article 21. The defense is not available if the carrier failed to observe required traffic document provisions contained in articles 3 (in relation to the passenger ticket), 4 (to the baggage check) and 8 (to the airway bill). The carrier's failure to observe such requirements makes it subject to unlimited liability in articles 3(2), 4(4), or 9. Accord MANKIEWICZ, supra note 14, at 80.

23. Warsaw Convention, art. 22. Any provision fixing a limit lower than that stipulated in article 22 is declared null and void by article 23. The limits in article 22 are stated in gold francs with a value corresponding to that of the 1929 French franc. For a discussion of the conversion problems, see, for example, MANKIEWICZ, supra note 14, at 113-14.

24. Warsaw Convention, art. 22(1). Article 22(1) permits the carrier and passenger to agree by special contract to a higher limit of liability. See MANKIEWICZ, supra note 14, at 110-11.

25. Warsaw Convention, art. 22(2) & (3). This limit may be exceeded if,

> the consignor has made, at the time when the package was handed over to the carrier, a special declaration of the value at delivery and has paid a supplementary sum if the case so requires.

In such circumstances, the limit becomes the declared sum unless the carrier proves that sum exceeds "the actual value to the consignor at delivery." For discussion of the provisions pertaining to the transportation of cargo and registered baggage, see MANKIEWICZ, supra note 14, at 111-13. The limit for carry-on articles is contained in article 22(3).

26. Articles 3(2), 4(4), 9, & 25 state the conditions for unlimited liability and are discussed by MANKIEWICZ, supra note 14, at 67-87, 122-3; MILLER, supra note 18, at chs. 5 & 11. Under article 3(2), unlimited liability applies, "if the carrier accepts a passenger without a passenger ticket having been delivered." Regarding baggage, liability becomes unlimited "if the carrier accepts baggage without a baggage check having been delivered," or if the baggage check lacks the required particulars contained in article 4(3)(d), (f), and (h), namely,

> (d) the number of the passenger ticket;
> (f) the number and weight of the packages;

(h) [a] statement that the transportation is subjected to the rules relating to liability established by this convention.

Article 9 provides for unlimited liability, "if the carrier accepts goods without an airway bill having been made out, or if the airway bill does not contain all the particulars set out in article 8(a) to (i) inclusive and (q)." Under article 25, liability is unlimited if the damage is caused by the willful misconduct (or default that the court hearing the case considers equivalent to willful misconduct) of the carrier or the carrier's agent. When interpreting this provision, courts are generally reluctant to find willful misconduct when air navigation rules are violated. The ambiguous drafting history of article 25 has, however, caused problems of interpretation.

27. See, for example, De Vivo, *The Warsaw Convention: Judicial Tolling of the Death Knell?*, 49 J. AIR. L. & COM. 71, 139 (1983); Fisher, *The Gold Issue: The Supreme Court Upholds the Limitation on Liability Established by the Warsaw Convention,* infra Appendix D (ch. 3), at 479; Note, *Up in the Air Without a Ticket: Interpretation and Revision of the Warsaw Convention,* infra Appendix D (ch. 3), at 342.

Fisher, *The Gold Issue . . . ,* infra Appendix D (ch. 3), at 481, emphasizes the inadequacy of the compensation available under the convention. This feature of the convention is generally contrary to the American tort law objective of compensation. The international credibility of the United States commitment to the convention is, therefore, maintained at a high cost.

28. Lowenfeld & Mendelsohn, supra note 14, discuss the hostility shown by the United States shortly after it ratified the convention. The hostility came to a head when the United States deposited its notice of denunciation in 1966. Briefly, the ultimate threat of withdrawal was prevented by the 1966 Montreal Agreement (see text at note 39 infra and accompanying text). The hostility toward the convention's liability system continues in the United States and other countries. Express refusals to comply with the convention are seen in the lack of uniform ratification of the amendments (see text at note 39 infra and accompanying text). Implied refusals to comply are evidenced by the courts' decisions circumventing the liability limits through their determinations of whether notice was adequate or whether willful misconduct exists.

29. The determination of scope is crucial to the convention's aim of creating a uniform regime of predictable legal rules. The greater the scope left to national law in determining liability, the less opportunity there is for achieving transnational uniformity. Generally, when establishing the convention's scope, problems have been encountered with the terms *international transportation* in article 1(1), and *the operations of embarking or disembarking* in article 17.

In regard to the term *international transportation,* the discussion in Stratis v. Eastern Airlines, 682 F.2d 406 (2d Cir. 1982) is relevant. There, the court focused on whether the passenger (Stratis) "had reason to know his overall flight was international" (682 F.2d at 412). Stratis was a discharged Greek seaman being repatriated as required by Greek and United States immigration law on a Delta flight from Baton Rouge to New Orleans, Louisiana, on an Eastern flight from New Orleans to New York, and on an Olympic Airway's flight from New York to Athens. He had only a domestic ticket for his Delta and Eastern flights. The Eastern plane crashed on approach to New York, and Stratis was injured. Olympic Airway's New York city office had prepared prepaid ticket advice — including notice of the convention's application for the international segment of Stratis's journey. This information had been communicated by telephone to the Olympic Airway counter at JFK International Airport. The ticket made for Stratis's international travel at that airport, however, had not been issued or validly stamped. Nevertheless, the court of appeals (682 F.2d at 412) focused on whether Stratis "had reason to know his overall flight was international," and concluded that "a passenger such as Stratis must be presumed to know that his flight is international in nature and that the Convention limitations apply." See Note, *Up in the Air Without a Ticket,* infra Appendix D (ch. 3), at 352 (stating that this holding opens the door for a searching and complex judicial inquiry).

30. The concept is discussed by MANKIEWICZ, supra note 14, at 149-154. Day v. TWA, 528 F.2d 31 (2d Cir. 1975), advances a test that has been followed and sometimes modified in subsequent cases. See, for example, Evangelinos v. TWA, 550 F.2d 152 (C.A. Pa. 1977). Evangelinos has been subsequently distinguished. The Day test focuses on the accident's location, the activity in which the injured person was engaged, and the defendant airline's control of the injured person at the location and while engaged in the activity occurring at the time of the accident. The Day court, however, noted the Warsaw delegates' concern for a flexible approach.

The Warsaw delegates' differing views on the meaning of this term are stated in WARSAW MINUTES, note 16 supra. The divergence has led to differing judicial interpretations. For instance, French courts in the past considered article 17 to encompass "only operations which exposed the passenger to the risk of the air." MANKIEWICZ, supra note 14, at 149, cites French cases holding that accidents on the apron before embarkation and after disembarkation are covered. Generally, American and other courts have held that operations begin with the check-in and cease once the passenger has ushered or collected his or her registered luggage. Today, hijacking and sabotage further complicate matters.

31. For what constitutes adequate notice and delivery for passenger tickets, see article 3; for baggage checks, see article 4; and for airway bills, see article 8. MILLER, supra note 18, at 92-93, discerns a shift from formal compliance to considering how the carrier complied. A central case on the requirements of adequate notice and delivery is Lisi v. Alitalia-Linee Aeree Italiane, 370 F.2d 508 (2d Cir. 1966), aff'd 390 U.S. 455 (1968). Lisi held that the delivery requirement of article 3 is meant "to provide the passenger with sufficient notice to afford him a reasonable opportunity to protect himself against the convention's limitation of liability" (370 F.2d at 513).

For cases following Lisi, see Albert, *Limitations on Air Carrier Liability,* infra Appendix D (ch. 3), at 143, n.24. MANKIEWICZ, supra note 14, at 73, points out that the courts following Lisi "differ on the criteria of legibility, or otherwise of the statements in question." Lisi has been subsequently distinguished in the second circuit. For criticism of the Lisi rule, see MANKIEWICZ, supra note 14, at 75-76. MILLER, supra note 18, at 98, observes that what constitutes adequate notice and delivery varies according to whether one is dealing with the passenger or the passenger's cargo or baggage. Limitations of liability on cargo are generally considered part of a commercial bargain not inequitably requiring restrictions, unlike liability limitations on passenger injury.

32. See, for example, Lisi v. Alitalia, note 31 supra.

33. See MANKIEWICZ, supra note 14, at 60; MILLER, supra note 18, at 82-91.

34. On the civil law influence in the convention, see MILLER, supra note 18, at 345.

35. Problems of translation occur both in countries where the convention is self-executing (as in Belgium, France, and the United States) and countries that require enactment of a statute or subordinate legislation to implement the convention (as in the United Kingdom, Netherlands, and Switzerland). See MANKIEWICZ, supra note 14, at 17-20; MILLER, supra note 18, at 339-49. Generally, the problems encountered result from the influence of each country's judicial process; the ambiguity of the legislative history; the tendency of common-law judges to rely on the common-law approach and, more generally, of judges to rely upon municipal law as a point of reference; and the different classification of legal issues in the various systems.

36. See, for example, McGilchrist, *Does the Warsaw Convention Govern Non-Contractual Liability?,* LLOYD'S MAR. & COM. L.Q. 685 (1983).

37. See text at note 39 infra and accompanying text.

38. On discontent with the maximum recovery amounts, see text at note 27 supra and accompanying text.

39. *Hague Protocol,* 478 U.N.T.S. 371 (1955): For commentary on the Hague Protocol, see Mankiewicz, *Hague Protocol to Amend the Warsaw Convention,* 5 AM. J. COMP. L. 78 (1956). By the summer of 1963, thirty states had deposited instruments of ratification. MANKIEWICZ, supra note 14, at his Appendix 1, identifies the amendments made by the Hague Protocol to the convention. These include a doubling of the liability limits; modification of the notice requirement for tickets and baggage; a new article 25 containing a factual description to be proved for willful misconduct and unlimited liability; and provision for legal fees. Problems, however, have been encountered with the Hague Protocol—in particular with its inadequate liability limits (even with the lawyers' fees provision). See MILLER, supra note 18, at 117. Moreover, the United States did not ratify the protocol, but only signed it on June 28, 1956.

Guadalajara Convention, ICAO Doc. 8181 (1961). The Convention Supplementary to the Warsaw Convention for the Unification of Certain Rules Relating to International Carriage by Air Performed by a Person Other than the Contracting Carrier was signed at Guadalajara on September 18, 1961 and came into force on May 1, 1964. See N. MATTE, TREATISE ON AIR-AERONAUTICAL LAW 444-454, at his Appendix 12 (1981). See also MANKIEWICZ, supra note 14, at 6-7. The Guadalajara Convention does not affect or modify liability limits, but has importance for jurisdiction and conflict of laws problems. It is primarily concerned with how the original and amended convention apply to both the contracting and actual carrier.

Montreal Agreement, ICAO Doc. LC/SC Warsaw—Report 2, 19/8/69: On November 15, 1965, the United States deposited its note of denunciation of the Warsaw Convention. A working group was established to prepare for the February Montreal Conference. As the time for denunciation grew nearer, various proposals were made to pacify the United States. Finally, the Montreal Agreement was adopted and denunciation avoided. The Montreal Agreement became effective on May 16, 1966; it applies to carriers going to, from, or via the United States. The agreement increases the personal injury and death liability limits to $75,000 (including legal fees) and to $58,000 (excluding legal fees). It also provides for more detailed notice requirements and the creation of absolute liability. The improvements made by the Montreal Agreement are only of limited value and effectiveness. See, for example, L. KREINDLER, AVIATION ACCIDENT LAW, infra Appendix D (ch. 3), at §§ 12-A-19 to 12-A-22.

The Guatemala City Protocol, ICAO Doc. 8932 (1971): The Guatemala Protocol essentially creates strict liability with an unbreakable limit: 1,500,000 gold francs (approximately $100,000) for "the aggregate of" personal injury and death claims "however founded"; 62,500 gold francs (approximately $4,150) for each passenger's delay; 15,000 gold francs (approximately $1,000) for destruction, loss, delay, or damage to registered baggage. Strict liability, however, is not adopted for carriage of goods. For a comprehensive discussion of the Guatemala City Protocol of 1971, see MANKIEWICZ, *The 1971 Protocol of Guatemala City to Further Amend the 1929 Warsaw Convention*, Appendix D (ch. 3) infra.

The Montreal Protocols, ICAO Doc. 9145 (1975) (Protocol No. 1); ICAO Doc. 9146 (1975) (Protocol No. 2); ICAO Doc. 9147 (1975) (Protocol No. 3); ICAO Doc. 9148 (1975) (Protocol No. 4): For a comprehensive discussion of the Montreal Protocols, see Fitzgerald, *The Four Montreal Protocols to Amend the Warsaw Convention Regime Governing International Carriage by Air,* Appendix D (ch. 3) infra.

40. Convention on the Recognition and Enforcement of Foreign Arbitral Awards, opened for signature, June 10, 1958, 21 U.S.T. 2517, T.I.A.S. No. 6997, 330 U.N.T.S. 3, codified in 9 U.S.C. §§ 201-08 (1982). For a comprehensive discussion of the Convention and of the various documents pertaining to it, see A. VAN DEN BERG, THE NEW YORK ARBITRATION CONVENTION OF 1958 (1981) (reviewed in 37 ARB. J. 61 [1982]; 18 TEX. INT'L L.J. 243 [1983]; 24 VA. J. INT'L L. 527 [1984]; 16 J. MAR. L. & COM. 129 [1985]) [VAN DEN BERG]. See also, Aksen, *Application of the New York Convention by United States Courts,* 4 Y.B. COM. ARB. 341 (1979); Contini, *International Commercial Arbitration: The United Nations Convention on the Recognition and Enforcement of Foreign Arbitral Awards,* 8 AM. J. COMP. L. 283 (1959); Mirabito, *The United Nations Convention on the Recognition and Enforcement of Foreign Arbitral Awards: The First Four Years,* 5 GA. J. INT'L & COMP. L. 471 (1975); Quigley, *Accession by the United States to the United Nations Convention on the Recognition and Enforcement of Foreign Arbitral Awards,* 70 YALE L.J. 1049 (1961); Sanders, *Consolidated Commentary on Court Decisions on the New York Convention 1958,* 4 Y.B. COM. ARB. 341 (1979) and 6 Y.B. COM. ARB. 202 (1981); Springer, *The United Nations Convention on the Recognition and Enforcement of Foreign Arbitral Awards,* 3 INT'L LAW. 320 (1969). For a comprehensive bibliography, see VAN DEN BERG, supra note 40, at 440-50. See generally G. GAJA, NEW YORK CONVENTION (multivolume series).

For a general discussion of international commercial arbitration, see Sanders, *Trends in the Field of International Commercial Arbitration,* 145 REC. DES COURS (Hague Academy Lectures) 205 (1975); de Vries, *International Commercial Arbitration: A Contractual Substitute for National Courts,* 57 TUL. L. REV. 42 (1982). Accord Higgins, Brown, & Roach, *Pitfalls in International Commercial Arbitration,* 35 BUS. LAW. 1035 (1980); Rhodes & Sloan, *The Pitfalls of International Commercial Arbitration,* 17 VAND. J. TRANS. L. 19 (1984). See also Proceedings, *Roundtable Discussion on*

Public International Arbitration between Professors Kenneth R. Simmonds, Ruth Lapidoth, and Hans W. Baade, 22 TEX. INT'L L.J. 149 (1987).

41. See VAN DEN BERG, supra note 40, at 1-10.

42. These two elements, in effect, are the most critical factors in establishing the institutional autonomy of arbitral adjudication. The history of arbitration law in various countries illustrates that the former judicial hostility to arbitration was expressed primarily in the form of challenges to the validity of arbitration agreements. See Carbonneau, *Arbitral Adjudication: A Comparative Assessment of Its Remedial and Substantive Status in Transnational Commerce,* 19 TEX. INT'L L.J. 33, 39-56 (1984) [*Arbitral Adjudication*].

In England, for example, the courts deemed arbitration agreements to be against public policy because they ousted the courts' jurisdiction and the guarantees of judicial justice. As a result, a party, anticipating an unfavorable award, could revoke its initial consent to arbitrate — claiming that the arbitration agreement was against public policy. American courts integrated the basic English judicial attitude into their case law, holding that an arbitration agreement was unenforceable through specific performance and could be revoked by either party before an award was rendered. Nineteenth-century French decisional law concurred with these results; the French courts held the arbitral clause (the agreement to arbitrate future disputes) invalid under French domestic law (see id. at 39-40, n.12 and sources cited).

The history of the English supervision of the merits of arbitral awards illustrates how the autonomy of the arbitral process could be effectively challenged on another ground (see id. at 40). When the initial reference to arbitration could not be defeated, the results of the process could be strictly reviewed by courts. An adjudicatory process unable to provide binding determinations had little basis upon which to found its legitimacy.

43. Accord VAN DEN BERG, supra note 40, at 28-43. See also Carbonneau, review of VAN DEN BERG in 24 VA. J. INT'L L. 527, 530-32 (1984).

44. See VAN DEN BERG, supra note 40, at 121-232.

45. See id. at 154-60.

46. See id.

47. See id. at 246-383.

48. See id. at 275-358.

49. See id. at 359-82.

50. See text at notes 30-32 supra.

51. See generally Sanders, *A Twenty Years' Review of the Convention on the Recognition and Enforcement of Foreign Arbitral Awards,* 13 INT'L LAW. 269 (1979); Sanders, *Consolidated Commentary on Court Decisions*

on the New York Convention 1958, note 40 supra; Van den Berg, *Court Decisions on the New York Convention 1958,* 11 Y.B. COM. ARB. 399 (1986).

52. But see VAN DEN BERG, supra note 40, at 28-43. Accord 24 VA. J. INT'L L. 527, 530-32 (1984).

53. The basic reference on French arbitration law is J. ROBERT, L'AR-BITRAGE DROIT INTERNE DROIT INTERNATIONAL PRIVE (5th ed. 1983) (translated into English as J. ROBERT & T. CARBONNEAU, THE FRENCH LAW OF ARBITRATION [1983], reviewed in 2 ARB. INT'L 266 [1986]). See also M. BOISSESON, LE DROIT FRANCAIS DE L'ARBITRAGE (1983); J.-L. DELVOLVE, AR-BITRATION IN FRANCE: THE FRENCH LAW OF NATIONAL AND INTERNA-TIONAL ARBITRATION (1982); B. MOREAU & T. BERNARD, DROIT INTERNE ET DROIT INTERNATIONAL DE L'ARBITRAGE (1985); 2 H. SMIT & V. PECHOTA, THE WORLD ARBITRATION REPORTER 1641 (1986) [H. SMIT & V. PECHOTA]; Derains, *France: National Report,* 6 Y.B. COM. ARB. 1 (1981) & 7 Y.B. COM. ARB. 35 (1982); Seppala, *French Domestic Arbitration Law,* 16 INT'L LAW. 749 (1982).

The following section of the text relies heavily upon several of my previous studies on French arbitration law, in particular on *Arbitral Adjudication,* note 42 supra. For a discussion of the French domestic court support for international commercial arbitration, see Carbonneau, *The Elaboration of a French Court Doctrine on International Commercial Arbitration: A Study in Liberal Civilian Judicial Creativity,* 55 TUL. L. REV. 1 (1980) [*French Court Doctrine*].

54. For a list of contracting states, see 11 Y.B. COM. ARB. 395 (1986).

55. See Carbonneau, *The Reform of the French Procedural Law on Arbitration: An Analytical Commentary on the Decree of May 14, 1980,* 4 HASTINGS INT'L & COMP. L. REV. 273, 275-76 (1981) [*French Procedural Reform*].

56. In particular, disputes regarding the obligations and dealings among business persons, merchants, and bankers. CODE DE COMMERCE art. 631 (Dalloz 1979-80). See Law of Dec. 31, 1925, [1926] SIREY LOIS ANNOT. 57-58 (Fr.). See also P. HERZOG, CIVIL PROCEDURE IN FRANCE 513, n.169 (1967).

57. See *Arbitral Adjudication,* supra note 42, at 53-54.

58. See *French Court Doctrine,* supra note 53, at 6-16.

59. CODE CIV. art. 2060 (Fr.). See Level, *Compromis d'Arbitrage,* in [1972] JURIS-CLASSEUR CIV. II arts. 2059-2061, at 4. See also *French Court Doctrine,* supra note 53, at 29, 6-7. The recently enacted law No. 86-972 of August 19, 1986, however, created an exception to article 2060, allowing the state and its entities to enter into arbitration agreements in contracts with foreign companies. See *New French Law Authorizes Arbitration for Government Entities,* 2 INT'L ARB. REP. 7 (Jan. 1987). See also Boisseson, *Interrogations*

et doutes sur une evolution legislative: L'Article 9 de la loi du 19 août 1986, [1987] REV. ARB. 3 (1987).

60. See Judgment of Apr. 10, 1957, Cr. d'appel 1re, Paris, 85 J. DR. INT'L-CLUNET 1002 (1958); Judgment of May 2, 1966, Cass. civ. 1re, Fr., [1966] DALLOZ-SIREY Jur. 575; Judgment of May 5, 1959, Cr. d'appel 1re, Aix-en-Provence, 87 J. DR. INT'L-CLUNET 1077 (1960). See also Batiffol, *Arbitration Clauses Concluded Between French Government-Owned Enterprises and Foreign Private Parties,* 7 COLUM. J. TRANS. L. 32 (1968); *French Court Doctrine,* supra note 53, at 29-30.

61. See Judgment of May 18, 1971, Cass. civ. 1re, Fr., 99 J. DR. INT'L-CLUNET 62 (1972); Judgment of June 14, 1960, Cass. civ. 1re, Fr., 49 REV. CRIT. DR. INT'L PR. 393 (1960); Judgment of June 30, 1976, Cass. civ. 1re, Fr., [1977] REV. ARB. 135 (1977). See also *French Court Doctrine,* supra note 53, at 36-40.

62. See *French Court Doctrine,* supra note 53, at 37-38.

63. See id. at 20-23.

64. Decree No. 80-354 of May 14, 1980, [1980] J.O. 1238, reprinted in [1980] DALLOZ-SIREY, Législation 207. See Delvolve, *La réforme du droit de l'arbitrage: l'intervention du juge,* [1980] REV. ARB. 607 (1980); Loussouarn, *La réforme du droit de l'arbitrage: les voies de recours,* [1980] REV. ARB. 671 (1980); Robert, *La législation nouvelle sur l'arbitrage,* [1980] DALLOZ-SIREY Chronique No. 25, at 189. See also *French Procedural Reform,* note 55 supra (the following commentary refers in the main to this previous analysis).

65. Decree No. 81-500 of May 12, 1981, [1981] J.O. 1398, reprinted in [1981] DALLOZ-SIREY, Législation 222. See Audit, *A National Codification of International Commercial Arbitration: The French Decree of May 12, 1981,* in RESOLVING TRANSNATIONAL DISPUTES THROUGH INTERNATIONAL ARBITRATION 116 [Sixth Sokol Colloquium] (T. Carbonneau ed. & contrib. 1984); Craig, Park, & Paulsson, *French Codification of a Legal Framework for International Commercial Arbitration: The Decree of May 12, 1981,* 13 LAW & POL'Y INT'L BUS. 727 (1981); Delaume, *International Arbitration under French Law: The Decree of May 12, 1981,* 37 ARB. J. 38 (1982); Goldman, *La nouvelle réglementation française de l'arbitrage international,* in THE ART OF ARBITRATION 153 (J. Schultsz & A. Van Den Berg eds. 1982); for further sources, see Audit, supra at 116-17, n.3. See also *Arbitral Adjudication,* supra note 42, at 77-79 (the following commentary refers in the main to this previous analysis).

66. Decree No. 81-500 of May 12, 1981, supra note 65, at art. 1492: "An international arbitration is one which implicates the interests of international commerce" (author's translation).

67. See *Arbitral Adjudication,* supra note 42, at 78-79.

68. See id. at 78.

69. See id. at 78-79. Other civil law jurisdictions recently have enacted legislation that moves them in the direction of adopting the concept of "anational" arbitration. On December 1, 1986, the Netherlands replaced the arbitral provisions of the 1838 Code of Civil Procedure with a revised regulatory framework for arbitration. The Netherlands Arbitration Act added a new book to the Code of Civil Procedure, consisting of articles 1020-1076. These new provisions, although based upon the regulation of arbitration through a territoriality principle, constitute a liberal statement of policy regarding arbitration. The legislation recognizes the principle of party autonomy, attributes full effect to the arbitration agreement, establishes a cooperative relationship between judicial and arbitral tribunals, and provides limited means for challenging awards. See Schultsz, *Les nouvelles dispositions de la législation néerlandaise en matière d'arbitrage,* [1988] REV. ARB. 209 (1988); Van den Berg, *The Netherlands,* 2 INT'L HANDBOOK COM. ARB. § The Netherlands (P. Sanders ed. April 1987); Van den Berg, *The Netherlands,* 12 Y.B. COM. ARB. 3 (1987); 3 MEALEY'S INT'L ARB. REP. 10 (July 1988).

On December 18, 1987, the Swiss Parliament enacted a law entitled the Swiss Private International Law Act that governs matters of international arbitration. The law contains a number of liberal provisions on arbitration, including one which recognizes the authority of arbitral tribunals to rule upon jurisdictional challenges. It generally gives effect to party choice and determination in matters of arbitration. See Briner, *Switzerland,* 2 INT'L HANDBOOK COM. ARB. § Switzerland (P. Sanders ed. Sept. 1988); Blessing, *The New International Arbitration Law in Switzerland: A Significant Step Towards Liberalism,* 5 J. INT'L ARB. 9 (1988); Budin, *La nouvelle loi suisse sur l'arbitrage international,* [1988] REV. ARB. 51 (1988); 3 MEALEY'S INTL'L ARB. REP. 5 (Nov. 1988).

In Belgium, the law of March 27, 1985, modified article 1717 of the Judicial Code, limiting the authority of Belgian courts to set aside an international or foreign arbitral award. For purposes of asserting jurisdiction, the article requires that one of the implicated parties have Belgium nationality, reside in Belgium, or have a commercial presence in Belgium. See Matray, *Belgium,* 2 INT'L HANDBOOK COM. ARB. § Belgium (P. Sanders ed. Dec. 1987); Paulsson, *Arbitration Unbound in Belgium,* 2 ARB. INT'L 68 (1986); Van Houtte, *La loi belge du 27 mars 1985 sur l'arbitrage international,* [1986] REV. ARB. 28 (1986).

70. See *Arbitral Adjudication,* supra note 42, at 79.

71. The legislation implementing the convention in England is: The Arbitration Act 1975, 1975 c.8, reprinted in 4 G. GAJA, THE NEW YORK

CONVENTION 15.1 (1978-1980) and A. WALTON & M. VITORIA, RUSSELL ON THE LAW OF ARBITRATION 548 (20th ed. 1982).
    72. For general sources on the English law of arbitration, see E. LEE, ENCYCLOPEDIA OF ARBITRATION LAW (1984); M. MUSTILL & S. BOYD, THE LAW AND PRACTICE OF COMMERCIAL ARBITRATION IN ENGLAND (1982); A. WALTON & M. VITORIA, note 71 supra; Hunter, *Arbitration Procedure in England: Past, Present and Future,* 1 ARB. INT'L 82 (1985); Jones, *History of Commercial Arbitration in England and the United States,* in INTERNATIONAL TRADE ARBITRATION 127 (M. Domke ed. 1958); Steyn, *England: National Report,* 8 Y.B. COM. ARB. 3 (1983); Steyn, *England: National Report,* 1 INT'L HANDBOOK ON COM. ARB. England-1 (1984); 1 H. SMIT & V. PECHOTA, supra note 53, at 2701-2762.
    73. See *Arbitral Adjudication,* supra note 42, at 40-42.
    74. Arbitration Act, 1950, 14 Geo. 6, ch. 27.
    75. See *Arbitral Adjudication,* supra note 42, at 42-44.
    76. See Park, *Judicial Supervision of Transnational Commercial Arbitration: The English Arbitration Act of 1979,* 21 HARV. INT'L L.J. 87, 92 (1980) [*Judicial Supervision*].
    77. Arbitration Act, 1979, ch. 42, reprinted in 5 Y.B. COM. ARB. 239-46 (1980). The secondary references on the 1979 Arbitration Act include: Abromson, *The English Arbitration Act of 1979: A Symbiotic Relationship Between the Courts and Arbitration Tribunals,* 5 SUFFOLK TRANS. L. J. 7 (1980); Comment, *Judicial Implementation of the United Kingdom Arbitration Act, 1979: Pioneer Shipping v. B.T.P. Tioxide ("The Nema"),* 24 HARV. INT'L L. J. 103 (1983); Donaldson, *Commercial Arbitration: 1979 and After,* 36 CURRENT L. PROB. 1 (1983); Elland & Goldsmith, *The Arbitration Act 1979,* 6 INT'L L. & PRAC. 63 (1980); Lord Hacking, *The "Stated Case" Abolished: The United Kingdom Arbitration Act of 1979,* 14 INT'L LAW. 95 (1980); Lord Hacking, *Where We Are Now: Trends and Developments Since the Arbitration Act [1979],* 2 J. INT'L ARB. 7 (1985); Jarvin, *London as a Place for International Arbitration: Some Observations in Light of the Arbitration Act 1979 and the Bank Mellat v. Helleniki Techniki case,* 1 J. INT'L ARB. 59 (1984); Kerr, *The Arbitration Act 1979,* 43 MOD. L. REV. 45 (1980); *Judicial Supervision,* note 76 supra; Park, *The Influence of National Legal Systems on International Commercial Arbitration: Recent Developments in English Arbitration Law,* in RESOLVING TRANSNATIONAL DISPUTES THROUGH INTERNATIONAL ARBITRATION, supra note 65, at 80; Samuel, *The 1979 Arbitration Act: Judicial Review of Arbitration Awards on the Merits in England,* 2 J. INT'L ARB. 53 (1985); Schmitthoff, *The United Kingdom Arbitration Act of 1979,* 5 Y.B. COM. ARB. 231 (1980); Shenton & Toland, *London as a Venue for International Arbitration: The Arbitration Act, 1979,* 12 L. & POL'Y INT'L BUS. 643 (1980); Smedresman, *The Arbi-*

tration Act, 1979, 11 J. MAR. L. & COM. 319 (1980); Thomas, *An Appraisal of the Arbitration Act 1979,* [1981] LLOYD'S MAR. & COM. L.Q. 199 (1981).

78. See Park & Paulsson, *The Binding Force of International Arbitral Awards,* 23 VA. J. INT'L L. 253, 272-73 (1983). See also Park, *The Lex Loci Arbitri and International Commercial Arbitration,* 32 INT'L & COMP. L.Q. 21, 40-41 (1983).

79. See *Arbitral Adjudication,* supra note 42, at 44-45, 62-64.

80. Id. at 64.

81. See Antaios Compania Naviera S.A. v. Salen Rederierna A.B. (The "Antaios") (No.2), [1984] 2 Lloyd's Rep. 235 (1984); B.T.P. Tioxide Ltd. v. Pioneer Shipping Ltd. and Armada Marine S.A. (The "Nema"), [1981] 2 Lloyd's Rep. 239 (H.L.) (1981); K/S A/S Bill Biakh & K/S A/S Bill Biali v. Hyundai Corp., Comm. Ct., QB, reported in 3 MEALEY'S INT'L ARB. REP. 7 (Sept. 1988). See also Comment, *Judicial Implementation of the United Kingdom Arbitration Act, 1979: Pioneer Shipping v. B.T.P. Tioxide (The "Nema"),* 24 HARV. INT'L L. J. 103 (1983); Thomas, *The Antaios: The Nema Guidelines Reconsidered,* [1985] J. BUS. L. 200 (1985); Martin, *International Arbitration (Great Britain),* LLOYD'S MAR. &COM. L. 23 (1988).

82. For a discussion of the prior status of the Canadian law on arbitration, see L. KOS RABCEWICZ-ZUBKOWSKI, COMMERCIAL AND CIVIL LAW ARBITRATION IN CANADA (1978); R. MCLAREN & E. PALMER, THE LAW AND PRACTICE OF COMMERCIAL ARBITRATION (1982); Claxton, *Commercial Arbitration Under Canadian Law,* 21 CAN. B. REV. 171 (1943); Guibault, *Les lois québecoises de conciliation et d'arbitrage,* 11 REV. BAR. 221 (1951); Kos-Rabcewicz-Zubkowski, *Commercial Arbitration in Canada,* 1 Y.B. COM. ARB. 16 (1977); Nadelmann, *Enforcement of Foreign Judgments in Canada,* 38 CAN. B. REV. 68 (1960); Perrault, *Clause compromissoire et arbitrage,* 5 REV. BAR. 74 (1945); 2 H. SMIT & V. PECHOTA, supra note 53, at 1143-1234; Verge, *De la souveraineté décisionnelle de l'arbitre,* 19 MCGILL L. J. 543 (1973).

83. See An Act to Implement the United Nations Convention on the Recognition and Enforcement of Foreign Arbitral Awards (Bill C 107); Law on the United Nations Convention Concerning Foreign Arbitral Awards (SC. 1986, C. 21) (received Royal assent on June 17, 1986). In accordance with the federal government accession, all of Canada's provinces and territories enacted legislation implementing the convention. See, for example, Foreign Arbitral Awards Act, Bill 67, 1985 British Columbia, 33d Parl., 34 Eliz. II, S.B.C. 1986, c. 14; An Act to Implement the United Nations Convention on the Recognition and Enforcement of Foreign Arbitral Award, Bill 98, 1986 Ontario, 1st Sess. 33d Leg. Ont., 35 Eliz. II; An Act to Implement the Convention on the Recognition and Enforcement of Foreign Arbitral Awards and to Adopt the Model Law on

International Commercial Arbitration, Bill 83, 1986 Nova Scotia, 2d Sess., 54th G.A.N.S., 35 ELIZ. II, enacted S.N.S. 1986, c. 12; An Act to Amend the Civil Code and the Code of Civil Procedure in Respect of Arbitration, Bill 91, 1986 Quebec, 1st Sess. 3d Leg., enacted S.Q. 1986, c. 73. See also Alberta, S. Alta. 1986, c. 1-66; Manitoba, S. Man. 1986, c. 32; New Brunswick, S.N.B. 1986, c. 1-12.2; Prince Edward Island, S.P.E.I. 1986, c. 14; Newfoundland, S. Nfld. 1986, c. 45; Northwest Territories, Ord. N.W.T. 1986(1), c. 6. Saskatchewan and the Yukon Territory, which adopted legislation to give effect to the New York Convention, were in the process of considering legislation to give effect to the UNCITRAL Model Law. By mid-1988, all Canadian provinces had enacted the UNCITRAL rules. See 3 MEALEY'S INT'L ARB. REP. 21 (Nov. 1988).

84. See An Act Relating to Commercial Arbitration, Bill C-108, 1986, 1st Sess., 33d Parl. 33-34-35 Eliz. II, enacted S.C., 1986, c. 22.

85. See generally *Canada,* in U.S. STATE DEPT., COUNTRIES OF THE WORLD 131 (1974).

86. See id.

87. See 2 H. SMIT & V. PECHOTA, supra note 53, at 1143, 1221. The provincial legislation was quite uniform. Typically, the parties could agree to submit either an existing or future dispute to arbitration. Such an agreement would have essentially the same effect as if the recourse to arbitration had been ordered by a court. See Ont. Rev. Stat. ch. 25 § 4 (1970); Alta. Rev. Stat. ch. A-43 § 2 (1980); Man. Rev. Stat. ch. A-120 § 5 (1970); B.C. Rev. Stat. ch.18 § 3 (1979); N.B. Rev. Stat. ch.A-10 § 5 (1973); Nfld. Rev. Stat. ch.187 § 178 (1970); N.W.T. Rev. Ord. Ch.A-4 § 5 (1980); N.S. Rev. Stat. ch.12 § 2 (1967); P.E.I. Rev. Stat. ch.12 § 4 (1974); Sask. Rev. Stats. ch.A-24 § 3 (1981).

Furthermore, the court could assist in the implementation of the arbitration proceedings by staying court proceedings, nominating an arbitrator, or supervising the incapacity of an arbitrator. See Alta. Rev. Stat. ch.A-43 §§ 3, 5, 11 (1980); B.C. Rev. Stat. Ch.18 §§ 5, 6, 13 (1979); Man. Rev. Stat. ch.A-120 § 7 (1970); N.B. Rev. Stat. ch.A-10 §§ 5, 7 (1973); Nfld. Rev. Stat. ch. 187 §§ 179, 181 (1970); N.W.T. Rev. Stat. ch.A-4 §§ 11, 12, 13 (1980); N.S. Rev. Stat. ch. 12 §§ 3, 6, 18 (1967); Ont. Rev. Stat. ch.25 §§ 7, 12 (1980); P.E.I. Rev. Stat. ch.A-14 §§ 6, 7 (1974); Sask. Rev. Stat. ch.A-25 §§ 5, 6, 10 (1981).

The enforcement of an award was obligatory; by leave of the court, an award could be enforced in the same manner as a judgment or order to the same effect. See Alberta § 12; British Columbia § 15; Manitoba § 24; New Brunswick § 18; Newfoundland § 187; Northwest Territories § 26; Nova Scotia § 3; Ontario § 13; Prince Edward Island § 13; Saskatchewan § 11. However, in four provinces, an appeal of the award was envisaged.

See Manitoba § 32(1); Ontario § 16; Prince Edward Island § 21; Saskatchewan § 14.

88. See Brierley, *International Trade Arbitration: The Canadian Viewpoint*, in CANADIAN PERSPECTIVES ON INTERNATIONAL LAW AND ORGANIZATION 826 (R. St. John MacDonald, G. Morris, & D. Johnston eds. 1974) [*The Canadian Viewpoint*].

89. See text at notes 74-76 supra.

90. See CODE PROC. CIV. arts. 940-51, ch.80 (1965), as amended ch.63 (1970).

91. See Que. Rev. Stat. ch.25 § 948 (1977).

92. See Que. Rev. Stat. ch.25 § 950, 951 (1977).

93. See Convention on the Recognition and Enforcement of Foreign Arbitral Awards, supra note 40, at art. II. See also VAN DEN BERG, supra note 40, at 123-25.

94. See Castel, *Canada and International Arbitration*, 36 ARB. J. 5, 6-10 (1981).

95. See *The Canadian Viewpoint*, supra note 88, at 834-35.

96. These conventions are: The Geneva Protocol on Arbitration Clauses of 1923; The Geneva Convention on the Execution of Foreign Arbitral Awards of 1927; The 1958 New York Arbitration Convention; and The Convention on the Settlement of Investment Disputes Between States and Nationals of Other States of 1965.

97. See *The Canadian Viewpoint*, supra note 88, at 831-32. See also Morris, *The Problem of Uniform Arbitration Legislation in Canada*, 13 ARB. J. 103 (1958).

98. See *The Canadian Viewpoint*, supra note 88, at 834.

99. See P. HOGG, CONSTITUTIONAL LAW OF CANADA 439-40 (2d ed. 1985) [P. HOGG]. See also *The Canadian Viewpoint*, supra note 88, at 834-35.

100. B. LASKINS, CANADIAN CONSTITUTIONAL LAW 3 (1951).

101. See P. HOGG, supra note 99, at 29-30.

102. See generally A. SMITH, THE COMMERCE POWER IN CANADA AND THE UNITED STATES (1963).

103. See P. HOGG, supra note 99, at 440 (citing Citizens' Ins. Co. v. Parson's, 7 App. Cas. 96 [1881]). "Since the *Parsons Case*, it has been accepted that, in general, intraprovincial power, under 'property and civil rights in the province' (S 93 [13]) and the federal trade and commerce power is confined to (1) interprovincial or international trade and commerce, and (2) 'general' trade and commerce." See id.

104. *The Canadian Viewpoint*, supra note 88, at 830.

105. Id. at 835.

106. See A. VAN DEN BERG, supra note 40, at 410 (Annex B). The convention now has more than seventy adherents.

107. See ch.4 infra. See also Holtzman, *Arbitration and the Courts: Partners on a System of International Justice,* [1978] REV. ARB. 253 (1978); Perlman & Nelson, *New Approaches to the Resolution of International Commercial Disputes,* 17 INT'L LAW. 215, 255 (1983); Ribicoff, *Alternatives to Litigation: Their Application to International Business Disputes,* 38 ARB. J. 3, 5 (1983).

108. See text at notes 82-84 supra.

109. See I. DORE, ARBITRATION AND CONCILIATION UNDER THE UNCITRAL RULES: A TEXTUAL ANALYSIS (1986). See also Bockstiegel, *The Relevance of National Arbitration Law for Arbitrations under the UNCITRAL Rules,* 1 J. INT'L ARB. 223 (1984); Herrmann, *The UNCITRAL Model Law: Its Background, Salient Features and Purposes,* 1 ARB. INT'L 6 (1985); Hunter, *International Commercial Arbitrations: The UNCITRAL Model Law,* 34 INT'L BUS. LAW. 189 (1984); McNerney & Esplugues, *International Commercial Arbitration: The UNCITRAL Model Law,* 9 B.C. INT'L & COMP. L. REV. 47 (1986).

110. See HERRMANN, *UNCITRAL's Work Towards a Model Law on International Commercial Arbitration,* 4 PACE L. REV. 537, 546-7 (1984).

111. Lucio, *The UNCITRAL Model Law on International Commercial Arbitration,* 17 U. MIAMI INTER-AM. L. REV. 313, 322 (1986).

112. Kerr, *Arbitration and the Courts: The UNCITRAL Model Law,* 34 INT'L & COMP. L.Q. 1, 16 (1985).

113. See Alvarez, *La nouvelle législation canadienne sur l'arbitrage commercial international,* [1986] REV. ARB. 529 (1986); Alvarez, *The Role of Arbitration in Canada: New Perspectives,* 21 U. B. C. L. REV. 247 (1987); Chiasson, *Canada: No Man's Land No More,* 3 J. INT'L ARB. 67 (1986); Mendes, *Canada: A New Forum to Develop the Cultural Psychology of International Commercial Arbitration,* 3 J. INT'L ARB. 71 (1986). See also Brierley, *Canadian Acceptance of International Commercial Arbitration,* 40 ME. L. REV. 287 (1988); Brierley, *Une loi nouvelle pour le Québec en matière d'arbitrage,* 47 REV. BAR. 259 (1987) (English translation in 13 CAN. BUS. L. J. 58 [1987-88]); Chiasson & Lalonda, *Recent Canadian Legislation on Arbitration,* 2 ARB. INT'L 370 (1986); Comment, *Canadian-American Perspectives on the United Nations Convention on the Recognition and Enforcement of Foreign Arbitral Awards,* 3 CAN.-AM. L. J. 219 (1986); Noecker & Hentzen, *The New Legislation on Arbitration in Canada,* 22 INT'L LAW. 829 (1988).

114. See Price Waterhouse, *Doing Business in Canada 7* (1983); *Canada,* in U.S. STATE DEPT., supra note 85, at 136.

115. Telephone interviews with Professors John Brierley (McGill University) and Leon Trakman (University of Dalhousie), May 5, 1987.

116. For a discussion and analysis of the traditional Latin American

attitude toward arbitration, see Garro, *Enforcement of Arbitration Agreements and Jurisdiction of Arbitral Tribunals in Latin America,* 1 J. INT'L ARB. 293 (1984). See also Nattier, *International Commercial Arbitration in Latin America: Enforcement of Arbitral Agreements and Awards,* 21 TEX. INT'L L. J. 397 (1986); Samtleben, *Arbitration in Brazil,* 18 U. MIAMI INTER-AM. L. REV. 1 (1986). For a discussion of the Inter-American Arbitration Convention, see Current Developments, *The Inter-American Convention on International Commercial Arbitration,* 75 AM. J. INT'L L. 982 (1981); Hoellering, *"Arbitration," Inter-American Convention,* 196 N.Y.L.J., at 1, col. 1 (Nov. 18, 1986); Norberg, *Inter-American Commercial Arbitration: Unicorn or Beast of Burden?,* 5 PACE L. REV. 607 (1985); Note, *International Commercial Arbitration: Domestic Recognition and Enforcement of the Inter-American Convention on International Commercial Arbitration,* 10 SYRACUSE J. INT'L L. & COM. 169 (1983). Accord 3 MEALEY'S INT'L ARB. REP. 19 (Nov. 1988) (reporting Congressional inaction on the convention).

117. See W. CRAIG, W. PARK, & J. PAULSSON, INTERNATIONAL CHAMBER OF COMMERCE ARBITRATION 5 (1984); Paulsson, *Arbitration Under the Rules of the International Chamber of Commerce,* in RESOLVING TRANSNATIONAL DISPUTES THROUGH INTERNATIONAL ARBITRATION, supra note 65, at 235, 255-60. Individual states in the United States also are becoming aware of the importance of international commercial arbitration and the need to support it. See *United States: Florida International Arbitration Act,* 26 INT'L L. MAT'LS 949 (1987).

118. See *China Becomes a Signatory to the New York Convention,* 2 MEALEY'S INT'L ARB. REP. 158 (Mar. 1987); Shaoshan, *A Brief Account of the New York Convention of 1958,* 2 CHINA PATS. & TMS. Q. 9 (Apr. 1987). See also DuQuan, *Fully Untilize (sic) the Methods of Mediation in Handling Foreign Economic and Trade Disputes,* 1 CHINA PATS. & TMS. Q. 33 (Oct. 1986); Gushu, *Settling Industrial Property Disputes Through Non-Judicial Procedures,* 1 CHINA PATS. & TMS. Q. 24 (Jan. 1986); Jinljang & Shujian, *Foreign-Related Disputes Handled by Chinese Arbitration Organs,* 2 CHINA PATS. & TMS. Q. 101 (June 1987); Yan, *A Comparative Study of the Uniform Commercial Code and the Foreign Economic Contract Law of China,* 93 COM. L. J. 63 (1988); Yougan, *Arbitration Cases Handled by the Foreign Economic and Trade Arbitration Commission, CCPIT,* 2 CHINA PATS. & TMS. Q. 101 (Jan. 1987). See generally Spanogle & Baranski, *Chinese Commercial Dispute Resolution Methods: The State Commercial and Industrial Administration Bureau,* 35 AM. J. COMP. L. 761 (1987); Symposium, *The People's Republic of China: International and Domestic Law in an Atmosphere of Change,* 23 WILLAMETTE L. REV. 615 (1987).

4 | The American Endorsement of Arbitration: Unequivocal Support Fueled by Misguided Objectives

In its historical evolution, the American law of arbitration[1] stands in an intermediary position between its French and English counterparts. It also bears some, albeit different, affinity with the Canadian experience. In keeping with the patterns developed in the French and English systems, a sense of commercial realism and lobbying efforts brought about landmark legislation that eventually undermined the judicial hostility toward arbitration, undoing the perception that it amounted to a contractual usurpation of judicial jurisdictional authority.[2] While the attitude of the American legal system initially paralleled the English reluctance to embrace arbitration wholeheartedly, contemporary American statutory and decisional law on arbitration are in keeping with the unequivocal French acceptance of arbitral adjudication.

Enacted in 1925, the Federal Arbitration Act (FAA)[3] is the landmark legislation that put an end to the era in which courts in the United States were willing to entertain suits brought in violation of arbitration agreements. According to the celebrated language of section 2 of the FAA, arbitration agreements are "valid, irrevocable, and enforceable."[4] The intendment of the federal legislation manifestly was to promote arbitration as a viable alternative to the judicial resolution of disputes. In its current form, the FAA retains substantially all of its original language. In the federal decisional law spearheaded by the United States Supreme Court, it continues to act as the legislative foundation for the judicial elaboration of a federal policy strongly favoring the recourse to arbitral adjudication.

As with most modern statutes on arbitration,[5] the federal legislation recognizes the principle of party autonomy in contract, the element that gives arbitration its fundamentally consensual nature. The federal statutory framework couples the party autonomy principle with arbitral flexibility. Within the restrictions posed by basic public policy requirements regarding adjudicatory justice, the parties to an arbitration agreement can fashion the procedural rules to be applied in the arbitral proceeding. Moreover, judicial jurisdictional authority is meant to assist the implementation and functioning of the arbitral process. Courts are the instruments by which to compel arbitration or appoint an arbitrator when a party is recalcitrant and refuses to comply with the provisions of a valid agreement to arbitrate. The courts are under a statutory obligation to give effect to the jurisdictional consequences of an arbitration agreement. A valid arbitration agreement compels the stay of any court proceeding regarding a dispute validly submitted to arbitration. Finally, the federal legislation provides for limited judicial supervision of awards. The grounds for setting aside an award center upon basic concerns of procedural due process.[6]

Before 1970, the United States—paralleling the English posture—was not a party to any international agreement on arbitration. In 1970, subject to the double reservation that the convention would be applied on the basis of reciprocity and only to disputes arising out of contractual or other relationships considered commercial under United States law, the United States ratified the 1958 New York Arbitration Convention. The ratification of the convention led to the enactment of the 1970 Arbitration Act, establishing a set of new provisions for dealing with litigation arising under the convention.[7]

The provisions of the New York Convention apply in cases in which an arbitration agreement or award arises out of a dispute in which one or both parties are foreign nationals.[8] When both parties are United States nationals, the convention governs only in those instances in which the "relationship involves property located abroad, envisages performance or enforcement, or has some other rational relation with one or more foreign states."[9] Like the English Arbitration Act of 1979, the American legislation defines international arbitration by reference to the formalistic requirement of party nationality. The governing definition in cases in which no party to the transaction is a foreign national, however, reflects a far more realistic standard than the English concept of "non-domestic" contracts. Like the French legislation, it focuses upon the actual economic impact of parties' commercial relationship to determine whether the award is international and thereby subject to the provisions of the convention.

As in other jurisdictions, judicial implementation is critical to the status of the convention in the American legal system. Following the rulings of the United States Supreme Court, the federal courts have exhibited a favorable disposition toward arbitration in general and toward international commercial arbitration in particular. A perusal of recent federal court cases, in fact, reveals that federal court decisions systematically uphold the continued viability and autonomy of the arbitral process.[10] The gravamen of the opinions centers upon furthering "the strong federal policy supporting arbitration"[11] — a phrase wrought and consecrated by the United States Supreme Court in its decisional law regarding the federal act and the convention.

The Court's opinions on arbitration can be roughly divided into three major groupings: first, earlier rulings that deal with the domestic law implications of arbitration, specifically the FAA's impact upon federalism concerns; second, more recent domestic rulings that demonstrate a reinforcement of the Court's favorable position toward arbitration and of its willingness to curtail federalism considerations to advance the process; and, third, rulings that deal exclusively with matters of international commercial arbitration. In these last rulings, the Court defines the interrelationship between national juridical requirements and the international process. The content of these rulings not only portends the creation of a general substantive American law on transnational commerce and arbitration, but also demonstrates the possible influence of such a law upon domestic commerce and arbitration matters. The radical character of the Court's most recent decision on arbitration, however, imperils the soundness and direction of its doctrine on arbitration.

Arbitration and Federalism

The Federal Arbitration Act was enacted during the era of *Swift v. Tyson*.[12] The import of *Swift* was that federal courts hearing state law cases on a diversity basis were bound by state court opinions only when the cases before them involved the construction of state constitutions or statutes. Where the latter were not involved, the federal courts were free to devise their own rules of decision independently of state courts' rulings.[13] *Erie v. Tompkins*[14] overruled *Swift v. Tyson*, providing that "there is no general federal common law,"[15] and that "Congress has no power to declare substantive rules of common law applicable in a state, whether they be local in their nature or general, whether they be commercial law or a part of the law of torts."[16] Accordingly, *Erie* reversed the prior doctrine, holding that federal courts, in cases in which their jurisdiction is based upon diversity of citizenship, are required to apply state law except when the controversy is governed by the U.S. Constitution or an act of Congress.[17]

Viewing the enactment of the FAA from the perspective of *Erie,* the question became whether the federal law on arbitration—providing for the enforceability of arbitration agreements—was merely a set of procedural regulations or legislation that created substantive rights. More specifically, in a diversity of citizenship case involving purely state interests, could the provisions of the FAA dislodge the application of a less favorable or perhaps contrary (but otherwise controlling) state statute or decisional law? Under *Erie,* the displacement of applicable state law on arbitration could be seen as a preemptive application of general federal common law. Although clearly protective of federalism principles, such an interpretation could have fragmented any national consensus on arbitration and undermined the FAA's clear mandate to make arbitration an autonomous and viable alternative adjudicatory process. In light of the latter consideration, another view of the federalism issue generated by the judicial implementation of the FAA in diversity cases could be advanced. Because *Erie* mandates the application of state law in all diversity cases but those in which the U.S. Constitution or federal legislation is controlling, the courts could deem the FAA applicable as a federal enactment, holding—in effect—that it represents more than the enactment of merely procedural regulations and that it actually creates substantive rights. According to a distinguished scholar in the area, "to be consistent with *Erie,* a court creating federal common law need only ground its authority to do so on some federal enactment other than the diversity grant."[18]

In this regard, the decision in *Prima Paint Corp. v. Flood & Conklin Mfg. Co.*[19] has seminal significance. Decided in 1967, *Prima Paint* establishes the separability doctrine as part of the developing decisional law on arbitration.[20] The separability doctrine holds that an arbitration clause is unaffected by the nullity of the main contract. For example, when the main contract is alleged to be invalid for reasons of fraud, that allegation does not affect the validity of the arbitration clause unless the fraud was also directed at that clause. The agreement to arbitrate has a separate juridical existence from the main contract.[21] Recourse can still be had to the arbitral process to decide those disputes that flow from the invalidity of the main contract. "Arbitration clauses as a matter of federal law are separable from contracts in which they are embedded, and . . . where no claim is made that fraud was directed to the arbitration clause itself, a broad arbitration clause will be held to encompass arbitration of the claim that the contract was induced by fraud."[22]

The significance of *Prima Paint* also resides in the Court's view of the FAA's systemic stature. The Court in *Prima Paint* underscored the primary intent and ultimate objective of the federal legislation and expressed its judicial resolve to give full effect to both these aspects of the act in relevant litigation.[23] The Court further stated that the question in *Prima Paint* "was not whether Congress may fashion federal substantive rules to govern questions arising in simple diversity cases, . . . but whether Congress may prescribe how federal courts are to conduct themselves with respect to subject matter over which Congress plainly has the power to legislate."[24] In other words, in the Court's view, *Prima Paint* did not involve the issue of federalism and states' rights, but rather whether Congress could provide substantive directives to the federal courts in areas in which Congress had specific legislative powers. The Court, in effect, had answered the federalism question while appearing to disregard it: Congress could create federal law where it had legislative authority to act. Therefore, in diversity cases in which questions arose concerning the validity of the recourse to arbitration, the federal courts were under an obligation to apply the relevant federal legislation in the area. Although the concept of interstate commerce could be construed very broadly, the only limitation upon the application of federal law appeared to be that the contracts in question must affect interstate commerce.

In *Prima Paint*, the Court also articulated what was to become a principal tenet of its evolving decisional law on arbitration: that the FAA's purpose to provide for the enforceability of arbitration agreements was manifest, and that that objective—buttressed by the reference to contractual freedom—must be given effect whenever possible. In the Court's own language, "in so concluding, we not only honor the plain meaning of the statute but also the unmistakably clear congressional purpose that the arbitration procedure when selected by the parties to a contract, be speedy, and not subject to delayed obstruction to the courts."[25] Challenges to the validity of arbitration agreements on the basis of state law provisions, therefore, were seen essentially as a dilatory tactic, meant to defeat the manifest purpose of the federal legislation. Despite the objections that can be made to the Court's reasoning,[26] it was now clear that the Court had espoused a strong and unequivocal position in regard to arbitration—a position that was not only supportive, but also protective of the institution of arbitral adjudication. This position continues to color, influence, and dictate the results in subsequent litigation on arbitration. Other cases interpreting the FAA, in fact, have been decided in a similar, and even stronger, vein.

The New Trilogy

Described by analogy to landmark labor arbitration cases as "the new arbitration trilogy,"[27] a series of cases reveals the strength of the policy that underlies the Court's construction of the FAA. The rulings in *Moses Cone v. Mercury Corp.*,[28] *Southland Corp. v. Keating*,[29] and *Dean Witter Reynolds v. Byrd*[30] make clear that the Court perceives a fundamental congressional objective underlying the FAA and that the Court will uphold that objective despite allegations that state law is controlling and requires a different result. These cases further demonstrate that the FAA embodies a federal rule of law of truly national scope.

Moses Cone involved circumstances relating to a contractual dispute between a hospital and a building contractor.[31] The hospital, located in North Carolina, entered into a contract with an Alabama construction company to build additions to its main building. The contract provided that disputes would be decided by the architect and, if the dispute were not decided within a specified time, it would then be submitted to binding arbitration. When a dispute arose and went unsettled beyond the specified time, the hospital filed an action against the construction company and the architect in a North Carolina state court. In its petition, the hospital sought a declaratory judgment that there was no right to arbitrate. The defendant construction company then filed an action in federal district court on the basis of diversity of citizenship, seeking an order to compel arbitration under the provisions of the FAA.[32]

Upon motion of the hospital, the federal district court stayed the federal court action pending resolution of the suit in state court. The federal court reasoned that the two suits involved identical issues, namely, the arbitrability of the claim under consideration.[33] On appeal, the federal appellate court reversed the ruling and issued instructions to compel arbitration.[34] The United States Supreme Court affirmed the appellate decision, grounding much of its reasoning in a categoric statement of doctrine upholding the FAA.[35]

Considering the possibility of fragmented proceedings in the resolution of this controversy, the court held that "the federal act requires piecemeal litigation when necessary to give effect to an arbitration agreement."[36] Moreover, the Court was concerned that the delay ordered by the trial court might defeat the underlying purpose of the federal legislation: "stay would have frustrated the statutory policy of rapid and unobstructed enforcement of arbitration agreements."[37] The intent of the legislation was to move the parties to an arbitration agreement out of court and into arbitration as quickly and as easily as possible.[38] Finally, the Court gave extensive reach to the federal legislation on arbitration. "Section 2 is a congressional declaration of a liberal federal policy favoring arbitration agreements, notwithstanding any state substantive or procedural policies to the contrary. The effect of the section is to create a body of substantive law of arbitrability, applicable to any arbitration agreement within the coverage of the act."[39] In effect, the Court's ruling made the provisions of the FAA applicable in state courts provided some sort of jurisdictional basis existed for applying federal law.

The *Keating* case was similarly decided, minimizing state statutory law on arbitration and upholding the underlying policy of the federal law. In *Keating*,[40] the issue centered upon the constitutionality of a section of the California Franchise Investment Law, which had been interpreted to require exclusive judicial consideration of claims brought under the statute.[41] Keating's claim, brought on behalf of Seven-Eleven franchisees against Southland Corporation, the Seven-Eleven franchisor, alleged, among other things, that Southland had breached its fiduciary duty and violated the disclosure requirements of the California Franchise Investment Law.[42] Pursuant to a contract provision, Southland moved to compel arbitration of all claims except those based on the franchise investment law. After a trial court determination holding the nonwaiver provisions of the franchise investment law valid,[43] the California court of appeals held that, if the franchise investment law rendered arbitration agreements unenforceable, it conflicted with the provisions of the FAA and was, therefore, invalid under the supremacy clause of the U.S. Constitution.[44] The California Supreme Court interpreted the investment law provision to require exclusive judicial consideration of claims brought under the statute; it held that claims asserted under the investment law were inarbitrable; and it further concluded that the California statute did not contravene the federal legislation on arbitration.[45]

The United States Supreme Court determined that the federal legislation created a duty not only upon the federal courts, but also upon the state courts to apply the federal policy on arbitration embodied in the FAA. "In enacting section 2 of the federal act, Congress declared a national policy favoring arbitration and withdrew the power of the state to require a judicial forum for the resolution of claims which the contracting parties agreed to resolve by arbitration."[46] Agreeing with the essential reasoning of the California appellate court opinion, the Court further held that, "in creating a substantive rule applicable in state as well as federal courts, Congress intended to foreclose state legislative attempts to undercut the enforceability of arbitration agreements. We hold that the California franchise investment law violated the Supremacy Clause."[47]

In undermining the state regulatory authority in the area of arbitration, the Court was especially concerned that state statutory policies could impair "the basic purpose of the federal statute."[48] In effect, by inserting restrictions on dispute resolution alternatives in other statutory frameworks, "states could wholly eviscerate the controlling congressional intent to place arbitration agreements 'upon the same footing as other contracts.'"[49] "We have rejected this analysis because it is in conflict with the Arbitration Act and would permit states to override the declared policy requiring enforcement of arbitration agreements."[50] The uniform application of the FAA would prevent forum shopping and oblige state courts in jurisdictions with narrow arbitration statutes to disregard their own law and apply the federal law.

The *Byrd* opinion is the final segment of the decisional law triptych. It reveals that the Court's position on the federal arbitration legislation is not simply grounded in a concern for dispute resolution efficiency. Rather, the Court's reasoning is anchored in a perception of a fundamental congressional intent underlying the FAA.

Byrd involved a dispute between a customer and the Dean Witter Reynolds securities brokerage firm.[51] *Byrd* filed a complaint against Dean Witter Reynolds in a U.S. district court, claiming jurisdiction based on the existence of a federal question as well as diversity of citizenship, alleging violations of the U.S. Securities Act of 1934 and of various state law provisions relating to securities regulation.[52] The broker-dealer contract, however, contained an arbitration agreement. Based upon that agreement, Dean Witter filed a motion to sever the pendant state claims and compel arbitration, staying arbitration pending the resolution of the federal court action. Both at the federal trial[53] and appellate[54] levels, the motion to sever the pendant state claims and compel arbitration was denied because of the "intertwining" doctrine,[55] barring the arbitration of state law claims that are factually inseparable from claims under the federal securities act. According to the appellate court reasoning, the intertwining doctrine maintained the federal courts' "exclusive jurisdiction over the federal securities claim"[56] by preventing the earlier arbitral determination of the state claim to bind the federal proceeding through collateral estoppel. Also, "by declining to compel arbitration, the courts avoid bifurcated proceedings and perhaps redundant efforts to litigate the same factual question twice."[57]

Despite the persuasiveness of this reasoning, the United States Supreme Court reversed the decision, holding that the pendant state claims should be compelled to arbitration.[58] In a unanimous opinion, the Court stated that "the Act leaves no place for the discretion by a district court, but instead mandates that district courts *shall* direct the portion to proceed to arbitration on issues as to which an arbitration agreement has been signed."[59] The Court was at pains to emphasize the underlying controlling congressional intent of the federal legislation on arbitration, namely, "that the purpose behind the act's passage was to ensure judicial enforcement of privately made agreements to arbitrate . . . and [we] therefore reject the suggestion that the overriding goal of the FAA was to provoke the expeditious resolution of claims."[60]

These decisions leave little doubt that the Court's recent decisional law has effectively federalized the American law of arbitration. In contradistinction with the Canadian experience, the national law on arbitration in the United States was not achieved by the concurrent enactment of legislation at the federal and state levels of government. Rather, over a period of years, the chief federal judicial organ progressively elaborated the full systemic implications of an earlier federal enactment. Using a triple constitutional reference—a broad view of interstate commerce under the Commerce Clause, a reference to the Supremacy Clause, and invoking the controlling congressional intent underlying the FAA—the Court concluded that state statutory provisions and court rulings must not contravene the FAA's basic provisions. Moreover, given the circumstances in *Keating*, this position, it seems, applies to cases that involve either interstate or even more localized forms of commerce.

Not unexpectedly, these recent opinions have generated a volume of scholarly criticism[61] decrying the rather evident infringement of state legislative authority over local commercial matters. The Canadian legislative approach certainly evinces greater respect for essential systemic relationships in the federal process. Canada, however, did not have an existing federal enactment. Moreover, the United States Supreme Court's action could be seen as the legitimate judicial extension of the enabling legislation's original intent over time and changing circumstances. No movement is currently under way to have the decisional law overriden by congressional action. While the Canadian approach can be seen as a perhaps less brutal exercise of power, both national experiences attest to the perceived need in each system to have a uniform national position on arbitration that is neither encumbered nor weakened by internal dissenting variations.

In summary, domestic litigation demonstrates that the Court has adopted a position supportive of the arbitral process's institutional autonomy and systemic viability. The Court's decisional law emphasizes the judicial duty to recognize the validity of arbitration agreements and their jurisdictional consequences. It appears clear that the Court wants to give full effect to the federal legislation's underlying intent of eliminating judicial hostility toward arbitration. It is also clear that the Court—while its interpretations are logical and grounded in a plausible jurisdictional base—is supplying additional content to the federal legislation and embellishing its original policy imperative. A more qualified form of support, however, could undermine the institutional autonomy and viability of arbitral adjudication. In order to have a cohesive and coherent national policy regarding arbitration, it may well be necessary to minimize state legislative authority in local commercial matters and to compel compliance by both state and federal courts with the FAA's express language.

International Arbitration Cases

The Court's forceful stance on arbitration also acts as the leitmotif of its decisional law on international litigation involving commercial arbitration. Here as well, the Court appears to give preeminence to the policy directive it perceives underlying the governing federal legislation (in this instance, the legislation being the 1970 Arbitration Act, which codifies the provisions of the 1958 New York Arbitration Convention).[62] Succinctly stated, the federalization of the American domestic law on arbitration is accompanied by a similar (and related) federalization of the American law on international commercial arbitration and, more generally, on international business transactions.

Scherk v. Alberto-Culver Co.,[63] the seminal case on international commercial arbitration, involved allegations that Alberto-Culver, the American purchaser of foreign trademarks, had been deceived by the fraudulent misrepresentations of Scherk, the Austrian seller, and that Scherk's conduct violated the provisions of the Securities Exchange Act of 1934. Several months after the initial sale, which was negotiated over a period of time in various countries, Alberto-Culver purportedly discovered that the trademarks it had purchased from Scherk were substantially encumbered. The purchase contract contained express warranties that title to the trademarks was unencumbered; the agreement also contained an arbitration clause, providing for the arbitral resolution of disputes arising under the contract.[64] The question presented in litigation before the federal courts was whether the substance of the 1934 Securities Exchange Act rendered the dispute inarbitrable, thereby nullifying the contractual provision for recourse to arbitration.

Previously, in litigation involving purely domestic interests, the Court had held that disputes allegedly involving violations of the Securities Act of 1933 were inarbitrable. In *Wilko v. Swan,*[65] an investor lodged an action against a securities brokerage firm, claiming that the firm had violated section 12(2) of the 1933 act. The brokerage contract contained a dispute resolution clause providing for the submission of disputes arising under the contract to arbitration.[66] Notwithstanding its view that the FAA embodied a strong congressional policy supporting arbitration, the Court deemed the arbitration agreement in *Wilko* to be unenforceable. The Court reasoned that the provision for arbitration countermanded the express policy of the 1933 act prohibiting investors from waiving certain statutorily established rights, namely, the rights to bring suit in any federal or state court, to select a forum from a wide choice of venue, to take advantage of the nationwide service of process provision, and to dispense with the amount in controversy requirement.[67] Moreover, section 12(3) of the act expressly gave investors a cause of action to redress claims of misrepresentation against a seller of securities, requiring the defendant to prove its lack of scienter.[68]

Therefore, despite a valid arbitration agreement, securities claims arising under the 1933 act could not be submitted to arbitration. The act's nonwaiver of rights provisions, in effect, manifested a congressional intent to create an exception to the FAA's validation of arbitration agreements. The policy imperative underlying the 1933 act exceptionally overrode its analogue in the FAA.

Despite the *Wilko* doctrine, which the lower federal courts found to be controlling in *Scherk*,[69] the Court nonetheless ordered the parties in *Scherk* to proceed with ICC arbitration as provided in the contract. In the Court's assessment, the critical factor that served to distinguish the cases was the "truly international"[70] character of the contract in *Scherk*: "The respondent's reliance on *Wilko* in this case ignores the significant and, we find, crucial difference between the agreement involved in *Wilko* and the one signed by the parties here. Alberto-Culver's contract to purchase the business entities belonging to Scherk was a truly international agreement."[71] Tracking the basic content of section 202 of the 1970 Arbitration Act, the Court defined the concept of a "truly international agreement" by reference to the constituent elements of the transaction: elements—like the parties' nationalities, where they conducted their principal business activities, the companies' place of incorporation, and the use of different national forums to assemble the deal—which reflected the transnational character of the venture.[72] The Court, however, gave principal import to the transaction's economic content and impact: "Finally, and most significantly, the subject matter of the contract concerned the sale of business enterprises organized under the laws of and primarily situated in European countries, whose activities were largely, if not entirely, directed to European markets."[73]

The Court's reference to the economic impact of the transaction aligned the American law on international commercial arbitration with the "anational" tenor of the French decree on international arbitration, avoiding the mechanical formalism of the British statute. Rather than half-heartedly concede the existence of the international process and subordinate its operation whenever possible to national legal strictures, the expansive reasoning in *Scherk* indicated that the Court perceived the United States ratification of the New York Arbitration Convention as part of a congressional pronouncement on matters of international trade—a legislative policy that included favoring the development of private international commerce. It was implied that the New York Convention and the 1970 Arbitration Act represented the United States' adherence to a global consensus on international trade. In the Court's assessment, the implementation of that policy justified and required the judicial elaboration of rules that minimized national legal obstacles to the performance of obligations under international contracts.

Although the 1933 Securities Act (controlling in *Wilko*) and the 1934 Securities Exchange Act (at issue in *Scherk*) arguably contained similar nonwaiver provisions,[74] the juridical effect of inarbitrability provisions in domestic statutes was substantially reduced, essentially eliminated, in cases involving international contracts. The dislodging of the contractual recourse to arbitration by the mandatory congressional provision for judicial remedies was ineffective in the *Scherk* setting because "such an [international] contract involves considerations and policies significantly different from those found controlling in *Wilko*. . . . The exception to the clear provisions of the Arbitration Act carved out by *Wilko* is simply inapposite to . . . [Scherk]."[75] The "considerations and policies," sufficient to undermine the application of otherwise mandatory domestic law, focused upon the needs and integrity of international commerce and the participation of U.S. business interests in the world marketplace:

> Such uncertainty will almost inevitably exist with respect to any contract touching two or more countries, each with its own substantive laws and conflict-of-laws rules. A contractual provision specifying in advance the forum in which disputes shall be litigated and the law to be applied is, therefore, an almost indispensable precondition to achievement of the orderliness and predictability essential to any international business transaction. Furthermore, such a provision obviates the danger that a dispute under the agreement might be submitted to a forum hostile to the interests of one of the parties or unfamiliar with the problem area involved.

> A parochial refusal by the courts of one country to enforce an international arbitration agreement would not only frustrate these purposes, but would invite unseemly and mutually destructive jockeying by the parties to secure tactical litigation advantages. In the

present case, for example, it is not inconceivable that if Scherk had anticipated that Alberto-Culver would be able in this country to enjoin resort to arbitration he might have sought an order in France or some other country enjoining Alberto-Culver from proceeding with its litigation in the United States. Whatever recognition the courts of this country might ultimately have granted to the order of the foreign court, the dicey atmosphere of such a legal no-man's-land would surely damage the fabric of international commerce and trade, and imperil the willingness and ability of businessmen to enter into international commercial agreements.[76]

In summary, arbitration—because of its adjudicatory neutrality, expertise, and privacy—had become the foremost remedial means to resolve international contract disputes. By ratifying the New York Convention—the universal charter of international arbitration—Congress had expressly endorsed the emerging international stature of arbitration and implicitly recognized that the world marketplace did business on transnational and not national terms. Accordingly, in its decisional law, the Court felt obligated to make the congressional endorsement a juridical reality. The *Scherk-Wilko* nexus required the Court to balance, segregate, and place priorities on divergent policy dictates: (1) the domestic interest in having claims of fraudulent misrepresentations in securities matters resolved by courts; (2) the FAA's mandate to enforce arbitration agreements; (3) the objective of furthering the interest of the world community and of the United States in international trade; and (4) the need to avoid compromising domestic legal imperatives, like the requirements of securities legislation, in international litigation without some fundamental justification.

In domestic matters, *Wilko* achieved a balanced form of prioritization by resolving the conflict between the first and second policy dictates in the form of an exception to the FAA that did not infringe upon the core interests of the arbitration legislation. *Scherk,* however, evidences an overriding prioritization of the policy interest favoring international commerce, placing that objective squarely above the other policy objectives. *Scherk* manifests the Court's intent to eliminate any opportunity for parochial judicial construction or extraterritorial judicial extension of domestic laws in the context of international cases involving arbitration. In effect, the Court recognizes a sphere of international activity that, although subject to national jurisdiction, must be regulated in keeping with its essentially autonomous transnational character. *Scherk* thereby allows the Court to lay the foundation for the elaboration of a substantive American law on private international commerce.[77]

The display of internationalism in *Scherk* stands in sharp contrast with a previous and well-established federal decisional law upholding the extraterritorial extension of United States antitrust laws.[78] Initially, the Court—with its decision in *American Banana Co. v. United Fruit Co.*[79]—adopted the rule of strict territoriality, holding that the regulatory reach of the Sherman Anti-Trust Act was confined to anticompetitive commercial practices taking place within the United States. In a series of subsequent cases[80] that culminated in the *United States v. Alcoa*[81] decision, the effect of a more aggressive executive branch antitrust enforcement policy was made felt. The rule of legislative territoriality was replaced by a more expansive construction of the Sherman Act's jurisdictional scope. That interpretation allowed the federal courts to assert jurisdiction in antitrust cases in which would-be violations took place abroad, provided the conduct in question bore a substantial connection with United States trade. In *Alcoa,* the controlling doctrine was reformulated in terms of "intended effects":[82] commercial activity pursued anywhere in the world by nationals of whatever country, that the courts could interpret as exhibiting an intent to place restraints upon American trade, was within the scope of United States antitrust jurisdiction.

More contemporary circuit court decisions in *Timberlane Lumber Co. v. Bank of America*[83] and *Mannington Mills v. Congoleum Corp.*[84] have tempered the parochial bias of the *Alcoa* rule and its disregard for international comity. Although neither opinion repudiates the statutory basis for asserting jurisdiction, the holding in each case modifies the legal standard for triggering the application of antitrust legislation. In effect, both courts abandoned the *Alcoa* "intended effects" test and replaced it with a more moderate balance-of-interests approach and a jurisdictional rule of reason.[85] According to these courts, the effects test was incomplete; in its provision for the assertion of jurisdiction, it inadequately accounted for the interests of other nations and for the actual relationship between the defendants and the United States. Under the jurisdictional rule of reason, assuming that "some" actual or intended effect could be established, the supposedly anticompetitive practices must be of sufficient magnitude to justify—in light of considerations of international comity—an assertion of domestic U.S.

jurisdiction.[86] The United States' interest in enforcement must outweigh the interests of the implicated foreign country. "When foreign nations are involved, it is unwise to ignore the fact that foreign policy, reciprocity, comity, and limitations of judicial power are considerations that should have a bearing on the decision to exercise or decline jurisdiction."[87]

Regardless of its current character, the decisional law on the extraterritorial application of U.S. antitrust laws has, in effect, been reversed by the Court's ruling in *Mitsubishi v. Soler.*[88] The long-awaited sequel to *Scherk, Mitsubishi* represented an opportunity for the Court to refine the implications of the international contract concept and place some restrictions on the wide policy directive articulated in *Scherk.* Because *Mitsubishi* involved the question of whether antitrust claims were arbitrable when they arose in the setting of an international contract, some commentators[89] anticipated that the case might represent an opportunity for the Court to establish essential boundaries between national priorities and the self-regulatory needs of international commerce. Like the public policy exception, the inarbitrability defense[90] is a well-recognized juridical limitation on arbitration, preventing it from infringing upon core systemic interests. The application of that defense in *Mitsubishi,* it was argued, would not have lessened the international commercial dispute resolution viability of the arbitral process.

Rather than restrict the *Scherk* doctrine, the *Mitsubishi* opinion reinforced and amplified it. Holding that antitrust claims arising from international contracts are arbitrable,[91] the Court avoided placing meaningful yet moderate national restraints on international arbitral adjudication. In effect, the Court impliedly affirmed the view that national Western economies have effectively been internationalized by world participation in international trade and that private transnational commerce functions by reference to its own, self-generated rules. *Mitsubishi* thus echoed the gravamen in *Scherk*: international trade is vital to the national interest, and the United States cannot expect the world to do business on primarily American terms.[92]

Evaluating the Twin Federalization of American Arbitration Law

The federalization of both the domestic and international American law of arbitration reflects too great a level of judicial innovation, and evidences too strong a doctrinal conviction, for their companion development to be explained as mere happenstance. Ostensibly with tacit congressional approval, the Court is adapting the FAA and the provisions of the 1970 Arbitration Act to contemporary domestic and international commercial adjudicatory realities. The Court attributes a privileged status to the congressional objective of validating arbitration agreements and legitimating arbitral adjudication in the hierarchy of protected values. Nor can the motivation that underlies such unequivocal support for a system of private, nonjudicial justice—beginning with *Prima Paint,* amplifying itself through the new trilogy, and gaining forceful expression in the *Scherk-Mitsubishi* internationalist doctrine— be adequately explained, as the *Byrd* Court opines,[93] merely by a mechanical judicial allegiance to a congressional dictate. The Court's rulings on arbitration embody concordant perceptions of the social role and necessity of commerce and of the limited dispute resolution utility of legal adjudication.

The decisional law on arbitration has survived the inevitable variations in the Court's political configuration. It has been espoused by liberal and conservative justices alike.[94] In the international cases, exceptional dissenting positions were taken by members of the Court as different as Justice Douglas (in *Scherk*)[95] and Justice Stevens (in *Mitsubishi*).[96] The steadfastness of the majority commitment to the FAA's policy directive reveals, in effect, an institutionalization of a federal policy on commerce: commercial activity is national in scope. The integrated national character of commerce should not be undercut by public law questions relating to systemic organization and political authority. Because of its private and self-regulatory character, commerce can escape public law constraints. To comingle constitutional debates and the intricacies of legality into commerce would paralyze the ability of merchants to function effectively and thereby imperil the national economy and commercial interests. Political values and the accompanying adjudicatory requirements have little relevance in the ideology of the marketplace.

With the Burger Court, the policy implied from the FAA's provisions merged with the concern about the litigation crisis and the accessibility of justice. The prevalent view, advocated by the former chief justice, was that the severe burden placed upon the courts by the volume of claims and protracted proceedings threatened to undermine the effective administration of justice.[97] The success of arbitration in labor and commercial matters[98] became the grounds upon which to advocate recourse to alternative means of dispute resolution in a variety of other areas. Although *Byrd* indicates that dispute resolution efficiency was not the principal motivation for the federal decisional law on arbitration, it is difficult to imagine that that concern did not inform and bolster the Court's perception that arbitration was a legitimate exercise in commercial self-regulation through self-determined adjudication.

The Court's unwavering support for commercial arbitration also challenged consecrated legal adjudicatory values. Its safeguarding of a privately initiated and controlled system of justice suggested that juridical adjudicatory methods were to be reassessed and convictions reconsidered. For example, the extensive protections available to the individual against state action in regard to fundamental political rights should not necessarily predominate in the adjudication of private law claims. Here, considerations of costs and expediency—also part of the ethic of fairness—should be weighed. The procedural flexibility, expertise, and possible efficiency proffered by arbitration responded to many of the elements of the dilemma generated by a dispute resolution framework saturated with lawyerly concerns and juridical procedures. Accordingly, the Court's institutionalization of a national policy on commerce was grouped with a growing awareness of the need to devise workable alternatives to judicial adjudication. In private law matters, the latter objective, it seemed, could be achieved by the promotion of self-determination in dispute resolution and the recourse to a nonjudicial and nonadversarial adjudicatory ethic.

The values espoused and promoted by the Court in domestic adjudication were already at work in transnational commerce. There, the different nationalities of contracting parties, the need for adjudicatory neutrality, expertise, and privacy, and the commercial necessity of maintaining viable business relationships despite disputes made the recourse to arbitration or other alternatives a virtual necessity. Rather than articulate a restrained acceptance of the process, the Court gave international arbitration an unqualified endorsement. A central feature of that endorsement was the minimization of domestic imperatives in transnational commercial cases. Again, the Court relied upon its pragmatic concern for the viability of commerce and its sense that traditional forms of legal regulation and juridical procedures were counterproductive in this setting. The internationalization of commerce meant that the U.S. national interest could only be served by participating in international trade on globally accepted terms. The extraterritorial extension of domestic laws, be they antitrust regulations or jurisdictional concepts, could only hinder American commercial interests. Moreover, the history of commercial self-regulation[99] supported the exemption of international commerce from national legal restrictions. Given the transnational support for arbitration, international arbitrators could legitimately deal with claims brought pursuant to United States or other national legislations that arose in the context of international commercial contracts.[100]

In keeping with the domestic experience, the principle of self-determination in international dispute resolution dislodged the application of systemic concerns in order to establish a cohesive national policy on commerce and to generate a body of law relating to a parallel and autonomous adjudicatory framework. Although arguably ill conceived,[101] the internationalist tenor of the rulings in *Scherk* and *Mitsubishi* give additional juridical support to the concept of an autonomous and "anational" international commercial arbitration process — a process distancing itself from any reference to municipal legal authority and operating free of national legal provisions but for those that specifically regulate private international law matters.[102] This stance coincides with recent developments concerning other facets of international commerce (specifically, in the jurisdictional area) where the Court has refused to transpose purely domestic legal standards (U.S. long-arm jurisdiction concepts) into transnational litigation.[103] The Court's sensitivity to issues of transnational commerce and its general activism in that area lay the groundwork for the progressive development of a substantive American law of private international law. Replacing the reliance on choice-of-law principles and national legal provisions, such a law would be comprised of substantive rules that account for the sui generis features and needs of international commercial cases.[104]

The Court's internationalism, presumably inspired and authorized by the 1970 Arbitration Act, raises a number of concerns. The determination that antitrust claims are arbitrable in an international contract setting leaves little room for the functioning of the inarbitrability defense (and the related public policy exception) contained in the New York Arbitration Convention.[105] With some reluctance and in the hope that a more measured balancing of interests might eventually be instituted, one could accept this development as a necessary part of the Court's accession to the concept of anational arbitration—although other aspects of the *Mitsubishi* opinion seem to undermine that concept.[106] Other criticism centers upon the concept of anational arbitration itself. There is a lively academic debate about whether the international arbitration process is truly separable from national legal processes.[107] The controversy is anchored in a positive law thesis that argues for the need to ground legal regulation and processes in an authorizing national sovereign source. Envisioning what might or ought to be, it is argued, cannot be mistaken for what is and must be.[108] Mirroring the English attitude on international arbitration, proponents of this view hold that the effort of international merchants to create their own adjudicatory system cannot be effective without the initial and continuing approval of national legal systems.[109] The responsibility and authority for creating legitimate legal norms lie exclusively within the province of municipal sovereignty.

The experience with the twin American federalization of arbitration law belies this interpretation of the development of international commercial arbitration. The municipal endorsement of arbitration—domestic or international—manifests a systemic willingness to accept arbitration as a parallel adjudicatory process. It further evidences a similar willingness to allow that mechanism to develop as a process and to formulate its own rules and modus vivendi. The viability of arbitration as an adjudicatory mechanism, in fact, depends upon its independence from judicial supervision as to both the arbitral proceeding and the award. Initial systemic espousal, therefore, implies an acceptance both of arbitration's legitimacy and of its independent evolution—including the laxity of procedure, party and arbitrator discretion, and flexible (even equitable) substantive rulings. Only fundamental abuses, amounting to a clear denial of procedural justice, need judicial correction.

The real issue of the law of international arbitration does not lie in whether the phenomenon of anational arbitration can be given an adequate theoretical foundation, nor in the United States Supreme Court's participation in advancing that concept of the process. The cohesion of international relations has always suffered from the continued, absolute assertion of sovereign municipal authority and parochial national self-interest; arbitration seems to have made significant inroads into limiting the application and operation of those factors—

by eliminating the recourse to fluid, open-ended, and unpredictable remedies, arbitration made the necessity of international commerce a reality. What is of significant moment are the indirect domestic consequences of the *Mitsubishi* ruling. The segregation of domestic and international policy imperatives resulting from the elaboration of a substantive private international law appears to be operative only at the level of insulating international adjudication from domestic law provisions. The rulings in the international cases, however, have exhibited a tendency to seep back into the domestic legal order. The *Mitsubishi* doctrine, for example, has generated considerable confusion and division among lower federal courts over whether purely domestic issues, formerly deemed unquestionably to be matters of public policy, are submissible to arbitration. In the aftermath of *Mitsubishi*, courts—ruling in both domestic and international cases—held that civil violations of the Racketeer Influenced and Corrupt Organizations statute (RICO) are submissible to arbitration, reasoning that the RICO legislation was no more significant in terms of the public interest than the Sherman Anti-Trust Act.[110] At least one court has held that antitrust disputes arising from domestic contracts are arbitrable.[111] Moreover, the *Scherk-Mitsubishi* doctrine has encouraged a significant minority of lower federal courts to question whether domestic securities fraud claims arising under either the 1933 or 1934 Securities Act are arbitrable.[112]

Obviously, the Court should clarify the domestic implications of its decisional law on international commercial arbitration. It seems that little benefit can be gained by reducing the scope of the inarbitrability defense in domestic law matters. The domestic process places significant public law value on matters of economic regulation and antiracketeering legislation; arguably, conflicts arising from such public law provisions should be resolved by tribunals invested with the public trust and adjudicatory authority. Although the Court attacked this rationale in *Mitsubishi*,[113] commercial arbitrators should have little credibility in addressing these regulatory issues, and such disputes have a much wider significance in the domestic order than ordinary contractual commercial controversies.[114]

There is, however, an inexorable logic to the "emphatic federal policy" favoring arbitration[115] that has already brought the aforementioned lower federal courts to render what were formerly unthinkable rulings. The compromise of federalism interests in the trilogy decisional law was itself a rather dramatic development, indicating that even fundamental considerations of political organization may fall in the face of the overriding policy of upholding the validity of arbitration agreements. The absolute character of that policy may well impel the Court to eliminate any juridical constraints upon the arbitral process in domestic law matters but for the FAA grounds for the enforcement of awards. The final result will be a fully uniform (and federalized) American arbitration law with totally concordant domestic and international branches—a law that, on the one hand, promotes the contractual recourse to arbitration as the primary mechanism for commercial dispute resolution and, on the other hand, advances a philosophy of adjudication that emphasizes, at least in regard to certain classes of disputes, the principle of autonomy and self-determination.

In many respects, despite some gaps, problems in implementation, and systemic conflicts, the contemporary development of arbitration law in the United States indicates not only the breadth and success of possible experimentation with alternatives, but also the limited scope and design of the legal approach to dispute resolution. Remedies, it seems, must comport with the nature of the disputes they are meant to resolve; their acceptance and viability are the measure of their truthfulness; and a proper marriage of disputes with remedies serves most, if not all, of the indispensable values—the right to be heard by an impartial panel that renders a relatively expeditous and fair determination.

McMahon: A Radical Postscript

Shearson/American Express Inc. v. McMahon,[116] decided in early June 1987 and involving a claim for securities fraud and misrepresentation under the 1934 Securities Exchange Act, is another of the Court's pronouncements in the area of American domestic arbitration law. The *McMahon* opinion further amplifies the already extensive reach of the "emphatic federal policy" favoring arbitration. It disposes of any residual doubts in domestic law surrounding the arbitrability of Exchange Act and RICO claims. The ruling, however, also alters certain well-settled principles of the developing American law on arbitration. It substantially discredits the precedential value of the *Wilko* decision, and eliminates the utility of the distinction—initially propounded in

126

Scherk—between the regulation of domestic and international arbitration.

Both the end achieved and the means employed in the opinion indicate that the Court will go to practically any length to uphold arbitration agreements. *McMahon* makes abundantly clear that the Court is impelled by an unbending objective: fostering the unfettered recourse to arbitration. In effect, the Court's desire to eliminate all vestiges of judicial hostility toward arbitration has given arbitration a privileged position in the cosmology of protected judicial values. Indeed, following *McMahon,* it is not at all implausible that the consideration afforded to arbitration (despite its private law character) is not so different, in kind or in degree, from the constitutional regard given to political speech, racial equality, or other fundamental public law values and rights. The uncompromising tenor of the doctrine generates questions about the wisdom of, and motivation for, the Court's stance.

Before *McMahon,* the related but separable rulings in *Wilko* and *Scherk* logically gave rise to the question of whether claims arising under the 1934 Securities Exchange Act were arbitrable in domestic transactions. After *Wilko,* lower federal courts[117]—in cases involving purely domestic contracts—had consistently held that these claims were inarbitrable for reasons of the public policy interest in security investor protection. The lower courts, it seems, took seriously the core element of the *Scherk* decision—that the internationalization of trade and national economies demanded that international commercial litigation be insulated from domestic juridical strictures (even imperative ones). Therefore, arbitrability as understood for purposes of international contracting differed quite substantially from arbitrability as applied to domestic commercial transactions. Although American merchants could not engage in international business exclusively on their terms, domestic notions of legality should still govern national commerce and commercial practices.

The *Scherk* reasoning represented a fair, open-minded, and pragmatic accommodation of national and international interests. In the relatively unfamiliar, specialized, and potentially politically contentious area of international trade, the Court provided a neutral form of leadership that allowed it to give proper scope to domestic regulatory policies and safeguard American interests in world trade. This balancing of interests dictated the result in the case. Proffering domestic legal protection to a sophisticated commercial enterprise allegedly defrauded by a foreign national was hardly worth compromising American international business interests. The Court, therefore, gave effect to the duly-consented-to arbitration agreement.

Mitsubishi,[118] the later companion opinion, reinforced and consolidated the display of judicial internationalism in *Scherk*. There, the Court held—despite persuasive domestic precedent to the contrary—that antitrust claims arising under an international contract were arbitrable. Although the tone of the opinion and segments of the Court's reasoning generated misgivings,[119] the unmistakable implication of the reasoning was that the Court had established a clear line of demarcation between matters international and domestic, that regulatory policies—which pertained to the public interest at a national level and which demanded adjudication through tribunals invested with public authority—did not maintain their public policy status once they were integrated into the transnational context.

Echoing *Scherk,* the Court in *Mitsubishi* reiterated the view that the community of international merchants had established arbitration as the remedial process for the resolution of international contract claims. Interpreting domestic American regulatory provisions to block the recourse to arbitration for certain types of international contract claims would imperil the viability of international commerce and larger American economic and commercial interests. Despite the equities involved and its clear authority to refuse arbitration under the public policy and inarbitrability provisions of the New York Arbitration Convention, the Court in *Mitsubishi* chose to restrict the reach of imperative domestic public policy requirements and to further its support for what appeared to be an emerging general American policy on private international law.

McMahon, however, demonstrates that *Scherk* and *Mitsubishi* are misunderstood if assessed as isolated international cases defining a special policy on transnational commerce and international arbitration. Following *Scherk* and contemporaneously with *Mitsubishi,* the Court decided the "new trilogy" of domestic arbitration cases—*Moses Cone, Keating,* and *Byrd*.[120] These cases gave new impetus and direction to the domestic law of arbitration. The "trilogy" cases established the foundation for a full-fledged national policy on arbitration. As a group, these cases stand for a variety of propositions that minimize, and perhaps eliminate, any federalism constraints on the policy underlying the FAA. According to these opinions, the "emphatic federal policy" favoring arbitration demands a virtual extinguishment of state authority in matters pertaining to arbitration. The FAA is not merely a composite of procedural enactments that apply only to federal courts, but rather the congressional enactment of substantive rules in an area where Congress has constitutional authority to act.[121]

Moreover, the Supremacy Clause mandates that the provisions of the FAA override contrary state legislative enactments;[122] ultimately, the policy and content of the FAA are binding upon both federal and state courts.[123] Even in those matters in which federal courts have exclusive jurisdiction, if related claims are submissible to arbitration, arbitration has to be compelled and federal jurisdiction stayed until the conclusion of the arbitral proceeding.[124] In effect, the intertwining doctrine could not survive the dominance of the FAA's policy and was eliminated in favor of the contractual recourse to arbitration. Even duplicative proceedings and adjudicatory inefficiency did not dissuade the Court in these domestic cases from upholding the congressional intent to legitimate the recourse to arbitration.

McMahon reinforces the direction born of the "trilogy"; however, it not only consolidates, but also expands the Court's domestic and international decisional law on arbitration. To achieve the objective of declaring that both Exchange Act and RICO claims are arbitrable, the Court engages in an uncharacteristic and disappointing display of narrow, strained, and distortive construction of statutes and prior decisional law. Although the Court's aim of eliminating any restrictions on arbitration is transparent, its methodology and doctrine are confusing, unpersuasive, and ultimately unsound. Indeed, it is difficult to understand why the Court is so determined to eradicate any and all juridical restraints upon arbitration. Surely, the imposition of some minimal limitations arising out of core public policy concerns would not threaten or undermine the autonomy of arbitral adjudication. For example, allowing consumers in the securities context to benefit from statutory protections exclusively through judicial forums would not preclude or restrict the recourse to arbitration in a commercial, arms' length setting where the institution of arbitration developed and continues to thrive. The Court's desire to give absolute effect to the FAA's policy of upholding arbitration agreements is both dogged and unnecessary to maintain the integrity of the arbitral process.

The reasoning in *McMahon* suffers from several methodological and conceptual deficiencies. Concerning the issue of the arbitrability of Exchange Act claims (a question that divided the Court 5–4), the majority opinion begins by incanting the now-consecrated view that a claim based upon statutorily conferred rights does not disrupt the ordinarily "hospitable" inquiry into the question of arbitrability.[125] To defeat the implied presumption favoring the arbitrability of claims, the statute that is the vehicle for creating the rights must contain, in either its language or its legislative history, a congressional command mandating exclusive recourse to the courts for the vindication of claims. Moreover, the burden is upon the party opposing arbitration to establish the existence of such congressional intent.[126] Having weighted the inquiry in favor of a finding of arbitrability, the majority opinion then engages in a series of strained constructions to guarantee the result implied by its initial proposition.

At the outset, the Court advances a painfully technical interpretation of the relevant provisions of the Exchange Act, arguing that the nonwaiver language of the act applies exclusively to the substantive obligations under the legislation.[127] Because the recourse to arbitration merely represents the selection of a different forum and remedial process, such an agreement—so the Court would have us believe—has no impact upon the substantive statutory rights in question. The nonwaiver provision of the act, therefore, does not apply to arbitration agreements because that choice of remedy does not affect the substantive guarantees of the act. In reaching this determination, the Court opines that arbitrators are capable of applying and interpreting the law.[128]

The Court, however, attributes no significance whatever either to the underlying purpose of the Exchange Act (to protect individual investors from overreaching by securities industry professionals) or to the intractable reality that arbitrators are likely to construe the applicable law very differently from judges, especially in light of the fact that the arbitral procedure is established and directed by the securities industry. In effect, the Court chooses to ignore the adhesionary character of the contract and the arbitration agreement, neglecting the evident need for consumer protection in these circumstances. The Court exhibits similarly tendentious and distortive reasoning in its attempt to align the result in *McMahon* with the principles of prior decisional law on arbitration.

For example, the majority opinion interprets the *Wilko* decision as barring the selection of a nonjudicial forum where arbitration is inadequate to protect the substantive statutory rights at issue.[129] *Scherk* is seen as providing that, where arbitration is deemed (presumably by the courts) sufficient to protect the rights at issue, there is no bar to a waiver of a judicial forum.[130] This construction of precedents extends the doctrine, first articulated in *Scherk* and more forcefully in *Mitsubishi,* that the existence of statutory rights does not preclude the recourse to arbitration unless there is a legislative command that mandates judicial disposition of alleged violations. According to the *McMahon* interpretation of *Wilko* and *Scherk,* statutory language providing for the nonwaiver of judicial remedies will be effective only when arbitration, the alternative, is deemed to be an inadequate remedial process for adjudicating statutory rights. Expressed more forthrightly, the syllogistic logic[131] yields the following new rule of law: express statutory language attributing exclusive jurisdiction to the courts will defeat a private agreement to arbitrate only when the courts determine that arbitration is an inadequate remedy to protect the statutory rights in question. The Court's review of the relevant precedent amounts to a reconstruction of the prior law.

In effect, *Wilko* stands for a very different proposition than the one advanced by the Court. According the express language of *Wilko,*[132] as between two competing congressional policies—upholding the validity of arbitration agreements under the FAA and protecting securities investors under the Exchange Act—the *Wilko* Court gave effect to the latter in light of the express statutory language in the 1933 act providing for exclusive judicial remedies and relief. The *Wilko* Court reasoned that, in such special circumstances, Congress had itself decided to make an exception to its general policy under the FAA. Moreover, *Scherk* is distinguishable from *Wilko* not because there exists a meaningful difference in statutory language or objective between the 1933 and 1934 acts, but rather because the domestic policy of security investor protection has little relevance to multinational parties engaged in an international commercial venture. The primary analytical factors that led in *Scherk* to a restriction of the *Wilko* doctrine to domestic circumstances are the presence of an international contract and the Court's willingness to elaborate special rules for transnational commercial activities.

McMahon ignores the special circumstances, express doctrinal content, and segregation of domestic and international considerations in the prior decisional law. The *McMahon* Court has thus created new law from the previously well-settled significance of these decisions. It is not surprising that these reconstructed rules are more suitable to developing an unlimited arbitrability doctrine.

The holding in *Mitsubishi* is similarly recast.[133] A fair reading of the *Mitsubishi* rule would represent it as stating that antitrust claims are arbitrable in the context of international contracts. As in *Scherk,* the triggering element of the opinion was the fact that the dispute and the agreement to arbitrate surfaced in the context of an international commercial transaction. If American parties could frustrate the recourse to arbitration by alleging violations of American antitrust law, the stability of international commerce achieved with predictable dispute resolution through arbitration would be undermined. According to *McMahon,*[134] however, *Mitsubishi* now stands for the proposition that the submission of statutory rights to arbitration does not represent an abandonment or elimination of those rights. Arbitral tribunals, like courts, are able to interpret and apply the governing law. Resorting to the arbitral rather than judicial adjudication of statutory claims merely represents a choice of dispute resolution forums.

This transparent reassessment of *Mitsubishi* is again calculated to support (*après la lettre*) the Court's increasingly expansive arbitration doctrine. It further appears that the objective of establishing a judicial policy on matters of private international law, discernible in the *Scherk* and *Mitsubishi* holdings as originally stated, has been engulfed by and lost in the larger, more doctrinaire, and unbending policy on arbitration.

In particular, *McMahon* gives short shrift to *Wilko.* According to the majority opinion,[135] rather than represent a statement of the importance of the policy of protecting securities investors from broker overreaching, *Wilko* symbolizes primarily a general distrust of arbitration and of the ability of arbitral tribunals to achieve viable adjudicatory results. Although the Court makes a half-hearted attempt to preserve *Wilko*'s precedential value,[136] it effectively discredits its reasoning and ultimate result — stating, for instance, that the *Wilko* view of arbitration does not square with the judicial evaluation in *Mitsubishi, Byrd, Keating, Moses Cone,* or *Scherk.*[137] The present view is that arbitral tribunals can handle complex disputes, that procedural flexibility in arbitration does not mean that substantive rights will be compromised or eliminated, and that arbitrators are able to apply the law (with the prospect of judicial review at the stage of enforcement standing as a safeguard against arbitrator abuse or incompetence).[138] Moreover, in regard to securities arbitration, the *McMahon* Court finds that the oversight authority of the Securities and Exchange Commission provides a guarantee against overreaching and unfairness.[139] Accordingly, the *Scherk* holding (despite its reasoning pertaining to international commerce) is extended to cover both domestic and international claims arising under the Exchange Act, and *Wilko* is limited to claims (presumably both domestic and international) arising under the Securities Act.[140]

With regard to the issue of the arbitrability of RICO claims,[141] the Court in *McMahon* is unanimous in its view that such claims can be submitted to arbitration. Although the RICO legislation could readily be seen as involving matters of public policy, no express language in the statute or its legislative history indicates a congressional intent to preclude party selection of alternative, nonjudicial remedies. Accordingly, under the revamped reasoning in *Mitsubishi,* the Court gleefully finds itself bound to conclude that RICO claims can be adjudicated through arbitration.[142] The RICO statute does provide for civil claims and arbitrators are able to take jurisdiction over such disputes. Apparently, arbitral (like judicial) jurisdiction extends to the awarding of treble damages.

It is startling that the disposition of this question generated no controversy among the members of the Court. Given the vehement dissents that accompanied some of the major cases in this line of decisional law,[143] some expression of disagreement could logically have been expected in light of the arguably vital public interests at stake. Perhaps, the Court finds the RICO statute duplicative of other regulatory legislation and burdensome to administer in actual litigation. In any event, the last vestiges of opposition to an unthwarted arbitration policy appear to have been finally voiced in *Mitsubishi.*[144]

Before *McMahon,* Justice Stevens's dissenting opinion in *Mitsubishi* had assumed a critical significance in the development of American arbitration law. Eloquent and persuasive, it made a cogent case for a more measured decisional law grounded in the need for rational restraints. It created the expectation that the Court's unwieldy vision of arbitration might be kept in check by an assessment of the process anchored in an intelligence of its history, reality, and design. Justice Stevens's concurring and dissenting opinion in *McMahon* very substantially disappoints that expectation. Agreeing that RICO claims can be submitted to arbitration, Justice Stevens only takes exception with the majority view that arbitration agreements should be enforced with respect to 1934 Security Exchange Act claims: given the "longstanding interpretation" upholding the *Wilko* bar in this area, "any mistake the courts may have made in interpreting the statute is best remedied by the legislative, not the judicial, branch." The brevity in tone and content of the opinion strongly suggests that the Stevens opposition to the incongruities of the majority's doctrine on arbitration has waned to acquiescence. His opposition to the concept of limitless arbitration gains expression in the empty formalism of judicial restraint.[145]

The majority opinion in *McMahon* makes evident that the Court wants the recourse to arbitration to go unimpeded in almost all circumstances. The most troubling and elusive component of the opinion is its underlying motivation and the need to have such an absolute and unrestricted policy on arbitrability specifically and on arbitration generally. The "new trilogy" in domestic law could be understood in terms of the need to articulate a policy on arbitration of truly national dimension. If state courts applying state law in commercial cases could undermine the basic purpose of the FAA, the congressional objective of legitimating arbitration might receive only episodic implementation. Moreover, in diversity cases, federal courts obligated to apply state law might also be compelled to undo the gravamen of the FAA. Accordingly, in matters of interstate commerce where Congress has the power to legislate, the goals of the FAA should receive uniform and systematic application by all judicial tribunals.

The determinations in *Scherk* and *Mitsubishi* were also sustainable by reference to a comprehensible policy objective. Simply stated, the needs of international commerce and trade are sui generis and differ from their domestic analogue. Because of its provision of neutrality and expertise, arbitration has become the principal dispute resolution mechanism in that area of activity. If it is problematic to have one party to a transnational commercial venture subject to the laws and judicial procedure of a foreign country, it is untenable to have the national law of one of the contracting parties frustrate the agreed-upon recourse to arbitration. Domestic restrictions on arbitrability, therefore, should not be integrated into the context of international transactions because such parochial action would eventually undermine the effectiveness and stability generated by the availability of the arbitral process. Although statutory rights available to American parties in the form of securities or antitrust legislation will probably be compromised under this internationalist doctrine, the interest in fostering the development of international commerce by freeing it of local juridical constrictions outweighs the policy of affording nationals—versed in the commercial climate—extraterritorial protection.

McMahon escapes the normal reach of policy justifications. The opinion effectively collapses the astute and creative distinction between matters of international arbitration and those pertaining to domestic arbitration. *Scherk* and *Mitsubishi* are no longer to be understood as creating special rules for international commercial litigation, but rather as producing propositions that generally apply to the arbitrability of all disputes. It is one thing to decide that domestic restrictions are unsuitable for application in an international context; it is quite another matter to decide that, because the domestic restriction is inapplicable in transnational matters, it has lost its governing effect in the domestic process as well. The rulings in *Scherk* and *Mitsubishi* were premised on the specialty of international commercial litigation, as exceptions to a usually controlling rule in the domestic legal order. Rather than simply ignore that aspect of the cases, the Court should have recognized the consequences of its reasoning and provided some justification for its ricochet integration of the international exception into the domestic legal order. After all, different legal regimes and policy interests are involved in these separable areas of activity. The unreasoned alignment of the international and domestic cases on arbitration, then, is both unfortunate and confusing. It robs both groups of cases of their specialty and particular policy directives, and allows the Court to elaborate a policy on arbitration that is abstracted from the meaningful restrictions of varying circumstances.

The only protection that the Court proffers against the potential compromise of rights and arbitral abuse is judicial review of awards at the enforcement stage. When applied under existing rules and procedures for review, such protection is likely to be ineffective. Arbitral awards generally do not contain reasons, and scrutiny is usually given only to basic procedural matters. If a more stringent review standard is applied—one, for example, applying to the merits, or that requires arbitrators to conform strictly to legal due process requirements, it is likely to do substantial damage to the autonomy of the arbitral process. A policy meant to give absolute free reign to arbitration will result in the gradual defacement of the process through an increase of judicial supervision.

The Court suggests in *McMahon* that its ruling is quite simply mandated by the congressional intent underlying the FAA.[146] Given the radical transformation of the American law of arbitration that *McMahon* achieved, however, that suggestion is unconvincing. A more likely explanation appears to reside in the Court's desire to take as much dispute resolution as possible out of judicial forums and to promote efficient judicial administration by lessening court dockets. But, if the American juridical culture is in crisis because of the predominance of the adversarial ethic and litigious dispositions, the answer to that problem, although it may reside in alternative approaches to dispute resolution, does not lie in simply shifting the maximum possible adjudicatory burden to arbitration. Arbitral adjudication works well for some disputes, especially those that are commercial and international in character, but it is not a panacea—it is not a remedial structure of universal application. There are some disputes that truly implicate core public concerns or involve parties whose bargaining position and knowledge are fundamentally unequal. In such cases, arbitration is inappropriate. Moreover, it is inappropriate to respond to a situation in which access to justice is a problem by making access completely impossible. Although the volume of claims is thereby reduced, such barriers do not improve the quality of justice that is dispensed.

The imbalance in the Court's analysis illustrates a willingness to compromise fundamental rights and values not for rational reasons, but out of a sense of desperation arising from the volume of litigation. Unfortunately, the Court's desperation may also lead it to compromise the effectiveness of arbitration itself and the integrity of the case law that advanced the favorable policy underlying the FAA. The dire prophecy of the Douglas dissent in *Scherk* appears to be materializing and influencing all aspects of the American law of arbitration. Rather than create a sound and structured juridical pathway for the exercise of contractual discretion in dispute resolution, the Court appears to have abdicated its function of providing necessary guidelines and balance to the institution of a cooperative relationship between the judicial and alternative processes. The unqualified recourse to the principle of freedom of contract is as dangerous as it is unintelligent. It transforms the invocation of that principle into undiscriminating sloganeering.

The experience with transnational law-making is generally instructive in a number of respects. It teaches that viable alternatives to judicial adjudication can be constructed when the legal ethic fails to achieve a functional framework for dispute resolution. Legal mechanisms are not exclusive or universal dispute resolution means. Rather, they constitute simply another form of recourse, albeit the most traditional and visible, for repairing injury and amending the loss of conflict. The role of sovereignty in public international relations and the need for adjudicatory neutrality, expertise, and privacy in transnational commerce make judicial adjudication dysfunctional in the setting of state-to-state conflicts and international contract disputes. States have recourse to more fluid remedies: diplomatic contact, continuing negotiations, efforts at conciliation through international agencies or other governments, and, finally, essentially nonbinding World Court determinations. The sovereign status of the parties leads them to prefer the adjustment rather than the adjudication of disputes in the hope that some form of working consensus will eventually emerge and result in a mutually agreed-upon solution.[147] National dignity will not tolerate the assertion of jurisdiction by a domestic court or the coercive enforcement of World Court judgments. Other avenues need to be available for discussion and producing compromise between disputing governments.

Similarly, international commerce, despite its private and basically nonpolitical character, suffers from a similar handicap; it cannot rely upon the traditional legal mechanisms for resolving contractual conflicts. Like state parties, international merchants—because of their allegiance to a particular national culture and legal system—seek to establish a neutral, nonnational adjudicatory process knowledgeable about the particularities of their activity. Unlike states, however, merchants consistently need stability and predictability in their associations; fluid, possibly lengthy, alternatives that never actually promise results would be unworkable in a commercial context. Merchants, therefore, seek a flexible, fair, but certain and binding dispute resolution alternative. Although questions now surround its continued desirability,[148] arbitration fulfills many of the adjudicatory needs of the international commercial community. In the supposedly lawless and juridically undercivilized world of international political and economic relations, the development of commercial arbitration is another example of how creative recourse to substitute processes can be used. The dearth of available remedies and the context of disputes allow for a more considered evaluation of the suitability of national judicial adjudication, illustrating that domestic adjudicatory perspectives on commercial transactions, legal formalism, and the choice-of-law methodology are inappropriate dispute resolution mechanisms.

In a broad generic sense, domestic legal systems also have modified their adjudicatory ethic. Notwithstanding their affiliation to a particular legal tradition, most legal systems have judge-centered civil adjudication processes.[149] In this framework, the court has primary authority; the parties play an important but moderated part in the conduct of the proceeding. Adversarial representation has its place, but it is not the predominant feature of the process. Underlying the framework is a sense that the proceeding should be fair to all parties concerned and should move forward with reasonable dispatch toward a substantive result. By comparison, civil litigation in the United States—despite the affinity between the English and American legal traditions—is exceptional in its structure and operation. Fundamental differences center upon the continued availability of the civil jury trial and the adversarial ethic's pervasive impact on the system. Socialist civil adjudicatory processes reflect the opposite, inquisitorial absolute. In these systems, judges possess elaborate procedural powers. Regardless of their differences, and perhaps as a result of their procedural sophistication, most domestic systems—and this is especially in evidence in the United States—experience difficulty in reconciling juridical values with the dispute resolution needs of society. Overcivilization in legal processes makes the adjudicatory framework respond to concerns and propound values estranged from the human and social reality of conflict. The access to—and cost of—justice, the all-or-nothing character of legal determinations, the narrowness and intricacy of legal inquiry breed discontent held in check only by coercion and the wearing effect of time.

Examining domestic frameworks from the vantage point of the international experience, some elements of that experience provide a possible foundation for reassessing the purpose and function of domestic judicial adjudication. Specifically, the recourse to self-determination and the molding of dispute resolution frameworks by reference to the nature of disputes and the special character of the implicated actors may provide the necessary insight for reformulating domestic adjudicatory ethics. The development of international commercial arbitration as an anational process, for instance, illustrates that dispute resolution processes and controlling substantive standards must accommodate the dispositions of disputes, the parties, and the nature of their activity. The art of dispute resolution contains no absolute truth. Its means are as variegated as its subject matter. Its guiding principle and exclusive form of truth is to devise procedures in various settings that advance the values of fairness and rationality that prevent conflicts from aggrandizing to counterproductive proportions. The international experience also teaches that, no matter how elaborate, procedural frameworks cannot act as a substitute for the parties' own evaluation of their circumstances and needs, and—most important—their willingness to achieve a mutually satisfactory outcome. The ultimate truth of adjudication is one born of the parties' understanding of their conflict, its costs, and how it might be resolved through consensual reciprocity.

Although civil adjudicatory frameworks in domestic legal systems should continue to evolve toward relying upon legal expertise in achieving determinations and toward containing the adversarial ethic by distributing adjudicatory responsibility among the litigants and the court, legal processes should be seen as merely one of several means to resolve private law conflicts. As in international business transactions, parties in dispute should be attributed a sense of responsibility and control that allows them to exercise a meaningful choice over which remedies are better suited to resolve their particular controversy. A measure of undercivilization in the framework that maintains social civilization might generate an equipoise between individual dispositions and social needs, rather than anarchy. Trusting individuals to manage their own fate and circumstances outside juridical constraints could engender a less problematic, more mature and humane society.

The following chapters examine the viability of the teachings gained from the international area in the context of two particularly troublesome areas of civil adjudication: divorce and personal injury disputes. Although international commercial arbitration may not be a "formula for world peace,"[150] its provision of insights into dispute resolution methodologies and procedures may make it a basis upon which to reeducate domestic societies and litigants about dispute resolution.

NOTES

1. General references on the American law of arbitration are: F. KELLOR, AMERICAN ARBITRATION: ITS HISTORY, FUNCTIONS AND ACHIEVEMENTS (1948); G. WILNER, DOMKE ON COMMERCIAL ARBITRATION: THE LAW AND

PRACTICE OF COMMERCIAL ARBITRATION (1984); Coulson, *Commercial Arbitration in the United States*, 51 ARB. J. 367 (1985); Hoellering, *Arbitration in the United States*, 76 AM. SOC. INT'L L. PROC. 175 (1982); Holtzmann, *National Report: United States*, 2 Y.B. COM. ARB. 116 (1977) and 9 Y.B. COM. ARB. 60 (1984). See also Carbonneau, *Arbitral Adjudication: A Comparative Assessment of Its Remedial and Substantive Status in Transnational Commerce*, 19 TEX. INT'L L.J. 33, 45-53, 65-77 (1984) (this previous study provides some of the background for the present chapter) [*Arbitral Adjudication*].

2. In an 1814 case, Tobey v. County of Bristol, 23 F.Cas. 1313 (C.C. Mass. 1845) (No. 14,065), Mr. Justice Story characterized the American judicial perception of arbitral adjudication in rather contradictory, albeit negative, terms:

> Courts of equity do not refuse to interfere to compel a party specifically to perform an agreement to refer to arbitration, because they wish to discourage arbitration, as against public policy. On the contrary, they have and can have no just objection to these domestic forums, and will enforce, and promptly interfere to enforce their awards when fairly and lawfully made, without hesitation or question. But when they are asked to proceed farther and to compel the parties to appoint arbitrators whose award shall be final, they necessarily pause to consider, whether such tribunals possess adequate means of giving redress, and whether they have a right to compel a reluctant party to submit to such a tribunal, and to close against him the doors of the common courts of justice, provided by the government to protect rights and to redress wrongs.

Id. at 1320-21. See also Note, *Enforcing International Commercial Arbitration Agreements and Awards Not Subject to the New York Convention*, 23 VA. J. INT'L L. 75, 83, n.30 (1982).

3. Ch. 213, §§ 1-15, 43 Stat. 883-86 (current version at 9 U.S.C. §§ 1-14 [1982]). Present arbitration legislation retains the vast majority of the original language.

During the congressional debate on the act in 1924, a proponent of the legislation explained its underlying purpose and rationale in the following terms:

> This bill is one prepared in answer to a great demand for the correction of what seems to be an anachronism in our law, inherited from English jurisprudence. Originally, agreements to arbitrate, the English courts refused to enforce, jealous of their own power and because it would oust the jurisdiction of the courts. That has come into our law with the common law from England. This bill simply provides for one thing, and that is to give an opportunity to enforce an agreement in commercial contracts and admiralty contracts an agreement to arbitrate, when voluntarily placed in the document by

the parties to it. It does not involve any new principle of law except to provide a simple method by which the parties may be brought before the court in order to give enforcement to that which they have already agreed to. It does not affect any contract that has not the agreement in it to arbitrate, and only gives the opportunity after personal service of asking the parties to come in and carry through, in good faith, what they have agreed to do. It does nothing more than that. It creates no new legislation, grants no new rights, except a remedy to enforce an agreement in commercial contracts and in admiralty contracts.

65 Cong. Rec. 1931 (1924) (Rep. Graham-Pa.).

See Baum & Pressman, *The Enforcement of Commercial Arbitration Agreements in the Federal Courts,* 8 N.Y.U. L. REV. 238 (1930); Note, *Contracts: Effect of the United States Arbitration Act,* 25 GEO. L.J. 443 (1937); Committee on Commerce, Trade, and Commercial Law, *The United States Arbitration Law and Its Application,* 11 A.B.A.J. 153 (1925).

4. United States Arbitration Act, ch. 213, § 2, 43 Stat. 883-86 (current version at 9 U.S.C. § 2 [1982]). See generally Heely, *An Introduction to the Federal Arbitration Act,* 13 J. MAR. L. & COM. 223 (1982); Overby, *Arbitrability of Disputes Under the Federal Arbitration Act,* 71 IOWA L. REV. 1137 (1986).

5. See *Arbitral Adjudication,* supra note 1, at 46, 50, and 54.

6. See id. at 45-46.

7. See id. at 66. 9 U.S.C. §§ 201-208 (1976).

8. 9 U.S.C. § 202 (1976).

9. Id.

10. See, for example, Atkins v. Louisville & Nashville R.R. Co., 819 F.2d 644, 649-50 (6th Cir. 1987); Bauhinia Corp. v. China Nat'l Mach. & Equip. Import & Export Corp., 819 F.2d 247, 250 (9th Cir. 1987); In re Diaz Contracting, Inc., 817 F.2d 1047, 1054 (3d Cir. 1987). For additional references, see Appendix A (ch. 4) infra.

11. See text at note 10 supra and accompanying text (sources cited).

12. 41 U.S. 1 (16 Pet.) (1842).

13. Id. at 18-19. In 1924, Congress apparently believed that, by making arbitration agreements enforceable in federal courts, the Federal Arbitration Act merely settled a "question of procedure" and did not create "substantive law". See *Incorporation of State Law Under the FAA,* 78 MICH. L. REV. 1391, 1398 (1980) (citing H.R. Rep. No. 96, 68th Cong., 1st Sess. 1 [1924]). Accordingly, if the FAA were merely a procedural rule applying to cases in the federal court system, even the later Erie prohibition would not bar its application. Although the underpinnings of the decision are far from being absolutely clear, Erie is generally interpreted as prohibiting only those federal rules of decision that affect state-created substantive rights. See Hirshman, *The Second Arbitration Trilogy: The Federalization*

of Arbitration Law, 71 VA. L. REV. 1305, 1316 (1985) (citing Erie v. Tompkins at 78-79) [Hirshman]. Cases since Erie, however, have held that the FAA creates substantive federal law; the United States Supreme Court has nonetheless upheld its application in diversity cases. See generally Atwood, *Issues in Federal-State Relations Under the Federal Arbitration Act,* 37 U. FLA. L. REV. 61 (1985); Kochery, *The Enforcement of Arbitration Agreements in the Federal Courts: Erie v. Tompkins,* 39 CORNELL L. Q. 74 (1953).

14. 304 U.S. 64 (1938). Erie was a diversity suit brought by a citizen of Pennsylvania for damages he sustained allegedly as a result of the activities of a New York railroad. The law of Pennsylvania favored the railroad, providing that the railroad had no duty in regard to people walking along the right of way unless its negligence was willful or wanton. The federal court in New York applied federal common law and found for the plaintiff. The United States Supreme Court reversed, holding that the Swift doctrine was unconstitutional because it allowed federal courts to make law where the federal government had no constitutional authority to do so. See generally Ely, *The Irrepressible Myth of Erie,* 87 HARV. L. REV. 693 (1974); Note, *Erie, Bernhardt, and Section 2 of the United States Arbitration Act: A Farrago of Rights, Remedies, and a Right to a Remedy,* 69 YALE L. J. 847 (1959).

15. 304 U.S. at 78.

16. Id.

17. Id.

18. Field, *The Scope of Federal Common Law,* 99 HARV. L. REV. 881, 888 (1986). For other writings on the domestic federalism question, see, for example, *Symposium, Federalism: Allocating Responsibility Between the Federal and State Courts,* 19 GA. L. REV. 789 (1985); La Pierre, *Political Accountability in the National Political Process: The Alternative to Judicial Review of Federalism Issues,* 80 N.W. U. L. REV. 577 (1985); Note, *The Law Applied in Diversity Cases: The Rules of Decision Act and the Erie Doctrine,* 85 YALE L. J. 678 (1976); Scheiber, *Federalism and Legal Process: Historical and Contemporary Analysis of the American System,* 14 L. & SOC'Y REV. 663 (1980); Segreti, *The Federal Preemption Question: A Federal Question? An Analysis of Federal Jurisdiction over Supremacy Clause Issues,* 33 CLEV. ST. L. REV. 653 (1984-85).

19. 388 U.S. 395 (1967). Prima Paint was preceded by Bernhardt v. Polygraphic Co. of America, Inc., 350 U.S. 198 (1956), which involved an action for breach of an employment contract brought before the federal district court on diversity of citizenship. The district court denied respondent's motion to compel arbitration, ruling that—under Erie—the arbitration clause in the contract was governed by Vermont law, which provided that agreements to arbitrate were revocable by either party before

the rendering of an award. On appeal, the United States Supreme Court upheld the district court ruling, holding that the FAA was inapplicable because the transaction did not involve maritime or commercial matters. Although the Bernhardt Court held that the FAA was substantive and not procedural for Erie purposes, it avoided addressing the question of whether the FAA controlled in cases that came before the federal courts exclusively on a diversity basis. See Hirshman, supra note 13, at 1320.

20. Prima contended that Flood and Conklin had fraudulently represented that it was solvent and therefore able to perform its contractual obligations. The contract between the parties contained a broad arbitration clause. The district court granted Flood and Conklin's motion to compel arbitration, holding that the claim of fraud in the inducement was properly a question for the arbitrators, not the court. The Second Circuit Court of Appeals dismissed Prima Paint's appeal, ruling that the FAA created "national substantive law and governs even in the face of a contrary state rule." The court of appeals cited Robert Lawrence Co. v. Devonshire Fabrics, 271 F.2d 402 (2d Cir. 1959), cert. granted 362 U.S. 909, cert. dismissed 364 U.S. 801 (1960) (holding that claims of fraudulent misrepresentation could be submitted to arbitration despite the requirements of New York state law; the FAA creates a body of substantive federal law that encompasses all the legal issues surrounding the arbitration clause; and the FAA does not require any reference to state rules of decision).

21. On the separability doctrine, see Prima Paint, 388 U.S. at 402. See also G. WILNER, DOMKE ON COMMERCIAL ARBITRATION, supra note 1, at § 8:01.

22. Prima Paint, 388 U.S. at 402.

23. Id. at 404.

24. Id. In his dissent, Justice Black argued that the majority went beyond the specific intent of the act: to make arbitration agreements enforceable in federal courts if they were valid and legally recognized under state law:

> The court holds that the Act gives federal courts the right to fashion federal law, inconsistent with state law, to determine whether an arbitration agreement was made and what it means. Even if Congress intended to create substantive rights by passage of the Act, I am wholly convinced that it did not intend to create such a sweeping body of federal substantive law completely to take away from the States their power to interpret contracts made by their own citizens in their own territory.

Id. at 422.

Justice Black also contended that the effect of the separability doctrine was to place arbitration agreements, not on an equal footing with other contracts — the avowed purpose of the FAA, but to afford them a privileged status beyond the ordinary legal impact of contract provisions. Prima

Paint's promise to arbitrate disputes, according to Black, was inseparable from its other contractual promises. Id. at 424.

25. Prima Paint, 388 U.S. at 404.

26. See Justice Black's dissent, 388 U.S. at 424-25.

27. See Hirshman, note 13 supra.

28. 460 U.S. 1 (1983).

29. 465 U.S. 1, 404 S.Ct. 852 (1984).

30. 106 S.Ct. 1238 (1985).

31. Moses Cone, 460 U.S. at 4-5.

32. Id. at 7.

33. Id.

34. See Mercury Construction Co. v. Moses H. Cone Memorial Hosp., 656 F.2d 933 (4th Cir. 1981).

35. Moses Cone, 460 U.S. at 13-29.

36. Id. at 20. The first question presented to the Court was whether the district court had properly stayed the federal action pending resolution of the parallel state claim. Id. at 4, 13. In addressing this question, the Court relied on Colorado River Water Conservation District v. United States, 424 U.S. 800 (1976), holding that—once federal jurisdiction is properly invoked—deference to parallel state court litigation is proper only in exceptional circumstances (see Colorado River, 424 U.S. at 813). The factors to be considered in determining whether exceptional circumstances exist are: (1) the inconvenience of the federal forum; (2) the desirability of avoiding piecemeal litigation; and (3) the order in which jurisdiction was obtained by the concurrent forums (see Moses Cone, 460 U.S. at 15). Applying these factors to the facts in Moses Cone, the Court found no showing of exceptional circumstances to justify the district court's stay. Id. at 19.

37. Moses Cone, 460 U.S. at 22-23.

38. Id.

39. Id. at 24.

40. 465 U.S. 1 (1984).

41. California Franchise Investment Law (CFIL), CAL. CORP. CODE § 31512 (West 1977). See Keating v. Superior Court, 31 Cal. 3d 584, 645 P.2d 1192, 183 Cal. Rptr. 360 (1982).

42. Keating, 465 U.S. at 4.

43. Keating v. Superior Court, 31 Cal. 3d 584, 599, 645 P.2d 1192, 1200, 183 Cal. Rptr. 360, 368 (1982).

44. Keating v. Superior Court, 167 Cal. Rptr. 481, 493-94 (1980).

45. Keating v. Superior Court, 31 Cal. Rptr. 584, 604, 645, 645 P.2d 1192, 1203-04 (1982).

46. Keating, 465 U.S. at 10.

47. Id. at 16.
48. Id. at 21.
49. Id. at 16.
50. Id. at 17, n.11.
51. 105 S.Ct. 1238 (1985).
52. Id. at 1239.
53. Id.
54. Id. (725 F.2d 552 [1984]).
55. Id. at 1240.
56. Id.
57. Id.
58. Id. at 1241.
59. Id.
60. Id. at 1242.
61. See Comment, *Dean Witter Reynolds, Inc. v. Byrd: The Unraveling of the Intertwining Doctrine,* 62 DEN. L. REV. 789 (1985); Hirshman, note 13 supra; Note, *Federal Preemption—Arbitration—Federal Arbitration Act Creates National Substantive Law Applicable in Federal and State Courts and Supersedes Contrary State Statutes,* 64 MISS. L.J. 561 (1984); Note, *Investor-Broker Arbitration Agreements: Dean Witter Reynolds, Inc. v. Byrd,* 20 U. S. F. L. REV. 101 (1985); Note, *Mixed Arbitrable and Nonarbitrable Claims in Securities Litigation: Dean Witter Reynolds, Inc. v. Byrd,* 34 CATH. U. L. REV. 525 (1985); Note, *Preemption of State Law Under the Federal Arbitration Act,* 15 U. BALT. L. REV. 128 (1985); Recent Developments, *The Federal Arbitration Act: A Threat to Injunctive Relief,* 21 WILLAMETTE L. REV. 674 (1985). See generally McDermott, *Significant Developments in the United States Law Governing International Commercial Arbitration,* 1 CONN. J. INT'L L. 111 (1985-86).
62. See text at note 7 supra and accompanying text.
63. 416 U.S. 506, reh'g denied, 419 U.S. 885 (1974). See *Arbitral Adjudication,* supra note 1, at 68-74.
64. 416 U.S. at 508.
65. 346 U.S. 427 (1953).
66. Id.
67. Id.
68. Id.
69. Id. at 512.
70. Id. at 515.
71. Id.
72. Id.
73. Id.
74. See *Arbitral Adjudication,* supra note 1, at 69.

75. 417 U.S. at 515-16.

76. Id. at 516-17.

77. For a discussion of the concept of private international law in its traditional sense and new acceptation, see Appendix B (ch. 4) infra.

78. See generally J. ATWOOD & K. BREWSTER, ANTITRUST AND AMERICAN BUSINESS ABROAD (2d ed. 1981); W. FUGATE, FOREIGN COMMERCE AND THE ANTITRUST LAWS (3d ed. 1982); Akehurst, *Jurisdiction in International Law,* 46 BRIT. Y.B. INT'L L. 145 (1973); Comment, *Shortening the Long Arm of American Antitrust Jurisdiction: Extraterritoriality and the Foreign Blocking Statutes,* 28 LOY. L. REV. 213 (1982); Fugate, *Antitrust Jurisdiction and Foreign Sovereignty,* 49 VA. L. REV. 925 (1963); Grundman, *The New Imperialism: The Extraterritorial Application of United States Law,* 14 INT'L LAW. 257 (1980); Lowe, *Blocking Extraterritorial Jurisdiction: The British Protection of Trading Interests Act, 1980,* 75 AM. J. INT'L L. 257 (1981); Note, *"Forum Non Conveniens" and the Extraterritorial Application of United States Antitrust Law,* 94 YALE L.J. 1693 (1985); Samie, *Extraterritorial Enforcement of United States Antitrust Laws: The British Reaction,* 16 INT'L LAW. 313 (1982); Stanford, *The Application of the Sherman Act to Conduct Outside the United States: A View From Abroad,* 11 CORNELL INT'L L.J. 195 (1978); Symposium, *Extraterritoriality of Economic Legislation,* 50 L. & CONTEMP. PROBS. 1 (1987).

On extraterritoriality generally, see EXTRATERRITORIAL APPLICATION OF LAWS AND RESPONSES THERETO (C. Olmstead ed. 1984); Maier, *Extraterritorial Jurisdiction at a Crossroads: An Intersection Between Public and Private International Law,* 76 AM. J. INT'L L. 280 (1982); Maier, *Interest Balancing and Extraterritorial Jurisdiction,* 31 AM. J. COMP. L. 579 (1983); Maier, *Resolving Extraterritorial Conflicts, or "There and Back Again,"* 25 VA. J. INT'L L. 7 (1984).

79. 213 U.S. 347 (1909).

80. See Kintner & Hallgarten, *Application of United States Antitrust Laws to Foreign Trade and Commerce: Variations on "American Banana"* *since 1909,* 15 B.C. IND. & COM. L. REV. 343 (1973). See also Thomsen v. Cayser, 243 U.S. 66 (1917); United States v. Pac. & Arctic Ry. & Navigation Co., 228 U.S. 87 (1913); United States v. Am. Tobacco Co., 221 U.S. 106 (1911); United States v. Sisal Sales Corp., 274 U.S. 268 (1927).

81. 148 F.2d 416 (2d Cir. 1945).

82. Id. at 442. See Ellis, *Comment to Miller: Extraterritorial Effects of Trade Regulations,* 111 U. PA. L. REV. 1129 (1963); Rahl, *Foreign Commerce Jurisdiction of the American Antitrust Laws,* 42 ANTITRUST L.J. 521 (1974); Zwarensteyn, *The Foreign Reach of the American Antitrust Laws,* 3 AM. BUS. L.J. 163 (1965). See also Occidental Petroleum Corp. v. Buttes Gas and Oil Co., 331 F.Supp. 92 (C.D. Cal. 1971), aff'd 461 F.2d 1261 (9th

Cir.), cert. denied 409 U.S. 950 (1972); U.S. v. R.P. Oldham Co., 152 F. Supp. 818 (N.D. Cal. 1957).

83. 549 F.2d 597 (9th Cir. 1976).

84. 595 F.2d 1287 (3d Cir. 1979).

85. Timberlane, 549 F.2d at 612-13; Mannington Mills, 595 F.2d at 1297-98.

86. Timberlane, 549 F.2d at 614; Mannington Mills, 595 F.2d at 1297-98.

87. Mannington Mills, 595 F.2d at 1296.

88. 105 S.Ct. 3346 (1985). For commentary on the case, see Campbell & Vollmer, *International Arbitration*, 7 NAT'L L.J., Aug. 19, 1985, at 24; Carbonneau, *The Exuberant Pathway to Quixotic Internationalism: Assessing the Folly of Mitsubishi*, 19 VAND. J. TRANS. L. 265 (1986) [*Quixotic Internationalism*]; Comment, *International Arbitration — Commerce — Arbitrability of Antitrust Claims: Mitsubishi Motors v. Soler Chrysler-Plymouth, Inc.*, 17 SETON HALL L. REV. 448 (1987); Comment, *International Arbitration: The Arbitrability of Antitrust Claims Arising Out of International Commercial Agreements — Mitsubishi Motors Corp. v. Soler Chrysler-Plymouth, Inc.: The Aftermath*, 8 N.Y. L. SCH. J. INT'L & COMP. L. 349 (1987); Lee, *Antitrust & Commercial Arbitration: An Economic Analysis*, 62 ST. JOHN'S L. REV. 1 (1987); Lipner, *International Antitrust Laws: To Arbitrate or Not to Arbitrate*, 19 GEO. WASH. J. INT'L L. & ECON. 395 (1985); Note, *International Arbitration and the Comity of Error: Mitsubishi Motors v. Soler Chrysler-Plymouth, Inc.*, 19 CONN. L. REV. 435 (1987); Recent Developments, *Arbitration: Arbitrability of Antitrust Claims in International Tribunals*, 27 HARV. INT'L L.J. 227 (1986); Robert, *Une date dans l'extension de l'arbitrage international: L'arrêt Mitsubishi c/ Soler*, [1986] REV. ARB. 173 (1986). See also Branson & Wallace, *Choosing the Substantive Law to Apply in International Commercial Arbitration*, 27 VA. J. INT'L L. 39, 50, 54, 57-64 (1986). See also Symposium, *The Future of Private International Arbitration: Beyond Mitsubishi*, 12 BROOKLYN J. INT'L L. 579 (1986).

For related articles that refer to Mitsubishi, see, for example, Allison, *Arbitration Agreements and Antitrust Claims: The Need for Enhanced Accommodation of Conflicting Public Policies*, 64 N.C. L. REV. 219 (1986); Cavanagh, *Detrebling Antitrust Damages: An Idea Whose Time Has Come?*, 61 TUL. L. REV. 777 (1987); Comment, *Arbitrating Civil RICO and Implied Causes of Action Arising Under Section 10(b) of the Securities Exchange Act of 1934*, 36 CATH. U. L. REV. 455 (1987); Fletcher, *Privatizing Securities Disputes Through the Enforcement of Arbitration Agreements*, 71 MINN. L. REV. 393 (1987); Note, *Arbitrability of Claims Arising Under the Securities Exchange Act of 1934*, [1986] DUKE L.J. 548 (1986); Note, *Arbitrability of*

Implied Rights of Action Under Section 10(b) of the Securities Exchange Act, 61 N.Y.U. L. REV. 506 (1986).

89. See *Quixotic Internationalism*, supra note 88, at 274-77. For commentary on the lower court determination of the case (723 F.2d 155 [1st Cir. 1983]), see Comment, *Mitsubishi: The Erosion of the New York Convention and International Arbitration*, [1984] WIS. INT'L L.J. 151 (1984); Recent Developments, *Arbitration: Public Policy Exception to Arbitration of Antitrust Issues*, 25 HARV. INT'L L.J. 427 (1984); Recent Decisions, *Arbitration: Transnational Antitrust Claims Are Nonarbitrable Under the Federal Arbitration Act and Article II(1) of the Convention on the Recognition and Enforcement of Foreign Arbitral Awards*, 17 VAND. J. TRANS. L. 741 (1984).

90. For a discussion of the separability doctrine, see G. WILNER, DOMKE ON COMMERCIAL ARBITRATION, supra note 1, §§ 8:01-:02; A. VAN DEN BERG, THE NEW YORK ARBITRATION CONVENTION OF 1958, 145-46, 156, 200, 372 (1983). See also Bedell, Harrison & Grant, *Arbitrability: Current Developments in the Interpretation and Enforceability of Arbitration Agreements*, 13 J. CONTEMP. L. 1 (1987); (regarding the related public policy defense) Sterk, *Enforceability of Agreements to Arbitrate: An Examination of the Public Policy Defense*, 2 CARDOZO L. REV. 481 (1981).

91. Mitsubishi, 105 S.Ct. at 3355.

92. See *Quixotic Internationalism*, supra note 88, at 280-81.

93. Dean Witter Reynolds, Inc. v. Byrd, 105 S.Ct. 1238, 1242-43 (1985).

94. Former Chief Justice Burger's departure, for example, has not modified the Court's position on arbitration. See McMahon v. Shearson/American Express, Inc., 107 S.Ct. 2332 (1987); Perry v. Thomas, 107 S.Ct. 2520 (1987).

95. Scherk v. Alberto-Culver Co., 417 U.S. 506, 529 (Douglas, J., dissenting). See *Arbitral Adjudication*, supra note 1, at 73-4.

96. Mitsubishi v. Soler, 105 S.Ct. 3346, 3361 (Stevens, J., dissenting). See *Quixotic Internationalism*, supra note 88, at 288-90.

97. See Address by Chief Justice Burger, ABA Midyear Meeting (Jan. 24, 1982), reprinted in 68 A.B.A.J. 274 (1982); *Chief Justice Burger's State of the Judiciary Address*, 109 N.Y.L.J., at 1, col. 4 (Feb. 4, 1982); *Time to Review Our Reliance on Adversary System: Chief Justice Faults Lawyers for Frivolous Suits, Discovery Abuse* (Address by Chief Justice Warren Burger at ABA Midyear Meeting, Las Vegas, Feb. 1984), L.A. Daily J., at 4, col. 3 (Feb. 15, 1984).

98. See generally (on commercial arbitration) 1-5 J. WETTER, THE INTERNATIONAL ARBITRAL PROCESS: PUBLIC AND PRIVATE (1979); G. WILNER, DOMKE ON COMMERCIAL ARBITRATION, note 1 supra; de Vries, *International Commercial Arbitration: A Contractual Substitute for National Courts*,

57 TUL. L. REV. 42 (1982); Mentschikoff, *Commercial Arbitration*, 61 COLUM. L. REV. 846 (1961). On labor arbitration, see J. CORREGE, V. HUGHES, & M. STONE (eds.), THE FUTURE OF LABOR ARBITRATION IN AMERICA (1976); F. ELKOURI & E. ELKOURI, HOW ARBITRATION WORKS (4th ed. 1985); O. FAIRWEATHER, PRACTICE AND PROCEDURE IN LABOR ARBITRATION (2d ed. 1983); M. HILL & A. SINICROPI, REMEDIES IN ARBITRATION (1981); S. KAGEL, ANATOMY OF A LABOR ARBITRATION (1st ed. 1978); C. UPDEGRAFF, ARBITRATION AND LABOR RELATIONS (3d ed. 1970); A. ZACK & R. BLOCH, LABOR AGREEMENT IN NEGOTIATION AND ARBITRATION (1983).

99. See Carbonneau & Firestone, *Transnational Law-Making: Assessing the Impact of the Vienna Convention and the Viability of Arbitral Adjudication,* 1 EMORY J. INT'L DISP. RES. 51, 57-63 (1986).

100. See Lowenfeld, *The Mitsubishi Case: Another View,* 2 ARB. INT'L 178 (1986).

101. See *Quixotic Internationalism,* supra note 88, at 296-98.

102. See Appendix B (ch. 4) infra.

103. See Asahi Metal Indus. Co. v. Superior Court of California, Solano Cty., 480 U.S. 102, 94 L. Ed. 2d 92, 107 S.Ct. 1026 (1987). See also Case Comment, *Asahi Metal Industry Co. v. Superior Court: The Stream of Commerce Doctrine, Barely Alive but Still Kicking,* 76 GEORGETOWN L.J. 203 (1987); Comment, *The Extraterritorial Assertion of Long-Arm Jurisdiction and the Impact on the International Commercial Community: A Comment and Suggested Approach,* 9 U. PA. J. INT'L BUS. L. 713 (1987); Note, *Jurisdiction: Personal Jurisdiction Over Alien Corporations—Asahi Metal Industry Co. v. Superior Court of California, 107 S.Ct. 1026 (1987),* 29 HARV. INT'L L. J. 207 (1988); Seidelson, *A Supreme Court Conclusion and Two Rationales That Defy Comprehension: Asahi Metal Indus. Co., Ltd. v. Superior Court of California,* 53 BROOKLYN L. REV. 563 (1987). On this question, see generally Hay, *Judicial Jurisdiction Over Foreign-Country Corporate Defendants: Comments on Recent Case Law,* 63 OR. L. REV. 431 (1984).

104. See Appendix B (ch. 4) infra.

105. See text at note 90 supra and accompanying text.

106. See *Quixotic Internationalism,* supra note 88, at 283-88.

107. For a discussion of the concept of private international law in this context, see Appendix B (ch. 4) infra.

108. See Carbonneau & Firestone, *Transnational Law-Making,* supra note 99, at 53, n.10:

> Municipal law can influence the arbitral process in a number of ways. First, the procedural rules of the forum may determine the manner in which the adjudication will be conducted. Second, substantive municipal law may govern the resolution of the dispute. Third, the validity of the award under various national laws may

be relevant to the award's enforceability. Unless the losing party acquiesces to the award, the prevailing party will lodge an enforcement action before a national court. Finally, questions arise concerning the relationship between the arbitral tribunal and the laws of the arbitral forum: whether and to what extent forum law can or should influence the course of arbitration solely because the tribunal is presiding in the forum.

The English view of the degree to which national laws and policy can or should influence the international arbitral process is marked by a strong disdain for arbitral anationalism. English judges and commentators refer disparagingly to a system of "floating" arbitration or arbitration "unbound." The traditional English view is that a system of procedural or substantive law for the resolution of disputes can exist only by virtue of sovereign authority. All adjudications conducted in England must be subject to a certain extent to the English judicial system and procedural rules. . . .

Mann's refusal to recognize international commercial arbitration as a form of adjudication independent of municipal law and national sovereigns reflects a strict Austinian view of the law. Essentially, Mann argues that there can be no party autonomy, hence no institutional autonomy, if autonomy is defined as independence from the strictures of national law. . . .

This attack upon the existing process is objectionable in a number of respects. On the one hand, the refusal to recognize the evident realities of international commercial activity and the necessity of having a dispute resolution process that transcends parochial national concerns reveal the sterility of the analysis. It begrudges the creative contributions of the dynamic interplay between the law and economic forces merely because they undo prior realities. On the other hand, the strident character of the analysis clouds the real problem: how to strike a workable balance between the transnational arbitral process and the integrity of vital national policy interests. . . .

109. See Appendix B (ch. 4) infra (references to Mann).

110. See *Quixotic Internationalism,* supra note 88, at 290-96.

111. See id. at 293, n.112.

112. See id. at 291, n.97. For further discussion of this point, see Appendix C (ch. 4) infra.

113. Mitsubishi, 105 S. Ct. at 3356-58.

114. See *Quixotic Internationalism,* supra note 88, at 275.

115. Mitsubishi, 105 S.Ct. at 3357. The strength of the federal policy favoring arbitration has made its influence felt upon the controversial question of whether arbitrators can award punitive damages. State courts are generally divided on the question—some see the arbitral mandate, once conferred, as basically unlimited, whereas others believe that all

arbitral powers should be expressly conferred by the terms of reference that accompanies the submission or the arbitral clause. Yet a third group of courts finds that the award of punitive damages by arbitrators is inappropriate in all cases. These courts view punitive damages as a social remedy and as a part of the law's exclusive hold on public policy matters. For further discussion of this point, see Appendix D (ch. 4) infra.

116. 107 S. Ct. 2332 (1987). For a discussion of the prior law, see, for example, Note, *Arbitrability of Securities Disputes Between Brokers and Customers — Phillips v. Merrill Lynch, Pierce, Fenner & Smith, Inc.,* 20 CREIGHTON L. REV. 1009 (1987); Peterson, *The Arbitrability of Claims Under the Federal Securities Laws,* [1987] J. CORP. L. 535 (1987). The following commentary was previously published in part in REV. ARB 1 (1988).

117. See 107 S. Ct. at 2346 (Blackmun, J., dissenting).

118. See text at note 88 supra.

119. See text at note 88 supra and accompanying text.

120. See text at note 27 supra.

121. See text at notes 38 & 39 supra (Moses Cone).

122. See text at notes 40-50 supra (Keating).

123. See id.

124. See text at notes 51-60 supra (Byrd).

125. 107 S. Ct. at 2337.

126. Id.

127. Id. at 2338.

128. Id. at 2340.

129. Id. at 2339.

130. Id. at 2338-39.

131. Id. at 2346, 2349 (Blackmun, J. dissenting).

132. See text at note 65 supra.

133. 107 S. Ct. at 2340, 2344-46.

134. Id. at 2344.

135. Id. at 2340-41.

136. Id. at 2341.

137. Id. at 2340.

138. Id. at 2341-42.

139. Id. at 2341.

140. Id. at 2343.

141. Id. at 2343-46.

142. Id. at 2345.

143. For instance, Justice Douglas in Scherk and Justice Stevens in Mitsubishi.

144. See Justice Stevens's dissent in Mitsubishi.

145. For a discussion of Justice Stevens's position on arbitration, see Appendix E (ch. 4) infra.

146. 107 S. Ct. at 2337-38. For other commentaries on McMahon, see Bedell, Harrison, & Harvey, *The McMahon Mandate: Compulsory Arbitration of Securities and RICO Claims,* 19 LOY. U. CHI. L. J. 1 (1987); Fletcher, *Learning to Live with the Federal Arbitration Act: Securities Litigation in a Post-McMahon World,* 37 EMORY L. J. 99 (1988); Ginger, *Managing Securities Disputes After McMahon: A Call for Consolidation and Arbitration,* 33 VILL. L. REV. 515 (1988); Leacock, *Extending Arbitration of Securities Disputes in American Law,* J. BUS. L. 271 (1988). The case is noted in: 19 ARIZ. ST. L. J. 793 (1987); 73 IOWA L. REV. 449 (1988); 101 HARV. L. REV. 280 (1987); 42 U. MIAMI L. REV. 203 (1987); 12 NOVA L. REV. 1375 (1988); 8 PACE L. REV. 193 (1988); 17 STETSON L. REV. 421 (1988); 62 TUL. L. REV. 284 (1987); 10 U. ARK. LITTLE ROCK L.J. 523 (1987-88).

In the wake of McMahon, the American Arbitration Association (AAA) quickly developed a set of specific institutional rules for securities arbitration, entitled "Securities Arbitration Rules," which became effective in September 1987. Previously, such cases had been governed by the rules for commercial arbitration. The alacrity of the AAA reaction indicated that the McMahon opinion was a source of new business for arbitral institutions and that arbitration in securities matters presented problems not normally associated with conventional arbitrations. With an increased volume of cases, new rules were needed to eradicate the industry bias in prior procedures and to account for the parties' disparity of position and for the likelihood that most claims would raise questions of regulatory law.

When compared to their commercial counterparts, the AAA rules for securities arbitration differ in only a few, albeit fundamental, respects. First, in regard to the number of arbitrators on the tribunal, the commercial rules provide that generally only one arbitrator shall be appointed unless the parties provide otherwise or the AAA deems a plurality of arbitrators necessary (Rule 17). The securities arbitration rules require a panel of three arbitrators whenever a claim exceeds the relatively modest sum of $20,000 (Rule 17). Second, the appointment of arbitrators is slightly more complicated under the rules for securities arbitration. The parties are given two lists of arbitrators — one listing arbitrators affiliated with the securities industry and the other nonaffiliated arbitrators. When the tribunal consists of three arbitrators, at least two must be nonaffiliated. If the arbitration is to be done by a sole arbitrator, that arbitrator must be nonaffiliated (Rule 13). Finally, in regard to the award, the rules for securities arbitration require arbitrators to "include a statement regarding the disposition of any statutory claims" (Rule 42), whereas the rules for commercial arbitration mandate only that the award be in writing and signed by a majority of the arbitrators (Rule 42).

While the rules for securities arbitration are molded to the special character of securities disputes, they may not alleviate the basic danger of having recourse to arbitration in a consumer and regulatory context. The practice of having three-member tribunals and a majority of non-affiliated arbitrators may not protect consumer interests sufficiently. It may only provide a formalistic safeguard. Industry practice may still set applicable standards and the public interest may never be defined, elaborated, or referred to in this private adjudicatory process. Unlike judges, arbitrators may not have the sense of independence necessary to adopt minority, economically questionable, or otherwise would-be deviant positions. Finally, mandating that securities arbitrators expressly acknowledge investor claims of statutory violations only provides superficial recognition of the public law character of the disputes. The rules do not mandate a reasoned assessment of the claim, and appeal to a court is no more readily available in these arbitral circumstances than in others.

Although these alterations do not attenuate the juridical dilemma created by the Court's decision, they do mitigate the harshness of the McMahon result. In McMahon, the Court was willing to have investor claims resolved through industry-controlled arbitration procedures (107 S.Ct. at 2341). By attempting to deal with disparities in position and the public law aspect of the cases, the new AAA rules at least are pointed in the direction of fairness and seek to protect the institution of arbitration from charges of glaring unsuitability and abuse. It bears reiterating, however, that these rules do not resolve the core problems raised by the arbitrability of securities claims: namely, the adhesionary character of the arbitral compact, the economic and positional inequality of the parties, and the depreciation of the public interest in preventing individual investor fraud and broker overreaching in a sophisticated and volatile market.

Moreover, in its opinion, the McMahon Court looked to Securities Exchange Commission (SEC) supervision as a means of justifying its confidence in industry-controlled securities arbitration procedures. If unfairness and injustice surfaced, the Court seemed to reason, the commission would be there to provide the necessary correction. "Black Monday" demonstrated the fallacy of the Court's reasoning and made the underlying problems with securities arbitration transparent. Following the stock market collapse, an avalanche of investor claims were submitted to the industry-controlled arbitral framework. Apparently, the SEC was unable to exercise its anticipated supervisory capabilities. The volume of pending cases and growing public dissatisfaction with arbitral procedures led the commission to consider asking for congressional legislation prohibiting mandatory predispute arbitration agreements in investor-broker contracts. It eventually resolved, however, merely to request a study of the problem. The depth of regulatory oversight from the commission envisaged by the McMahon Court simply does not exist. See Christian Science Monitor, Oct. 21, 1988, at 8.

SEC inaction and public outcries of injustice with mandatory arbitration in securities cases may lead to legislative attacks upon the arbitral process. The McMahon opinion, in fact, gave rise to a determination in some legislative quarters to oppose the Court's reordering of fundamental juridical priorities. A few months after the McMahon decision, the Massachusetts state legislature enacted provisions prohibiting the use of mandatory arbitration clauses in investor-broker contracts. Under the legislation, which took effect in January 1989, brokers must inform prospective clients of their legal right to judicial redress of their grievances. Moreover, brokers must still do business with investors who refuse to agree to arbitrate. While the legislation is directed to consumer protection, it casts arbitration in an unfavorable light, stigmatizing it as an adjudicatory mechanism that can be manipulated by special interests and can become an instrument of abuse. A discredited and misunderstood process, then, may be the ultimate legacy of the Court's liberal endorsement of arbitration.

Because the Massachusetts law conflicts directly with the federal law on arbitration and the content of the Court's arbitral doctrine, it has been challenged on constitutional grounds. While the statute may not survive legal challenge, it provides the impetus for triggering a congressional response to the McMahon doctrine. See Securities Industry Assoc. v. Michael J. Connolly, [1988] U.S. Dist. Lexis 14587, decided Dec. 19, 1988, reported in 3 MEALEY'S INT'L ARB. REP. 17 (Oct. 1988). Correcting reckless judicial positions through legislative action, however, can be perilous. Legislatures are prone to act primarily when abuses are substantial, plainly visible, and implicate financially important or numerically significant and vocal interests. Rather than command mere adjustments, the correction is likely to be either a sweeping measure or a provision so riddled with compromise that viable solutions are evaded. Either course of action could undermine arbitration's traditional standing.

The history of American arbitration law would then have gone full circle. In the early days of rehabilitation, New York legislation provided the basis for positive federal action; now, the Massachusetts provision may give rise to restrictive congressional counteraction. Tainting the arbitral process with illegitimacy could seep to the core of its institutional stature. The overexuberant liberal judicial endorsement will have lain the foundation for arbitration's eventual demise. An intelligent sense of the institution and a moderate consideration of its needs could have avoided such a costly correction.

The Court's decisional law on arbitration is now poised for yet another development that may lead the Court to strengthen its existing doctrine and thereby guarantee some form of federal legislative reprisal. The Court recently agreed to review, 57 U.S.L.W. 3337 (Nov. 14, 1988), the Fifth Circuit Court of Appeals' decision in Rodriquez De Quijas v. Shearson/ Lehman Bros., Inc., 845 F.2d 1296 (5th Cir. 1988), holding that claims arising under the 1933 Securities Act could be submitted to arbitration. In its opinion, the Fifth Circuit emphasized the McMahon Court's assessment that the Wilko precedent, which banned arbitration in this area, was begotten of an age in which courts were hostile to arbitration. The appellate court then brought this assessment to its logical conclusion, holding that the McMahon reasoning reversed Wilko. If the Court upholds this decision (as it is likely to do), it will render the inarbitrability defense completely meaningless. Such action should push public tolerance of the Court's liberalism on arbitration to the outer limits. Problems in judicial administration do not justify a general deprivation of legal remedies in matters where judicial recourse is expressly mandated by statute. The Court's solution to the litigation crisis brought on by the predominance of the adversarial ethic is too simplistic and single-minded, and it is fundamentally misdirected. It has generated a patent breach of essential legal guarantees. Worse, it has exploited arbitration to provide a surrogate solution, a means to avoid recognizing the true problems and exploring real solutions.

147. See *A Colloquy Alternative Dispute Resolution in International Trade and Business* (Wilner's remarks), 40 ME. L. REV. 223, 237, 239, 244-47, 248 (1988). [On May 15, 1989, the Court upheld the Fifth Circuit decision in *Rodriquez*. See (1989) W. L. 488 21 (U.S.).]

148. See Jarvin, *La loi-type de la C.N.U.D.C.I. sur l'arbitrage commercial international*, REV. ARB. 509, 513 (1986).

149. See ch. 2, at notes 23-62 supra.

150. Mitsubishi, 105 S.Ct. at 3374 (Stevens, J. dissenting).

5 | Alternatives to Divorce Litigation

Discordant Perceptions of Marriage and Marriage Pathology

The Legal View

From a legal perspective, the marriage relationship is a bundle of rights and duties, akin in many respects to a partnership or joint venture association.[1] It is evident, however, that even from the perspective of legality the fabric of marriage is more than a loose confederation of the disparate strands of contract law interwoven by the thread of party autonomy. Marriage implies a larger social interest and transcends purely individual concerns.[2] Indeed, the law, through statutes and judicial rulings, defines the nature and content of the essential matrimonial duties and ordinarily provides for the regime governing marital property.[3] During the existence of the marriage, society expects that the spouses will cooperate to maintain their association and allocate responsibilities in the furtherance of common tasks and goals — broadly defined as the emotional development and material well-being of the family unit and of its individual members.

Accordingly, marriage merges the individual's contractual prerogatives with social imperatives relating to the family. The grouping of two persons in a matrimonial association, therefore, simultaneously excludes and includes an impersonal state interest. The dynamics of this curious triangular association are particularly evident when the personal relationship is being terminated. At this stage, in the name of public policy, a court of law usually intervenes to deal with disputes that ensue from the dismantling of the matrimonial association.[4]

Disputes that attend the breakdown of a marriage resist facile legal description, making governing standards concerning substance and procedure difficult to define. Conflicts between divorcing spouses, in addition to implicating the public interest, sound both in torts and contracts.[5] For instance, a divorce may involve questions bearing upon marital conduct, the division of property, financial maintenance, and the custody of children—issues governed by contrastive substantive predicates.[6] Moreover, differences arising between divorcing spouses are accompanied by volatile emotions, personal antagonisms, and feelings of retribution, making the procedural adjudication of legal issues potentially strident.[7] To achieve effective results, then, the rules and procedures applied by courts should reflect the sui generis aspects of matrimonial disputes and the unique and varied features of divorcement.

The Personal View

From the perspective of individual human ideals, marriage consists at its core of an intimate and pleasurable relationship which, despite the vicissitudes of life, holds physical and emotional benefits for both parties.[8] The contemplated sharing generates not only a sense of mutual commitment, but also a bond of trust, making the spouses dependent upon and vulnerable to one another. The relationship can also involve and implicate the rights and welfare of innocent, noncontracting third parties: the children, who frequently become weapons in the divorce battle.[9] The spouses have relinquished their ideal aspirations, and focus upon their disappointment. They may disagree about whether the relationship should cease; in any event, they are often prone to affix personal blame on each other.

Potential Causes

The factors that give rise to such a situation are as multifarious as are the human psyche and the variegated mores of contemporary society.[10] The couple may have married at an early age and developed toward emotional adulthood at different paces, inducing persistent and increasing tension between them. Latent psychological conflicts may have precipitated episodes of domestic violence, infidelity, abuse of stimulants, or a pattern of such incidents in response to perceived inattention or a lack of affection.[11] Anger may have been expressed in destructive ways. Continuous misunderstanding resulting from unrecognized depression over a period of years may have eroded the interest and will of one of the spouses to salvage the relationship. In all these circumstances, there may be transference[12] from a psychologically debilitating childhood: emotions toward a parent who failed or disappointed the individual as a child are expressed against the spouse and destroy the healthy adult dimension of the relationship.

Contemporary social ethics may also provide some explanation for the breakdown of marriages. The debate surrounding gender equality, for instance, has already had a visible impact upon substantive domestic relations law. Joint custody statutes[13] embody a legislative reassessment of the ability of men to engage in parenthood—a reevaluation advocated by an emerging fathers' rights movement. The economic integration of women into the work force and their increasing financial self-sufficiency have contributed to the transformation of alimony statutes from fault-based provisions (allegedly protective of helpless, innocent wives and punitive as to overbearing, culpable husbands) to a gender-neutral and need-determined standard that promotes economic rehabilitation.[14] Such changes in social thinking about men and women probably have an impact upon the decision to enter into or to terminate marriage.

Another gender-related factor may be the contrastive attitudes between men and women toward interpersonal relationships. Because of different cultural, sociological, and psychological assumptions that underlie their upbringing and eventual integration into society, men and women traditionally bring disparate expectations and dispositions to marriage.[15] Encouraged by social custom to restrict the expression of their emotions and to gain identity from external accomplishments, men tend to interpret marriage in terms of, and perhaps subordinate it to, the attainment of more objective career goals. Although useful and productive in business and professional relationships, male "tunnel" vision—implying a clear and unswerving focus upon objectives and the means for achieving them—reduces (at least ostensibly) the importance and complexity of personal relationships. For men, conflicts between job objectives and marital life-styles may well compromise the stability of marriage. By contrast, women are taught to have a larger view and appreciation of personal relationships. Their "global" vision implies a preference for deviating from a goal, either temporarily or permanently, in order to preserve relationships.[16] Unless spouses understand their respective perceptions of relationships, the inevitable misunderstanding and frustration may become overwhelming and prove fatal to the marriage.

It might be conjectured that the redefinition of social morality (seen in the prevalence of spouse-equivalent relationships, the availability and use of birth control, the legalization of abortion) should have some bearing on how people perceive marriage and divorce. Also, the decline or resurgence of religious beliefs, the greater or lesser popularity of psychotherapy and other forms of counselling, purely economic considerations (for example, the effect of tax laws on marriage), even drug or alcohol abuse, may all be relevant to providing insight into the underlying motives for a high incidence of divorce[17] in contemporary American society.

In the final analysis, however, the social factors and personal reasons given for the instability and disruption of matrimonial relationships are virtually indistinguishable. For example, a disagreement between spouses on gender roles in the family and society not only exemplifies the influence of contemporary mores upon the marriage relationship, but also indicates that the couple is experiencing difficulties in communicating. Their disagreement may well reflect their inability to achieve any sort of personal consensus on so-called life-styles. Such conflicts eventually erode affective bonds and engender feelings of "loss of love" and incompatability, perhaps leading the spouses to find needed affection with someone else. Being unfaithful in circumstances of increasing marital dissatisfaction is also a particularly poignant and brutal way in which to communicate basic unhappiness about the relationship.

The decision to enter into or to terminate a marriage emerges as a profoundly personal choice. The view that marriage, although a contractual association between individuals, has significant social policy implications and, therefore, warrants the assertion of a strong state regulatory interest, becomes accordingly more of a rhetorical pronouncement than a meaningful statement about the authority of the state over individuals in marriage. Even the prospect of lengthy, distasteful, and hurtful divorce proceedings will do little to bring about a reparation of shattered matrimonial expectations or undo the conviction that the investment of self in a marriage has culminated in an irremediable loss. In fact, rather than deter the parties, the occasion for legal haggling more than likely satisfies the spouses' need to make the pain of their matrimonial failure felt. The law, in effect, is powerless to abrogate or amend, and can only contain, spousal disaffection. With regard to the influence of laws and the legal system,[18] there seems to be an irreducible human element to marriage and divorce that will be neither coerced nor cajoled or abridged by the legal order's abstract conception of matrimony.

The Legal System's Failure of Accommodation

The legal system does not openly respond to the emotions experienced by divorcing spouses, ranging from disappointment and anxiety to depression, sadness, and grief, and always including anger (sometimes to the point of rage).[19] As to both its content and its procedure, the legal process attributes only a modicum of recognition to the emotional trauma that underlies the severance of affective bonds founded upon a formerly mutual trust.[20] Legal rules and procedures do not reflect the dichotomous interests in and views of marriage; they do not attempt to coalesce the objective emphasis on rights and public policy strictures with the individual's subjective emotional perception of the relationship and its breakdown.[21] The law practices a policy of simple containment grounded in a Hobbesian vision of social ordering.

In an attempt to deal with marital conflict in manageable practical terms, the legal process of divorce focuses primarily upon objective conduct and the disposition of financial matters.[22] In some jurisdictions, the law still affords the spouses the additional, although questionable, boon of assessing their respective behavior according to an external standard of fault and legal causation.[23] In most jurisdictions, a spouse has the right to dissolve the marriage either on grounds of the other spouse's specific conduct (matrimonial fault as expressed, for example, through the concepts of infidelity, cruelty, and constructive or actual abandonment), or for reasons of incompatibility (a nonfault premise), or, yet again, on a simple uncontested basis (default).[24] The courts are not meant nor equipped to provide relief in the form of therapy or counselling. From the perspective of intra- and interpersonal conflict, they merely proffer remedies for resolving "surrogate,"[25] albeit concrete, conflicts, thereby avoiding the more fundamental personal grievances of the implicated individuals.

The divorcing couple's perception of the legal setting for divorce is, in many respects, inconsonant with the objective attributes of the process of judicial adjudication. The spouses misunderstand the legal system's assessment of, and approach to, their problems and infuse their underlying personal conflicts into the legally cognizable claims.[26] The courts, then, are confronted with an emotional tug-of-war that they allow to masquerade as a set of practical concerns. In the classical circumstances of a unilateral divorce, the abandoned spouse, at a minimum, is embittered and may be prone to vindictive retaliation. The abandoning spouse, anxious to conclude and forget the relationship, will not only be resentful of legal tactics meant to frustrate a prompt discontinuance of the marriage and to establish accountability for its breakdown, but may also find in litigation a means of reprisal and a vehicle for communicating disapproval and defensive anger. In a situation where the law might see a cause of action for adultery or grounds for granting alimony or sole custody, the couple senses deeply rooted pain and a vehicle for expressing rage through recrimination.

Moreover, the "battleground" atmosphere of the courtroom devalues rationality and invites the spouses to adopt a distorted view of their situation and to engage in single-minded advocacy. The spouses' conflicts are usually exacerbated rather than attenuated by the gamesmanship of adversarial posturing.[27] Legal proceedings, in fact, become an invitation to extend the conflictual relationship and to engage in an exercise of personal vindication. Litigation is a socially acceptable means by which to portray matrimonial conflicts, to dramatize a sense of having been victimized, and to unravel the plight of a personal dilemma that could not be redressed in the reality of marriage. Protracted court actions may often be fueled by the hope that a parentified court will approve of past conduct and require the culprit to admit patent insensitivity, beseech forgiveness, and expunge the fault by acquiescing to punishment. The usual result is further acrimony—eliminating all but a forcible determination of disputes by a court of law.[28]

Judicial procedures for divorce, then, appear to operate upon the basis of fundamental incomprehension among the parties, the adjudicatory mechanism, and the subject matter of the proceeding. Despite the practical ordering function of such a structure for marital dispute resolution, the system leaves much to be desired from the perspective of humanistic priorities.

Possible Alternatives

Without compromising its essential ordering and stabilizing mission, the legal process for divorce might be supplemented by alternative mechanisms. The human complexity of divorce disputes calls for a choice of remedies. Rather than obliging spouses to deal with the breakdown of their relationship through the prism of adversarial contentiousness, alternative processes would permit them to face their emotional and practical dilemma squarely, allowing them to assume responsibility for, and a measure of control over, the conclusion of their matrimonial relationship. As a general rule, the parties should gain a sense of achievement, acceptance, and a more lucid understanding of their former relationship from such an experience. It might enhance their capacity to engage in parenting after divorce and provide them with insight as to future relationships. In addition, nonadversarial proceedings would lessen state intrusion into the couple's private life.[29]

In summary, a comprehensive remedial framework for divorce should attempt to respond more adroitly to the human character of divorce disputes and accommodate the various competing interests implicated by divorcement: the now somewhat questionable state interest in the permanency of marriage—perhaps more accurately described as an interest in a well-established and defined personal status for all citizens; the spouses' individual interest in their marriage and the rights that accompany it; the welfare of the children; and the financial and property considerations usually associated with the termination of a marriage. Such a framework should also be neutral about considerations of legal culpability. The determination of spousal guilt or innocence in regard to marriage breakdown is probably impossible to make in most cases; moreover, legal standards do not really touch upon the true causative roots of marital failure.[30] Finally, given the variety of individual circumstances in divorce, the alternative framework should provide for the greatest number of remedial options in order to respond as effectively as possible to existing dispute resolution needs.

Arbitration as an Alternative

A number of commentators[31] have advocated the use of arbitration as a substitute remedy in the area of divorce, emphasizing its dispatch, economy, and nonadversarial quality. Their recommendations have centered principally upon the inclusion of arbitral clauses in separation agreements as a means of restoring consensus among couples who initially had reached an accommodation.[32] The history of arbitration, however, reveals that its adjudicatory characteristics are particularly well-suited to the specific features of labor and commercial controversies.[33] The proposals for divorce arbitration usually are part of a wider consideration of alternative mechanisms. As a result, they focus primarily upon the need to replace the adversarial process with noncontentious proceedings and fail to pay sufficient attention to the sui generis nature of arbitral adjudication.

Recommendations that arbitral techniques be applied to issues of marital dissolution need to be anchored in a thorough analysis of the specific character of the arbitral remedy, creating the necessary foundation by which to evaluate whether arbitration will respond to the singular anatomy of divorce disputes and will eliminate the deficiencies of the present process. Given that it usually requires consensus and that it is an adjudicatory (rather than conciliatory) mechanism, arbitration—as traditionally understood—may have a very limited vocation as an extrajudicial means of resolving divorce disputes.

Contrasting Commercial and Divorce Disputes

The characteristics of arbitral adjudication coincide with the basic disposition of a cohesive and interdependent commercial community, bolstering its pragmatic ethic and economic self-interest.[34] Merchants do not share lawyerly concerns about the litigation process. Adversarial wrestling for truth rubs coarsely against the grain of good faith and arms' length dealings and might undermine the present or future basis for commercial relationships. The legal resolution of disputes becomes a disruptive entanglement, insensitive to the primary commercial concern for transactional costs, time, the value of opportunities, and the need to reach expedient accommodations. The possibility always exists that, even were the law governing the merits of the dispute tailored to reflect commercial dispositions, judges might misconstrue the guiding commercial norms that should govern the outcome of the dispute. The proffer of expertise, flexibility, and expedited determinations through the vehicle of arbitral adjudication allows the special interests of commerce to be mirrored in a form of dispute resolution that can be voluntarily consented to and that is likely to reach final conclusions.

Despite some superficial similarities, both the context and content of domestic relations disputes stand in stark contrast to their commercial analogues. In the commercial setting, parties engage in transactions for profit, and the interests of society usually are served by the pursuit and acquisition of wealth. When the emergence of a dispute disrupts the venture, the resulting damage can be measured and the object of the dispute defined in terms of money—the initial and principal aim of the transaction. The conflict is predominantly, if not exclusively, pecuniary in character, and the ultimate consideration financial in nature: which party will absorb the cost of the economically ill-fated venture as a cost of doing business. However aggressively merchants may pursue their self-interest in resolving the dispute, they nonetheless realize that they must continue to operate in the commercial community and pay allegiance to its pragmatic code of conduct.[35]

In the circumstances of divorce, there is no such code of conduct, nor the possibility of a continued conjugal association. Moreover, marriage is not usually a venture entered into for profit, and the losses that accompany divorcement are emotional, not monetary. To be sure, marriage and divorce entail significant financial consequences for the spouses, and society has a legitimate interest in seeking to protect the welfare of a divorcing couple's offspring, to effect an equitable division of the common marital assets and liabilities, and to provide means through alimony of readapting a disadvantaged spouse to a status of economic viability or providing maintenance where economic rehabilitation is no longer feasible. Society's treatment of the couple as a business entity in the process of liquidation, however, is an artificial way of measuring the spouses' emotional loss in terms of financial detriment.[36] Whereas money is the real object of disputes between merchants, it becomes a mistaken symbol for divorcing spouses—the pelf for their pain, humiliation, anger, and latent psychological conflicts.[37]

Even in parenting circumstances, divorcing couples are a deteriorating (rather than a cohesive) partnership; they are no longer inspired by a consensus view born of mutual self-interest nor do they subscribe to a functional modus vivendi attributing primacy to pragmatic accommodation rather than disputation. Finally, commercial arbitrators are usually merchant peers whose expertise comes from experience. In a divorce situation, it would be difficult to find such peers for adjudicatory purposes.[38]

Other Obstacles

Given the usually consensual nature of arbitration, the success of an arbitral remedy in divorce is largely, if not entirely, dependent upon the disposition and motivation of the couple. On the one hand, an agreement to arbitrate nonstatus disputes is not likely to be forthcoming from spouses whose relationship remains emotionally tense and dominated by disagreement. On the other hand, spouses capable of collaborating on the selection of such an adjudicatory mechanism probably do not need it. They could reach an out-of-court settlement with little difficulty, it seems, through pretrial negotiations. These considerations suggest that arbitration, at least in its consensual form, would probably become a token remedy and would not really respond to any actual needs of divorcing couples.

The implementation of a divorce arbitration process is likely to generate other problems. Although conceived primarily as a consensual form of adjudication, arbitration can be made mandatory by legislative fiat.[39] Provision for compulsory recourse to divorce arbitration, presumably for nonstatus disputes,[40] would necessitate a legislative determination in the enabling statute as to whether resulting awards are binding or nonbinding. An award that contains a nonbinding determination does not need to be subject to any rigorous form of judicial scrutiny for its enforcement; in order to achieve any sort of adjudicatory effect, both parties must concur in the result. As a matter of practicality, this compulsory alternative remedy would do no more than test the mettle of the parties' disagreement against a first barrier.[41]

Compulsory binding arbitration would, of course, constitute a more efficient and effective remedial process.[42] Here, courts would scrutinize awards at the stage of enforcement simply because they contain a final or nearly final disposition regarding the parties' rights and obligations. The critical question evidently centers upon the magnitude of the scrutiny to be exercised. Too extensive a form of review would jeopardize the viability and autonomy of the arbitral process as an alternative process of adjudication by making its determinations completely vulnerable to judicial second-guessing. Laxity of review may well trigger constitutional challenges on due process grounds.[43] Given these considerations, compulsory arbitration is unlikely to be functional in the context of domestic relations disputes. Society, acting through the legislative will, cannot realistically dictate rationality and self-imposed order where parties are determined and have an unfortunate but basic right to act otherwise. The experience in other, admittedly distinct yet relevant, areas of dispute resolution[44] illustrates that the successful arbitration of conflicts is achieved when recourse to the alternative remedial framework is voluntary, agreed-upon, and founded upon a group consensus that supports the process.

Moreover, according to the classical tenets of arbitration law,[45] when the subject matter of a dispute pertains to matters of public policy, it cannot be submitted to arbitration. Consequently, a couple seeking a divorce could not empower an arbitrator to render an award declaring that the couple is divorced; matters of status and capacity have always been deemed to be within the ambit of public policy. Recourse to arbitration, however, could be had to resolve the incidental disputes that attend a change of status and over which the parties retain contractual control, namely, financial claims relating to alimony and the division of the spouses' common assets and liabilities.[46] Also, the legal system is likely to limit considerably the authority of arbitral tribunals concerning child custody matters (the right to custody, visitation, and support)[47] because the welfare of a minor third party is directly at issue. In effect, the scope of application of a divorce arbitration process (in terms of arbitrability) may be quite restricted, making it a remedy of qualified utility.

The essential question of whether divorce arbitration, if it is to be adopted as a substitute adjudicatory model, can or should achieve substantive predictability about results also needs to be addressed.[48] The predictability of results on the basis of law may not be possible or even desirable in the context of divorce arbitration. Under one possible variant, the divorcing couple could require the arbitrator to reach a determination according to the usually applicable rules of law. The couple would thereby have placed some restriction upon the arbitrator, guaranteeing to some extent that the resulting award would not be completely whimsical. Such an approach presents a number of evident problems. First, it reduces the incentive to have recourse to arbitration. Why would the couple invoke arbitration instead of filing a court action if the only advantage is procedural flexibility? If the couple is seeking this sole advantage or wishes simply to have a court proceeding in all but name, then their engagement in arbitration is probably ill-conceived. Second, divorce arbitrators may not be trained jurists. An effective process, for instance, would probably have mental health professionals as well as attorneys serve as arbitrators; obliging psychologists or family therapists to render an award according to law may riddle the process with problems and eventually reveal itself to be unrealistic and unsatisfactory.

Third, a ruling on the basis of law would probably compel the issuance of a written legal opinion along with the award (the latter being merely a statement of conclusions about the issues). Otherwise, no ascertainable basis would exist for the ruling, and the attempt to create a standard of accountability or substantive objectivity would fail. In all likelihood, such a practice would invite court supervision of the merits. If arbitral tribunals were to apply the relevant state law allegedly in conformity with judicial standards, the courts of that jurisdiction might feel obligated, for reasons of public policy, to supervise the arbitral determination. The judicial confirmation of reasoned awards might lead to a system of persuasive or binding precedents for subsequent divorce arbitrations. In effect, divorce arbitration could become nearly equivalent to judicial adjudication, robbing the alternative process of much of its raison d'être. Parties, then, would still be faced with the possibility that the logic of the law might command an outcome out of keeping with an equitable appraisement of their circumstances.

Because arbitral tribunals receive their authority from a private and not a public source, they are not bound to apply the governing law unless the parties so provide. For example, in commercial arbitration, arbitral tribunals usually rule on the basis of a flexible substantive predicate (taking commercial usage and trade practices into account) and rarely, if ever (at least in domestic American practice), render legally reasoned written opinions to support their award.[49] Given the basic purpose for invoking arbitration, a more appropriate substantive predicate for the arbitral adjudication of domestic relations disputes may reside in requiring arbitrators to rule not according to established legal rules or decisional law, but rather according to a basic respect for law.[50] Under this general standard, arbitrators would seek guidance from, rather than apply, the governing law, modifying or disregarding the latter where—in their estimation—it conflicts with considerations of equity or the basic interests of justice in the given case.[51]

Arbitrators given a malleable substantive adjudicatory predicate would have large authority in determining disputes. Paradoxically, having arbitrators rule according to a general substantive standard that merges legal and equitable considerations, in some respects, might make awards with written reasons and accompanying judicial supervision more rather than less necessary. Potential abuse, however, could be avoided through the careful selection of the arbitrators. This choice may be left to the parties or to the arbitral institution under which the proceeding is organized. If to the latter, some form of legislative regulation of the institution or certification of arbitrators might be necessary. The need for court supervision could thereby be eliminated entirely or restricted to basic procedural concerns. Moreover, integrating flexible substantive standards into the process to deal with financial matters may be entirely appropriate given the nature of the rights and interests at stake.[52]

The drawbacks to this recommendation are, however, evident. It leaves the parties vulnerable to the arbitral tribunal's discretion on matters of substance (making the trusting of arbitrators by the parties the backbone of the process), and it might encourage tribunals to reach "pie-splitting" determinations.[53] Either result may significantly compromise the integrity of the process and lessen its viability as an alternative adjudicatory mechanism.

Finally, the integration of lawyers into the divorce arbitration process could also present difficulties. An adjudicatory mechanism which, as a general rule rather than as a matter of party agreement, excluded the right to legal representation might be too fragile—as a matter of principle—to dispense even a private form of justice and could well be constitutionally suspect. Although the participation of attorneys could, on the one hand, increase the quality of the adjudication and provide for the better protection of rights, their accustomed-to role in adversarial litigation could, on the other hand, transform the arbitration into a privately instituted court proceeding. Lawyerly dispositions would need to be modified to fit the contours of flexible adjudication in which the brokering of disputes is achieved principally through equitable accommodation. The parties' objective in having recourse to an alternative mechanism should moderate the ethic of litigation. Eventually, a divorce arbitration bar might emerge, lessening considerably the inherent tension between adversarial training and arbitral flexibility.

An Assessment

The cardinal misgiving normally associated with any proposal regarding the incorporation of an alternative dispute mechanism in the domestic relations area is that implementation requires, at a threshold, a minimum level of agreement on the part of the divorcing couple.[54] Despite the commonplace disaffection with divorce proceedings, some question exists whether spouses experiencing a matrimonial breakdown can cooperate sufficiently to agree upon a substitute adjudicatory process. The temptation to act on emotions and to resort to what is known and accepted, to trust the courts, may well be irresistible. Providing for compulsory divorce arbitration would not resolve the problem. Substantial constitutional objections can be levied at such a scheme, and spouses who are coerced to arbitrate can undermine the process through dilatory tactics and other maneuvers. Despite its inherent fragility, consensual arbitration seems to be the only form of arbitral adjudication that can be proffered as an alternative.

Balancing the gains against the losses that can be derived from the recourse to divorce arbitration is the only feasible way in which to measure the suitability of the process as an alternative mechanism. Divorcing couples might be attracted to arbitration for a number of reasons. Procedural and substantive flexibility (as well as the factor of privacy) should lessen overt animosity and attenuate even its covert expression, allowing for a quicker and less costly resolution of disputes. Moreover, parties could benefit from the psychological training of certain arbitrators; determinations could reflect the substantial expertise of fully qualified professionals who serve as arbitrators. Finally, the arbitral tribunal would not be pressed by administrative imperatives to hear other cases or to otherwise dispose of a crowded docket.

The arbitral alternative also has real drawbacks. Depending upon its legislative definition for divorce, the doctrine of arbitrability, for example, may substantially restrict the scope of arbitral jurisdiction. The limited arbitrability of divorce disputes would, in turn, probably call for a fairly simple and economical divorce arbitration framework in order to maintain the attractiveness of the alternative mechanism, increasing the likelihood that rights might be compromised and making the mechanism further suspect. The modest utility of the mechanism would heighten the pressure on arbitrators to reach determinations that accommodate both parties, rather than to adjudicate. At this point, resolving divorce disputes through arbitral adjudication appears to offer little more than achieving an out-of-court settlement. If a settlement is the initial objective and can be obtained, divorcing couples are probably ill-advised to agree to arbitrate and subject themselves to the systemic and procedural complications of a novel process.

In the final analysis, the chief attribute of divorce arbitration would be to provide a flexible, private, nonadversarial setting for dispute resolution that lessens the hostility between the parties. The complexity and difficulties that accompany the establishment of such a remedial framework, as well as the development of a coordinate relationship between it and the court system, seem to outweigh its principal advantage. If the objective is to promote rationality among divorcing couples about dispute resolution and to avoid public proceedings as well as the formalities and intricacies of law, it would seem preferable to eliminate any adjudicatory character to the alternative framework. Arguably, divorce arbitration should remain available as an option for couples who want to dispense with adversarial histrionics, but who are unable or unwilling to communicate effectively enough to reach a settlement. Transforming existing court procedures for divorce into a type of arbitral mechanism may also, in fact, be a more effective way to achieve humanistic dispute resolution ends.

Mediation: A Nonadjudicatory Alternative Mechanism

Its Potential and Basic Character

When the breakdown of a marriage is at issue, traditional adjudicatory processes, whether judicial or arbitral in character, are generally deficient. They are stymied in their effectiveness by an incapacity to address fully the emotional dimension of the controversies surrounding matrimonial dissolution. A more significant remedial proposition resides perhaps in the adoption of a nonadjudicatory alternative process that would redistribute decision-making authority in divorce, emphasizing individual rationality and responsibility in matrimonial dispute resolution and, concomitantly, reducing the role of state regulation.

Divorce mediation[55] can function as an appendage to the legal system, providing divorcing couples with a structured opportunity to reach a consensual agreement on the financial and parenting consequences that will accompany the eventual modification of their matrimonial status. Because matters of status and capacity are of public policy, the formal pronouncement of divorce remains within the jurisdictional province of the courts. Mediation bears some resemblance to arbitration—for example, sessions are conducted by a neutral third party in a private, nonadversarial setting— but differs from it and any other form of recourse for resolving matrimonial disputes in a number of important essentials.

Although it combines features of both processes, mediation is neither an adjudicatory nor a therapeutic remedy.[56] It has an extensive cross-cultural history as a dispute resolution mechanism.[57] Mediation endeavors to achieve the pragmatic end of adjudication—the finality of determinations—by attending simultaneously to the intertwining practical and emotional dimensions of marital conflict. Whereas arbitrators reach a binding disposition of disputes and hold the authority to do so from the inception of the proceeding, mediation yields a binding result only when the spouses themselves have arrived at a written agreement.

The various divorce mediation models[58] have a number of salient advantages over judicial (or even arbitral) divorce proceedings. The time and cost of the duration of the mediation process are reasonably predictable and quantifiable; usually, mediators' fees consist of a fixed hourly rate, and the participants can reach an agreement within seven to ten one-hour sessions that take place over the course of two to three months.[59] Because the procedure is nonadversarial, obtrusive legalistic considerations—for example, intricate procedural embroglios, the reconciliation of precedents, choice-of-law, and interpretative concerns relating to whether and what type of substantive law governs the merits—are eliminated. Although subsequent, albeit limited, court supervision of the mediated agreement would apply, and the document would be required to identify the relevant issues, track the basic contours of the forum's domestic relations law, and align itself with public policy imperatives, the spouses' agreement over what is fair and just in their particular situation basically is the controlling standard.

Divorcing couples with minor children should be especially attracted to mediation because it safeguards their offspring from undergoing the trauma of litigation and allows them, and not the judicial organ of the state, to determine what is in the best interests of their children.[60] Mediation can teach parents to communicate on more businesslike terms and to learn how to compromise. Mediation merges well with the preference for joint custody of children by divorced parents, the substantive standard that applies in an increasing number of jurisdictions.[61] It also complements statutory provisions for no-fault divorce that exist in some form in a majority of states.[62] Divorce mediation has the considerable advantage of addressing each case on an ad hoc basis within the confines of a private and structured framework; in every instance, the general form and structural phases of the process are molded to the specificity of the individual situation. Although paced and guided by a mediator, the spouses retain ultimate control over the process. Because the result is a product of personal involvement and is largely self-determined, initial and continuing compliance with the mediated agreement should be facilitated, lessening the possibility of a reconsideration or litigation.[63]

This humanistic design explains mediation's appeal and its potential viability for achieving justice in divorce matters. Mediation's chief recommendation resides in its comprehensive response to the dispute resolution needs of divorcing couples. Rather than ignoring or simply seeking to contain the emotional substratum of marriage breakdown, the mediation process addresses it head-on and proffers the spouses an opportunity to lessen their feeling of unbounded upheaval, contravening the view that the tumult of their predicament commands a warring solution. Through mediation, divorcing couples can gain control over the termination of their relationship and become the architects of their own destiny.

Forsaking the Old Creed

The chief advantages of divorce mediation also constitute its principal frailty. The implementation of a nonjudicial and nonadjudicatory mechanism for dealing with matrimonial breakdown, even as nothing more than an appendage to the legal process, would compel a reassessment of society's conception of divorce.[64] A dispute resolution process tailored to purely individual needs that operates nearly exclusively upon an ad hoc personal standard of justice and promotes primarily the right of self-determination in family matters minimizes considerably the state regulatory interest, reducing it to a formalistic and supervisory role. Its prescription not only would require legislative approbation—in all likelihood, conferred with some initial reluctance[65]—but would also demand that potential participants demystify their thinking about the meaning of the family, the function of the legal system, and the personal implications of marital disharmony.

For divorcing couples and for society at large, a willingness to be educated, which may provoke feelings of embarrassment and fear, and to accept and experience therapeutic methods, are indispensable to the effective incorporation of divorce mediation in the arsenal of dispute resolution processes. The quest for vindication and self-destructive vengeance before a court would succumb to a more poised perception of personal loss — that the marital relationship is no longer viable and, despite the painful emotions associated with termination, that necessary practical concerns need to be confronted and resolved in the solid terrain of human rationality. Divorce would no longer imply a dismantling of the family under the aegis of legal principles and procedures, but rather a restructuring of the family unit in light of the emergence of a new personal reality between the spouses.

Legislative Compulsion or Personal Volition

In theory, the social benefits of divorce mediation might be so considerable that mandatory recourse to it would be warranted in all cases, at least at the outset of each case. In the interests of fairness and to avoid constitutional challenges, mandatory mediation would not be binding and would not oblige spouses to reach a mediated agreement. Rather, it would require the couple to engage in a minimum number of mediation sessions, allowing them to evaluate for themselves the viability of the remedy in their circumstances.[66]

Even with legislative approval and a moderate command, however, divorce mediation must remain inextricably tied to the willingness of divorcing couples to forego the traditional pattern of litigation and to assume responsibility for their own lives. No matter how skillful or resourceful, mediators cannot supply spouses with the necessary minimum motivation. A divorcing couple or spouse, loathe to accept the finality of termination and having feelings of rage and bitterness, may need the constraining effect of courtroom procedures and an external frame of reference to reach a disposition of practical issues. In these circumstances, compelling participation in divorce mediation may well end in failure.[67] Couples may view mandatory divorce mediation as a perfunctory and irksome delay to having their day in court, finding in the therapeutic orientation ineffectual platitudes at best and, at worse, unwarranted intrusiveness. They may also misperceive the mediator's role as an adjudicatory one, and doubt his or her ability and competence to deal with the concrete legal and financial issues that confront them. Finally, regardless of whether the mediation process is chosen or imposed, spouses may desire to have the procedural and substantive guarantees and the eventual finality that accompany recourse to judicial adjudication.

Choosing Mediators

Assuming that a social and individual reevaluation of divorce could gradually be undertaken and that divorcing couples would espouse an ethic of personal accountability for their lives, important practical problems relating to the implementation of mediation need to be addressed. Given the significance of the family issues and personal rights at stake, the selection and certification of mediators become a critical concern.[68] Like the process they serve, divorce mediators are still in the making. Ideally, their training should mirror the sui generis approach and comprehensive objectives of divorce mediation. Mediators need to combine disparate, somewhat heteroclitic skills: a thorough awareness of the legal framework for divorce (including the statutory and judicial disposition of substantive issues and the art of brokering practical disputes) and an equally solid grounding in the therapeutic techniques of communication (the art of brokering emotional conflicts).

Currently, the corps of mediators[69] is comprised principally of mental health professionals, such as psychiatric social workers, family therapists, psychologists, and psychiatrists, and, to a much lesser extent, attorneys who presumably specialize in domestic relations. The techniques of therapy that facilitate and foster communication obviously are central to the divorce mediation process; consequently, mental health professionals, already certified in that expertise, may be best prepared and disposed to assume the role of mediator. The process, however, implicates family and social interests, implies an at least indirect entrustment of rights, and embraces rationality primarily to resolve practical marital disputes, thereby rendering an appreciation of legal concerns equally vital. Ultimately, the outcome of the mediation process must in some fashion be integrated into, and validated by, the legal system's ethic of basic fairness over procedure and substance. The deficiency created by having the predominant group of existing mediators come from the mental health professions could be remedied in a number of ways, most of which call for more substantial attorney participation.

Having attorneys interact with the divorce mediation process in their usual adversarial capacity is perilous and, in fact, threatens to compromise the viability of the process. Unless they espouse the dispute resolution values embodied in the divorce mediation, lawyers are likely to become a dysfunctional element in the process, not only jealous of its intrusion into their domain of competence, but also unable to adapt professionally to a situation of controlled and defused, rather than polarized and contentious, conflict.

At the same time, the rights at issue and the interests of society demand some lawyerly presence and participation. Determining that lawyers should be excluded because their professional demeanor and conduct would denature the character of the process, and that psychologically oriented mediators should simply make do with the legal implications of divorce disputes, even when the participants have knowingly consented, would place a greater onus upon the courts to supervise the mediation procedure and result. Possible judicial intervention or rejection may well undermine the emerging viability of divorce mediation, clouding it in a haze of indeterminacy and an appearance of incompetence. A dual-mediator model, joining mental health professionals and attorneys as mediators, may well be a more sagacious response to these acknowledged difficulties.

The advantages of the dual-mediator model over the single, psychologically oriented mediator model can be quite considerable. Faithful to the intended interdisciplinary approach of the process, the dual-mediator model holds a much greater guarantee of professional competence in both aspects of the mediation approach. Moreover, with a team of two mediators, it becomes possible to achieve a gender balance in the process, thereby eliminating the possibility, which exists with a single mediator, that one of the spouses might feel alienated because the other spouse and the mediator are of the same sex.[70] Having the legal and psychological orientations coalesce directly in practice might well lead to a more rapid and less tentative definition of mediation's particular professional stature and social purpose. It may also yield the not inconsiderable advantage of minimizing interprofessional competition and support the type of reeducation indispensable to achieve a proper integration of the divorce mediation process in society. Finally, the necessary linkage and rapport with the judicial process should be facilitated.

Team mediation does present its own set of disadvantages. For example, it may increase the cost and may add to the number of mediation sessions. It presumes that the tensions among different professional trainings can be reconciled through personal collaboration between individuals who will develop a healthy respect for each other's differing professional concerns and approaches. Team mediation also assumes that fully incorporating a lawyerly component in the process, unlike having lawyers stand at the periphery of a single, psychologically oriented mediator model, will not disrupt the workability of the process. This may require that the attorneys who participate gain some formal understanding of the mental health profession. Finally, team mediation that includes an attorney trained as a mediator complicates considerably the deontological considerations that apply to the activity of being a mediator. Individual professionals who engage in team mediation should be guided and governed by a code of ethical conduct that transcends their respective professions and regulates directly the

| 175

unique professional services they render. In addition, attorneys who participate in team mediation might be confronted with allegations of unethical conduct in that they are simultaneously representing conflicting interests and encouraging an unauthorized person to engage in the practice of law.[71]

Whether a suitable pairing of mental health and legal professionals can be achieved is largely dependent upon the happenstance of personality and circumstances. Both types of professionals should receive the same training in mediation. It is not unreasonable to assume, however, that some legal practitioners have gradually developed the view that adversarial litigation may be inappropriate in some divorce cases and through their practice have gained some awareness of, and sensitivity to, the psychological dimension of their clients' disputes. By the same token, confidence in rationality as a means of treating matrimonial discord and other family disorders cannot ignore that emotional conflicts and their resolution often have serious practical implications affecting legal rights and social interests. By definition, a competent therapist should not fail to acknowledge and appreciate that aspect of patients' problems. Having lawyerly skills function in the context of a more humanistic dispute resolution framework and extending the influence of therapy to the more material concerns of individuals should have nearly universal appeal.

Making an Appraisal

Available documentation[72] demonstrates that divorce mediation remains largely an experimental phenomenon. The process and its implementation are still too novel to draw any definite statistical conclusions about workability and effectiveness. The potential systemic deficiencies of team mediation specifically, and of divorce mediation generally, could be cured by reference to a set of three factors: legislative approval, court supervision, and party consent.

The deontological issues surrounding attorney participation in divorce mediation present perhaps the most difficult problems to resolve.[73] Until special standards have been defined for mediation practice, full disclosure[74] to participants concerning the purpose, goal, and approach of the process and the concept of neutral family law lawyering[75] may constitute the most expedient and reasonable device by which to accommodate the various competing interests: the ethical requirements of the legal profession; the protection of the rights and expectations of the consuming public; the desirability of promoting alternative mechanisms for resolving divorce disputes; and the developmental needs of the divorce mediation process.

Proposals for divorce mediation do not suffer greatly from accusations of atavism. Despite their emphasis upon the individual resolution of personal disputes, however, they are not meant to dismantle the existing apparatus for justice in domestic relations controversies. The challenge is to admit inadequacies where they exist, mold present professional abilities to suit the task, and devise appropriate processes in light of an accurate reading of the reality of divorce disputes. None of this can be achieved without systemic consensus and cooperation or agreement upon the overriding social goal. The sophistication of the current apparatus will be transformed into a different type of refinement, not a decentralized and rudimentary method for achieving justice.

In fact, the most formidable obstacle to alternative dispute resolution through divorce mediation is neither systemic, professional, nor conceptual in character. Legislatures will ultimately allow individuals to decide their own matrimonial destiny; courts would rather not deal with divorce cases; and the implicated professions eventually will accept the conflict resolution ideas that underlie the mediation process. As with arbitration, the greatest resistance will probably emanate from divorcing couples who may be unsuited for any but a litigious resolution of their marital disputes.

Mediation appears to respond primarily to younger, well-educated, usually professional and materially comfortable couples and parents who are accepting of psychological analysis and thinking.[76] As a result, mediation may well become a remedial option exclusively for middle- and upper-middle-class divorce. Any wider vocation may be confined to child custody controversies.[77] In addition, mediation works best for parties skilled at verbal communication. People unaccustomed to discussing their problems may not succeed in a process that requires them to say what they feel. In such a situation, they may defer to the mediator and ultimately may become dissatisfied with the outcome.[78]

It is also generally recognized that mediation requires the parties to be in roughly equal bargaining positions.[79] If either party is significantly intimidated by the other, the process cannot work. Many mediation centers, for example, refuse to handle spouse abuse cases because they represent the extreme of unequal power situations.[80]

Mediators may recommend counseling or psychotherapy in such cases, but the divorce itself is sent back to the judicial process. Another situation unconducive to successful mediation emerges when one spouse (usually the wife) assumes a martyr role in the hope of achieving a reconciliation. In such a case, the self-deprecating spouse is likely to accede to all demands and end up with an unfavorable settlement.[81] Although comprehensive statistics are not available, the number of spouse abuse cases and those in which the spouses are otherwise in unequal bargaining positions suggest that mediation may be far from a panacea.

Individual spousal dispositions also are a crucial factor. What should mediators do with willing but particularly obdurate participants who persistently disagree? Who should decide when an attempt at mediation has failed? Should the legal system require all divorcing couples, especially those who are parents, to participate in a mandatory number of sessions? Might a central court of mediation be established to address the foregoing questions? What about conflicts that arise regarding the implementation of the mediated agreement[82]—is court action necessary, or should the agreement contain an arbitration or mediation clause to deal with such problems? Although ideally structured to achieve qualitative dispute resolution in divorce matters, mediation—about recourse, pursuit, and finality—places a necessary but precarious reliance upon the willingness of individuals to espouse a rational course of conduct in the middle of disagreement.

Judicial Arbitration

The general dissatisfaction with adversarial litigation in divorce, the sheer number of matrimonial breakups, and the physical burden divorce places upon the judicial process should prompt legislatures to make voluntary or mandatory alternative mechanisms available to divorcing couples. An effective social framework for divorce should encourage recourse to negotiations conducted by party representatives and acceptance of settlement agreements. When estranged spouses are unable to settle their differences through attorneys, they still do not need to be thrown into the litigious fray. Although mediation would be the preferred extrajudicial alternative, it is not for everyone. A specialized form of judicial adjudication, therefore, might be employed when the truculent, uncompromising reality of disagreement persists.

These specialized divorce courts would merge coercive judicial powers with the procedural and substantive flexibility of arbitration: a form of "judicial arbitration." In short, when coercive judicial authority is required in divorce, a sense of rationality must still predominate. Marital dissolution thus accomplished through a nonadversarial judicial procedure would be better for the couple, their children, and for society generally. It should also contribute to reducing judicial caseloads.

It might be argued that judicial arbitration is no different from what an enlightened judge might do under the present process. Rather than achieving systemic change, judicial arbitration merely adds another layer to an already complex judicial mechanism. Nonetheless, although the present process may have enlightened participants, the adversarial ethic does not allow their attitude to be fully integrated into dispute resolution procedures. There are no guarantees that these more realistic, enlightened attitudes will be shared or applied. Moreover, it is unfair to have the parties' fate depend upon whether they fortuitously hire the appropriate attorneys and have their case heard by the right judge. The proposed system calls for the pervasive adoption of a new dispute resolution ethic and adjudicatory methodology in divorce and requires the abandonment of adversarial litigation.

Arguably, changes in the applicable substantive law might achieve similar, perhaps better, results without a modification of existing procedures.[83] Fixed rules of law, such as the primary caretaker concept in custody matters,[84] so the debate goes, might eliminate the uncertainty of determination and the opportunity for contentious argument. The epistemology of legal training, however, promotes semantic ambiguity as a fundamental truth. Ironclad predicates are, in fact, antithetical to lawyerly dispositions and adversarial adjudication. The irreducible insufficiencies of the current process and the private, emotional character of the conflicts compel the recourse to self-determination. Alternative mechanisms must be advanced as the primary remedy, and an arbitral judicial process seen as a last resort.

Nonadjudicatory Options

The first stage of the recommended judicial arbitration framework would be triggered when either one of the spouses, or the couple, files a petition for divorce with the state trial court. After the tolling of a statutorily prescribed time limit (either six or 12 months), either spouse, upon motion, could obtain a divorce. In the interval, the divorcing spouses—at their option—could simply wait out the required time for obtaining a divorce, engage in counselling with a view to reconciliation, or attempt to settle the loose ends of their dissolving union. Although unlikely, some jurisdictions might require the divorcing spouses to attend a few counselling or conciliation sessions during this waiting period. Legislatures could either establish a publicly funded marriage counselling and conciliation process, designate approved private counselors and conciliators, or have the couple undertake the initiative completely on their own.

Assuming basic agreement on termination and a sufficient level of rational cooperation among the spouses, the proposed framework should allow couples to engage in mediation during the waiting period. Some legislative regulation of the mediation process should apply— for example, rules relating to the qualification of court- or privately-appointed mediators, basic procedural and substantive standards for mediation, and indications of whether single or team mediation models apply. In light of the central importance of party dispositions in mediation, all disputes, even those relating to child custody, should be submitted to mediation only when there is clear spousal willingness to explore and experiment with the remedy. Coercive participation is essentially antithetical to the principles underlying mediation. When the spouses invoke mediation, the role of the court should be limited to the formal granting of the divorce decree and approval of the mediated agreement.

If the spouses are unable to reconcile and unwilling to engage in mediation, they could authorize their respective attorneys to negotiate a settlement regarding the practical incidents of their eventual divorce. To achieve maximum efficiency, attorneys who engage in such divorce negotiations should be compelled to operate within the established time limit for obtaining a divorce. The use of negotiation through legal representation, akin in many respects to pretrial settlement, can be especially beneficial because it allows attorneys to function in their usual capacities and makes few demands upon the court system. Under this approach, a court would simply issue the requested decree and assure the fairness of the negotiated agreement.

Judicial Arbitration

Assuming that conciliation, mediation, and negotiation are unavailing, recourse could be had to judicial arbitration. In this setting, arbitration would not function as a consensual and private form of justice initiated by party agreement, but rather as an institutionalized form of flexible adjudication. Legislatures could institute a process of judicial arbitration for all divorce cases not pliant to other dispute resolution means. The procedural restraints on the judge-arbitrator would consist almost exclusively of allowing each party an equal and fair opportunity to present its case. Ordinarily, such arbitral court proceedings should be regulated by a time limit rule (say, three months from the date the divorce is granted). The time limit could be extended to a maximum of six months at the court's discretion when the court finds truly exceptional circumstances to exist. In some respects, the judge would still function as a passive referee between the parties, but the flexible procedure should allow the judge to control the quantum of discovery and to minimize delay through procedural tactics.

To expedite and simplify matters and conserve judicial resources, the spouses might be required to reach an agreement on the practical concerns as a condition precedent to the granting of a divorce. After all, the divorcing couple has had the time and a number of opportunities to achieve consensual agreement. Postponing the resolution of such matters, at the very least, could give rise to problems of proof. The immediate clarification of the estranged spouses' financial and property rights might prevent the unwitting or intentional duping of third parties and the litigious morass that usually follows. Moreover, the spouse upon whom a divorce is imposed would probably immediately initiate a suit for property division, alimony, and child support and custody in an effort to retaliate. Although the consolidation of the actions would delay the possibility of remarriage, it would do so only by three or six months. Even in circumstances of truly difficult disagreement, the judge-arbitrator could interpret a spouse's failure to agree as vindictive and dilatory. Rather than find that exceptional circumstances exist and prolong the proceeding, the court could rule that such conduct amounts to a breach of the duty to adjudicate in good faith and take the party's lack of cooperation into account in its judgment.

Joining the actions, however, may prove to be unduly coercive —an excessive compromise of rights that undermines the integrity of the dispute resolution framework. In addition to creating an incentive for the abandoned spouse to extort an excessive property or alimony settlement from the other spouse by threatening to delay the latter's remarriage, consolidation may associate the granting of a divorce so closely with financial issues as to inflame the debate surrounding practical concerns. It would also eliminate the possibility that the passage of time and a process of attrition might defuse the situation, providing a type of default remedy. These concerns argue for the adoption of a less draconian rule that allows the court to grant a divorce once the statutory period has tolled, but also requires the court to rule provisionally and set a hearing date (under the time limit rule) for outstanding practical differences.

Procedural and evidentiary rules governing judicial arbitral proceedings would be general and flexible in character. For example, each party would have a right to be represented by legal counsel; there would be a right to call witnesses and to engage in cross-examination; the parties would be allowed to present whatever evidence they deem necessary to establish their case. After an initial hearing, if both parties agree, the judge could reach a determination exclusively on the basis of a written record. The arbitral court could call any witnesses it deems necessary or have recourse to experts for advice on technical determinations. Again, a party's lack of cooperation could amount to a breach of the duty to adjudicate in good faith and could be taken into account in the final ruling. A rather diffuse sense of procedural fairness would be the governing rule.

Given their general character, the equitable application of domestic relations legal rules by a judicial arbitral tribunal would not be out of keeping with the results that presently obtain. For example, in a child custody dispute, a domestic relations judge sitting as a judicial arbitrator would rule in a fashion similar to an ordinary court of law, applying the best interests of the child standard. Similar results are also likely in alimony determinations. Today, in most jurisdictions, alimony is a purely financial matter involving considerations of need, ability to pay, and economic rehabilitation. A judge-arbitrator could resolve alimony disputes under the general guidelines of the currently applicable statutes. The allocation and distribution of common marital assets and liabilities might present greater problems. Some jurisdictions have elaborate laws governing marital property division. A court sitting as an arbitral tribunal could be empowered to apply established rules with a regard to equity and fairness. Such a standard comports with the adjudicatory standards applying in most domestic and international arbitrations, namely, that the tribunal rule according to a basic respect for law.

Given its public jurisdictional authority, a court exercising arbitral authority would render a judicial judgment, not an arbitral award. The usual standard of a merits review would apply to the arbitral court judgment. Unless the parties agree to a waiver, the possibility of appellate review would require the judge-arbitrator to render a reasoned award stating the court's conclusions on the merits and articulating succinctly the reasoning that underlies those conclusions. Appellate courts, ruling according to arbitral adjudicatory standards, would not disturb the judgment below without a finding of manifest procedural unfairness or a basic disregard of law. This standard, although it limits the right of appeal, currently applies in most states for domestic relations matters and reflects the unique vantage point of trial courts on the dispute, the witnesses, and the parties. The application of such a standard in a process of judicial arbitration, therefore, would not compromise basic rights.

In light of the flexible substantive predicate to be applied by arbitral courts, legislatures—in an effort to allay concern about the possible compromise of substantive legal rights—might oblige them to sit as a panel of three judges that would reach its determinations by majority vote. Although dissenting or concurring opinions could be allowed, the precedential value of rulings should be limited. Most substantive issues should be resolved (arguably, as they are presently) on an ad hoc basis, patterned upon the particular circumstances of the individual case. Moreover, legislatures might require judges or other professionals sitting on such panels to have special qualifications. A typical panel of three members could consist of the elected or appointed domestic relations judge in the jurisdiction, sitting as president of the tribunal, an attorney, and a mental health professional. Such procedural complication, although not unduly burdensome, may, however, be counterproductive in terms of time and the efficiency of adjudication. Given that the present system functions with a single judge, a three-member panel may be unnecessary.

Given attorneys' traditionally adversarial role in court proceedings, the most difficult obstacle to implementation may reside in the integration of legal representation into the judicial arbitral model. The presence of litigators might transform the arbitral proceeding into the usual combative contest. The time limit rule, however, would oblige all parties, including legal representatives, to respond to the stated arbitral intent of the proceeding. Some consideration might be given to the elaboration of a special code of ethics for domestic relations practice, emphasizing the advantages of neutral lawyering and requiring some mental health training for family law lawyers.

Conclusion

Judicial arbitration, together with the opportunity to bring about resolution by private agreement and other means, appears to constitute a remedial framework that responds more fully to the dispute resolution needs of divorcing couples. It eliminates the predominance of the adversarial ethic and avoids parentlike juridical intrusions into the private emotional lives of divorcing spouses. Most important, it allows the principles of individual accountability and self-determination to have their necessary impact upon matrimonial matters. In effect, the structure of such a framework combines the wisdom of the comparative experience of legal systems—that is, their movement toward judge-centered proceedings allowing for moderate party participation—and the teachings of the international experience in dispute resolution—identifying the sui generis traits and resolution needs of disputes and molding mechanisms accordingly. Adapting traditional mechanisms and proffering dispute resolution alternatives in divorce enables society to achieve its civilizing design upon individuals by privileging rationality rather than blindly resorting to obsolete and formalistic rituals.

NOTES

1. See, for example, LA. CIV. CODE ANN. art. 119 (West 1986). Articles 119 and 120 of the Louisiana Civil Code articulate the respective rights and duties of married persons. The parties to the marriage owe each other fidelity, support, assistance, and the obligation of conjugal cohabitation. Id. The courts have defined the specific content of these duties in the context of particular cases. See, for example, Smith v. Smith, 382 So. 2d 972 (La. App. 1st Cir. 1980); Hingle v. Hingle, 369 So. 2d 271 (La. App. 4th Cir. 1979); Favrot v. Barnes, 332 So. 2d 873 (La. App. 4th Cir. 1976), rev'd on other grounds, 339 So. 2d 843 (La. 1976), cert. denied 431 U.S. 966 (1977). Article 120 was repealed by Acts 1985, No. 271, § 1, leaving the duty of conjugal cohabitation to be implied from the content of article 119. Further revisions of the Code in 1987 transformed former article 119 into article 98, which provides: "Married persons owe each other fidelity, support, and assistance" (Acts 1987, No. 866, § 1, effective Jan. 1, 1988).

In regard to the duty of conjugal cohabitation, the Revision Comments for 1987 provide that "the spouses are free to live together as necessary to fulfill their obligation mutually to support, assist, and be faithful to each other." LA. CIV. CODE ANN. art. 98 (West 1988).

LA. CIV. CODE ANN. art. 86 (West 1987) provides that "[the] law considers marriage in no other view than as a civil contract." The 1987 revisions to article 86 do not modify the essential substance of the provision. Article 86 now reads in pertinent part: "Marriage is a legal relationship between a man and a woman that is created by civil contract." LA. CIV. CODE ANN. art. 86 (West 1988). The express definition of marriage is, therefore, secular and devoid of religious overtones. It functions within a conceptual framework of individual freedom of contract. See Carbonneau, *Analytical and Comparative Variations on Selected Provisions of Book One of the Louisiana Civil Code with Special Consideration of the Role of Fault in the Determination of Marital Disputes,* 27 LOY. L. REV. 999, 1013, 1014 (1981); Comment, *The Best Interest of the Divorcing Family: Mediation Not Litigation,* 29 LOY. L. REV. 55, 58 (1983) (Louisiana law). Similarly, common-law jurisdictions define marriage by statute as a civil contract. See H. CLARK, THE LAW OF DOMESTIC RELATIONS IN THE UNITED STATES 31-120 (2d ed. 1988) [H. CLARK].

2. Because marriage implicates both personal rights and social policy, it is more than a mere contract. Therefore, the state may nullify provisions of a prenuptial agreement as void against public policy. See, for example, Holliday v. Holliday, 358 So. 2d 618 (La. 1978) (provision of prenuptial agreement waiving right to temporary alimony declared invalid). Accord Monk v. Monk, 376 So. 2d 552 (La. App. 3d Cir. 1979) (postseparation agreement waiving right to permanent alimony in consideration of community property settlement upheld). According to Homer Clark, the position in common-law jurisdictions on this issue is virtually identical. "Broadly speaking these agreements are valid and enforceable, and in fact favored by the law, if they meet certain requirements." H. CLARK, supra note 1, at 7. Accord UNIF. MARITAL PROP. ACT (U.M.P.A.) 10(g), 9A U.L.A. 35 (Supp. 1983).

3. As to the financial regime that applies to marriage, see LA. CIV. CODE ANN. arts. 2336 & 2346 (West 1988); H. CLARK, supra note 1, at 589-618.

The Louisiana Civil Code provides that "marriage is a contract intended in its origin to endure until the death of one of the contracting parties." LA. CIV. CODE ANN. art. 89 (West 1987). The substance of this article was eliminated by the 1987 revisions to the Code. According to Clark, the interest of the state "formerly lay in the direction of preserving marriages and ensuring that divorces were only granted after satisfactory proof that conduct constituting one of the fault grounds for divorce had occurred." H. CLARK, supra note 1, at 539 (footnote omitted).

4. See LA. CIV. CODE ANN. art. 140 (West 1988) (providing that "separation . . . can not be made the subject of arbitration"). For the position in common-law jurisdictions, see H. CLARK, supra note 1, at 574-79.

5. A breach of a matrimonial duty, on the one hand, violates the civil agreement between the spouses and, on the other hand, may invade a corporeal or emotional personality interest protected by the law of tort. For a more detailed discussion of this point, see H. CLARK, supra note 1, at 496-528.

6. For instance, the concept of matrimonial fault is usually relevant in some jurisdictions to the grounds for divorce, but does not factor into the custody question, nor does it usually affect the division of property. For a description of the role of fault in divorce matters in the various state jurisdictions, see Carbonneau, *A Consideration of Alternatives to Divorce Litigation,* [1986] U. ILL. L. REV. 1119, 1137-38, n.47 (1986) (the text of this chapter relies heavily upon the content of that article) [*Alternatives to Divorce*]. See also Comment, *The Best Interest of the Divorcing Family: Mediation Not Litigation,* supra note 1, at 58-68 (describing the role of fault in the Louisiana law of separation and divorce); H. CLARK, supra note 1, at 496-528, 619-708, 786-849.

7. For a humorous illustration of this point, see, for example, Gilberti v. Gilberti, 338 So. 2d 971 (La. App. 4th Cir. 1976). See also Trosclair v. Trosclair, 337 So. 2d 1216 (La. App. 1st Cir. 1976); O'Neill v. O'Neill, 196 So. 2d 669 (La. App. 3d Cir. 1967).

8. See, for example, M. GREEN, MARRIAGE (1984).

9. Children are subject to the authority of their parents. In Louisiana, their biological relationship gives them inheritance rights, known as forced heirship. See LA. CIV. CODE ANN. arts. 1493 & 1495 (West 1988). For a detailed discussion of the legal status of children in the family, see, for example, H. CLARK, supra note 1, at 149-203, 786-849.

10. See generally *The Revolution in Family Law,* 5 FAMILY ADVOCATE 1 (1982).

11. See L. BARUTH & C. HUBER, AN INTRODUCTION TO MARITAL THEORY AND THERAPY (1984). See also Kaslow, *Divorce and Divorce Therapy,* in HANDBOOK OF FAMILY THERAPY (A. Gurman & D. Kriskern eds. 1981). Accord Whitaker & Miller, *A Reevaluation of "Psychiatric Help" When Divorce Impends,* 126 AM. J. PSYCHIATRY 57 (1969).

12. According to Hinsie and Campbell, transference
in psychoanalytic therapy, [is] the phenomenon of projection of feelings, thoughts, and wishes onto the analyst, who has come to represent an object from the patient's past. The analyst is reacted

to as though he were someone from the patient's past; such reactions, while they may have been appropriate to the conditions
that prevailed in the patient's previous life, are inappropriate and
anachronistic when applied to an object (the analyst) in the present.
L. HINSIE & R. CAMPBELL, PSYCHIATRIC DICTIONARY 751 (4th ed. 1976). See
also C. JUNG, CONTRIBUTIONS TO ANALYTICAL PSYCHOLOGY (H. Baynes &
C. Kegan trans. 1928); H. NUNBERG, PRINCIPLES OF PSYCHOANALYSIS (1955);
Winnicott, *Clinical Varieties of Transference,* in D.W. WINNICOTT: COL-
LECTED PAPERS 295 (1958).

Psychological experts claim that transference can also take place in
ordinary life situations—between spouses, in professional relationships,
in friendships, and in daily impersonal encounters. According to popular
psychological literature, transferring childhood feelings and behavior into
the present "is fairly common in life, and there are elements of it present
in any contact with authority. . . ." T. HARRIS, I'M O.K.—YOU'RE O.K. 229
(1973).

13. See, for example, Krebs, *Joint Custody: Is It Really in the Best
Interest?,* in T. CARBONNEAU, THE FAMILY AND THE CIVIL CODE 499 (1983).
See also C. VETTER, CHILD CUSTODY: A NEW DIRECTION (1982); M. WHEELER,
DIVIDED CHILDREN (1980). For a critical judicial assessment of the concept
of joint custody, see Turner v. Turner, 455 So. 2d 1374 (La. 1984).

14. See *Alternatives to Divorce,* supra note 6, at 1139-49.

15. For a general discussion of these concepts, see, for example, R.
BARNHOUSE, IDENTITY (1984); C. GILLIGAN, IN A DIFFERENT VOICE (1984);
A. ULANOV, THE FEMININE IN JUNGIAN PSYCHOLOGY AND IN CHRISTIAN
THEOLOGY (1971).

16. Id.

17. Two types of models have been developed to explain marital success
and failure: a social-psychological model focusing upon barriers and attractions, and an economic model emphasizing costs and benefits. The
social-psychological model predicts marital success as a function of the
interplay between attractions (factors encouraging marriage) and barriers
(factors discouraging divorce). When attractions and barriers are both
strong, divorce is unlikely; as both decline, so does the stability of the
marriage. See Levinger, *A Social Psychological Perspective on Marital Dissolution,* 32 J. SOC. ISSUES 21 (1976).

Economic models predict marital success according to the costs and
benefits of maintaining the marriage—in emotional as well as financial
terms. Variables include financial success, attachment to the spouse, ex-
tramarital attachments, presence of children, variations between the spouses
in education and church membership, expectations of the marital relationship, and attitudes of the surrounding community regarding divorce.

If these variables combine in such a way that it is more costly to sustain the marriage than it is to terminate it, then it is more likely to fail. See Becker, *A Theory of Marriage Pt. 1*, 81 J. POL. ECON. 813 (1973); Becker, A Theory of Marriage Pt. 2, 82 J. POL. ECON. § 11 (1974).

Economic and social-psychological models generally produce similar conclusions that can also be predicted by demographic trends. Women are more likely to divorce when they are financially independent: this result may be due to either the resulting economic leverage or the removal of a general psychological barrier to divorce. The presence of children contributes to marital stress, yet it inhibits divorce: this effect may be due to the additional financial or emotional costs of children (with a recognition of even greater postdivorce costs), or it may be explained by a sense of duty toward the children. The explanative and predictive values of the two approaches appear to be roughly comparable.

Social and demographic trends, together with psychological and economic analyses, may account for at least a portion of the increase in the divorce rate, but they are not sufficient. Not all independent women divorce; even women with less than happy marriages may not choose divorce. Having a strong religious affiliation and parents who are divorced are other factors that may account for some of the variance, but certainly not all of it. These approaches analyze trends, but not the ultimate causes behind those trends. Fully adequate explanatory models do not yet exist.

18. See Sepler, *Measuring the Effects of No-Fault Divorce Laws*, 25 FAM. L. Q. 65, 89 (1982). See also McGraw et al., *A Case Study in Divorce Law Reform and Its Aftermath*, 20 J. FAM. L. 443 (1982).

19. Coogler gives an especially vivid and critical account of the misunderstandings that exist between divorcing couples, their lawyers, and the judicial system. Coogler argues that, in choosing the adversarial system for divorce, parties

> often do not realize they have made the choice until they find themselves caught up in it with apparently no way out. There is little or no explanation in advance of commitment. There is no offer of a choice between it and anything else.
>
> Without their awareness, the choice is made for most couples when either one or both parties decide to consult an attorney. Often their purpose in seeking the consultation was to find an answer to the question, What are my legal rights? This would seem to be a rational beginning for dealing with a matter in which one is without prior experience. Most people do not have information in advance when they are confronted with death or divorce.
>
> Lawyers, like undertakers, are presumed to have the answer to questions in their field, but unlike undertakers, lawyers never answer

the questions. They are not answered because there are no answers to what the client wants to know.

There is no other field of law in which the court is given such complete and, for all practical purposes, uncontrolled discretion as in divorce cases. To answer the client's question, the lawyer would have to guess what the judge might do, except that one can never be sure which judge will hear the case. Studies have shown, and observers of the legal process confirm, that different judges may make quite different decisions upon substantially the same factual situation.

This uncertainty does not stop most lawyers from giving what sounds like an answer while qualifying each statement made. The one thing the client is very sure of from the consultation is that it is all very hard to understand. From this follows a decision to leave it up to the lawyer who then compliments the client for having made a very wise choice as a check for the retainer fee is written.

. . .

What they do not know about the adversarial system is that the lawyer, as an advocate, is required to represent, or advocate, *solely* the interest of his client. *He cannot represent both parties,* as is commonly supposed. The lawyer represents his client within the "light of his professional judgment." But the client's interest is always perceived as being in opposition to the interests of the other party. The lawyer cannot and does not regard the parties as having a common problem which he or she will help resolve.

The represented party, feeling that there is a knowledgeable person "on my side," experiences considerable relief after all the feelings of fear and helplessness that have gone before. At this point there is little awareness of being postured against the other party — "What should he/she have to fear from me?" The heightened feelings of fear and helplessness the other party experiences by not having anybody on his/her side are not anticipated.

It is rare that the employment of one attorney does not lead to the employment of a second, unless the parties simply do not have the financial resources. The need for a second attorney usually comes into focus when the parties realize that many areas of agreement are needed which they had not previously considered. The possible implications of an attorney's routine demands for financial disclosure can be so threatening as to send an unrepresented party to another attorney in a near panic.

Once a second attorney is employed, the only factor limiting escalation of the competitive struggle between husband and wife is the financial resources of the family. In some cases, the struggle may continue not just through the divorce, but for the lifetime of the parties.

O. COOGLER, STRUCTURED MEDIATION IN DIVORCE SETTLEMENT 6-8 (1978) (emphasis in the original) [O. COOGLER].

This criticism may indicate nothing more than clients' dissatisfaction with the lack of predictability of the eventual outcome. Arguably, if more answers in the form of fixed substantive rules were available, clients would be more satisfied with the legal process of divorce. For a discussion of this point, see Glendon, *Fixed Rules and Discretion in Contemporary Family Law and Succession Law,* 60 TUL. L. REV. 1165 (1986); Glendon, *Family Law Reform in the 1980's,* 44 LA. L. REV. 1553 (1984). According to Glendon, "The most serious problem with the law currently governing the child-related and economic effects of divorce is not its broad grants of discretion, but its incoherence at the level of principle" (60 TUL. L. REV. at 1171).

20. For example, in punishing adultery, the law primarily focuses upon the occurrence of intercourse and the possibility of introducing illegitimate offspring into the family line. It does not concentrate upon the tortious nature of the offensive conduct—including the emotional impact upon the other spouse—nor does it attempt to evaluate the motivation for such conduct. Generally, such issues are outside the purview of legally cognizable claims.

21. See O. COOGLER, note 19 supra.

22. Namely, the grounds for divorce, and the determination of issues pertaining to child custody and support, alimony, and property division.

23. See *Alternatives to Divorce,* supra note 6, at 1137, nn.46-52 and accompanying text.

24. See id. at 1137, n.47.

25. According to psychological literature, the concept of "surrogate" means "one who takes the place of another. In a child's growth and development, original affective attitudes and feelings towards a parent may in time be transferred to a *sibling,* a teacher, a relative, a friend. With each new surrogate there is less resemblance to the original attachment." A PSYCHIATRIC GLOSSARY 144 (4th ed. 1975) (emphasis in the original).

26. See O. COOGLER, note 19 supra.

27. Criticism of the adversarial process—centering upon its expense, delay, and negative effect upon litigants—is not confined to domestic relations disputes. According to Lieberman, such criticism applies to the process in most, if not all, areas of litigation. See J. LIEBERMAN, THE LITIGIOUS SOCIETY, cited in ch. 1, supra, in note 1 and accompanying text. See generally J. AUERBACH, UNEQUAL JUSTICE (1976).

Vituperative accounts of the adversarial process are particularly pronounced when the process is evaluated for its operation upon family matters. See Keynote Speech by Frank Sander, ABA National Conference on Alternate Means of Dispute Resolution (June 1982), cited in ch. 1, supra, note 3 and accompanying text.

28. Indeed, although the couple may not anticipate that this situation will ultimately befall them, they may gradually enmesh themselves in it. See O. COOGLER, supra note 19, at 11-12.

29. Family mediation furthers the policy of minimum state intervention. The arguments for minimum state intervention in determinations of child care and custody have been widely debated, and they are now quite familiar. Parents should be presumed to have the capacity, authority, and responsibility both to determine and to do what is best for their children as well as what is best for their entire family constellation, regardless of how that constellation might be rearranged by divorce. Psychological theory as well as constitutional considerations argue for parental autonomy and family privacy when there is no direct evidence that the interests of children are jeopardized in the process. Parents, whether married or divorced, should have the opportunity to meet the needs of their children and to maintain family ties without state interference. Folberg, *A Mediation Overview: History and Dimensions of Practice,* 1 MEDIATION Q. 3, 10 (1983). Given the public interest in marriage and the family, some form of court supervision and lawyer participation would be necessary. The benefits of such coordinated organization should yield systemic cooperation rather than competition. See generally Elster, *Solomonic Judgments: Against the Best Interest of the Child,* 54 U. CHI. L. REV. 1 (1987).

30. See text at note 20 supra and accompanying text.

31. See Herrman, McKenry, & Weber, *Mediation and Arbitration Applied to Family Conflict Resolution: The Divorce Settlement,* 34 ARB. J. 17 (1979); Meroney, *Mediation and Arbitration of Separation and Divorce Agreements,* 15 WAKE FOREST L. REV. 467 (1979); Rigby, *Alternate Dispute Resolution,* 44 LA. L. REV. 1725 (1984); Spencer & Zammit, *Mediation-Arbitration: A Proposal for Private Resolution of Disputes Between Divorced or Separated Parents,* [1976] DUKE L. J. 911 (1976).

See also Coulson, *Family Arbitration: An Exercise in Sensitivity,* 3 FAM. L.Q. 22 (1969); Philbrick, *Agreements to Arbitrate Post-Divorce Custody Disputes,* 18 COLUM. J.L. & SOC. PROBS. 419 (1985); Spencer & Zammit, *Reflections on Arbitration Under the Family Dispute Services,* 32 ARB. J. 111 (1977). See generally Comment, *Arbitration: A Viable Alternative?,* 3 FORDHAM URB. L. REV. 53 (1974); Comment, *The Enforceability of Arbitration Clauses in North Carolina Separation Agreements,* 15 WAKE FOREST L. REV. 487 (1979).

32. For a discussion of arbitral clauses in separation, see Meroney, *Mediation and Arbitration of Separation and Divorce Agreements,* note 31

supra; Spencer & Zammit, *Mediation-Arbitration: A Proposal* ..., note 31 supra; Comment, *Enforcement of Arbitration Clauses,* note 31 supra.

33. See *Alternatives to Divorce,* supra note 6, at 606, n.7.

34. See Carbonneau, *Rendering Arbitral Awards with Reasons: The Elaboration of a Common Law of International Transactions,* 23 COLUM. J. TRANSNAT'L L. 579, 581-86 (1985) [*Rendering Arbitral Awards*]. For a discussion of the advantages traditionally associated with arbitration, see, for example, Mentschikoff, *Commercial Arbitration,* 61 COLUM. L. REV. 846 (1961). See also de Vries, *International Commercial Arbitration: A Contractual Substitute for National Courts,* 57 TUL. L. REV. 42 (1982); Kerr, *International Arbitration v. Litigation,* [1980] J. BUS. L. 164 (1980).

35. See *Rendering Arbitral Awards,* supra note 34, at 581-86.

36. See Bezou v. Bezou, No. 81-11606 (CDC-Orleans June 3, 1983) (illustrating the type of frustration that can arise from the attempt to apply legal rules and concepts to divorce disputes).

37. In personal injury cases, money also stands as a symbol for the victim's loss — corporeal and emotional. In the case of tortious injury, however, there is usually an identifiable aggrieved party and a tortfeasor, as well as objective damages that can be measured with some precision. The law of tort, despite its recognized contemporary mission of providing compensation, still hesitates to provide recovery for purely emotional loss. See, for example, RESTATEMENT (SECOND) OF TORTS § 436A (1963-64). Although there is some overlap, tort and divorce disputes are separable from one another and impose different burdens and problems upon the legal process. In divorce, usually the loss is purely one of a personal relationship; money should only factor in the adjustment of the respective economic positions of the parties following dissolution.

38. See text at notes 34-35 supra and accompanying text.

39. For a more extensive discussion of this point, including a list of relevant sources, see *Alternatives to Divorce,* supra note 6, at 1157-59.

40. See id.

41. See id.

42. See id.

43. For a discussion of these constitutional issues, see generally Comment, *An Analysis of State Legislative Responses to the Medical Malpractice Crisis,* [1975] DUKE L.J. 1417 (1975); Comment, *Legislative Response to the Medical Malpractice Crisis,* 39 OHIO ST. L.J. 855 (1978); Comment, *Recent Medical Malpractice Legislation: A First Checkup,* 50 TUL. L. REV. 655 (1976); Comment, *Testing the Constitutionality of Medical Malpractice Legislation: The Wisconsin Medical Malpractice Act of 1975,* [1977] WISC. L. REV. 838 (1977); Note, *Comparative Approaches to Liability for Medical Maloccurrences,* 84 YALE L.J. 1141 (1975); Note, *Constitutional Law: Lou-*

isiana Medical Malpractice Review Panel Upheld Under Equal Protection Scrutiny, 53 TUL. L. REV. 640 (1979); Redish, *Legislative Responses to the Medical Malpractice Insurance Crisis: Constitutional Implications,* 55 TEX. L. REV. 759 (1975); Sakayan, *Arbitration and Screening Panels: Recent Experience and Trends,* 17 FORUM 682 (1981-82).

44. See text at notes 34-35 supra and accompanying text.

45. See G. WILNER, DOMKE ON COMMERCIAL ARBITRATION §§ 12:00-02 (1984). For example, matters of status and capacity are deemed to be "non-arbitrable" because they involve the state's public policy, and are within the exclusive jurisdiction of the courts of law. For an extensive discussion of the term, see J. ROBERT & T. CARBONNEAU, THE FRENCH LAW OF ARBITRATION Pt. I, § 1:03, at 1-13 to 1-22.

46. See, for example, Rigby, *Alternate Dispute Resolution,* supra note 31, at 1751. Contra Winks, *Divorce Mediation: A Nonadversary Procedure for the No-Fault Divorce,* 19 J. FAM. L. 615, 631, n.76 (1980-81).

47. The Tardits case, Judgment of Feb. 15, 1966, Cr. d'appel, Orléans, [1966] D. S. Jur. 340, is an illustration of this distinction between non-arbitrable public policy disputes and arbitrable incidental disputes attaching to a larger controversy implicating public policy. See Carbonneau, *The Elaboration of a French Court Doctrine on International Commercial Arbitration: A Study in Liberal Civilian Judicial Creativity,* 55 TUL. L. REV. 1, 36-38 (1980).

48. For a more extensive discussion of this point, including a list of relevant sources, see *Alternatives to Divorce,* supra note 6, at 1160-62.

49. For a more extensive discussion of this point, see *Rendering Arbitral Awards,* supra note 34, at 603-10.

Ordinarily, in commercial and other forms of arbitration, arbitral awards are subject to appeal on limited grounds — for essentially procedural violations. See G. WILNER, DOMKE ON COMMERCIAL ARBITRATION, supra note 45, at pt. XI, §§ 32.00-35.03. Historically, judicial review on the merits of arbitral awards was allowed and even required. This was especially true in England. See Carbonneau, *Arbitral Adjudication: A Comparative Assessment of Its Remedial and Substantive Status in Transnational Commerce,* 19 TEX. INT'L L.J. 33, 39-61 (1984). Eventually, a review of the merits was precluded, attesting to the adjudicatory autonomy of arbitration. See *Rendering Arbitral Awards,* supra note 34, at 581-86.

50. See *Rendering Arbitral Awards,* supra note 34, at 608-10.

51. This equitable adjudicatory authority is expressed by the concept of *amiable composition,* which allows arbitrators to rule according to their basic sense of fairness and justice and to disregard, where they think appropriate, the rules of law. See Carbonneau, *The Elaboration of a French Court Doctrine . . . ,* supra note 47, at 2, n.2.

52. As noted earlier, if arbitrators are allowed to rule on child custody questions, the usually flexible standard of review may have to yield to a more stringent form of judicial scrutiny, possibly in the form of de novo review. In addition, arbitrators would probably be obligated to apply governing legal rules. See supra note 46 and accompanying text.

53. This is a common complaint made by lawyers regarding arbitration. It reflects their adversarial, one-sided perspective of dispute resolution, which demands a single answer to conflict situations.

54. See *Alternatives to Divorce,* supra note 6, at 1165-67.

55. The principal sources on divorce mediation are: O. COOGLER, supra note 19; J. FOLBERG & A. TAYLOR, MEDIATION: A COMPREHENSIVE GUIDE TO RESOLVING CONFLICTS WITHOUT LITIGATION (1984); J. PEARSON & N. THOENNES, DIVORCE MEDIATION: STRENGTHS AND WEAKNESSES OF ALTERNATIVE MEANS OF FAMILY DISPUTE RESOLUTION (1982). See also *Symposium on Critical Issues in Mediation Legislation,* 2 OHIO ST. J. DISP. RES. 1 (1986). For an extensive listing of the literature on divorce mediation, see *Alternatives to Divorce,* supra note 6, at 602, n.2.

56. See Kelley, *Mediation and Psychotherapy: Distinguishing the Differences,* 1 MEDIATION Q. 33 (1983). See also Yahm, *Divorce Mediation: A Psychoanalytic Perspective,* 6 MEDIATION Q. 59 (1984).

57. See, for example, J. FOLBERG & A. TAYLOR, MEDIATION . . . , supra note 55, at 1-7; Rigby, *Alternate Dispute Resolution,* supra note 31, at 1729-33, 1740-43.

58. Although there are many mediation styles, the literature suggests two fundamental models, of which the diverse styles are variations. Coogler's structured mediation model is formal and, true to its name, highly structured. It requires the participants to sign agreements stipulating interim settlements and a commitment to mediation. All mediation sessions must be joint, and an advisory attorney appointed as consultant. See generally O. COOGLER, supra note 19. See also Coombs, *Mediation and Counseling in Child-Custody Disputes,* 17 FAM. L.Q. 469, 471 (1984). Advocates of this approach maintain that the formalities lend a sense of predictability to the procedure and help ensure that the parties will cooperate. Disadvantages include a lack of flexibility plus the possibility of preventing participants from consulting with private attorneys. See J. FOLBERG & A. TAYLOR, MEDIATION . . . , supra note 55, at 137. There is also the possibility that participants may not fully understand the implications of the agreements they sign at the outset of the process.

"Comprehensive mediation," in contrast with "structured mediation," does not involve a consulting attorney, nor does it require the participants to sign agreements to participate. It also permits individual sessions and allows each party to have individual counsel. See Coombs, supra this note, at 472. Although it is more flexible, comprehensive mediation can resemble the traditional adversarial system, permitting each party to have legal counsel and allowing individual mediation sessions.

Structured mediation has been criticized as potentially unfair to the weaker party in a relationship, who might feel pressured to agree in a joint session. See Rifkin, *Mediation from a Feminist Perspective,* 2 LAW & IN-EQUALITY 21 (1984). See also Lerman, *Mediation of Wife Abuse Cases: The Adverse Impact of Informal Dispute Resolution on Women,* 7 HARV. WOMEN'S L.J. 57 (1984). In such a situation, comprehensive mediation might be the more appropriate approach.

Many mediation programs combine features of both structured and comprehensive mediation. For example, one mediation program in New York provides advisory counsel at an intake session, but permits each party to have private counsel, who may attend mediation sessions. Moreover, both parties are invited to attend all sessions, but joint attendance is not required, nor is an interim agreement necessary. See CENTER FOR DISPUTE SETTLEMENTS (Rochester, N.Y.), FAMILY AND DIVORCE MEDIATION PRO-GRAM (n.d.) (brochure). This is only one of many varieties of mediation currently in effect. Ultimately, the ideal types of structured and compre-hensive mediation may be of greater interest to writers and advocates than to practitioners. See generally Blades, *Mediation: An Old Art Revitalized,* 3 MEDIATION Q. 59 (1984).

59. Although proposed as a cost-efficient alternative to lengthy litiga-tion, mediation may not always be more economical. If each party must attend four to six mediation sessions, which cost $100 per hour or more, and have private counsel to approve the mediated agreement, there may be little in monetary savings. If structured mediation is used (requiring only a single attorney as consultant to both parties), the cost may be lower, but the parties may not have been adequately represented. See Crouch, *The Dark Side of Mediation,* in ALTERNATIVE MEANS OF FAMILY DISPUTE RESOLUTION 339 (American Bar Assoc. 1982).

Although a complete response to the statement of these potential de-ficiencies can only be gained from actual experience, conjectural reflection suggests that either these deficiencies can be remedied or their impact minimized. For instance, when compared to adversarial litigation, team mediation is unlikely to result in a greater expenditure of time and money. A single mediator, advised by a consulting attorney, may constitute the most economical format, but it has the possible negative consequence of placing the participating couple at a real, or perceived, disadvantage in relation to the mediator who is advised. This contributes to feelings of helplessness and distrust that might strongly impinge upon the viability of the process. While single, psychologically oriented mediation that provides the couple with ancillary legal services may, theoretically, present the most likely possibility of less expense and fewer sessions, outside attorneys' disagreement with the procedure or outcome could generate a substantial amount of additional costs that could undermine the entire mediation. The latter prospect would clearly be wasteful of resources, culminating, perhaps, in a contested divorce action, as well as a breach of contract or malpractice suit between the couple and the mediator. In the interest of procedural integrity, even the dual-mediator model should require that the spouses retain separate counsel to review the mediated agreement prior to signature. However, both the presence of an attorney on the mediation team and the participation of the spouses in the agreement process should minimize the potentially disruptive effect of outside legal advice.

60. See, for example, Rosanova, *Mediation: Professional Dynamics,* 1 MEDIATION Q. 63, 63 (1983). See also, for example, R. GARDNER, FAMILY EVALUATION IN CHILD CUSTODY LITIGATION (1982); D. SAPOSNEK, MEDIATING CHILD CUSTODY DISPUTES (1983); Patrician, *Child Custody Terms: Potential Contributors to Custody Dissatisfaction and Conflict,* 3 MEDIATION Q. 41 (1984); Waldron, Roth, Fair, Mann, & McDermott, *A Therapeutic Mediation Model for Child Custody Dispute Resolution,* 3 MEDIATION Q. 5 (1984).

61. See, e.g., Milne, *Divorce Mediation: The State of the Art,* 1 MEDIATION Q. 15, 15 (1983). For a discussion of joint custody, see Cox & Cease, *Joint Custody,* 1 FAMILY ADVOCATE 10 (1978); Schulman, *Who's Looking After the Children?,* 5 FAMILY ADVOCATE 31 (1982).

62. See Milne, *Divorce Mediation: The State of the Art,* note 61 supra.

63. See J. FOLBERG & A. TAYLOR, MEDIATION . . . , supra note 55, at 1-15.

64. See Milne, *Divorce Mediation: The State of the Art,* supra note 61, at 28-31.

65. See, for example, Lemmon, *Divorce Mediation: Optimal Scope and Practice Issues,* 1 MEDIATION Q. 45, 52 (1983). See also *Alternatives to Divorce,* supra note 6, at 1178-79, n.176.

In other words, divorcing couples would need to defuse their irrational thinking about marriage breakdown and its personal implications. The estranged spouse would not be viewed as a culprit for past emotional wrongs, nor would the legal system be viewed as a means of redressing the shortcomings of a spouse's childhood upbringing. However unfortunate divorce may be in the eyes of either or both of the spouses, termination should be perceived as a necessary reality in appropriate circumstances, requiring the family to assume another form. The all-or-nothing or life-or-death interpretation of divorce can only increase the anxiety and difficulty in what is an already perplexing and painful situation.

66. For a more extensive discussion of this point, including a list of relevant sources, see *Alternatives to Divorce,* supra note 6, at 1170-71, 1178-79, n.176.

67. See id. at 1171, 1180, nn.179-80.

68. See id. at 1171-73.

69. See, for example, Moore, *Training Mediators for Family Dispute Resolution,* 2 MEDIATION Q. 79 (1983). Current training seems to consist of a series of lectures lasting up to five days. Id. at 87. These campaigns are sometimes modeled on a format of itinerant, episodic, privately confected blitz programs of instruction. Such a brief training period seems inadequate to produce a corps of rigorously qualified professionals, even for persons already professionally trained in related areas such as family law or social work. See also J. FOLBERG & A. TAYLOR, MEDIATION . . . , supra note 55, at 244, 249; *Ethics, Standards, and Professional Challenges,* 4 MEDIATION Q. 1-93 (J. Lemmon ed. 1984).

70. See Black & Joffee, *A Lawyer/Therapist Team Approach to Divorce,* 16 CONCILIATION CTS. REV. 1 (1978); Gold, *Interdisciplinary Team Mediation,* 6 MEDIATION Q. 27 (1984). See also J. FOLBERG & A. TAYLOR, MEDIATION . . . , supra note 55, at 143-44.

71. MODEL RULES OF PROFESSIONAL RESPONSIBILITY rule 2.2 provides for lawyers to act as intermediaries between clients. An intermediary role requires the attorney to inform each client of the risks involved, to notify clients of decisions to be made, and to withdraw at the request of any client, or if the lawyer believes that the intermediary role is no longer in the best interests of the clients. The comments to this rule stipulate that "a lawyer cannot undertake common representation of clients between whom contentious litigation is imminent or who contemplate contentious negotiations." Id. This would seem to preclude intermediating in all but the most amicable divorces.

While mediation is listed in the comments as an approved form of intermediation, "the Rule does not apply to a lawyer acting as . . . mediator between or among parties who are not clients of the lawyer, even where the lawyer has been appointed with the concurrence of the parties." Id. This suggests that a lawyer may serve as mediator in a consulting or advisory role without regard to ethical rules, but must be much more careful if performing professional services as an attorney. Some of the potential conflict could be alleviated by requiring each spouse to retain separate counsel to review the mediated agreement prior to signature. In this instance, the mediating lawyer would be acting as consultant rather than legal advisor and would not be affected by the rule.

For a discussion of professional responsibility issues in divorce mediation, see J. FOLBERG & A. TAYLOR, MEDIATION . . . , supra note 55 at 244-

50. See also Bishop, *The Standards of Practice for Family Mediators: An Individual Interpretation and Comments,* 17 FAM. L.Q. 461 (1984); Crouch, *The Dark Side Is Still Unexplored,* 4 FAM. ADVOC. 27 (1982); Gaughan, *Taking a Fresh Look at Divorce Mediation,* 17 TRIAL 39 (1981); Riskin, *Toward New Standards for the Neutral Lawyer in Mediation,* 26 ARIZ. L. REV. 329 (1984); Silberman, *Professional Responsibility Problems of Divorce Mediation,* 16 FAM. L.Q. 107 (1982); Special Section on Mediation, *Standards of Practice for Family Mediators,* 17 FAM. L.Q. 455 (1984). See generally, Note, *Family Law: Attorney Mediation of Marital Disputes and Conflict of Interest Considerations,* 60 N.C. L. REV. 171 (1981); Note, *Protecting Confidentiality in Mediation,* 98 HARV. L. REV. 441 (1984).

72. For a more extensive discussion of this point, including a list of relevant sources, see *Alternatives to Divorce,* supra note 6, at 1175.

73. See id.

74. See id. at 1175; Riskin, *Toward New Standards . . . ,* note 71 supra.

75. See Bernard, *The Neutral Mediator: Value Dilemmas in Divorce Mediation,* 4 MEDIATION Q. 61 (1984); Dibble, *Bargaining in Family Mediation: Ethical Considerations,* 4 MEDIATION Q. 75 (1984); Smart & Salts, *Attorney Attitudes Toward Divorce Mediation,* 6 MEDIATION Q. 65 (1984). See also text at note 71 supra and accompanying text.

76. For a more extensive discussion of this point, including a list of relevant sources, see *Alternatives to Divorce,* supra note 6, at 1175-77.

77. See id.

78. A number of additional criticisms can be levied at the mediation process. Mediation has been advanced as a way to relieve some of the pressures on a heavily overburdened court system, thereby speeding up the divorce process. Although courts are clogged with divorce-related issues, not all divorces are contested. One estimate shows that 85 to 90% of divorce cases are settled before trial, either by mutual agreement of the parties, or through attorney negotiation. See *Alternatives to Divorce,* supra note 6, at 1137, n.44. The mediation services in Los Angeles, Denver, Minneapolis, and Connecticut do not appear to do any better. Although this question has not been formally investigated, it may be that the people who mediate successfully would also successfully reach agreements without mediation.

Although successful mediation might relieve some of the pressures on the courts, it does not save much time. In Denver, successful mediators receive final decrees in an average of 9.7 months after initiation of proceedings. In contrast, it took 11.9 and 11.1 months, respectively, for a control group and for those who had actively rejected offers to mediate. The difference is statistically significant at the .05 level, but it concerns only two months at most and does not indicate an overwhelming acceleration of the divorce process. In sum, mediation may help unclog the courts and speed up the process, but it does neither to any great extent. See Pearson & Thoennes, *A Preliminary Portrait of Client Reactions to Three Court Mediation Programs,* 3 MEDIATION Q. 21 (1984).

The small minority of cases that are battled in the courtroom may be the ones most in need of mediation, but they may involve couples who will never agree in any proceeding. Indeed, in Denver, the difference in relitigation between successfully mediated settlements and those never referred to mediation is quite small: 11% of the former and 15% of the latter had returned to court 15 months after the settlement. While mediation may be a great improvement over endless litigation, it may not be better than successful negotiation with individual counsel. It is not at all certain that the parties who engage in endless litigation are deterred by mediation. See id.

One critic of mediation points out that mediators have a vested interest in settling controversies that might be better solved outside the mediation forum. He notes that mediation's emphasis on compromise might produce settlements that make no "objective" sense. See Crouch, *The Dark Side of Mediation,* supra note 59, at 344-45. Child custody issues, a common subject for mediation, may provide illustrations of irrational, "compromised" mediation settlements. One mediation text provides examples of ideal settlements, including one in which the parents divide custody of their two children such that the siblings are together in the same home only three days a week. See D. SAPOSNEK, MEDIATING CHILD CUSTODY DISPUTES, supra note 60, at 306 (1983). Such a settlement may please the parents and be a good compromise for them, but it is not necessarily best for the children (for whom sibling relationships and continuity are extremely important).

79. For a discussion of this point, including a list of relevant sources, see *Alternatives to Divorce,* supra note 6, at 1176, nn.169-71.

80. See id.

81. See id. at 1176; Winks, *Divorce Mediation: A Nonadversarial Procedure for the No-Fault Divorce,* 19 J. FAM. L. 615, 650 (1980-81).

82. See *Alternatives to Divorce,* supra note 6, at 1177, n.172.

83. See text at note 19 supra and accompanying text.

84. See Garska v. McCoy, 278 S.E.2d 357, 363 (W. Va. 1981). See also Minnesota Developments, *A Step Backward: The Minnesota Supreme Court Adopts a "Primary Caretaker" Presumption in Child Custody Cases: Pikula v. Pikula,* 70 MINN. L. REV. 1344 (1986).

6 | Adjudicatory Realities, Deficiences, and Remedies in Tort Law

Introduction

The Debate

Like divorce actions in their impact upon litigants and adjudicatory resources, personal injury suits raise both institutional and public concern about the viability of traditional adjudicatory methodologies. The concern has recently escalated to a thoroughgoing debate among interested groups. Lawyers and consumer advocates,[1] for example, accuse the insurance industry of price gouging, taking advantage of its antitrust exemptions, and hiding the real facts about insurance costs from the public. According to these stalwarts of the current system, the insurance industry's former practice of deliberately underpricing premiums to generate cash for investment is the cause of the astronomic rise in current premiums—not the unpredictability of risk owing to litigation. The decline in interest rates simply made the practice of underpricing short-sighted and unrealistic.[2] In addition, reports indicate that the insurance industry remains very profitable despite the alleged crisis, realizing $50 to $75 billion in net gains during the last ten years.[3]

Furthermore, statistical studies[4] provide convincing evidence that the system of tort litigation continues to function in a socially effective way. Media (and hence public) attention focuses upon a small minority of exceptional cases. Exorbitant recoveries, suits brought against remote "deep pocket" defendants, and the award of compensation in extraordinary circumstances constitute only a small percentage of the cases.[5] Also, the total money awarded in tort litigation comes from a small fraction of cases, and the number of tort actions has not risen disproportionately in relation to population increases.[6] Finally, plaintiff attorneys—who work on a contingency basis—do not make any more as a group than defense attorneys who work on an hourly basis.[7] Given the financial risk and investment of resources for plaintiff attorneys, the contingency fee system generally works to eliminate specious claims while providing access to justice for meritorious cases.[8] Therefore, although there are some abusive results, the system, as a rule, works to maintain social stability, adjudicatory fairness, and the democratic character of the process.

At the level of principle, it is further argued that civilized society cannot function without legal accountability for harm done. Business necessities and economic considerations should not overwhelm the societal and individual interest in the protection of legal rights. However criticized and criticizable the jury may be, both the federal and state constitutions guarantee the right to a civil jury trial.

For their part, corporate defendants and insurance companies generally decry the so-called litigation craze, claiming that it has reached destructive proportions and is beyond the bounds of common sense. They point to the nefarious consequences of suits[9] lodged by private parties against commercial enterprises, physicians and other professionals, and their insurers: doctors (especially surgeons and obstetricians) are heading for early retirement, companies are unable to stay in business for lack of resources to deal with litigation, and handsome verdicts for specious claims are undermining the integrity of the legal system. Moreover, the specter of unlimited tort liability has made insurance coverage either unavailable or astronomically expensive,[10] thereby undermining the essential economic foundation that supported the process. Previously, the imposition of legal liability without reference to culpability merely raised moral and ethical issues; now, it threatens to undermine the viability of commercial activity. Finally, lawyers' greed stimulated by contingency fee arrangements encourages frivolous suits brought against "deep pocket" corporate parties whose activities are only vaguely—if at all—related to the incident.[11] The single-minded advocacy for consumers and the superficial, emotional appeal to democratic values cloud the real issues of debate. Liability is imposed for having the ability to pay, not for engaging directly in blameworthy conduct.[12]

The proponents of fundamental reform call for lessons to be learned from outcomes in actual cases. The suit brought by Charles Bigbee against a telephone booth manufacturer is a popular reference.[13] Bigbee was injured when a drunk driver drove his car into the telephone booth that Bigbee was using. Bigbee alleged that the booth was defectively designed; by being so close to a busy street, it placed him at unreasonable risk. After more than ten years of litigation, the California Supreme Court upheld a jury verdict for Bigbee, ruling that a jury could find that the defendant manufacturer's failure to protect the booth from such an occurrence made the incident reasonably foreseeable.[14] The upshot of the Bigbee case, it is said, is that corporate enterprises' ability to pay makes them universal tortfeasors; they are, in effect, the new disadvantaged victims of tort law in the late twentieth century. Injury may be an expected feature of modern life for individuals, but the risk of corporate or professional legal accountability has literally become limitless. The only remaining predictability in the system is that, because the unpredictable will happen, "deep pocket" corporate parties will be made to pay, no matter how remote their conduct or activity. Moreover, juries make excessively generous awards for intangible, noneconomic loss such as pain and suffering.[15] In practice, such awards do not directly benefit the victim and usually go to pay for attorneys' fees. In fact, after years of protracted litigation, the injured victim usually gets only a modest share (30 to 40%) of the ultimate recovery.[16] Finally, the discovery of new causes of action in tort, like the toxic tort typified by the asbestos litigation, has placed yet another juridical burden upon economic activity and development.[17] Plaintiff attorneys are inviting the courts and juries to engage in social "robinhoodism," and the appeal to social conscience blinds the judgment of these institutions to other, more realistic considerations.

The foregoing debate is further complicated by interested groups' jockeying for advantage before the public and state legislatures through public relations campaigns and lobbying efforts.[18] The controversy is staggering in terms of its volume, depth, intensity, and implications. The fundamental, sometimes ferocious, division of opinion among the various interests involved makes the discord extremely resistant to solution, outdoing both traditional and nontraditional pathways to possible reconciliation.

The Speciality of Tort Disputes

Unlike divorce conflicts, personal injuries claims do not involve an emotional substratum that can potentially be harnessed by therapeutic techniques. Nor are tort grievances as intimately personal, even when they involve attacks upon reputation. Whereas alimony and community property matters can be controlled by the disaffected spouses' contractual discretion, the content of a tort action is not so easily dislodged from the province of public policy. The association of individual corporeal integrity with the public interest in security and deterrence limits the reach of party autonomy in tort litigation.[19] Finally, along with their public policy character, tort actions have a more objective and realistically quantifiable content than do their analogues in divorce;[20] as a result, they lend themselves more readily and appropriately than divorce conflicts to juridical classification and the legal processing of disputed claims.

Although a major part of the difficulty with tort litigation lies in its lack of predictability, the dilemma of tort claims cannot be significantly minimized by the recourse to arbitration. In international commerce, arbitration serves as a means of providing transactions with predictability concerning dispute resolution. Unlike international merchants, however, the actors in tort litigation are not bound by a common self-interest in the face of dispute, nor are they associated members of an integrated, self-disciplined, cohesive community. Their relationship is fortuitous, rather than the result of an agreed-upon contract.

Tort litigation, in short, is a highly political affair.[21] It is an adjudicatory framework that brings into opposition a range of social philosophies as irreconcilable as the conservative view of a ruggedly self-reliant response to life's vicissitudes and the liberal interpretation of the imposition of legal liability in tort as an exercise in humanitarian social welfare. The former view is epitomized by the assumption of risk doctrine[22] invoked by defendants to prevent regulation of their activity, and the latter position is variously assumed by the court or the jury in an implied fiduciary capacity on behalf of plaintiffs. To invoke the commonplace description, tort proceedings are a "battleground of social theory."[23]

Given these characteristics, the public, not the private, international experience is germane to testing the feasibility of dispute resolution alternatives in tort conflicts. Like state-to-state disputes, allegations of negligence implicate not only private rights, but also a much larger set of public concerns—akin, in many respects, to the principle of and interests arising from national sovereignty. The merits of every tort case implicate the public welfare, ultimately call into play competing political interests, and require the balancing of divergent positions. Like the dispute resolution process between sovereign states, tort proceedings could be usefully informed and eventually stabilized by the integration of a plurality of remedies: a dispute resolution framework anchored in a fluid ethic that defuses conflictual opposition.

For example, compensatory judgments in personal injury cases can be said to represent an implied socialization of societal risk through a policy of wealth redistribution.[24] Some maintain that such adjudicatory outcomes are an inappropriate use of judicial authority.[25] In effect, courts are using their systemic stature to implement a disguised form of commercial taxation. From this perspective, legal accountability in tort can be seen as an attack against the free enterprise system. From the opposite vantage point, having courts issue quasi-legislative rulings lessens the influence of special interests in articulating a national policy toward social risks, individual victims, and commercial enterprises. More neutrally, the presence or absence of juries can be viewed as a brief for democratic or elitist justice.

Relegating judicial adjudication to a last resort, modifying it, or eliminating it entirely, a system of alternative procedures might respond more ably to the problematic aspects of tort disputes and help to instill a more acceptable, less divisive balance between competing political ideologies and opposing social philosophies. In addition, these alternative remedies should perform an educative function. As with divorce disputes, they should enable parties to develop responsibility for, and exercise self-determination in, dispute resolution. The basic thrust of alternative dispute resolution frameworks should be to establish personal understanding (an individual truth) as the basic foundation for societal dispute resolution.

Features of Tort Law

The Substantive Law

Roughly speaking, tort law[26] functions as the private analogue of criminal law. Although a cause of action in tort need not satisfy statutory elements or fulfill a mens rea requirement, the law of tort does impose liability for harmful conduct that is adjudged intentional, reckless, or negligent (unreasonable and careless conduct in the circumstances).[27] A finding of liability in tort does not result in liberty-deprivation sanctions, but rather in the tortfeasor's payment of compensation to the injured victim. The imposition of monetary sanctions also seeks to deter future, potentially harmful conduct.[28] The advent of no-fault or strict liability[29] in tort created an imbalance between these twin objectives, eventually placing greater store in the compensatory goal of tort law to the detriment of its retributive function. In fact, tort liability principles have supposedly become a morally neutral, economically based corpus of rules by which courts (with implied legislative acquiescence) have propounded a juridically devised concept of social justice.

Historically, tort law was a restrictively and an infrequently imposed form of legal liability.[30] Early in its modern development, its controlling tenet was that a finding of legal culpability was the exception rather than the rule. A plaintiff's failure to establish strictly any one of several judicially created elements to a cause of action resulted in dismissal of the action. Moreover, plaintiffs who overcame technical barriers bore a heavy burden to establish that the defendant's conduct fell below the standard of reasonable care. The philosophy that life entailed inevitable accidents and unavoidable injuries—risks assumed by victims as part of life in society—weighed heavily in judicial determinations.[31] Not unexpectedly, the position of judicial conservatism and restraint corresponded to ideological tendencies in the wider make-up of society, namely, economic laissez-faireism.[32] The legal principles that constituted tort law, therefore, were generally interpreted with a view to preventing commercial enterprises from becoming social insurers of individual welfare.[33] Legality was seen as affording remedies only against truly blameworthy and morally reprehensible conduct. As a social instrument, the mission of the law was to prevent the hampering of social and economic activity with unnecessary claims by unfortunate victims and over regulation by the courts.

This version of tort policy—favoring industrial development—was revamped by the same social dynamic that created it. The gradual transformation of society into a technological, mass-producing and mass-consuming entity engendered a corresponding change in the judicial construction and implementation of tort law. The cohabitation of machines and people in concentrated urban centers gave the concepts of negligence and legal causation an entirely new acceptation, juridical vocation, and social mission. Courts began to view children more benevolently as helpless and in need of protection rather than as "mischievous" or "thoughtless";[34] widespread economic activities in society—like public transportation[35]—created a likelihood of harm that was not necessarily assumed by victims in a "busy world";[36] the episodic confrontation of cars and trains on public roads gave new meaning to

| 205

what might be deemed imprudent on the part of defendant enterprises.[37] The concept of "unavoidable accidents"[38] for which legal liability and blame could not fairly be imposed was ultimately stricken from the lexicon of judicial interpretation and has been replaced by the concept of individually inescapable social risk: a revised sense of fairness now demands that those who engage in and profit from risk-generating activities afford monetary compensation to their unfortunate victims as a cost of doing business. Blame has become irrelevant, and retribution has been neutered. Wealth and its transfer have emerged as the principal, albeit legally unprincipled, factors in the liability (and no longer culpability) calculus. An umbrella of juridically instituted social welfare protects against the ineluctable dangers of living in a fast-paced, constantly evolving, materially productive society.

Product Law as an Example

The genesis and evolution of the tort law of product liability illustrate the gradual emergence of the social philosophy that underlies contemporary jurisprudence in tort. They also explain the underpinnings of the current controversy in tort brought about by judicial activism. In early product liability cases,[39] courts did not even recognize a tort law cause of action for damages occasioned by product mishaps. By premising potential legal liability on an exclusively contractual basis, this decisional law—motivated by a desire to protect nascent enterprises—erected privity of contract as a barrier to potential lawsuits.[40] Victims of product maloccurrences could not sue the manufacturer of the harmful product unless they had been the direct purchaser in the line of sale.

The proliferation of new products and the volume of production, however, eventually brought a change in principle, accompanied by the recognition of a cause of action in tort. Unsuspecting and technically inexpert buyers or users of products, so the new reasoning went, should not be disqualified from pursuing legal remedies simply because they failed to satisfy commercial law requirements. According to the rule in *MacPherson v. Buick Motor Co.*,[41] they were consumers, not merchants; by their very nature, some products—like cars—if improperly made, created a high level of risk and danger in society: they became "[a] thing of danger."[42] A person injured by a faulty product could, as a result, sue the manufacturer and recover—provided the product's improper construction was linked to the manufacturer's unreasonable conduct.[43]

In the words of an eminent tort scholar,[44] the "march" toward strict liability had begun. Once they benefited from a cause of action in tort, product cases yielded to the pressure of and participated in the general movement toward an economically based form of liability predicated upon social justice principles. The revolution achieved by the *MacPherson* doctrine was a necessary but limited step; plaintiffs still suffered from the handicap of establishing manufacturer negligence, a requirement that obliged them to shoulder the discovery of highly technical matters. "Innovative" judicial application of the doctrine of *res ipsa loquitur,*[45] however, lightened the burden very considerably, allowing plaintiffs to race far ahead of panting manufacturers. Disregarding Justice Traynor's call to clarity and honesty in legal doctrine,[46] the majority of the California Supreme Court in *Escola v. Coca Cola Bottling Co.*[47] ignored the salient implications of the circumstances of the case and discovered that plaintiff injury through product use gave rise to a presumption of product defect and manufacturer negligence, even though the factual elements of the case afforded the defendant little or no opportunity to adduce evidence to the contrary.[48] The summit was finally reached in *Greenman v. Yuba Power Products Inc.*[49] when Justice Traynor, renewing the logical continuity of legal reasoning, established the founding elements of a strict product liability cause of action in tort. Because the notion of contractual warranties had been the conceptual precursor of the tort action and provided merchants with a no-fault remedy, why should plaintiffs—no longer hampered by the barrier of privity—not benefit from a similarly simple and efficient basis of liability in tort?

Incorporated into section 402A of the *Restatement of Torts,*[50] the *Greenman* doctrine accomplished the second leg of the revolution. Damages occasioned by products were integrated into the full elasticity of tort law. Injured plaintiffs[51]—bombarded by advertising as consumers—no longer needed to establish manufacturer negligence, but rather that the product was defective and had caused their harm.[52] Although it was intellectually possible to view proof of defectiveness as basically indistinguishable from the requirement of establishing negligence (especially in light of section 402A's reference to an "unreasonably dangerous" defect),[53] the courts—in the vast majority of cases—failed to focus upon that potential ambiguity. To the contrary, the reigning jurisprudential mood led courts once again to remedy possible conceptual barriers to plaintiff recovery through the use of legal presumptions. That the plaintiff's injury was related to the product was deemed a sufficient ground to support a presumption of product defectiveness against the manufacturer.[54] The door was now open for the introduction of even more far-reaching compensatory concepts, such as enterprise liability,[55] invited misuse,[56] and market share liability.[57]

This survey of product law illustrates that tort law rules—perhaps more than their analogue in any other area of law (with the possible exception of public international law)—are informed primarily by the Holmesian factor of experience.[58] In articulating standards, courts place little reliance upon the elements of logic and analysis, except as they relate to the achievement and justification of policy objectives. The generalized character of the rules facilitates their use as instruments of policy implementation. There is, therefore, little in the way of meaningful traditional law in tort, and a considerable amount of judicial creativity—especially at the appellate level of proceedings where the legal rules and determinations can be conclusively adjusted to social policy ends.

The Politics of the Process

Salient features of the procedural administration of tort claims coincide with and have encouraged the development of substantive tort law as an instrument of social policy implementation. Tort litigation at the trial level is notoriously unpredictable. Judges can differ in their professional attitudes and personal convictions; no decision-maker is ever fully impartial or guided exclusively by juridical precepts, and exercising judgment is an art, not a quantifiable physical science. Also, expectations concerning witnesses or available evidence can be disappointed as the trial process begins and develops. More important, there is the jury:[59] the single, most fundamental factor of unpredictability in the litigation process. On the one hand, the jury can be viewed as a means of redressing the power imbalance between plaintiffs and corporate defendants. By their composition, juries should have an innate affinity with, and sympathy for, the plaintiff. On the other hand, it is a misconception to believe that juries consistently function to the advantage of plaintiffs. The jury verdict in *Marsee v. U.S. Tobacco*[60] provides a telling illustration that juries do not necessarily redress the power imbalance among litigating parties. There, the jury denied recovery for the death of a teenage boy who used snuff and died of tongue cancer at the age of nineteen. The facts of this case poignantly dramatized the overwhelming misfortune of a disadvantaged and innocent party and the considerable advantage of the commercial enterprise. Yet, the jury chose to uphold a conservative view of the case, apparently finding risk-assuming conduct by the decedent and sufficient doubt on the question of probable factual causality.[61]

Also, as the cases brought against cigarette manufacturers[62] illustrate, individuals who initiate lawsuits against large commercial enterprises are—by the nature of things—at a severe procedural disadvantage from the outset of the lawsuit. As a rule, corporations have financial access to the best legal services, whereas private individuals can only retain those attorneys they can afford. Although the contingency fee arrangement—permitting lawyers to advance costs of the litigation to their clients—has facilitated matters, plaintiffs usually need significant injury and a good case on the law to persuade lawyers that the risk is worth taking. Corporate defendants hoping to elude a jury determination have budgets that can support protracted discovery and pretrial motions. For example, rather than allow suits against them to go to trial with appropriate dispatch, cigarette manufacturers adopted a policy of deliberately delaying proceedings in the hope of wearing down the other side before the merits could be addressed.[63] Due process requirements and the passive role of the judge in adversarial proceedings make different adjudicatory practices unlikely.

The attempt by defendants to avoid the jury through procedural tactics skews the process and undermines much of its substantive integrity. In adversarial warfare, however, every maneuver must be responded to in kind—thus a generally distortive dynamic is set in motion. Plaintiff attorneys hang on in the pretrial phase and then, in an attempt to gain an adversarial advantage, use psychological techniques in jury selection and mock juries before and during the trial to anticipate the reaction of the seated jury. Defense attorneys do likewise, and the spiraling tactical contest reinforces and perpetuates the weaknesses of the process. Despite their central decision-making role, juries already have difficulty understanding applicable legal standards and are prone to decide matters on the basis of subjective impressions and personal beliefs. Fostering the recourse to that nonlegal predicate for decision-making through manipulation and the theatrical production of appearances erodes the credibility of trial proceedings. It creates a substantial and unacceptable distance between the theory and the implementation of law—a gap that is allegedly demanded by the ineluctable practicalities of adversarial gamesmanship.

Ultimate Systemic Consequence

Traditionally, the objective of tort adjudication was to arrive at a determination of whether conduct was legally wrongful. Despite the embracing of a compensatory rationale, adjudicatory outcomes still carry the stigma of blameworthiness. No one enjoys or easily tolerates being unjustly accused of having committed a legal wrong. Moreover, the legal process must express its commitment to humanitarian compensation in conventional legal terms and concepts—analytical language that harbors little conceptual affinity to social welfare objectives and results in opaque communications. Therefore, although the content of the debate is ultimately political, the discourse is cast in terms of juridical considerations: causation, negligence, victim fault, proof of defectiveness, and the measurement of damages. The resulting incomprehension breeds further antagonism among opposing interests. Litigious posturing over a period of time is usually necessary before the parties, in the name of expediency and efficiency, acquiesce to a solution of compromise. In a minority of instances, the resentment that builds from the clash of legal accountability principles and the compensatory objective cannot be sufficiently diminished. Only a fully litigious confrontation provides finality in the form of a jury determination ultimately upheld on appeal.

As noted, collective and individual jury behavior is impossible to predict for either side. The lack of predictability that results from the presence of the jury in the trial process ordinarily makes both parties uneasy and may be the primary reason for the high level of settlement in tort actions. Estimates are that nearly 95% of tort actions are concluded by way of settlement.[64] Unpredictable jury determinations induce the financially advantaged defendant to take a possibly lesser loss and the injured plaintiff to gain a quicker and more certain, if less generous, recovery.

The bias in substantive tort law and the procedural uncertainty of tort litigation work hand in hand to achieve what appears to be an intended (or at least inescapable if unintended) systemic consequence. Courts have adjusted the applicable legal principles to avoid the automatic disqualification of plaintiff actions. Judicial opinions further indicate that, in most circumstances, questions of law in actual litigation will be construed to favor plaintiff recovery. Litigation, however, is—it seems—equally precarious for both parties. To the defendant's economic leverage and foot-dragging, the plaintiff answers with the prospect of an eventual jury determination brought upon by histrionics and sympathy. The gamble is, however, considerable on both sides. Each party faces the prospect of an unstable decision-making predicate and the possibility of a complete loss at the hands of inexpert impressions. The various elements of the tort system, therefore, appear to encourage the granting of some form of compensation by the recourse to a more rationally based alternative. Neither party is really guilty or innocent, or really wants to play Russian roulette with its interests. The overwhelming majority of parties, therefore, choose settlement over the adjudication of their claims.

The critical problem in the development of tort law, then, is not the judicial use of legal doctrine to fashion a particular brand of social justice nor the recourse to litigious parodies of substantive legal truth by trial attorneys. The view that modern society is dangerous, includes unavoidable injury, and should provide compensation to its victims is not an unwarranted interpretation of the contemporary social contract. Trial attorneys are under an ethical duty to their clients to play the adversarial game by its rules, no matter how illogical and unprincipled. The real issue is whether the systemic factors that—by implication rather than forthrightly—encourage settlement are the best rationale and procedure for resolving tort disputes. Although compensation should be available, placing an excessive burden on commercial enterprises or compromising their economic viability is socially self-destructive. Settlement after extensive legal posturing may be too costly in monetary, legal policy, and human terms. In any event, an implied policy encouraging settlement does little to reduce the inflammatory social debate and to create a consensus position in society. Alternative procedures—founded upon a more explicit rational dispute resolution ethic—might lessen the perception of crisis as well as its reality.

Tort Reform

The specific perimeters of the present controversy surrounding tort reform[65] can be summarized by the attempt of lawyers, corporate enterprises, professional associations, consumer groups, and insurance companies to cast blame upon each for creating the crisis in tort litigation or imagining that it exists. The irreconcilable, politically embedded opposition has led the proponents of change to approach the legislative process, seeking to redress the perceived imbalance by way of a political command. Specifically, the victims of would-be judicial and jury bias seek to have legislatures dictate that concepts of joint and several liability be applied more restrictively to limit corporate liability and to have ceilings placed upon the monetary amount recoverable for noneconomic damages.[66]

Also, during the early eighties, strong efforts were undertaken to have a nationally uniform product liability law enacted by the United States Congress.[67] The substance of the bill supported manufacturer interests; it included such limitation of liability features as a statute of repose for products and advanced a negligence principle as the standard of liability.[68] The level of criticism lodged against, and the public attention given to, the tort litigation system even led the American Bar Association to take steps that acknowledged that some type of problem existed. At the 1987 midyear meeting, the American Bar Association recommended, pending further study, that judges exercise their authority to reduce tort awards that are "clearly disproportionate to community expectations."[69] In addition to other difficulties, the evident problem with the recommendation is that the reference to "community expectations" simply restates the problem. The community, however defined, is fundamentally divided over its expectations in this area. More important, the passionate character of the debate impedes efforts to clarify the situation: no one really knows whether substantial problems do in fact exist with the tort litigation process. While there are evident abuses in a minority of cases, the outrage they generate should not lead to a blanket denial of rights in all cases.

The continuing criticism and public attention have encouraged many state legislatures to enact tort reform measures either of a moderate or extreme kind.[70] These measures center upon the more common complaints made by the reformist camp, namely, the application of joint and several liability provisions and awards for noneconomic and punitive damages.[71] There are serious questions, however, about whether legislative solutions can be effective in achieving greater justice in tort litigation. Apart from the overriding question of whether the current system is actually deficient, these legislative enactments may not reflect a considered, neutral judgment about the solution to a social problem.

212 |

They may symbolize a political response to public pressure generated by public relations campaigns, a permanent or temporary shift in the power balance of the state legislature, or the astute lobbying efforts of a particular special interest group. Usually, such measures are the product of political compromise and are, therefore, ineffective to deal with the reality of the problem they address. For example, the legislative imposition of medical malpractice review panels has not lessened the intensity of that aspect of the tort litigation crisis.[72] In most cases, these panels operate primarily to advance the interests of only one of the affected groups: the doctors. By comparison to legislatures, judicial tribunals at least have a more neutral institutional stature and — in theory — can give a more legitimate expression to a societal consensus about what is fair in these circumstances. Moreover, in those states that have adopted tort reform measures, premiums for insurance coverage have not declined in any significant way,[73] attesting to the ineptitude of the special interest solution. Insurance business practices may, in fact, be at the heart of the present controversy over the availability of resources for compensation.

The real tragedy of the present system (and where legislative or judicial efforts should be focused) lies in another feature of the tort process. An immense superstructure of law has fueled an intensely political debate centering upon the questions of who pays, how much, and in what circumstances for societal risk. The transposition of a social humanitarian objective into the legal process has generated untoward costs, substantial confusion about the meaning of legal liability, and results that imperil the integrity of legal doctrine and the social viability of the adjudicatory system. It is an unruly system whose present operation appears to have exceeded its initial utility for achieving its social objective. In the confrontation of group self-interests within the confines of the present system, the public interest always emerges as the real loser.[74]

On the one hand, legislative endorsement of enterprise and insurance industry proposals for tort reform minimizes individual access to courts, limits the right to the redress of grievances, and will eventually lead to a denial of necessary compensation in deserving cases. On the other hand, the current process achieves its fundamental objective of finding juridical means to obtain compensation for persons who have suffered harm only at considerable expense. Although Bigbee eventually achieved recovery from a remote corporate party, it took ten years of litigation to arrive at that result. Many trial court outcomes—those that gain most public attention—are reduced significantly through protracted appellate proceedings, final outcomes that have a much lesser public visibility.[75] Thus, under the current system, plaintiffs must have suffered sufficient injury to interest an attorney in a contingency fee, be willing to tolerate and able to survive protracted proceedings, and be satisfied with an ultimate recovery significantly (as much as 70%) less than the original award after costs. The public—either collectively through higher product prices or individually through substantially reduced recoveries—bears the costs of a judicially supervised, de facto social insurance program.

As noted earlier,[76] the operation of the process implicitly coerces settlement. Instances in which aberrant results are obtained are exceptional, occurring only when the systemic pressure to resort to settlement fails. Faced with the prospect of costly and unpredictable litigation, rationality dictates that negotiated settlement is the preferred option in the circumstances for both parties. When that option fails in this judicially legislated system, the jury is still available to make the legislative determination on the social issues implicitly generated by the litigation. Because cases recalcitrant to settlement are rare, abuse of decision-making authority can be corrected by appellate processes without calling the integrity of the tacit systemic ethic into question.

The general operation of society, the advancement of the public interest, the position of plaintiffs, and business operations could be greatly facilitated by an express recognition and formalization of that tacit systemic ethic, and not its elimination or modification. Given the complexities of society and of litigation, to promote settlement surreptitiously is no longer a workable policy instrument. It works too great a hardship upon plaintiffs and has generated a political debate—enmeshed in professional self-interest—that threatens to undermine the integrity of the legal adjudicatory process. For fear of losing advantage, neither side is willing to assume a position of compromise. Any retrenchment of position would be analogous to a national government's abandonment of its shield of sovereignty in a state-to-state dispute. The public international experience in dispute resolution teaches that traditional adjudicatory means are ineffective in the resolution of politically charged controversies that implicate fundamental interests. It is now time to heed for a second time Justice Traynor's call to simple, honest doctrine[77] and to devise a system of dispute resolution in tort that externalizes the settlement rationale of the current process.

Possible Alternatives

Socialization of Risk

Although probably unthinkable and arguably impractical, the true answer to the political controversy raised by the system of tort litigation is to legislate a program of comprehensive social compensation for accident victims. Such a program would place political responsibility "where it ought to be,"[78] and would obviate the institution of litigation with the sole objective of finding a defendant financially able to compensate injured victims.

Such a program would eliminate the need for new dispute resolution remedies. The problems with the existing process would simply not exist. It would allow tort adjudication to perform the less creative, albeit more politically suitable, function of deterring and affixing legal blame for unlawfully dangerous conduct. The formal institutionalization of a compensatory mechanism for accident loss would allow the courts to address the issue of legal blameworthiness more forthrightly. In fact, the general availability of social compensation should allow liability determinations to result from the application of a professional art and could, once again, be limited to circumstances of exceptionally egregious conduct without placing victims in a condition of destitution. Liability determinations could lead to the tortfeasor's payment of money damages to the system of social compensation (as a partial reimbursement) and—more exceptionally—to the injured victim (in the form of punitive damages). The law of tort could thereby still perform a deterrence function. Maximum recovery ceilings could be placed upon both types of damages; generally, the measurement of damages would exclude any reference to noneconomic harm; and punitive damages— the only allowable form of noneconomic recovery—would be available only in the truly exceptional case. General predictability of recovery should allow most damages (except for punitive damages) to be covered at least partially by personal liability insurance.

The funding for such a system is a critical factor. It is likely to resurrect much (perhaps more) of the political turmoil that characterizes the current debate on tort law. The inevitable intensity of the controversy leads to the suspicion that the proposal of a program of socialized risk would reinforce rather than resolve the existing political conflicts. Be that as it may, in the general outline of the proposed scheme, state governments would perform a role analogous to the one they currently play in mandatory automobile insurance. Legislatures would issue the command, set minimum amounts, enforce compliance, and encourage the creation of private insurance companies to deal with emerging needs. Such a procedure would combine elements of privatization with the general socialization policy. Private companies would act as a financial base upon which to erect a state regulatory and social policy.

To deal with inability to comply because of financial incapacity, state governments could themselves provide a form of basic coverage, including hospitalization, disability, and life insurances. The support for such a fund would be gained in part from liability reimbursements, but primarily through individual and corporate taxation. If accidents are an inevitable part of social existence and the provision of compensation is part of the price of doing business, a modest tax could be levied on income, products, and/or corporate organization and activities. Again, the key to any (even and perhaps especially a political) program to deal with social loss resides in the ability of individuals and the community to espouse a rational and demystified view of problems. Although all residents would be required to pay the same percentage tax, state coverage would be made available on a graduated scale based on income. Individuals whose income level qualifies them for only partial coverage or disqualifies them from any coverage would be required to purchase stated minimum amounts from private sources.

The program's general objective would be to prevent injury-producing events from creating devastating losses for individuals or their survivors. The underlying rationale is that the misfortunes of life and their consequences are better entrusted to the public will rather than to private litigation and judicial adjudication. The provision of humanitarian compensation to individuals should be seen as a matter of collective right and responsibility. Legal blame should either be excluded altogether or triggered only in egregious circumstances to achieve reimbursement and deterrence. Moreover, such a program is not based primarily upon insensitive principles of economic calculations, but rather is embedded in a structure of fundamental values. It is in society's best interest to maintain the integrity of legality, recognize the intractable risk of social existence, and respond to social problems with rationally based and productive solutions.

Although cost distribution is an increasingly popular device (even in private enterprise) simply because it makes economic sense, a plan to collectivize the costs of personal injury will probably fail because it is likely to generate divisive and uncompromising political controversy. It will produce an unending debate between those who believe in government intervention and responsibility for social welfare and those who cherish individual initiative and self-reliance as the essential modalities of civilized political life. As with public international law disputes, political convictions frustrate the recourse to simple, expedient, and pragmatic alternatives. Self-evidently workable solutions cannot be engaged because of the threat they pose to fundamental political choices. To some extent, the uncompromising attitudes on large general issues foster mythical and mystical perceptions that confine understanding to all-or-nothing propositions. Such superficial assessments are at times difficult to integrate into the more disparate and ambiguous character of actual reality where real solutions are necessary.

Assuming that the proposal for collectivizing social risk and injury would be untenable even as a guiding principle of reform, the adjudicatory process remains the only institutional means by which to confront the problem. Its task is to deal with an acknowledged social need while containing the political passions that underlie the implicated interests. Moreover, the accommodation of the competing considerations must be accomplished through the use of established juridical concepts and by reference to the existing realities of the procedural process. By a vast majority, both institutional actors and private participants in the present process agree that settlement is the most feasible means for resolving tort disputes. The formalization of that practice in a variety of alternative mechanisms—functioning in conjunction with the judicial process—might facilitate the task of the adjudicatory framework, help to reduce costs, and achieve a higher quality of justice in society.

Mediation

The experience with state-to-state disputes teaches that political conflicts are most effectively resolved by having a number of nonbinding remedies available to the parties. Also, the lessons of dispute resolution in divorce illustrate that impassioned conflicts, although they may proceed from a similar general mold, are not all alike and will respond to different resolutory mechanisms. Parties involved in a personal injury matter should, therefore, be afforded a panoply of diverse prelitigation remedies. Assuming a basic awareness and understanding of circumstances, the choice of remedies should enable the parties to develop and exercise meaningfully their ability to engage in self-determined dispute resolution.

The mediation methodology[79] constitutes a first (perhaps final) step, offering a nonadjudicatory means of addressing conflict. In effect, the recourse to mediation would represent the paradigmatic circumstances of "bargaining in the shadow of the law."[80] The mediation alternative could make the possibility of negotiated settlement available to the parties in a more humane fashion and presumably at less financial cost. It also intends to give the parties an understanding of their dispute and how and why it might be more effectively resolved through rational exchange and compromise. The mediator would function in a mixed capacity, acting both as a conciliator and negotiator. The mediator's responsibility would be to offer the parties an impartial outside perspective on their dispute, use communication skills to bring them closer to a consensus about the desirability of resolution, and suggest ways for achieving a mutually agreeable accommodation of their interests. Mediators could be selected by the parties or appointed by the court from a legislatively established list of academics, mental health professionals, or certified mediators. In any event, mediators who undertake the mediation of personal injury disputes should combine a professional or practical understanding of conflicts (how they arise and how they can be resolved) with a general knowledge of the dispute resolution results that usually obtain in the tort litigation system.

The scheme of rules for mediation should exclude adversarial posturing and dilatory tactics from the process. Despite opposing interests, legal representation should be molded to fit the informality and arms' length character of the dispute resolution framework. In the setting of mediation, legal representation needs to strike a balance between advocacy and cooperation, thereby facilitating the creation of a working consensus among the parties and the effort to achieve settlement. Attorneys, for example, could submit written statements on behalf of clients, stating the facts and the client's general position as well as specific arguments on the issues, and advise clients during the mediation session(s) and before a formal agreement.

After reviewing the submissions, the mediator would meet with the parties and their legal counsel—informing them initially of the purpose and goals of the proceeding and of the benefit of mutual cooperation in resolving disputes. The mediator might set the tone and direction of the session by suggesting a few touchstone ideas. For example, a physical or emotional harm, once perpetrated, can only be repaired by money or the exchange of some other substitute, not righted through restitution. A companion notion—that physical injury is accompanied by real emotional detriment and sometimes substantial inconvenience—should also be integrated into the basic assumptions of the process. Moreover, absolute categorical positions are both unrealistic and counterproductive in the circumstances of conflict. No matter how indefensible behavior may appear initially, legal and even moral arguments can always be mustered in support of the other side. Prolonging disagreement, postponing the day of reckoning, or unwillingness to accept some amount of loss will usually generate more injury and costs. Finally, intransigence makes the all-or-nothing gamble of adversarial adjudication a virtual necessity. Rationality and a sense of practicality should dispel windfall fantasies, the irrational desire for complete vindication, and the irresponsibility of desired nonaccountability.

The mediator could then comment upon the divergent positions taken in the written statements, asking the parties (who would have the benefit of the advice of counsel) to consider a number of compromissory positions in discussing specific points of disagreement. Casting a disinterested, resolution-oriented perspective on problems and suggesting possible solutions for consideration should stimulate the parties to envisage their conflict with greater rationality and generate creative insights on both sides that allow for a truly self-determined conclusion.

Although mediated resolutions cannot be coerced, state legislatures might nonetheless require prospective personal injury litigants to attend one or several mediation sessions. All parties would thereby have at least an opportunity to gain knowledge about the nature of disputes and the diverse methods of resolution. They could also develop a more informed understanding of what lies ahead in terms of traditional adjudication and change their conduct in that setting to some extent. Moreover, the rate of settlement in the current process indicates that the vast majority of litigants are prone to accept compromise and a rational appraisal of the reality of dispute. The framework for dispute resolution should at least test whether the parties have any desire to achieve an orderly, logical, and constructive informal settlement of their claims.

As with its analogue in divorce, the successful mediation of personal injury claims would culminate in a contractual agreement that memorializes the parties' mutually agreed-upon resolution of their differences. The specific terms of the agreement should be drafted in a final collective session among the mediator, the parties, and their legal counsel. To legitimate the mediation process and to give the agreement the express force of law, the final contract should be reviewed by a court and integrated into a formal judicial judgment. Finally, to give the process greater appeal, the state could pay for most mediation costs but the attorney's fees. Because mediation should result in lowering court costs, the savings could be used to support the mediation process. Moreover, certified mediators could perform their functions on a *pro bono publico* basis or for a minimal fee.

Arbitration

Although mediation formalizes the tacit settlement practice of the current process, it will not achieve universal success. The mediation methodology is likely to be functional only for a certain, albeit large, class of personal injury disputes. It should, for example, achieve satisfactory results in cases involving ordinary parties whose bargaining positions and strengths are roughly comparable. Statistical studies show that these cases constitute the bulk of tort litigation and are already responsive to settlement through adversarial means. The opposition of interests should yield even more quickly to settlement in a process that expressly fosters compromise.

Suits brought by individuals against corporate enterprises either for direct harm or upon a more remote causal basis are likely to be less malleable to interests accommodation through mediation. Although corporate enterprises generally favor the recourse to alternative mechanisms (like arbitration and the mini-trial)[81] in their commercial dealings, the parties' disparity of position in personal injury matters and the potentially provocative basis for liability may render mediation unworkable. In these circumstances, a combination of adjudicatory alternatives might be attempted.

Such cases, for example, could be submitted to a form of arbitral fact-finding before litigation.[82] The arbitral tribunal—consisting of legal professionals with diverse but relevant expertise and experience—would perform functions roughly comparable to those of English masters in trial preparations.[83] Under a set of flexible and nonadversarial procedural rules and operating in reference to an established time limit, the tribunal would generally supervise the parties' discovery efforts, directing them when necessary to gather and present information the tribunal finds necessary for the ensuing litigation. After the parties' submissions, the arbitrators — after hearing the parties — would also refine the factual and legal matters at issue. The purpose of the arbitral proceeding would be to take discovery and similar matters out of the contentious process. This procedure should limit the play of the adversarial ethic upon judicial resources and the jury. Once the proceeding is closed, the arbitral tribunal would deliver its neutral findings to the court. The statement of the essential facts and the description of the applicable law should also clearly describe whatever consensus existed and has been created among the parties as well as the divisions between them. The court should evaluate the record, and either accept it or request that the arbitral tribunal clarify points or fill gaps. Once approved, the arbitral record would be presented by the court to the jury, and the formal trial would consist primarily of brief rebuttals and closing arguments before the jury.

Depending upon the scope of reform measures, arbitral factfinding as an adjunct to the judicial process could be supplemented with a number of options that further facilitate dispute resolution. For example, having established the basic factual and legal elements of the case, the arbitral tribunal could also — if both parties agree — render an award resolving some or all of the claims. In these circumstances, with judicial approval and supervision, the parties would enter into a submission agreement, stating that they have agreed to arbitrate the claims enumerated in the agreement and to accept the tribunal's award as the final and binding determination. In these circumstances, the tribunal could be authorized to request assistance from the court to clarify legal questions. Unlike the old English stated case procedure,[84] only the arbitrators would have authority to make such requests, and the request would be for legal guidance and not a judicial ruling. To encourage party recourse and add integrity to the process, the eventual award should contain the tribunal's rulings accompanied by a modest set of reasons justifying those conclusions. The content of the award would reflect a basic consensus among the arbitrators after deliberation on the record and should be subject only to the limited forms of recourse provided for in the Federal Arbitration Act.[85] Such an outcome would generally correspond to the result reached through current pre-trial conferences that lead to settlement.

To provide a further incentive to convert the fact-finding determination into a final award, the court could give the parties its evaluation of the arbitral record and its recommendations on the law. At this point, the parties should also have a good idea of the general direction of an arbitral ruling. Fundamental disagreement may, however, persist. For example, a corporate party may be unwilling, as a matter of principle, to accept the juridical basis for its alleged liability. One or both parties may assume that the arbitral determination is likely to be unfair. In these circumstances, the process could be supplemented with a judicial option that would be exercised at the court's discretion and be intended for application in exceptional circumstances. Upon its own motion, the court could issue a summary judicial disposition of the case. Using the record of facts and arguments presented during the arbitral proceeding, the court could find that the issues, on their face, are ripe for determination and render a judgment. The judgment would be subject to appellate review on the ordinary grounds for appeal.

Arbitration could also be used as a true adjudicatory mechanism from the outset of the process. Assuming that tort disputes are arbitrable,[86] parties who mutually find adversarial adjudication unsuitable but are unable to mediate their differences could engage in the traditional form of consensual arbitration. In this setting, party contract discretion could work in tandem with legislative reforms; for example, the option of converting a fact-finding arbitral proceeding into an adjudicatory determination would, in effect, greatly enhance the ultimate recourse to consensual arbitration. Moreover, rather than having arbitration function solely as a fact-finding mechanism and a preface to litigation, state legislatures could require the recourse to arbitral adjudication as a mandatory precursor to litigation or to supplant legal adjudication altogether. In the latter case, the legislature would direct that all personal injury claims be submitted to mandatory binding arbitration. In the former circumstances, before the suit, claims would be submitted to mandatory nonbinding arbitration or to an arbitral tribunal's advisory jurisdiction.

When arbitration is mandatory and nonbinding, it is constitutionally permissible for state legislatures to require initial recourse to arbitral rather than judicial adjudication. The provision for mandatory nonbinding arbitration does not directly result in the denial of due process of law, equal protection of the laws, or in constitutionally prohibited discrimination. The problem with mandatory nonbinding arbitration is that it privileges the position of the financially advantaged party by adding another layer to a process that may already be only barely accessible to the economically disadvantaged party—without making finality any more likely.[87] On the other hand, mandatory binding arbitration raises a host of other problems, already discussed in regard to divorce disputes.[88] It not only raises significant constitutional questions, but is also misplaced in a remedial framework that seeks to foster self-determination, individual rationality, consensus, and mutual cooperation in dispute resolution.

Instead of, or in addition to, arbitral fact-finding, mandatory binding, or nonbinding arbitration, state legislatures might provide for advisory opinions through arbitral adjudication in cases in which there is a substantial disparity in the parties' positions and continuing steadfast opposition. Unless an accommodation of interests can be reached before the conclusion of such an arbitral proceeding, the advisory procedure would result in the judicial adjudication of the dispute by a modified form of civil jury trial. Advisory arbitral opinions might constitute the best means by which to reconcile the interest in adjudicatory fairness and the need to minimize the impact of the adversarial ethic on tort dispute resolution.

In the advisory framework, the legislature would require that all personal injury suits be submitted preliminarily to arbitration for advisory adjudicatory evaluation. The arbitral tribunal, consisting of a panel of three experts in law and dispute resolution, would establish a factual record by having depositions taken, receiving documentary evidence, and hearing lay and expert witnesses. Also, the parties would submit briefs on the legal issues in dispute. Pursuant to ordinary arbitral practice, the governing procedure would be anchored in the twin dictates of fairness and flexibility. Under the general supervision of the tribunal, the arbitrators and the parties would, in effect, share responsibility for the conduct of the proceeding, which should move forward with reasonable dispatch. The tribunal would take an active part in the discovery of evidence and the questioning of witnesses. It would evaluate evidence and arguments in accordance with a basic respect for law. Finally, a party's failure to comply or cooperate could be taken into account in the tribunal's advisory opinion.

After deliberating on the record and by reference to the arguments presented, the tribunal would issue an advisory opinion setting out the essential facts of the case, the basic legal issues in question, and the applicable law. The tribunal would then include its recommendations about how the case should be decided, explaining in detail its reasons for supporting such a determination. This appraisal should also include an assessment and apportionment of damages. In an effort to encourage party acceptance of the arbitral determination, state legislatures might impose ceilings on recovery in the arbitral opinion but not in regard to an eventual jury verdict. If the parties did not move to have the tribunal convert the advisory opinion into a final award, the court—upon receipt of the opinion—would set a date for trial.

At the outset of the trial, the court would inform the jury that an impartial group of expert arbitral adjudicators has established the legal and factual record of the matter, reveal the contents of the advisory opinion to the jury (except its reference to the measurement of damages), and give its general evaluation of the opinion. After the court's presentation to the jury, the parties would have the opportunity to make a brief presentation and their closing arguments to the jury, emphasizing and criticizing various aspects of the advisory opinion within an allotted period of time. After being instructed, the jury would then recess to study the advisory opinion and return to the courtroom to pose questions concerning the matter to the court in the presence of and with the participation of legal counsel. It would thereafter enter into deliberation. Again, the rule of order would be that proceedings should move forward with reasonable dispatch.

Although the right to a civil jury trial is guaranteed by both the federal and state constitutions,[89] no constitutional imperative prohibits integrating arbitral determinations with trial proceedings or requires the adversarial ethic to dominate absolutely every aspect of the trial process. If parties want a legislative determination of their controversy and of the social issues it implies in the form of a jury verdict, the process should allow that community determination to be guided primarily by expert and impartial legal appraisals rather than dilatory procedural tactics or a display of theatrical jousting.

As with divorce disputes, the framework of alternatives in tort ranges from procedurally flexible remedies that emphasize third-party-assisted self-determination to procedurally more restrictive remedies that limit the exercise of litigious party discretion. When the conflict is not susceptible to self-determination, the framework provides a variety of opportunities to enable the parties to respond to accumulated experience and avoid an actual trial. If legal adjudication is selected as the means of recourse, it should provide juridical answers to the parties' dilemma and should not produce results inconsonant with the legal integrity of the process. Moreover, when the mediated settlement option fails, the framework attempts to make creative use of arbitration both as a fact-finding and as an adjudicatory methodology. Finally, when coercive legal finality becomes a necessity, the framework seeks to modify traditional judicial procedures to give legal expertise the upper hand over adversarial warfare and have that expertise shape the ultimate jury determination.

Conclusion

The foregoing recommendations outline what might be done to institute alternative mechanisms that facilitate and improve dispute resolution in tort. The recommendations do not address fully all aspects of possible implementation, but rather propose a general scheme of reorientation. Their objective is to integrate humanistic priorities into the dispute resolution framework (the reference to rationality, self-determination, and inward personal truth) and to minimize the deficiencies of the traditional legal adjudicatory methodology (single-minded advocacy, distortions of truth and the evasion of substantive law, the influence of economic and political leverage, and the undue reliance on external, impersonal standards).

In its operation, the proposed alternative framework seeks to have third parties instruct litigants, caught in the turmoil of conflict, on how to cooperate sufficiently to reach a consensus position, rather than simply do the job for them and rob them of any role in resolving their problems. Accordingly, the alternative framework places a premium upon the willingness of parties in conflict to reach third-party-assisted but self-determined results and substantially devalues the utility and minimizes the role of the adversarial ethic. Beyond these initial, albeit fundamental considerations, questions remain regarding the funding of the process, the certification of mediators and adjudicators, and the willingness of legislative bodies to dislodge tort disputes from the province of public policy. The consideration of these problems, however, must await initial experimentation with the basic principles that have been suggested. Using the example of the development of international commercial arbitration, experience with limited trial implementation should provide an indication of feasibility, how the process will or should be made to evolve, and whether a societal consensus can be developed.

The theory and structure of the specific alternative remedies appear to reduce the deficiencies of the current tort litigation process without generating substantial inadequacies of their own. Mediation has a clear potential for achieving the already pervasive systemic result of settlement without the need to engage in the duplicity and frustration of adversarial posturing. More important, it gives the parties an understanding of dispute resolution and allows them to combine that knowledge with their own basic rationality to achieve a mutually agreed-upon and self-determined outcome. Limiting adversarial access to the jury should not create a disincentive to settlement. Although substantive legal expertise would surround the jury and its function, the inexpert character of the jury will not change. Moreover, by their appeal to rationality, the proffer of self-determination, and their reliance on professional adjudicatory skills and knowledge, alternative mechanisms should induce a willingness to compromise and reinforce the settlement ethic.

In its traditional adjudicatory format, consensual arbitration offers some advantages over the process of legal adjudication, especially in terms of its procedural flexibility. Those advantages, however, may appeal only to a small number of parties who can agree that adversarial adjudication is untenable but cannot cooperate sufficiently to engage in a self-empowering process. Using the arbitral framework in a fact-finding or advisory capacity represents a more creative use of arbitration to deal with the minority of cases that resist compromise and agreed-upon settlement. The chief contribution of these arbitral alternatives is that their integration into the current adjudicatory framework can justify a significant reduction of the role of the adversarial ethic—the science of jury manipulation and procedural obfuscation.

The cardinal disadvantage of the recommended framework is that, by using alternative mechanisms, the political controversies implied and generated by tort disputes will be resolved, in the main, without any public reference.[90] It is true that the light of public scrutiny will not glow into the shadows of private decision-making. Arguably, however, when settlement is achieved currently within the judicial process, basically similar results apply. The public interest, it seems, can be more appropriately served by placing public trust in individual responsibility and rationality, rather than in public officials who—under the current system—are at best passive and, at worst, beleaguered in the execution of their duties by the politics of adversarial combat. Alternative remedies would prevent the undermining of the legal system's integrity—unburdening it of its political task when legislative bodies are unable to perform effectively because of the influence of special interests. The systemic shadow of the current process—having social policy wear a juridical mask and purchasing approval in the secrecy of legislative corridors and offices—are certainly more ominous than whatever dark dangers can be seen in the exercise of personal responsibility and accountability in private dispute resolution. If a public espousal of the problem through social welfare remains unthinkable, the ad hoc system of compensation should become truly ad hoc rather than masquerade in the costume of legality.

NOTES

1. See, for example, Greengard, *Is the Tort System Heading for a Crash?*, 14 BARRISTER 8, 9-11, 37-38 (1987) [Greengard]. For a comprehensive discussion of contemporary developments and theories in tort law, see Contents, 10 AM. J. TRIAL ADV. 193-364 (1986); Symposium, *Alternative Compensation Schemes and Tort Theory*, 73 CALIF. L. REV. 548 (1985). See also Smith, *The Critics and the "Crisis": A Reassessment of Current Conceptions of Tort Law*, 72 CORNELL L. REV. 765 (1987); Stewart, *Crisis in Tort Law? The Institutional Perspective*, 54 U. CHI. L. REV. 184 (1987).

2. See, for example, Greengard, supra note 1, at 10. But see U.S. ATTORNEY GEN., AN UPDATE ON THE LIABILITY CRISIS TORT POLICY WORKING GROUP 22-31 (Mar. 1987), reprinted in 1 MEALEY'S LITIG. REP. NAT'L TORT REFORM 1742, 1753-58 (Apr. 7, 1987) [UPDATE ON LIABILITY CRISIS].

3. See Greengard, supra note 1, at 10. But see UPDATE ON LIABILITY CRISIS, supra note 2, at 22-31. Accord *GAO Says Industry Profited More Than $80 Billion Over Decade*, 1 MEALEY'S LITIG. REP. NAT'L TORT REFORM 1919 (May 6, 1987). See also Reshe, *Was There a Liability Crisis?*, ABA J. 46 (Jan. 1989).

4. See Greengard, supra note 1, at 37-38. See also *Oregon Trial Lawyers Study Shows No Increase in Jury Verdicts*, 1 MEALEY'S LITIG. REP. NAT'L TORT REFORM 1990 (May 20, 1987).

5. See id. at 11, 37. Accord Rand Report, *The Civil Jury in the 1980's,* note 59 infra.

6. See Greengard, supra note 1, at 37.

7. See id. at 38.

8. See id. For a positive appraisal of the current system of tort law, see SPECIAL COMM. ON THE TORT LIAB. SYS., AMER. BAR ASS'N, TOWARDS A JURISPRUDENCE OF INJURY: THE CONTINUING CREATION OF A SYSTEM OF SUBSTANTIVE JUSTICE IN AMERICAN TORT LAW (1984). See also Phillips, *In Defense of the Tort System,* 27 ARIZ. L. REV. 603 (1985). Accord Fleming, *Is There a Future for Tort?* 44 LA. L. REV. 1193 (1984) and 58 AUSTL. L.J. 131 (1984). See generally Abraham, *Individual Action and Collective Responsibility: The Dilemma of Mass Tort Reform,* 73 VA. L. REV. 845 (1987); Priest, *Modern Tort Law and Its Reform,* 22 VAL. U. L. REV. 1 (1987); Wade, *Tort Law as Ombudsman,* 65 OR. L. REV. 309 (1986); White, *Tort Reform in the Twentieth Century: An Historical Perspective,* 32 VILL. L. REV. 1265 (1987).

9. See Greengard, supra note 1, at 10.

10. See id.

11. See id. at 9-10.

12. See id.

13. See id.

14. See id. at 9.

15. See id. at 37-38.

16. See id. at 38. See also UPDATE ON LIABILITY CRISIS, supra note 2, at 52-53.

17. See J. KAKALIK, P. EBENER, W. FELSTINER, & M. SHANLEY, COSTS OF ASBESTOS LITIGATION (1983); Jackson v. Johns-Manville Sales Corp., 750 F.2d 1314, 1335-41 app. *Dimensions of Asbestos Litigation* (5th Cir. 1985) (Clark, C.J., dissenting). See also Brodeur, *Annals of Law: The Asbestos Industry on Trial* (pts. 1-4), 61 THE NEW YORKER 49 (June 10, 1985, at 49; June 17, 1985, at 45; June 24, 1985, at 37; July 1, 1985, at 36); Comment, *An Examination of Recurring Issues in Asbestos Litigation,* 46 ALB. L. REV. 1307 (1982); Comment, *Asbestos Litigation: The Dust Has Yet to Settle,* 7 FORDHAM URB. L.J. 55 (1978-79); Note, *Market Share Liability and Asbestos Litigation: No Causation, No Cause,* 37 MERCER L. REV. 1115 (1986); Special Project, *An Analysis of the Legal, Social, and Political Issues Raised by Asbestos Litigation,* 36 VAND. L. REV. 573 (1983).

18. See, for example, W. PABST, AN AMERICAN HOSPITAL ASSOCIATION PROFESSIONAL LIABILITY SURVEY (1981); PUB. AFF. DEP'T., AM. TRIAL LAW. ASSN., THE AMERICAN MEDICAL ASSOCIATION IS WRONG: THERE IS NO MEDICAL MALPRACTICE INSURANCE CRISIS (1985). Accord U.S. DEP'T OF HEALTH, EDUC. & WELFARE, MEDICAL MALPRACTICE REPORT OF THE SECRETARY'S

COMMISSION ON MEDICAL MALPRACTICE (1973); D. LOUISELL & H. WILLIAMS, MEDICAL MALPRACTICE (Supp. 1984) (multivolume series). See also P. DANZON, MEDICAL MALPRACTICE THEORY, EVIDENCE, AND PUBLIC POLICY (1985), noted in 99 HARV. L. REV. 2001 (1986); Danzon, *The Frequency and Severity of Medical Malpractice Claims,* 27 J. L. & ECON. 115 (1984); Kelner & Kelner, *Medical Malpractice: Is There a Crisis?,* 191 N.Y.L.J. 1 (Feb. 8, 1984); Londrigan, *The Medical Malpractice "Crisis": Underwriting Losses and Windfall Profits,* TRIAL, May 1985, at 22. See generally J. KING, JR., THE LAW OF MEDICAL MALPRACTICE IN A NUTSHELL 319-32 (2d ed. 1986); C. KRAMER & D. KRAMER, MEDICAL MALPRACTICE (5th ed. 1983); B. WERTHMANN, MEDICAL MALPRACTICE LAW: HOW MEDICINE IS CHANGING THE LAW (1984). See generally GEN. ACCT. OFFICE, REPORT MEDICAL MALPRACTICE CRISIS (1987), summarized in 1 MEALEY'S LITIG. REP. NAT'L TORT REFORM 2138 (June 17, 1987).

19. See generally M. FRANKLIN & R. RABIN, TORT LAW AND ALTERNATIVES 396-400 (4th ed. 1987) ("The New York legislature has adopted a series of statutes declaring 'void as against public policy and wholly unenforceable' efforts of various groups to contract out of liability for their own negligence and that of their servants, agents, or employees." Id. at 396.)

20. For a discussion of the measurement of damages in tort, see RESTATEMENT (SECOND) OF TORTS §§ 901-32 (1977).

21. The phrase is partly borrowed from Zacharias, *The Politics of Torts,* 95 YALE L.J. 698 (1986).

22. For a discussion of assumption of risk, see Murphy v. Steeplechase Amusement Co., 250 N.Y. 479, 166 N.E. 173 (Ct. App. 1929), noted in 15 CORNELL L.Q., Dec. 1929, at 132. See also text at note 32 infra and accompanying text.

23. W. KEETON, D. DOBBS, R. KEETON & D. OWEN, PROSSER AND KEETON ON THE LAW OF TORTS § 3, at 15 (5th ed. 1984) [PROSSER AND KEETON].

24. See generally G. CALABRESI, THE COSTS OF ACCIDENTS (1970); Klemme, *The Enterprise Liability Theory of Torts,* 47 U. COLO. L. REV. 153 (1976); Landes & Posner, *The Positive Economic Theory of Tort Law,* 15 GA. L. REV. 851 (1981); Posner, *A Theory of Negligence,* 1 J. LEGAL STUD. 29 (1972). But see England, *The System Builders: A Critical Appraisal of Modern American Tort Theory,* 9 J. LEGAL STUD. 27 (1980); Fletcher, *Fairness and Utility in Tort Theory,* 85 HARV. L. REV. 537 (1972). See also R. RABIN, PERSPECTIVES ON TORT LAW 152-236 (2d ed. 1983); G. WHITE, TORT LAW IN AMERICA AN INTELLECTUAL HISTORY 218-23 (1980).

25. See, for example, Adams v. Bullock, 227 N.Y. 208, 125 N.E. 93 (Ct. App. 1919) ("To avert the possibility of this accident and others like it . . . , the defendant must have abandoned the overhead system, and put

the wires underground. Neither its power nor its duty to make the change is shown. To hold it liable upon the facts exhibited in this record would be to charge it as an insurer." 227 N.Y. at 211, 125 N.E. at 94.)

26. See generally F. HARPER, F. JAMES, JR., & O. GRAY, THE LAW OF TORTS (2d ed. 1986) (six-volume set); PROSSER & KEETON, note 23 supra. See also RESTATEMENT OF TORTS (1934-39) (four-volume set); RESTATEMENT (SECOND) OF TORTS (four-volume set) (1963-77).

27. See Losee v. Buchanan, 51 N.Y. 476 (1873) ("No one can be made liable for injuries to the person or property of another without some fault or negligence on his part." 51 N.Y. at 491); O. HOLMES, THE COMMON LAW 108-113 (1881) ("The business of the law of torts is to fix the dividing lines between those cases in which a man is liable for harm which he has done, and those in which he is not." Id. at 79.) See also R. RABIN, PERSPECTIVES ON TORT LAW, supra note 24, at 1-81.

28. For a discussion of the deterrence function of tort law, see Schofield, *Davies v. Mann: Theory of Contributory Negligence,* 3 HARV. L. REV. 263, 269-70 (1890); Stoll, *Penal Purposes in the Law of Tort,* 18 AM. J. COMP. L. 3 (1970); Williams, *The Aims of the Law of Tort,* 4 CURRENT LEGAL PROBS. 137, 144-51 (1951). Accord E. BERNZWEIG, BY ACCIDENT NOT DESIGN 65-71 (1980); Fleming, *The Role of Negligence in Modern Tort Law,* 53 VA. L. REV. 815 (1967).

29. For a discussion of strict liability and the historical debate surrounding fault and strict liability, see Gregory, *Trespass to Negligence to Absolute Liability,* 37 VA. L. REV. 359 (1951); Malone, *Ruminations on the Role of Fault in the History of the Common Law of Torts,* 31 LA. L. REV. 1 (1970); Rabin, *The Historical Development of the Fault Principle: A Reinterpretation,* 15 GA. L. REV. 925 (1981); Schwartz, *Tort Law and the Economy in Nineteenth-Century America: A Reinterpretation,* 90 YALE L.J. 1717 (1981). See also R. RABIN, PERSPECTIVES ON TORT LAW, supra note 24, at 123-236.

30. See G. WHITE, TORT LAW IN AMERICA, supra note 24, at 8-14. See also L. FRIEDMAN, A HISTORY OF AMERICAN LAW 467-87 (2d ed. 1985); M. HORWITZ, THE TRANSFORMATION OF AMERICAN LAW, 1780-1860, 85-101 (1977); text at note 29 supra and accompanying text.

31. See O. HOLMES, THE COMMON LAW, supra note 27, at 94 ("The general principle of our law is that loss from accident must lie where it falls, and this principle is not affected by the fact that a human being is the instrument of misfortune. But relatively to a given human being anything is accident which he could not fairly have been expected to contemplate as possible, and therefore to avoid.")

32. See, for example, G. WHITE, TORT LAW IN AMERICA, supra note 24, at 63-113 ("Assumption of risk strikes the twentieth-century observer as

the archetypal doctrine of an age entranced with the idea that each man was equally capable of protecting himself against injury. In its most extreme applications the doctrine seems almost a parody of itself, an abstraction, that from current perspectives, lost all touch with reality." Id. at 41.)

33. See, for example, Baltimore & Ohio R.R. Co. v. Goodman, 275 U.S. 66, 48 S. Ct. 24, 72 L. Ed. 167 (1927), noted in 16 CALIF. L. REV. 238 (1928), 26 MICH. L. REV. 582 (1928), 76 U. PA. L. REV. 321 (1928), 37 YALE L.J. 532 (1928).

34. Adams v. Bullock, 227 N.Y. at 210, 125 N.E. at 93 ("But no vigilance, however alert, unless fortified by the gift of prophecy, could have predicted the point upon the route where such an accident would occur. . . . At any point upon the route a mischievous or thoughtless boy might touch the wire . . . or fling another wire across it.")

35. See Pokora v. Wabash Ry. Co., 292 U.S. 98, 54 S. Ct. 580, 78 L. Ed. 1149 (1934), noted in 15 B.U. L . REV. 90 (1935), 23 CALIF. L. REV. 112 (1934), 33 MICH. L. REV. 457 (1935), 13 TEX. L. REV. 132 (1934).

36. Greene v. Sibley, Lindsay & Curr Co., 257 N.Y. 190, 177 N.E. 416 (Ct. App. 1931) ("Looking back at the mishap with the wisdom born of the event, we can see that the mechanic would have done better if he had given warning of the change of pose. Extraordinary prevision might have whispered to him at the moment that the warning would be helpful. What the law exacted of him, however, was only the ordinary prevision to be looked for in a busy world." 257 N.Y. at 192, 177 N.E. at 417.)

37. See text at note 35 supra and accompanying text.

38. See text at note 31 supra and accompanying text.

39. For a discussion of product liability law, see L. FRUMER & M. FRIEDMAN, PRODUCTS LIABILITY (1960-1987) (multi-volume series). See generally Bieman, *Strict Products Liability: An Overview of State Law,* 10 J. PROD. LIAB. 111 (1987). For the early English and American products cases, see Winterbottom v. Wright, 10 Mees. & W. 109, 152 Eng. Rep. 402 (Ex. 1842); Longmeid v. Holliday, 155 Eng. Rep. 752 (Ex. 1851); Heaven v. Pender, 11 Q.B.D. 503 (1883); Loop v. Litchfield, 42 N.Y. 351 (Ct. App. 1870); Losee v. Clute, 51 N.Y. 494 (Ct. App. 1873).

For a discussion of the privity requirement in the tort context, see Bohlen, *The Basis of Affirmative Obligations in the Law of Tort,* 44 AM. L. REG. (n.s.) 209, 280-309 (1905). For a discussion of the American law of product liability, see D. OWLES, THE DEVELOPMENT OF PRODUCT LIABILITY IN THE UNITED STATES (1978).

40. See Winterbottom v. Wright, 152 Eng. Rep. at 405 (Lord Abinger: "There is no privity of contract between these parties; and if the plaintiff can sue, every passenger, or even any person passing along the road, who was injured by the upsetting of the coach, might bring a similar action.

Unless we confine the operation of such contracts as this to the parties who entered into them, the most absurd and outrageous consequences, to which I can see no limit, would ensue.")

41. 217 N.Y. 382, 111 N.E. 1050 (Ct. App. 1916), noted in 16 COLUM. L. REV. 428 (1916), 29 HARV. L. REV. 866 (1916), 3 VA. L. REV. 628 (1916), 25 YALE L.J. 679 (1916). See generally Prosser, *The Assault Upon the Citadel (Strict Liability to the Consumer)*, 69 YALE L. J. 1099 (1960); Prosser, *The Fall of the Citadel (Strict Liability to the Consumer)*, 50 MINN. L. REV. 791 (1966).

42. 217 N.Y. at 389, 111 N.E. at 1053 ("If the nature of a thing is such that it is reasonably certain to place life and limb in peril when negligently made, it is then a thing of danger.")

43. Id. at 390, 111 N.E. at 1053 ("In such circumstances, the presence of a known danger, attendant upon a known use, makes vigilance a duty. We have put aside the notion that the duty to safeguard life and limb, when the consequences of negligence may be foreseen, grows out of contract and nothing else. We have put the source of the obligation where it ought to be. We have put its source in the law.")

44. F. STONE, TORT DOCTRINE (12 LOUISIANA CIVIL LAW TREATISE 1977 & Supp. 1982) (The word is from the title of Stone's comparative tort course taught at the University of Grenoble, France.)

45. For a discussion of the *res ipsa loquitur* doctrine, see C. MORRIS & C. MORRIS, JR., MORRIS ON TORTS 117-25 (2d ed. 1980). See also Comment, *Res Ipsa Loquitur: Tabula in Naufragio*, 63 HARV. L. REV. 643 (1950).

46. See 24 Cal. 2d 453, 464-68, 150 P.2d 436, 442-44 (1944) (Traynor, J., concurring).

47. 24 Cal. 2d 453, 150 P.2d 436 (1944), noted in 33 CALIF. L. REV. 637 (1945).

48. See 24 Cal. 2d at 461, 150 P.2d at 440.

49. 59 Cal. 2d 57, 377 P.2d 897, 27 Cal. Rptr. 697 (1963). See also Henningsen v. Bloomfield Motors, Inc., 32 N.J. 358, 161 A.2d 69 (1960) (implied warranty of safety runs with product to ultimate user).

50. RESTATEMENT (SECOND) OF TORTS § 402A (1963-64) reads:

(1) One who sells any product in a defective condition unreasonably dangerous to the user or consumer or to his property is subject to liability for physical harm thereby caused to the ultimate user or consumer, or to his property, if

(a) the seller is engaged in the business of selling such a product, and

(b) it is expected to and does reach the user or consumer without substantial change in the condition in which it is sold.

(2) The rule stated in Subsection (1) applies although

(a) the seller has exercised all possible care in the preparation and sale of his product, and

(b) the user or consumer has not bought the product from or entered into any contractual relation with the seller.

Caveat:

The Institute expresses no opinion as to whether the rules stated in this Section may not apply

(1) to harm to persons other than users or consumers;

(2) to the seller of a product expected to be processed or otherwise substantially changed before it reaches the user or consumer; or

(3) to the seller of a component part of a product to be assembled.

51. See Escola, 24 Cal. 2d at 467, 150 P.2d at 443, wherein Justice Traynor, in his concurring opinion, states, "The consumer no longer has means or skill enough to investigate for himself the soundness of a product . . . and his erstwhile vigilance has been lulled by the steady efforts of manufacturers to build up confidence by advertising and marketing devices . . . ." This view formed the basis of the Greenman court's imposition of strict liability upon the manufacturer, *viz.*, "We need not recanvass the reasons for imposing strict liability on the manufacturer." 59 Cal. 2d at 63, 377 P.2d at 901 (citing Escola, Traynor, J., concurring).

52. See Greenman, 59 Cal. 2d at 64, 377 P.2d at 901.

53. For a discussion of the "ring of negligence" in Section 402A, see Cronin v. J.B.E. Olson Corp., 8 Cal. 3d 121, 501 P.2d 1153, 104 Cal. Rptr. 433 (1972). See also Prosser, *Strict Liability to the Consumer in California,* 18 HASTINGS L.J. 9, 23 (1966). See generally Gilmore, *Products Liability: A Commentary,* 38 U. CHI. L. REV. 103 (1970); Henderson, *Product Liability and Admissibility of Subsequent Remedial Measures: Resolving the Conflict by Recognizing the Difference Between Negligence and Strict Tort Liability,* 9 J. PROD. LIAB. 187 (1986); Keeton, *Conditional Fault in the Law of Torts,* 72 HARV. L. REV. 401 (1959); Keeton, *Manufacturer's Liability: The Meaning of "Defect" in the Manufacture and Design of Products,* 20 SYRACUSE L. REV. 559 (1969); Wade, *On the Nature of Strict Tort Liability for Products,* 44 MISS. L.J. 825 (1973).

54. See, for example, Jackson v. Melvey, 56 App. Div. 2d 836, 392 N.Y.S.2d 312 (1977) (sufficient to show that steering wheel locked on three-week-old car and that owner had taken car back to dealer a week earlier because of steering problem). See also Keeton, *Product Liability and the Meaning of Defect,* 5 ST. MARY'S L.J. 30 (1973).

55. See Hall v. E.I. Du Pont De Nemours & Co., 345 F. Supp. 353 (E.D.N.Y. 1972). See also Campbell, *Enterprise Liability: An Adjustment of Priorities,* 10 FORUM 1231 (1975); Kornhauser, *An Economic Analysis*

of the Choice Between Enterprise and Personal Liability for Accidents, 70 CALIF. L. REV. 1345 (1982).

56. See LeBouef v. Goodyear Tire & Rubber Co., 451 F. Supp. 253 (W.D. La. 1978), aff'd 623 F.2d 985 (5th Cir. 1980).

57. See Sindell v. Abbott Laboratories, 26 Cal. 3d 588, 607 P.2d 924, 163 Cal. Rptr. 132, cert. denied 449 U.S. 912 (1980), noted in 69 CALIF. L. REV. 1179 (1981); 14 IND. L. REV. 695 (1981), 42 U. PITT. L. REV. 669 (1981). See also Delgado, *Beyond Sindell: Relaxation of Cause-in-Fact Rules for Indeterminate Plaintiffs,* 70 CALIF. L. REV. 881 (1982); Fischer, *Products Liability: An Analysis of Market Share Liability,* 34 VAND. L. REV. 1623 (1981); Robinson, *Multiple Causation in Tort Law: Reflections on the DES Cases,* 68 VA. L. REV. 713 (1982).

58. See generally O. HOLMES, THE COMMON LAW, note 27 supra.

59. For a discussion of the jury system, including defenses and criticisms, see P. DiPERNA, JURIES ON TRIAL: FACES OF AMERICAN JUSTICE (1984), reviewed in 84 MICH. L. REV. 1030 (1986); A. GINGER, JURY SELECTION IN CIVIL AND CRIMINAL TRIALS 2d (1984) (two-volume set). See generally V. HANS & N. VIDMAR, JUDGING THE JURY (1985). Accord Rand Report, *The Civil Jury in the 1980's* (1987), summarized in 1 MEALEY'S LITIG. REP. NAT'L TORT REFORM 1556 (Mar. 3, 1987); Rand Report, *Punitive Damages: Empirical Findings* (1987), summarized in 1 MEALEY'S LITIG. REP. NAT'L TORT REFORM 1731 (Apr. 7, 1987). See also discussion in ch. 2, supra, at note 77 and accompanying text.

60. The case was decided July 1986, Oklahoma City, Oklahoma.

61. See id.

62. See discussion in ch. 1, supra, at note 28 and accompanying text.

63. Interview with Marc Z. Edell (Morristown, N.J.) (plaintiff's counsel in Cipollone v. Liggett Group, Inc.).

64. The new science of jury manipulation is reflected in S. HAMLIN, WHAT MAKES JURIES LISTEN: A COMMUNICATIONS EXPERT LOOKS AT THE TRIAL (1985).

Estimates for tort settlements appear in: M. FRANKLIN & R. RABIN, supra note 19, at 21; Greengard, supra note 1, at 11, 37.

65. See, for example, Symposium, *Developments in Tort Law and Tort Reform,* 18 ST. MARY'S L. J. 669 (1987).

66. See Appendix A (ch. 6) infra.

67. See U.S. DEP'T OF COMMERCE, MODEL UNIFORM PRODUCT LIABILITY ACT, reprinted in 44 FED. REG. 62,714 (Oct. 31, 1979). See Atkeson & Neidich, *A Status Report on Proposals for a Federal Product Liability Act,* 38 BUS. LAW. 623 (1983); Dworkin, *Federal Reform of Product Liability Law,* 57 TUL. L. REV. 602 (1983); Schwartz, *The Federal Government and the Product Liability Problem: From Task Force Investigation to Decisions*

by the Administration, 47 U. CIN. L. REV. 573 (1978); Twerski, *National Product Liability Legislation: In Search for the Best of All Possible Worlds,* 18 IDAHO L. REV. 411 (1982). See also *Student Forum on the Model Uniform Product Liability Act,* 49 U. CIN. L. REV. 111 (1980).

Efforts to modify existing product liability law at the federal level have been renewed. The Reagan administration proposed legislation reforming product liability that would base liability upon a fault standard, modify or eliminate joint and several liability in most cases, and limit recovery for noneconomic damages. The proposed legislation received mixed congressional reaction; several congressional measures modifying or opposing the administration's legislation were introduced. See 1 MEALEY'S LITIG. REP. NAT'L TORT REFORM 1551-52, 1643, 1644, 1645-46, 1647, 1732-33, 1843, 1921, 1986-87, 1988, 1989-90; 2 MEALEY'S LITIG. REP. NAT'L TORT REFORM 14-16.

68. See text at note 67 supra and accompanying text.

69. See *Tort Reform: ABA Acts on Excessive Awards,* 14 BARRISTER 11 (1987). See also *ABA Adopts Tort Reform Recommendations,* 1 MEALEY'S LITIG. REP. NAT'L TORT REFORM 1535 (Mar. 3, 1987).

70. See text at note 66 supra and accompanying text.

71. See id.

72. See, for example, Nocas, *Arbitration of Medical Malpractice Claims,* 13 FORUM 254 (1977); Terry, *The Technical and Conceptual Flaws of Medical Malpractice Arbitration,* 30 ST. LOUIS U. L. J. 571 (1986). See also discussion in ch. 1, supra, at notes 19 & 22 and accompanying text.

73. See Greengard, supra note 1, at 10-11.

74. See O'Connell, *Neo-No-Fault Remedies for Medical Injuries: Coordinated Statutory and Contractual Alternatives,* 49 L. & CONTEMP. PROBS. 125 (1986).

75. See Greengard, supra note 1, at 38.

76. See text at notes 64-65 supra and accompanying text.

77. See text at note 46 supra and accompanying text.

78. See text at note 41 supra and accompanying text.

79. On mediation, see discussion in ch. 5, supra, at notes 27-31, 55-84 and accompanying text.

80. The phrase is taken from Mnookin & Kornhauser, *Bargaining in the Shadow of the Law: The Case of Divorce,* 88 YALE L. J. 950 (1979).

81. See, for example, G. WILNER, DOMKE ON COMMERCIAL ARBITRATION (1984 & Supp.); Hoellering, *The Mini-Trial,* 37 ARB. J. 48 (1982).

82. For a discussion of arbitration as a fact-finding mechanism, see, for example, R. BERNSTEIN, HANDBOOK OF ARBITRATION PRACTICE 159-86 (1987); A. REDFERN & M. HUNTER, LAW AND PRACTICE OF INTERNATIONAL COMMERCIAL ARBITRATION 241-61 (1986).

83. See discussion in ch. 2, supra, at notes 25-28 and accompanying text.

84. See discussion in ch. 3, supra, at notes 72-88 and accompanying text.

85. See discussion in ch. 4, supra, at notes 4-6 and accompanying text.

86. See text at note 19 supra and accompanying text.

87. See text at note 72 supra and accompanying text.

88. See discussion in ch. 5, supra, at notes 31-53 and accompanying text.

89. See discussion in ch. 2, supra, at notes 35-37 and accompanying text.

90. See discussion in ch. 1, supra, at note 1 and accompanying text (sources cited, especially Galanter, Edwards, and Fiss).

7 | Concluding Observations and Proposals for Future Directions

A Final Look at Educational and Epistemological Goals

The preceding discussion is intended in part to illustrate the relevance and necessity of the study of international and comparative law in American legal education. To achieve more salutary dispute resolution ends, a more universal, intellectually based form of legal education that transcends narrow professional training needs to be devised. In a substantive but primarily in a methodological sense, the study of foreign legal systems and transnational law-making is indispensable to achieving a reformulated basic program.

Meaningful insights are rarely gained and, when gained, soon exhausted if they do not arise from a genuine confrontation of different, sometimes antagonistic forces. Mere dialectical opposition, however, is not enough; understanding will arise only from the effort to appreciate and synthesize differences. The attempt to reconcile the core elements of contradistinctive values invariably produces the requisite distance to achieve more perceptive knowledge. Such a process is necessary to an understanding not only of the meaning of reality and of human relationships, but also of social institutions, the existence of disputes, the mission of legal regulation, and the role of lawyers in both the legal system and society.

Global interdependence, both in political and commercial terms, is an irreversible fact. As a result, domestic legal processes—as the Scherk and Mitsubishi opinions clearly demonstrate—need to adapt to a larger, rapidly evolving transnational reality that is not underpinned by a cohesive, self-contained, or even federated juridical culture. The methodology that proceeds from the uniformity of substantive law and the rigor of procedural requirements will not suffice in that setting as a problem-solving apparatus. Nor will recalcitrant isolation and deliberate avoidance of perplexing new realities lead to the formulation of a sufficiently universal juridical calculus. An openness to, and understanding of, major legal traditions and systems—both as to surface and core similarities and distinctions—are indispensable to fashioning a suitable form of legality for international relations. Pitting diverse traditions together, isolating their elements of likeness and contrast, and seeking a common ground that maintains separate identities but acts as a basis for systemic interchange and improvement, are the principal scholarly goals of comparatists and the central challenge of international law in its attempt to establish and maintain orderly relations and fairness among national governments and in promoting the development of international commerce. The effort to counterbalance, reconcile, and synthesize opposing international forces through the prism of national legal systems, however, should not be unidirectional. Once achieved, a comparative, transnational understanding of the various national entities in the international process should redirect its attention to the influence of international elements upon national processes, elucidating national dynamics through the international reference.

For example, the recourse to judge-centered civil adjudicatory processes in most national legal systems should, at least, engender questions about the American practice of civil jury trials and the prevalence of the adversarial ethic in American civil procedure. The confrontation of different procedural traditions may well reinforce existing values and procedures, but—given the current controversy over litigation in America—the inquiry should, and must, be undertaken. The consideration of transnational dispute resolution not only conveys insight into the complexity of conflict avoidance and dispute resolution in sovereign relations and how national legal systems have contributed to the elaboration of an "anational" system of arbitration; it also sheds new light upon the view of American tort law as "a battleground of social theory." It makes useful suggestions as to how to structure alternatives to deal with policy-laden, essentially political, domestic conflicts. Furthermore, judicial arbitration in divorce and mediated settlement in tort reveal that comparing opposites—without infringing upon their distinctiveness—can yield the foundation for adjudicatory combinations that have real problem-solving potential.

Therefore, the study of international and comparative law has both an intrinsic value and a larger intellectual mission that can, and should, act as the conceptual and substantive background for academic training in law. Both areas are necessary to effective United States participation in international politics and trade, and they have unparalleled value as a means by which to promote a more penetrating understanding of law as a social and cultural instrument.

Another central theme of this book deals with the relationship among truth, legal adjudication, and the human personality, and the implications of this relationship for alternative dispute resolution. The concern about truth arises from traditional and contemporary perceptions that the law—its methodology and adjudicatory mechanisms— either avoids or defaces truth. According to Giraudoux, "no poet ever interpreted nature as freely as a lawyer interprets truth."[1] While a result reached or a statement made in trial may be legally correct, it is sometimes morally erroneous and self-evidently unacceptable. The use of mock juries, or the recourse to procedural obfuscation to benefit from economic advantage, illustrates the untruthfulness of legal proceedings. Yet a dispute resolution process is necessary to maintain social order: the social contract and the principle of civilization call for providing individuals with the means by which to resolve their conflicts without resorting to forcible self-help.[2] The legitimacy of those means resides in their ability to be fair, consistent, and truthful. Truth is essential to the moral integrity required for a cohesive sense of personal and social identity.

The discovery of truth appears alien to the substantive analytical methodology of the law and to the practicalities and the principles of the litigation process. Legal rules can always be riddled with semantic ambiguity through analytical challenges. In the theory of law, statements of doctrine never seem to have any positive, irrebuttable core. The indecision of legal rules gives critical importance to the litigation process, where guiding juridical precepts have even less meaning. Informed by the adversarial ethic, civil proceedings become a contest of economic strategy and physical endurance. Legal rights are determined and legal duties affixed on the basis of motions and cross-motions, matching a parade of experts with a similar line-up that, hopefully, has a better designated hitter. To carry the sports analogy a step further, litigation is a sort of tag-team wrestling match: a direct power play between the parties with little in the way of meaningfully applied rules, a contest prized primarily for its gross entertainment value.

Transferring the task of ascertaining legal meaning from substantive rules to the litigation process eliminates the meaningfulness of legality. Unguided by substantive standards, the practical necessities of the adversarial process place an unbridgeable gap between the promise of legal substance and the outcome of the process. Truth, in whatever acceptation it receives, is destroyed by the single-minded and relentless pursuit of litigious victory. Within the framework of the legal system, the litigation process acquires a dynamic of its own. The lawyer's professional obligation of zealous representation—interpreted to require invoking every possible procedural advantage and developing a science of jury manipulation—does not include the objective of ascertaining truth, but rather that of having the client's position prevail no matter what its objective veracity.

The destabilization of the legal system's search for truth through the analytical inadequacy of legal provisions, the practicalities of process factors, and the predominance of the adversarial ethic, have generated a crisis in the values normally associated with legality. The overcivilization of the analytical and procedural apparatus has nearly extinguished the values of integrity, honesty, and simple truthfulness in legal regulation; untruths can hide behind a procedural or argumentative mask and prevail over what is morally and factually truthful. Juridical institutions are thus imprisoned by the force of their own internal logic. The two-sided view of substantive considerations has resulted in a total lack of vision, incapacitating the law to provide any guidance; the preoccupation with procedural regularity, fairness, and impartiality has become so all-consuming as to blind the system to flagrant abuse and to make it intolerant of anything but a procedural basis for decision. While the substantive law teaches that there are no intrinsic answers to problems except those the procedural process provides, the procedural process, for its part, teaches that lawyerly shrewdness, or an inexpert and impressionable jury, are the only factors that matter.

Faced with the ineptitude of this pedagogy, individuals can only look to themselves for recourse. The tragic flaw of the present legal adjudicatory process lies not only in the incestuous and isolating quality of its internal dynamic, but also in its failure to envisage civil litigants as something other than the Holmesian "bad men":[3] its failure to develop human understanding, rationality, and responsibility in the confrontation of conflict. The containment of destructive passions and retributive instincts are simply not enough because they reflect an incomplete view of the human soul. At some inward level, people in conflict seek a pathway to humane resolution; they should be encouraged to take personal responsibility and authority for a solution rather than be limited to counterproductive avenues and an invitation to terminate in self-destruction.

Impotent neutrality, contentious distortion, and cynical assumptions need to be replaced by more humanistic procedures. The experience with transnational arbitration shows that people, when given sufficient motivation and institutional permission, can deploy considerable creativity in devising dispute resolution mechanisms that respond to their actual needs, thereby satisfying the public trust. To be sure, some form of third-party intervention remains a necessary element because an external perspective provides the parties with a more objective, less self-interested vantage point on their conflict. By conveying necessary information about disputes and the means of resolution, the societal framework for dispute resolution should assist parties to self-empower and thereby reach a mutually determined resolution of their conflict. From a civilian perspective, the truth of the substantive law might regain its impact when it is assessed by the parties in relation to their own sense of truthfulness.

Proposals for Future Directions

The ADR Debate

The debate about the social and moral value of adversarial justice and the legitimacy and professional viability of alternative modes of dispute resolution is progressing. The evolving literature is sometimes punctuated by the diatribes that usually flourish in the discussion of fundamental issues. At other times, the discourse lapses into the tedium of expository prose, where polemical flare is superseded by the subtlety of requisite caveats and knowledgeable corollaries. In any event, the current literature on how people in dispute should be made to agree harbors some rather considerable disagreement.

There is the primary ADR view, advanced most visibly by former Chief Justice Burger,[4] that alternative mechanisms need to be instituted because of the failings of the legal system and of the law. According to Burger, the process of legal adjudication saps an inordinate proportion of available social resources and has become a means by which to fill an individual existential void left by the deterioration of the secular and religious community. Legal proceedings relieve the loneliness of existence by allowing the individual to strike out at faceless surroundings and to leave an identifying mark in the wall of social anonymity. However unintended, the use of litigation to quell the poetic pleas of the soul, however, is a misguided endeavor. The quest for relief from the isolation of individuality places a false and overwhelming burden upon institutional mechanisms for social ordering. Legal proceedings stray from their original stabilizing design and exact too high a toll for their performance of a misconceived role.

Seen from the perspective of the social contract, a civilization exclusively anchored in litigious adjudicatory mores no longer adequately intermediates between the dictates of natural freedom and the necessity of social constraints. It ceases to function as an instrument of moral human development. The former chief justice and other likeminded proponents, therefore, recommend a shift toward natural freedom precepts. Exercising their freedom of contract, parties involved in dispute should consider informal and nonjudicial means of dispute resolution ("especially arbitration") to achieve the finality of their conflict.

There have been two primary responses to this advocacy for ADR. First, there is disagreement on the basic proposition regarding the existence of a "litigation crisis." The work of Marc Galanter[5] especially has been instrumental in pointing to the empirical frailty of assertions that American society is suffering from the disease of "hyperlexis"—the paralysis of American society through an overly abundant recourse to litigation. For example, the claim that jury verdicts in personal injury cases are exorbitant and founded upon empathy for the plaintiff is not supported by available studies. Although there are a few aberrant cases in which large recoveries were obtained, the vast majority of jury-determined damage awards do not show a trend toward excessively generous verdicts. Reformist advocacy based upon the existence of a litigation crisis, therefore, is founded upon impressionistic accounts that cannot be corroborated (and are, in fact, contradicted) by hard evidence. Moreover, investigators also claim that ADR proponents undervalue the actual operation of existing judicial procedures—their "nonadjudicative dimension."[6] In more than 90% of the cases, parties who engage in adversarial litigation reach a settlement of their differences.[7] ADR objectives, then, are already being fostered and realized under present procedures.[8] According to the studies, the only statistically significant change in litigation patterns has been a shift away from contract and property claims to claims sounding in tort, family law, and public law matters.[9]

Typically, these statistical findings have themselves been challenged by others as being too narrowly established. Critics allege that the studies fail to give a comprehensive or accurate view of litigation patterns.[10] More important, however, the underlying concern of those who see a crisis in the legal process does not center upon the objectivity of statistics, but rather upon the perception, admittedly more subjective, that the pervasive influence of adversarial justice is harming the integrity of American society and undermining the value it should afford to truth, morality, and human dignity. Rather than its physical dimensions, it is the practice itself and its ethos that are being brought into question.

The movement away from lawsuits in contract and property disputes may bespeak the capacity of the existing system to self-regulate. The underlying motivation for such a development should be explored to determine whether it might or should be expanded to have some impact upon the disputes now being resolved by courts. By the same token, settlement achieved through the threat of adversarial litigation may be very far removed from the type of settlement process proposed by the ADR movement. While compromises in litigation are struck for reasons of efficiency and expediency, that form of settlement, achieved through the usual competitive and confrontational techniques, is effective only in comparison to an ultimate adversarial determination. The "nonadjudicative dimension" of the litigation process does not foster a different vision of dispute resolution; it does not approximate Frank Sander's "multi-door courthouse"[11] in which parties choose a remedy they find appropriate to their dispute; and it does not encourage the learning of a mutual, problem-solving approach to the resolution of conflict.

Although more accepting of ADR objectives, other commentators have criticized ADR on the basis of specific developments within the movement. Chapter 4 of this book, for example, argues that the United States Supreme Court's unqualified support for arbitration may work ultimately to the detriment of arbitral adjudication. The adaptation of remedial alternatives from specialized contexts to general application is a task both delicate and dangerous. Promoting efficiency in judicial administration by undermining the consensual character of arbitral adjudication eventually will be counterproductive; in all likelihood, it will result in the demise of a viable means of contractual dispute resolution. The integration of ADR mechanisms into the mainstream of American legal culture requires an attention not only to policy objectives, but also to the character of the alternative mechanisms and of the affected disputes.

Others have focused upon the adjudicatory viability and legitimacy of ADR mechanisms.[12] Judicial functions are longstanding and can be evaluated by reference to well-defined factors—for example, the permissible limits for the exercise of public jurisdictional authority, the public nature of the proceedings, the use of legal precedent, the elaboration of reasons, and the availability of appeal. If ADR processes are instituted and accepted, they will, by definition, operate outside the usual analytical framework for evaluating adjudicatory processes. The bargain struck within the confines of privately instituted justice cannot be held to the ordinary standards of adjudicatory accountability. If private consensus and mutuality are to replace the legitimation of public sanction, should some form of external assessment be imposed to guard against potential abuses? Would such supervision undermine the effectiveness of these mechanisms?

Public law lawyers have engaged in the most vituperative criticism of ADR. Owen Fiss, the most prominent antagonist, has inveighed against the tenets of ADR, stating that they result in a "trivialization" of the adversarial process and of the social function of judicial adjudication.[13] The exercise of public jurisdictional authority is a necessary instrument to maintaining the balance of political power within American society. Judicial adjudication yields principled results essential to the preservation of civil liberties and political rights. The courts perform indispensable functions through the adjudicatory process: they make reasoned choices, protect minority interests, curb governmental action, and articulate decisional rules that represent difficult social value choices. Alternative means for achieving settlement are "the civil equivalent of plea-bargaining"[14] under which society foregoes the opportunity to define its political culture through the courts. According to Fiss, ADR proponents are short-sighted and altogether too willing to sacrifice fundamental values and the indispensable role of social institutions to considerations of mere time and money. Finally, ADR is being used by political figures (like Burger) to achieve an underlying political agenda. Self-empowered justice and party autonomy in dispute resolution are at the service of the rightist ideology of deregulation and anti-statism.

To a private law lawyer, the Fiss critique is an illuminating portrait of the public lawyer's mind and vision of society. The fundamental dynamic of social organization consists of vying political forces; maintaining an equilibrium between majoritarian rule and minority interests is the key to political organization. Law and judical adjudication cement the balance and redress it when necessary. The public mission of the courts is to make difficult, sometimes unpopular, choices in the competition between contradistinctive rights and values. The public law vision, however, has little regard for personal humanity; in the world of public law, individuals are holders of rights; they gain significance as possible victims of discriminatory state action or other forms of illegality. The judge, making oracular pronouncements, is the final arbiter of political competitions, the protector of rights and values against unlawful conspiracies, and the ultimate source of validating and principled wisdom.

This world of political struggle is basically alien to the ADR adjudicatory vision. Much of Fiss's critique is fueled by examples of constitutional controversy.[15] The history and character of nonjudicial remedies reveal that the primary application of ADR mechanisms is in private law matters—to conflicts involving purely individual concerns and where parties are pitted against one another as individuals. In this context, persons are not seen as the repositories of political rights and their conflict as a choice between competing political values. Rather, they are human beings involved in a personal dilemma generated by commonplace social relationships. ADR reform has little to contribute to the divisive character of political struggles, and it does not challenge the hegemony of judicial authority in public law matters. It can be perceived as a threat to public law values only by those whose perception of social life is confined to, and to some extent blinded by, the political and conspiratorial dimension of human behavior. ADR is directed to more ordinary disputes where the state and its political interests are largely absent, where the parties are engaged in a competition concerning their private rights, and where the principle of mutuality and consensus can be made functional. Although it may eventually modify human behavior generally in dispute situations and teach even political actors other means of dealing with conflict, ADR seeks to inaugurate a new adjudicatory ethic exclusively in the private law area.

ADR is, however, in its developmental stage. There are serious questions being raised not only concerning the integrity of its intellectual and doctrinal foundations, but also regarding what it has done and what it can realistically accomplish. Also, there appears to be confusion about what it wants to do. The basic thrust of the ADR movement is founded upon two principal, albeit distinct and possibly conflicting, tenets.

First, society should create and espouse alternative pathways to justice primarily for reasons of practicality, efficiency, and economy. Because of the volume of demand and the intricacies of procedure, courts are relatively inaccessible. Legal proceedings exact a substantial human and resource cost. Litigation is, therefore, counterproductive in most cases. The use of nonjudicial and perhaps nonadjudicatory procedures could yield fair yet expedient results. Disputing parties could be made whole in ways more constructive than litigation. Arbitration, the alternative adjudicatory ethic adopted in commerce and labor, may also be good for other areas of private law conflict.

Second, ADR reform attacks the adversarial ethic and lawyering practices from a larger dimension. Here, much of the "pocket book" pragmatism wanes and the ideological debate, implicitly or expressly, begins. In this second view of ADR and its objectives, there is a confrontation between the "is" and the "ought" of adjudication—a clash of dichotomous perceptions of disputes, social order, institutional roles, and human relationships. According to these proponents of ADR, adversarial proceedings need to be abandoned primarily because they are antihumanistic—they achieve the finality of disputes through a degradation of the human spirit. Adversarial representation destroys the possibility of reconstructing human relationships and makes the exercise of rationality alien to the resolution of conflict.

The humanistic strain of the ADR movement posits a framework for conflict resolution that is ideologically intolerant of the reductionist approach and monetarism of the law office and the courtroom. Criticism centers not so much upon lawyers' ethics as upon the ethic of lawyering itself. Constraining individuals to act within minimalist levels of civilized behavior is not civilization at all. Base, antagonistic resolution should be replaced with a sensitivity to the human dilemma underlying conflict and a professional attitude that supports and fosters mutual adjustment. Through negotiation, mediation, arbitration, or combinations thereof, parties must be given the opportunity to understand their dispute and its ramifications, to integrate it into the entire setting of their relationship and their lives, and to devise and evaluate a variety of noncontentious solutions through a professionally guided problem-solving approach.

Manifestly, this second founding tenet of ADR has the greater visionary appeal. It embodies the promise of a "new adjudicatory day" and, if Derek Bok[16] is right, it heralds the future state of social civilization—perhaps even at a global level. Of the two objectives of ADR, however, it is also undoubtedly the one that raises the most suspicions and misgivings; inevitably, it has faced and will face greater resistance and opposition. Pending a coercive legislative imposition of ADR—a means of integration antithetical to ADR's humanistic philosophy— society and individuals, both in the abstract and in circumstances of actual conflict, must perceive the ADR approach as superior to adversarial representation and want an ADR methodology to supersede the ordinary role of legal proceedings. That choice cannot be made without conveying the necessary information to all levels of society— educating or reeducating not only professionals, but also the general public. The proposed ethic can never take hold and be integrated into the actual operation of society unless comprehensive education is made available and a debate of wide proportions ensues.

As a general rule, the existing literature has not risen to the task in any systematic fashion. To some extent, the status of the literature reflects the emerging character of ADR and confusion about its direction and implications. As a professional discipline, negotiation[17] is just beginning to find a preliminary coherent structure; mediation,[18] however, is at an even more rudimentary stage of development; and arbitration,[19] despite its longstanding use in specialized matters, is undergoing a redefinition of its basic character in view of a potentially larger vocation. Commentaries range from purely promotional entreaties to didactic expositions, to recondite analyses, and finally to attempts to construct abstract models of desired professional conduct in dispute circumstances. Many of the most cohesive intellectual accounts have, at best, only an academic relevance.[20]

Currently, ADR is like a wheel spinning in a void, unable to catch a groove that allows it to channel its energy into the larger mechanism of society.[21] There is an evident need to expand the scope of consideration and to present the ADR humanism to a larger public. Dealing with the modification of professional attitudes is only part of the effort. Such an approach is likely to have little impact—a trickle effect— upon those whose attitude matters perhaps the most—the actual beneficiaries of adjudicatory service. The following discussion outlines a proposal for comprehensive education in ADR. It establishes an educational blueprint for the present providers and users of adjudicatory services and also looks to the future where real change can be effected.

Professional Education

In addition to revitalizing and expanding the study of international and comparative law, the integration and attainment of humanistic priorities in the dispute resolution process will require some profound changes in the way lawyers are trained and educated.[22] The development of advocacy and analytical skills will no longer be sufficient. More comprehensive dispute resolution goals will require a wider vision of disputes and an understanding of various dispute resolution skills and techniques. The central emphasis of the first-year legal curriculum on substantive subject areas and reasoning skills should be modified to include a substantial interdisciplinary consideration of how, and why, disputes arise in society and what methods—in addition to legal adjudication—exist to attempt a resolution of those conflicts. The purpose and goals of lawyering should be integrated into a larger cosmology of social and political theory that attempts to impart a sense of how lawyers and the legal system fit into the grand design of social civilization. Even when the function of the attorney is to advocate on behalf of a client, a perception of the larger implications of the necessity of dispute resolution in society can allow that task to be performed in a more socially integrated way. The concept of lawyering, in any event, needs to be disengaged from the confining mold of adversarial advocacy and the narrow skills it implies.

Lawyers need to emerge as universal problem-solvers who have a variety of skills at their disposal and who can relate to other professional disciplines to achieve qualitative, humane dispute resolution in society. No matter what its underlying motivation may be, former Chief Justice Burger's characterization of lawyers as "healers of human conflict"[23] is particularly apt to describe a new mission for legal education. Because private law disputes always involve people, and their perceptions and feelings about property or about others, attorneys should have some formal exposure to the study of the human psyche—more specifically, how people generate, interpret, and respond to conflict and how they might be likely to achieve an intra- and interpersonal resolution of the conflicts they experience. Arguably, divorce clients, for example, are seeking this sort of human understanding as much as purely legal advice. An understanding of the psychology of sovereign behavior is necessary to explain why so many nonbinding and nonadjudicatory remedies are necessary to achieve workable dispute resolution in state-to-state conflicts. Knowing how merchants behave and why they behave as they do are indispensable to understanding the suitability of international commercial arbitration as a remedial mechanism in transnational business. An effective response to tort disputes cannot be made without knowing how people perceive loss, misfortune, and social fairness. Lawyers should be given enough formal exposure to these areas of human psychology to enable them to act as counsellors and tutors to their clients as well as their advocates.

The consideration of other dispute resolution methods needs to supplement the interdisciplinary study of disputes and the exposure to the ethic of legal adjudication. Having gained an understanding of how disputes arise and what they imply in human and social terms, law students should be introduced to the panoply of possible remedies—of which adversarial litigation should be only one possible remedy. Law students should be afforded a comprehensive exposure to, and practical training in, negotiation, mediation, and arbitration as part of their initial introduction to the study of law. Once students have had an opportunity to consider the purpose of legality within a wider human, social, and intellectual context, they can thereafter undertake the conventional curriculum offerings and skills training. Attorneys cannot be expected to function effectively in a humanistically oriented dispute resolution framework without having had a substantial formal exposure to humanistic education in their field—which, by definition, for lawyers means an awareness of, and an ability to respond to, the multifarious dimensions of the human experience with conflict.

The first year of law school should be reorganized to include a large component of humanistic and interdisciplinary courses that focus upon a wide evaluation of the methodology of law and the social function of the legal process. The aim of these courses would be to give law students a sense of the attorney's function as a "healer of human conflict." A two-semester, first-year program might take the following pattern:

Fall Semester Courses
1. *An Interdisciplinary Introduction to Disputes and Social Con-*

249

flicts. This course would be taught from a sociological, psychological, philosophic, and legal perspective, and would deal with the origin, development, and content of disputes. How and why do individuals enter into conflict? What are the individual and social implications of disputes? How can disputes be classified, both singly and in relation to one another? What does the history of disputes tell us about the nature of society and of individuals?

2. *Dispute Resolution Methodologies and Mechanisms.* This course would position the process of legal adjudication in the context of other remedies that might be invoked in conflictual circumstances. Students would receive instruction on the basic principles and practices of negotiation, mediation, and arbitration. These alternative mechanisms would be compared to the functioning of the current adjudicatory process, and contrasts established between the adversarial ethic and other dispute resolution ethics.

3. *Comparative Juridical Cultures and Values.* This course would have the objective of introducing students to the methodology of comparative law and to the operation of both the American and foreign legal systems. Emphasis would be placed upon the distinctions and similarities in the way in which those systems approach the regulation of social conflict. In addition to the traditional systemic differences, the analysis would center upon the role of law in society, the stature of lawyers, and the nature of adjudicatory processes. Finally, some reference should be made to transnational legal processes and the means used for resolving disputes at that level of activity.

4. *The Lawyer's Role and Responsibility in Society.* This course would replace and amplify the substance of the current offering in Professional Responsibility. It would have students approach the ethical dilemmas posed by the adversarial ethic at a stage in their academic evolution when they can give such problems the most serious, untainted consideration. In addition, the focus of the course would exceed the usual perimeters of the Code of Professional Responsibility by addressing the larger questions of lawyers' duty to society, their other obligation and ability to interface with other professionals, and their responsibility in maintaining the integrity of the adjudicatory process. The approach would also focus upon lawyers' responsibility to their clients and to the other parties to a conflict.

5. *Legal Writing and Research.* This course would be the only

hold-over from the traditional first-year, first-semester law school curriculum. It would introduce students to the essential mechanics of legal reasoning and case analysis — necessary preparation for undertaking the traditional substantive law courses that begin in the Spring semester.

SPRING SEMESTER COURSES

1. *Psychological Dynamics of the Human Personality and Basic Principles of Counselling.* In addition to providing a basic introduction to human behavior and emotional dispositions, this course would focus upon the effect of conflicts upon people — what their likely reactions are to certain types of disputes and how they can be helped in coping with them. Also, the emotional dynamics of the adversarial ethic and advocacy would be explored with reference to other philosophies of dispute resolution.
2. *Civil Procedure.* This course, would consist of the regular offering in the area, modified in content by the basic direction given to the first-year program.
3. *Contracts.*
4. *Tort.*
5. *Introduction to Public Law and Constitutional Law.*

The integration of these new courses into the law school curriculum would require adjustments to the second- and third-year offerings and might even require lengthening the academic training in law (contrary to the popular thesis of abbreviation). For example, constitutional law, criminal law, and constitutional criminal procedure should be offered separately in the upper-level curriculum; the basic first-year private law courses (civil procedure, torts, property, and contracts) should be extended into the first semester of the second year; and students should be afforded a significant curricular opportunity to test out adjudicatory and alternative techniques of problem-solving. A fully comprehensive education in law should include a complete view of the role of law in society, an exposure to the ordinary substantive law courses, and an opportunity to confront actual problem-solving circumstances under academic and practical supervision. The upper-level curriculum should include practical training in negotiation, mediation, and arbitration, as well as substantive courses emphasizing the larger dispute resolution vocation of attorneys.

Public Education

The objective of modifying professional legal education is to create a new class of lawyers—lawyers who, in a private law context, can function as professional dispute resolution advisers or counsellors. The consultation with such a lawyer would involve a complete accounting of the facts and the context of the dispute followed by an examination of the various remedies that might be pursued. Adversarial representation would be a possible course of action by which to seek a resolution, but it could be used in combination with other means, or a completely nonadversarial strategy might be pursued.

As an expert in dispute resolution, the lawyer could and should make necessary recommendations. This more global and less partisan approach, however, requires clients to be actively involved in the process and, ideally, to make many of the critical decisions in dispute resolution. Unless law offices offer tutorial services for clients on approaches to dispute resolution, the lawyer's counselling function is unlikely to have any measurable impact upon the rendition of legal services. It assumes that clients are generally aware of the available remedies and of the character of dispute resolution processes.

As a consequence, educational reforms need to be undertaken not only in law schools and through continuing legal education programs, but also at all levels of society. Civic instruction, given by interdisciplinary teams of teachers over a period of time at the primary, secondary, and adult levels, needs to be devised, encompassing a systematic program in dispute resolution and its function in society. Structuring a curriculum for the specific setting of each group would depend upon the experience of educators expert in the field. An educational model of general application, consisting of three essential stages, however, can be advanced and should convey a basic understanding of the role of the individual and society in dispute resolution.

Educational Model

FIRST STAGE: *Personal and Social Relationships.* The first stage should focus, preliminarily, on the individual within the family setting emphasizing the importance of the family structure and its significance to the individual. Instruction and illustrations should focus upon the emergence of conflict between family members (parent versus child, sibling versus sibling), how such conflict grows, and how it is eventually arrested or reconciled. An inventory of classical conflicts should be established, and the typical behavior of the various family members in response to these conflicts evaluated. The constructive means of resolving the identified conflicts should be contrasted to destructive solutions. Both positive and negative means of conflict avoidance should also be explored.

The core family relationship model can then be transposed to a social setting—both the differences and similarities of family and social relationships should be underscored. The individual human and social being needs to establish a basis beyond the family group. Social and professional existence is a type of family beyond the family—here, parents are represented by various authority figures and, to some extent, friends become siblings. The relationships within this adopted social family also breed conflicts that typically can be identified and to which certain behaviors can be ascribed. How are conflict resolution and avoidance achieved in this setting in order to limit negative and encourage positive impact?

Having gone through the genesis of the individual and his or her integration into various networks, emphasis needs to be placed upon the contradistinctive demands of the individual, the group, and other individuals. The individual may not appreciate the restraints of schooling, but the group demands conformity to a schedule and other patterned behavior. Recreational and social interests may conflict. Particular dress may lead to general ridicule. Affections may not be reciprocated.

Although the reality of such conflicts should not be minimized, they should be portrayed as a challenge that should ultimately result in balancing needs within the individual and in a moderation of conduct. Here, the motivation for relationships and the cost of their disruption would need to be considered. The idea of inevitable loss and compromise should also be explored, as well as the idea of growth through loss and of the value of adaptability within the limits of principle. Finally, some attention needs to be given to the development of values and ideologies within the person and the group.

Finally, a composite picture of an autonomous and socially integrated individual can be sketched. The teaching here should focus upon the complexity of a person's relationships and the complexity of the worlds to which he or she belongs. Underlying the intricate patternings are usually some basic needs and feelings that are complicated by the layerings of maturity, experience, and civilization. Ordinarily, an understanding of both the simplicity and the complexity of wants is necessary to arrive at a solution once a disruption in a relationship has taken place. The value of adjustments, of intermediating between opposing interests, should be emphasized along with the relativity of beliefs. Finally, some indication should be given of the impact of career choices upon personal dispositions, values, and relationships.

SECOND STAGE: *Approaches to Disagreement, Conflicts, and Disputes.* Once the individual networking from a biological family to a social and professional group is understood, the difficult lessons of adult life can be broached. Newspaper accounts teach us every day that people become enmeshed in intractable conflict and attempt to win their struggle whatever the cost. Some more measured view of social and professional relations needs to be posited, without having the discussion devolve into an unrealizable form of idealism. The primary initial lesson is that people with equal or comparable personal and social worth enter into legitimate disagreement frequently and almost inevitably throughout life. The existence of disagreement does not lessen their individual integrity, but it simply means they perceive some segment of reality from a different perspective.

Disagreement can rise to the level of conflict when positions are steadfast, the parties appear irreconcilable, and the disagreement takes place in the context of a continuing relationship (either one that preceded the disagreement or was generated by it). Conflict can also emerge when one or both parties interpret the disagreement as involving some form of tangible or intangible loss. The conflict may escalate to an actual dispute when one or both parties perceives the loss or disagreement to be significant and neither sees a means for solution.

Both parties may be right or wrong. In all likelihood, their actual position on the merits is, at this stage, irrelevant. What is of critical significance is their perception of disagreement, conflict, and dispute. What does discord mean to them as people? How do they respond to and deal with it? How will they want to approach circumstances in which they perceive significant loss or hurt?

Various hypothetical examples taken from everyday life in a number of dispute areas could be used to illustrate the character of such disputes and the likely and/or desired behavioral response to them. The purchase of consumer items of varying value at different stages of life (clothes, a used car, appliances, a home, various investments) from a known or unknown seller in a large, small, or medium-sized community should contain fertile examples for discussion. Analysis should focus upon classifying the disputes and the parties; a comprehensive consideration of all the factors germane to the dispute setting should be encouraged. Also, the break-up of romantic relationships could be usefully contrasted and compared to the dissolution of marriages. Why should the law regulate one and not the other? How meaningful is the dispute between divorcing spouses to the rest of society? What role should social mores play? Can emotional torment be repaired? What concerns should be uppermost among the various considerations? Finally, disputes about the payment of rent, the care of property, employment situations, and the like might be considered to give a comprehensive view of dispute areas.

The thorough consideration of actual situations should focus upon the human reality underlying the disagreement, conflict, and dispute. The discord involves two persons who believe they have experienced some form of loss at the hands of the other. Both persons have their particular sensitivity to defend and their strengths and weaknesses as people. In the circumstances of discord, each will see the other as an opponent whose deficiencies have brought about the dispute. The challenge resides in defusing the embellishment of the controversy: ridding it of its absolute trappings of good and bad and having the parties understand what they really want to accomplish in these circumstances. Along with the basis for disagreement, each party should be encouraged to see an area of possible agreement and the reasons for the other party's position. They should be aware that the tangible conflict over price, property interests, and child custody may be a metaphor for other conflicts with others (triggered by ricochet in these circumstances). They should understand that the conflict is interpreted by each of them in personal terms, as a factor in their relationship, and as part of their identification with the whole of society.

Once this larger perspective of the dispute is instilled, the parties at least have a better basis for understanding their disagreement and conflict. They can then decide whether it amounts to an actual dispute and, if so, how they wish to pursue its resolution. Some mention should be made in the final consideration about whether, and why, this type of approach somehow coincides with the participants' individual sense of justice.

THIRD STAGE: *Social Mechanisms for Resolving Disputes.* This final stage of the educational model completes the instruction. Once the origin, development, and implications of a dispute are understood, the question becomes one of achieving a resolution. Here, the goal is to offer systematic and relatively elaborate expositions on the legal process and other means to achieve the termination of conflict.

First, a historical survey of the law and legal processes, including a reference to their underlying objectives, should be undertaken. Legal systems should be grouped into various traditions, and those traditions compared and contrasted. This universalist approach should be followed by a synthetic description of the typical operation of the legal process—the function of the lawyer and the judge and the character of legal proceedings. A relatively clear demarcation should be established between public and private law matters. Participants also need to be instructed upon how lawyers are trained, the program of instruction and method of teaching in law schools, and how law firms function and are organized. Emphasis needs to be placed upon both the potential and limitations of lawyering. Finally, readings in political theory might help to convey a sense of the law's social mission.

The actual function of the adversarial process in American society should then be addressed. Readings on the rationale for the adversarial process should be introduced and contrasted to comparative accounts of procedure in foreign legal systems and to the criticisms of the adversarial ethic. It is important both to convey a sense of the advantages and disadvantages of the process and to give an accounting of what adversarial representation means. Mock depositions, cross-examinations, and attendance at a trial might be useful illustrations to convey basic understanding.

Finally, once a thorough and objective view of the adversarial process has been presented, participants should be exposed to the various aspects of the ADR debate. Is there a litigation crisis? Does ADR compromise essential social interests? Can it be applied to both public law and private law disputes? To all forms of private law disputes? Should ADR be mandated by the legislative will or remain a completely consensual process?

Most important, this segment of the instruction should inform participants about various alternatives to adversarial representation. How do conciliation, negotiation, mediation, and arbitration differ? What are their respective advantages and disadvantages? How does adversarial negotiation compare to problem-solving negotiation? Is mandatory mediation a good idea? What does arbitrability mean? Do these mechanisms sufficiently protect legally conferred rights? Can lawyers effectively participate in these nonadversarial processes? The use of simulated sessions should again be useful in conveying an understanding of these mechanisms.

Like participatory democracy, a system of primarily self-determined civil justice requires a basic understanding of fundamental concepts and procedures. An effective system of justice cannot depend solely upon the knowledge and abilities of a small minority who engage in professional graduate study or take a few episodic college survey courses in law. If schools have, as one of their principal goals, the effective preparation and integration of young people into adult life processes and society, then junior high and high school curricula should give them the opportunity to understand disputes and apply those principles to their current and future lives.

Conclusion

To achieve and give expression to legal truth and its constituent values — fairness, impartiality, and consistency — the adjudicatory process must be both effective and humanistic. It must not only contain, but also reverse, the destructive force of social disputation. Dispensing results that are accepted and acceptable, the adjudicatory process should impart upon the parties, and society at large, a teaching about the need for social order, the genesis and resolution of disputes, and the avoidance of conflict in the future.

The adversarial ethic operating in the context of the civil jury trial falls far short of achieving any humanistic design in dispute resolution. Moreover, its effectiveness may be eroding gradually as the societal impatience with its underlying tenets and outcomes grows. Its truth-seeking premise is largely mythical — illogical and unrealistic; in any event, its functioning has been inefficient, costly, and emotionally debasing. The inertia of tradition should not be allowed to impede a redefinition of the lawyers' and the legal process's mission with respect to the resolution of conflict between individuals. A large sense of social responsibility would make the finality of disputes emerge from a more knowledgeable and principled, perhaps self-empowering process—not the insolvent epistemology of adversarial confrontation.

It is only by giving people a full opportunity to penetrate into the deeper motivation of human experience that humanistic priorities can be achieved and society can have a truly civilizing influence upon its members. Melting the lances of contentious misunderstanding and dismounting the steeds of adversarial confrontation could inaugurate a new reign of humanistic practices in the face of personal antagonisms and social discord.

NOTES

1. J. GIRAUDOUX, TIGER AT THE GATES 45 (C. Fry, trans. 1955).

Fictional representations of the law have always generated interest among lawyers. Recently, the interest has taken a more organized turn. See, for example, Collins & Hattenhauer, *Law and Language: A Selected, Annotated Bibliography on Legal Writing,* 33 J. LEGAL EDUC. 141 (1983); Domnarski, *Law-Literature Criticism: Charting a Desirable Course with Billy Budd,* 34 J. LEGAL EDUC. 702 (1984); Finet, *Franz Kafka's Trial as Symbol in Judicial Opinions,* 12 L. STUDIES FOR. 23 (1988); Symposium, *Law and Literature,* 39 MERCER L. REV. 739 (1988). Academic lawyers have begun to apply literary theories and techniques to the analysis of judicial opinions and statutes. In this framework, the Constitution becomes a "text"—a source of exegetical commentary in decisional law. The efforts to integrate a literary approach into the study and evaluation of law have engendered debate. See, for example, West, *Authority, Autonomy, and Choice: The Role of Consent in the Moral and Political Visions of Franz Kafka and Richard Posner,* 99 HARV. L. REV. 384 (1985); Posner, *The Ethical Significance of Free Choice: A Reply to Professor West,* 99 HARV. L. REV. 1431 (1986); LaRue, *Posner on Literature,* 85 MICH. L. REV. 325 (1986); West, *Submission, Choice, and Ethics: A Rejoinder to Judge Posner,* 99 HARV. L. REV. 1449 (1986).

The incorporation of literary analysis into legal doctrine, however, minimizes the significant ideological differences between law and literature. Although writers are fascinated by the law and its operation, their interest centers upon a dichotomy of values and their rejection of the law's debasement of human dignity. The lesson to be drawn from the literary representations of law is that poets and lawyers engage in contradistinctive enterprises that have fundamentally irreconcilable goals and epistemologies. The poet endeavors to capture an eternal truth in a self-contained esthetic vision. The lawyer seeks to triumph in a contentious contest that sub-ordinates truth to the attainment of litigious victory and, to some extent, social order. The lawyer's world is one of daily, material reality where immediate interests are controlling and the universal is noticeably absent.

Balzac, for example, was one writer who studied and actually practiced law for a period of time. The references to the law in THE HUMAN COMEDY reveal his antipathy for the legal process and his effort to construct a more humanly acceptable form of justice. See my article *Balzacian Legality: A Proposal for Natural Law Juridical Standards of Legitimacy,* 27 LOY. L. REV. 1 (1981) ("Although he does not require that the legal system eliminate human disloyalty and maliciousness entirely, Balzac wants it to fulfill a truly creative function within society: not only by establishing a semblance of order among unruly human passions, but also, much like the writer in relation to his work, by instilling a sense of fairness, truth and humanity in human relations—in a word, by grafting onto the operation of society the immutable tenets that are anchored in and emerge from man's essential moral nature." Id. at 33.) The ideas Balzac advanced are central to the general thesis of this book.

Many other prominent literary figures have had less than flattering, and sometimes completely condemning, views of the professional activity of lawyers and of the operation of the legal process. There is the celebrated line in Shakespeare's Henry VI: "The first thing we do, let's kill all the lawyers" (II Henry VI, act IV, scene ii, line 70). Shakespeare's vision of the law and lawyers has been extensively explored and documented in legal literature. See, for example, Note, *Shakespeare and the Legal Process: Four Essays,* 61 VA. L. REV. 390 (1975).

Kafka is reported to have described his experience in the study of law as equivalent to eating sawdust. See E. PAWEL, THE NIGHTMARE OF REASON: A LIFE OF FRANZ KAFKA 117 (1984). Although characteristic of his general perception of human experience, Kafka in THE TRIAL portrayed the process of legal adjudication as a particularly hideous, nightmarish encounter be-tween individuals and legal institutional authority. Dickens was no less critical of the quality and content of legal proceedings. In BLEAK HOUSE, the law and lawyers are depicted as an "establishment" that has "dissolved [its] partnership with truth and justice." Dickens further insists on the moral bankruptcy of legal practice in THE OLD CURIOSITY SHOP when he writes that "if there were no bad people, there would be no good lawyers." For these references to Dickens, see Edwards, *Do Lawyers Still Make a Difference?,* 32 WAYNE L. REV. 201, 201, n.2 (1986).

Edwards also quotes from Montaigne who adopted a more tolerant, stoically accepting, but no less critical, view of the lawyer: "There's no reason why a lawyer . . . should not recognize the knavery that is part of his vocation. An honest man is not responsible for the vices or the stupidity of his calling, and need not refuse to practise them. A man must live in the world and avail himself of what he finds there." Id. at 202, quoting IV ESSAIS DE MONTAIGNE 152-53 (Charpentier, Variorum ed. 1876).

2. For a discussion of self-help as a legal concept in public international law, see RESTATEMENT OF FOR. REL. LAW (U.S.) § 905 (1987); H. KELSEN, PRINCIPLES OF INTERNATIONAL LAW 15-17, 22-23, 58-62 (1952); Schachter, *Self-Help in International Law*, 37 J. INT'L AFF. 231 (1984); Schachter, *The Right of States to Use Armed Force*, 82 MICH. L. REV. 1620 (1984).

3. Holmes, *The Path of the Law*, 1 B. L. SCH. MAG. 1, 3 (1897). ("If you want to know the law and nothing else you must look at it as a bad man, who cares only for the material consequences which such knowledge enables him to predict, not as a good one, who finds his reasons for conduct, whether inside the law or outside of it, in the vaguer sanctions of conscience.")

4. Address by Chief Justice Burger, ABA Midyear Meeting (Jan. 24, 1982), reprinted in 68 A.B.A.J. 274 (1982). See also Burger, *Using Arbitration to Achieve Justice*, 40 ARB. J. 3 (1985).

5. See, for example, Galanter, *Reading the Landscape of Disputes: What We Know and Don't Know (and Think We Know) About Our Allegedly Contentious and Litigious Society*, 31 U.C.L.A. L. REV. 4 (1983) For supplemental references to ADR literature, see Appendixes A, B, & C (ch. 1) infra.

6. See Trubek, Sarat, Felstiner, Kritzer, Grossman, *The Costs of Ordinary Litigation*, 31 U.C.L.A. L. REV. 72, 124 (1983).

7. See Galanter, *Reading the Landscape of Disputes*, note 5 supra.

8. See Trubek et al., *The Costs of Ordinary Litigation*, supra note 6, at 124.

9. See Galanter, *Reading the Landscape of Disputes*, note 5 supra.

10. See R. POSNER, THE FEDERAL COURTS: CRISIS AND REFORM 76-77 (1985).

11. See Sander, *Varieties of Dispute Processing*, 70 F.R.D. 79, 130-33 (1976).

12. See Resnik, *Managerial Judges*, 96 HARV. L. REV. 374 (1982) and Resnik, *Failing Faith: Adjudicatory Procedure in Decline*, 53 U. CHI. L. REV. 494 (1986).

13. See Fiss, *Against Settlement*, 93 YALE L. J. 1073 (1984).

14. See id. at 1075.

15. See, for example, id. at 1076-78, 1082-90.

16. See Bok, *A Flawed System of Law Practice and Law Teaching*, 33 J. LEGAL EDUC. 570, 583 (1983).

17. See, for example, R. FISHER & W. URY, GETTING TO YES: NEGOTIATING

AGREEMENT WITHOUT GIVING IN (1981); R. FISHER & S. BROWN, GETTING TOGETHER: BUILDING A RELATIONSHIP THAT GETS TO YES (1988); Menkel-Meadow, *Toward Another View of Legal Negotiation: The Structure of Problem-Solving*, 31 U.C.L.A. L. REV. 754 (1984).

18. See, for example, J. FOLBERG & A. TAYLOR, MEDIATION: A COMPRE-HENSIVE GUIDE TO RESOLVING CONFLICTS WITHOUT LITIGATION (1984).

19. For a list of sources on arbitration, see notes in ch. 4 supra.

20. For a sampling of the current writings in various areas of ADR, see, for example, L. RISKIN & J. WESTBROOK, DISPUTE RESOLUTION AND LAWYERS (1987).

21. The federal and state activity relating to ADR remains embryonic; programs are instituted in a piecemeal fashion and other attempts at implementation are largely episodic. See generally 1 & 2 BNA ALTERNATIVE DISPUTE RESOLUTION REPORT (1987-1988) [BNA]. Current state legislation is directed principally to family law matters and to cases involving relatively modest sums that do not present significant legal or factual complications. ADR mechanisms also have been used in some states to temper the difficulty of dealing with highly complex evidentiary cases by segregating parts of the dispute and submitting them to ADR. In Hawaii, for example, mediation is being used to process $30 million of suits brought in a thirteen-year-old stadium construction dispute. See BNA, 2/4/88, at 35. Moreover, several communities have had recourse to ADR mechanisms in an attempt to resolve longstanding disputes or environmental controversies. A negotiated solution was reached, for instance, in a community claiming to have been damaged by the industrial use of PCB. See BNA, 3/17/88, at 93. See also BNA, 1/7/88, at 3. Professional liability insurers offer discounts and special deductibles to parties willing to engage in ADR to resolve claims. See BNA, 2/18/88, at 51. The present emphasis is clearly upon efficiency and economy on an ad hoc basis—to apply ADR processes in those areas in which rapid and inexpensive determination can be achieved and adversarial litigation can be avoided without too great a compromise of legal rights.

There have been congressional hearings on two bills designed to encourage the use of ADR by federal agencies (BNA, 5/12/88, at 171; 4/28/88, at 163; 8/20/87, at 187; 6/9/88, at 203): the Negotiated Rulemaking Act of 1987 and the Administrative Dispute Resolution Act of 1988. The proposed legislation seeks to gain congressional approval for nonadversarial mechanisms in regulatory and administrative disputes. Also, the president's 1989 Budget recommends the use of private arbitrators in pending tax cases. There is apparently a backlog of some eighty thousand cases involving $20 billion of uncollected revenues. Under the proposal, arbitration, however, would be excluded in precedent-setting cases. See

BNA, 3/3/88, at 67. ADR is also provided for in the Agricultural Credit Act of 1987 as agricultural loan mediation programs (BNA, 1/7/88, at 10, 10/15/87, at 245) and in the Uniform Product Safety Act of 1987 in the form of a provision for the "mediation of actions" (BNA, 1/7/88, at 10).

Arbitration procedures also have figured prominently in the text of the recent Free Trade Agreement between Canada and the United States. See BNA, 3/17/88, at 91, 1/21/88, at 20. Jurisdiction for trade disputes involving anti-dumping, countervailing duties, and other claims would be transferred to a "supranational" or "binational" panel of arbitrators consisting of experts nominated by the executive branch of each country. The awards would be binding and not appealable to national courts.

As noted previously in chapter one and the foregoing appendix (ch. 6), some state legislatures have instituted mediation programs in family law and child custody matters and required arbitration in tort and other civil cases. See BNA 3/3/88, at 75. These civil suits usually do not involve large amounts and are not legally or factually complicated. In agricultural states, there has been considerable interest in establishing mediation programs between agricultural debtors and creditors. See BNA, 2/18/88, at 59-60; 8/20/87, at 188; 5/28/87, at 60. Much of the recent state legislation deals with the certification of mediators, their potential legal liability, and the confidentiality of mediation proceedings. Typically, these laws or bills provide that mediation proceedings are confidential, that mediated agreements are not confidential unless the parties so provide, and that mediators are not civilly liable unless they acted in bad faith, with a malicious intent, or in wanton disregard of the parties' interests. See BNA, 3/31/88, at 108 (Florida); 3/3/88, at 77 (Virginia & South Dakota); 2/18/88, at 58 (New Hampshire); 2/4/88, at 36 (Florida); 10/15/87, at 245 (North Carolina); 6/25/87, at 114 (West Virginia); 5/28/87, at 60 (Arizona & Montana); 5/25/87, at 197 (Alabama).

Legislation in California appears to be particularly on the cutting edge of developments. Responding apparently to developments in federal law (the McMahon case), a new bill provides that arbitration agreements in adhesion contracts are enforceable. In such circumstances, however, arbitrators will be selected in a manner specified by the legislation rather than in a manner provided for in the contract. See BNA, 3/3/88, at 75. This proposed legislation coincides with the AAA's initiative following McMahon to establish independent arbitral panels for customer-broker disputes as an alternative to industry forums. See BNA, 9/17/87, at 213. Also, a new law in California requires more stringent adjudicatory standards in arbitrations involving a long-term health care facility. When arbitrators are ruling on a health or safety violation, they must specify in writing the areas of disagreement, what evidence was deemed probative, and the reasons for decision. See BNA, 2/18/88, at 58.

22. For a discussion of the modification of the law school curriculum in light of ADR, see, for example, Sander, *Alternative Dispute Resolution in the Law Curriculum: Opportunities and Obstacles*, 34 J. LEGAL EDUC. 229 (1984); Topic, *Developments in Alternative Dispute Resolution*, 37 J. LEGAL EDUC. 26 (1987).

23. See address by Chief Justice Burger, note 4 supra.

Appendixes

SECTION I. CHAPTER 1
Appendix A. *Additional References on the Litigation Crisis and ADR*

Additional references on the litigation crisis and the ADR movement include: M. DEUTSCH, THE RESOLUTION OF CONFLICT (1973); J. HIMES, CONFLICT AND CONFLICT MANAGEMENT (1980); P. STEIN, LEGAL INSTITUTIONS THE DEVELOPMENT OF DISPUTE SETTLEMENT (1984); Alschuler, *Mediation with a Mugger: The Shortage of Adjudicative Services and the Need for a Two-Tier Trial System in Civil Cases,* 99 HARV. L. REV. 1808 (1986); Cady, *Curbing Litigation Abuse and Misuse: A Judicial Approach,* 36 DRAKE L. REV. 483 (1986-87); Eisenberg, *The Bargain Principle and Its Limits,* 95 HARV. L. REV. 741 (1982); Eisenberg, *Private Ordering Through Negotiation: Dispute Settlement and Rulemaking,* 89 HARV. L. REV. 637 (1976); Fleming, *Reflections on the ADR Movement,* 34 CLEV. ST. L. REV. 519 (1986); Franaszek, *Justice and the Reduction of Litigation Costs: A Different Perspective,* 37 RUTGERS L. REV. 337 (1985); Gerber, *Victory vs. Truth: The Adversary System and Its Ethics,* 19 ARIZ. ST. L.J. 3 (1986-87); Gilkey, *Alternative Dispute Resolution: Hazardous or Helpful?,* 36 EMORY L.J. 575 (1987); Mnookin & Kornhauser, *Bargaining in the Shadow of the Law: The Case of Divorce,* 88 YALE L.J. 950 (1979); Resnik, *Managerial Judges,* 96 HARV. L. REV. 374 (1982); Sarat, *The Litigation Explosion, Access to Justice and Court Reform: Examining the Critical Assumptions,* 37 RUTGERS L. REV. 319 (1986); Sipes, *Reducing Delay in State Courts — A March Against Folly,* 37 RUTGERS L. REV. 299 (1985); Thensted, *Litigation and Less: The Negotiation Alternative,* 59 TUL. L. REV. 76 (1984).

See also O. COOGLER, STRUCTURED MEDIATION IN DIVORCE SETTLEMENT (1978); J. FOLBERG & A. TAYLOR, MEDIATION: A COMPREHENSIVE GUIDE TO RESOLVING CONFLICTS WITHOUT LITIGATION (1984); Green, *Growth of the Mini-Trial,* 9 LITIGATION 12 (1982); Goldstein, *Alternatives for Resolving Business Transaction Disputes,* 58 ST. JOHN'S L. REV. 69 (1983); Heintz, *Medical Malpractice Arbitration: A Viable Alternative,* 34 ARB. J. 12 (1979); Hoellering, *Remedies in Arbitration,* 20 FORUM 516 (1985); Note, *Private Judging: An Effective and Efficient Alternative to the Tra-*

ditional Court System, 21 VAL. U. L. REV. 681 (1987); Snow & Abramson, *Alternatives to Litigation: Court-Annexed Arbitrations,* 20 CAL. W. L. REV. 43 (1983).

But see R. ABEL, ed., POLITICS OF INFORMAL JUSTICE 1981, reviewed in 37 J. LEGAL EDUC. 334 (1984); LITIGATION IN AMERICA, 31 U.C.L.A. L. REV. 1-127 (1983) (Galanter, *Reading the Landscape of Disputes: What We Know and Don't Know [and Think We Know] About Our Allegedly Contentious and Litigious Society,* id. at 4); Delgado, Dunn, Brown, Lee, & Hubbert, *Fairness and Formality: Minimizing the Risk of Prejudice in Alternative Dispute Resolution,* [1983] WIS. L. REV. 1359 (1983); Edwards, *Alternative Dispute Resolution: Panacea or Anathema?,* 99 HARV. L. REV. 668 (1986); Fiss, *Against Settlement,* 93 YALE L.J. 1073 (1984); Fiss, *Foreword: The Forms of Justice,* 93 HARV. L. REV. 1 (1979); Fiss, *Out of Eden,* 94 YALE L. J. 1669 (1985); Galanter, *The Day After the Litigation Explosion,* 46 MD. L. REV. 3 (1986); Galanter, *The Legal Malaise; or, Justice Observed,* 19 L. & SOC'Y REV. 537 (1985). Accord *Comments on Galanter,* 46 MD. L. REV. 40-85 (1986) (Civiletti, Dobbs, Phillips, Saks, & Samuelson); Kanowitz, *Alternative Dispute Resolution and the Public Interest: The Arbitration Experience,* 38 HASTINGS L.J. 239 (1987); McThenia & Shaffer, *For Reconciliation,* 94 YALE L.J. 1660 (1985). See also *The Litigation Explosion Debate,* 11 JUST. SYS. J. 259 (1986).

Appendix B. *Additional References on the Debate Relating to Adversarial Justice*

Additional references on the adversarial system and its viability include: T. MARVELL, APPELLATE COURTS AND LAWYERS: INFORMATION GATHERING IN THE ADVERSARY SYSTEM (1978); Alexander, *Trial by Champion,* 24 SANTA CLARA L. REV. 545 (1984); Barrett, *The Adversary System and the Ethics of Advocacy,* 37 NOTRE DAME L. REV. 479 (1962); Barrett, *The Constitutional Right to Jury Trial: A Historical Exception for Small Monetary Claims,* 39 HASTINGS L.J. 125 (1987); Forrester, *Are We Ready for Truth in Judging?,* 63 A.B.A.J. 1212 (1977); Fuller, *The Adversary System,* in TALKS ON AMERICAN LAW 30 (H. Berman ed. 1961); Golding, *On the Adversary System and Justice,* in PHILOSOPHICAL LAW 98 (R. Bronaugh ed. 1978); Gorsky, *The Adversary System,* in PHILOSOPHICAL LAW 127 (R. Bronaugh ed. 1978); Landsman, *A Brief Survey of the Development of the Adversary System,* 44 OHIO ST. L. J. 713 (1983); Landsman, *Reforming the Adversary Procedure: A Proposal Concerning the Psychology of Memory and the Testimony of Disinterested Witnesses,* 45 U. PITT. L. REV. 547 (1984); Landsman, *The Decline of the Adversary System and the Changing Role of the Advocate in that System,* 18 SAN DIEGO L. REV. 251 (1981); Landsman, *The Decline of the Adversary System: How the Rhetoric of Swift and Certain Justice Has Affected Adjudication in American Courts,* 29 BUFFALO L. REV. 487 (1980); Luban, *The Adversary System Excuse,* in THE GOOD LAWYER: LAWYERS' ROLES AND LAWYERS' ETHICS 83 (D. Luban ed. 1984), reviewed in 84 MICH. L. REV. 1011 (1986); Schwartz, *The Professionalism and Accountability of Lawyers,* 66 CALIF. L. REV. 669 (1978).

Appendix C. *ADR Bibliography*

The following sources contain general discussions of alternative dispute resolution. *The Growing Field of Alternative Dispute Resolution,* 7 AM. ARB. ASSOC. LAW. ARB. LETTER 1-7 (No. 4 Dec. 1983); Sander, *Family Mediation: Problems and Prospects,* 2 MEDIATION Q. 3, 3-5 (1983); ARBITRATION AND THE LAW (AM. ARB. ASSOC. 1982) (General Counsel's Annual Report); L. FREEDMAN, LEGISLATION ON DISPUTE RESOLUTION (1984) (A.B.A. Spec. Comm. on Dispute Resolution Monograph No. 2 [1984]); Kritzer & Anderson, *The Arbitration Alternative: A Comparative Analysis of Case Processing Time, Disposition Mode, and Cost in the American Arbitration Association and the Courts,* 8 JUST. SYS. J. 6 (1983). See also Comment, *The Alternative Dispute Resolution Act of 1986: A Critical Analysis,* 31 ST. LOUIS U. L.J. 981 (1987).

The following sources contain discussions of alternative dispute resolution mechanisms in specific areas: (commerce) Hoellering, *The Mini-Trial,* 37 ARB. J. 48 (1982); *The Effectiveness of the Mini-Trial in Resolving Complex Commercial Disputes: A Survey,* 17 THE LAWYER'S BRIEF 3 (Mar. 31, 1987); (environmental matters) Watson & Danielson, *Environmental Mediation,* 15 NAT. RESOURCES LAW. 687 (1983); (medical malpractice) Aslanian-Bedikian, *Arbitrating a Medical Malpractice Claim,* 62 MICH. B. J. 788 (1983); Comment, *Alternatives to the Medical Malpractice Phenomenon: Damage Limitations, Malpractice Review Panels and Countersuits,* 34 WASH. & LEE L. REV. 1179 (1977); Note, *Medical Malpractice Arbitration: A Comparative Analysis,* 62 VA. L. REV. 1285 (1976); (neighborhood/community justice) J. LEMMON, ed., COMMUNITY MEDIATION, 5 MEDIATION Q. 1-90 (1984); (patent disputes) Farley, *The Role of Arbitration in the Resolution of Patent Disputes,* 3 TOURO L. REV. 47 (1986); Goldstein, *Arbitration of Disputes Relating to Patent Validity or Infringement,* 72 ILL. B. J. 350 (1984); (real estate) Levy, *Resolving Real Estate Valuation Disputes Through Arbitration,* 14 REAL ESTATE REV. 61 (1984); (torts generally) Hoellering, *Remedies in Arbitration,* 20 FORUM 516 (1985); (on nonadversarial remedies in family law) Cochran, *Mediation of Marital Disputes Before It Is Too Late: A Proposal for Premarital Contract Provisions for Mediation of Disputes within the Intact Family,* 15 PEPPERDINE L. REV. 51 (1987); Finlay, *Towards Non-Adversary Procedures in Family Law,* 10 SIDNEY L. REV. 61 (1983); Foster & Freed, *Child Custody and the Adversary Process: Forum Conveniens?,* 17 FAM. L.Q. 133 (1983); (on arbitration in family law) Coulson, *Family Arbitration: An Exercise in Sensitivity,* 3 FAM L.Q. 22 (1969); Philbrick, *Agreements to Arbitrate Post-Divorce Custody Disputes,* 18 COLUM. J. L. & SOC. PROBS. 419 (1985); Spencer & Zammit, *Reflections on Arbitration Under the Family Dispute Services,* 32 ARB. J. 111 (1977); Comment, *Arbitration: A Viable Alternative?,* 3 FORDHAM URB. L. REV. 53 (1974); (on conciliation) Foster, *Conciliation and Counselling in the Courts in Family Law Cases,* 41 N.Y.U. L. REV. 353 (1966); Lightman & Irving, *Conciliation and Arbitration in Family Disputes,* 14 CONCILIATION CTS. REV. 12 (1976); McIntyre, *Conciliation of Disrupted Marriages by or Through the Judiciary,* 4 J. FAM. L. 117 (1964); Wolff, *Family Conciliation: Draft Rules for the Settlement of Family Disputes,* 21 J. FAM. L. 213 (1982); (on mediation in family law) Evarts & Goodwin, *The Mediation and Adjudication of Divorce and Custody: From Contrasting Premises to Complementary Processes,* 20 IDAHO L. REV. 277 (1984); Pearson & Thoennes, *Mediating and Litigating Custody Disputes: A Longitudinal Evaluation,* 27 FAM. L.Q. 497 (1984); Phear, *Family Mediation: A Choice of Options,* 39 ARB. J. 22 (1984); Winks, *Divorce Mediation: A Nonadversary Procedure for the No-Fault Divorce,* 19 J. FAM. L. 615 (1980-81); Zumeta, *Mediation as an Alternative to Litigation in Divorce,* 62 MICH. B.J. 434 (1983).

SECTION II. CHAPTER 2
Appendix A. *The Procedural Experience of Mixed Jurisdictions: Louisiana as an Example*

Although lessons can be drawn from the evolution of English civil procedure, additional insights might be gained from assessing the experience of mixed jurisdictions with contrasting adjudicatory principles and techniques. See generally J. DAINOW, ed., THE ROLE OF JUDICIAL DECISIONS AND DOCTRINE IN CIVIL LAW AND IN MIXED JURISDICTIONS (1974); Cross, *The Eclecticism of the Law of Louisiana*, 55 AM. L. REV. 405 (1921); Pound, *The Influence of the Civil Law in America*, 1 LA. L. REV. 1 (1938); Stein, *The Attraction of the Civil Law in Post-Revolutionary America*, 52 VA. L. REV. 403 (1966). Through their amalgamation of the features of various legal traditions, these legal systems symbolize the full potential of the comparative law inquiry. Their hybrid legal culture makes them domains for gauging the respective operation and merit of diverse systemic devices, dispositions, and ideas. In the cosmology of legal systems, the state of Louisiana occupies an intermediary, somewhat ambiguous position. On the Louisiana legal system, see generally A. YIANNOPOULOS, ed., JURISPRUDENCE AND DOCTRINE IN CIVIL LAW AND IN MIXED JURISDICTIONS (1974); Barham, *Methodology of the Civil Law in Louisiana*, 50 TUL. L. REV. 474 (1976); Baudouin, *The Influence of the Code Napoleon*, 33 TUL. L. REV. 21 (1958); Dart, *The Legal Institutions of Louisiana*, 3 SO. L. Q. 247 (1918); Tate, *Civilian Methodology in Louisiana*, 44 TUL. L. REV. 673 (1970).

The diversity of colonial influences and the state's eventual political integration into the United States led it to absorb, albeit to varying degrees, the attributes of contradistinctive legal traditions. The amalgam of traits is present in both substantive and procedural law. As a consequence, Louisiana's juridical culture, in both historical and contemporary terms, is dominated by a tension between the contrastive civil-law and common-law influences—a conflict between a loyalty to historical origin and the practical reality of geopolitical circumstances. See generally G. DARGO, JEFFERSON'S LOUISIANA: POLITICS AND THE CLASH OF LEGAL TRADITIONS (1975); B. SCHWARTZ, THE CODE NAPOLEON AND THE COMMON-LAW WORLD (1956); Barham, *A Renaissance of the Civilian Tradition in Louisiana*, 33 LA. L. REV. 357 (1973); Carbonneau, *Les facteurs affectant la codification du droit en Louisiane*, 40 REV. JUR. & POL. 581 (1986); Crabites, *Louisiana Not a Civil Law State*, 9 LOY. L. J. 51 (1928); Daggett, Dainow, Hebert, &

McMahon, *A Reappraisal Appraised: A Brief for the Civil Law of Louisiana*, 12 TUL. L. REV. 12 (1937); Ireland, *Louisiana's Legal System Reappraised*, 11 TUL. L. REV. 585 (1937); Tullis, *Louisiana's Legal System Reappraised*, 12 TUL. L. REV. 113 (1937).

The history of the Louisiana law of civil procedure reveals that differing procedural principles were reconciled progressively into a common whole. See McMahon, *The Louisiana Code of Civil Procedure*, 21 LA. L. REV. 1, 1, 20 (1960). The Louisiana Code of Civil Procedure, enacted in 1960, reflects the synthesis of opposing legal ideas and values that is the hallmark of Louisiana law. LA. CODE CIV. PROC., [1960] 2 LA. ACTS (Supp. 1986). For an appraisal of the Code of Civil Procedure as a recent legislative enactment responding to past practice and establishing a prospective procedural regime, see, for example, *Symposium: Louisiana Code of Civil Procedure*, 35 TUL. L. REV. 473-596 (1961). For a discussion of the effect of subsequent practice upon the provisions of the Code of Civil Procedure, see, for example, *Louisiana Procedure Symposium*, 22 LOY. L. REV. 1-271 (1976). The most synthetic and illuminating commentary on the Code of Civil Procedure as enacted in 1960 is: McMahon, *The Louisiana Code of Civil Procedure*, supra [hereinafter McMahon]. See also McMahon, *The Background, Structure, and Composition of the Louisiana Code of Civil Procedure*, 7 LA. BAR J. 246 (1960).

The events that preceded the enactment of the Code illustrate that there had been a constant vying between influences, edging toward a consolidated identity. The early Practice Act of 1805 sought to promote integration into the prevailing national legal culture by establishing trial by jury and concomitantly instituting oral testimony in court proceedings. ACTS OF THE LEGISLATIVE COUNCIL OF THE TERRITORY OF ORLEANS OF 1805 (also known as the Livingston Practice Act). See McMahon, *The Case Against Fact Pleading in Louisiana*, 13 LA. L. REV. 369 (1953); Tucker, *Proposal for Retention of the Louisiana System of Fact Pleading; Exposé des Motifs*, 13 LA. L. REV. 395 (1953).

The incorporation of the jury into the trial process — the gravamen of American common-law adjudicatory procedure — demanded the additional incorporation of intricate rules of evidence based on the American model. Oral testimony by witnesses in court generated a need for the common-law techniques of direct and cross-examination. But, despite the 1805 Act and its incorporations, strong Spanish influences remained present in Louisiana's procedural law (see McMahon, supra, at 10).

The Codes of Practice of 1825 and 1870 demonstrate that the system of Louisiana's adjectival law continued to represent a merger of continental and Anglo-American borrowings blended into a unique amalgam of co-existing law (see id. at 6-10). The profoundly common-law influence, the jury trial and its attendant procedural implications that most threatened to dislodge the civil-law heritage, had been minimized by subsequent practice and legislation. The provision for a plenary review of the facts on appeal, a distinctive feature of civil-law procedure, made the institution of the civil jury trial basically an empty shell of the procedural law. Indeed, very few parties would bear the costs of an initial trial by jury only to have the legal and factual determinations completely reconsidered by an appellate court sitting without a jury (see id. at 13).

As a result, the rules of evidence, the use of oral testimony, and the recourse to cross-examination were of much less consequence in defining the procedural identity of the system. As in other civil-law jurisdictions, the judge in effect became the central decision-maker in the trial process. An otherwise significant common-law inroad had been placed in abeyance, and the adjectival law regained a basic equilibrium. Given the sophistication and overwhelming importance of common-law procedure in the United States, it is amazing that the romanist and continental influences remained so resilient in Louisiana.

For present purposes, the central teaching of the 1960 Code resides in the language of article 5051, which provides that:

> The articles of this Code are to be construed liberally, and with due regard for the fact that rules of procedure implement the substantive law and are not an end in themselves. LA. CODE CIV. PROC., art. 5051 [1960] 2 LA. ACTS (Supp. 1986).

This is more than a mere statement of pragmatic procedural policy; it represents a systemic objective of subordinating adjectival law and insisting upon the substantive resolution of controversies. It stands as an attitude of principle directly contravening the received wisdom of the early English common law that "there are no rights without remedies." In the words of one eminent commentator, the Louisiana Code of Civil Procedure "embodies procedural rules designed to permit the trial of a case to serve as a search for the truth, and to have its decision based on the substantive law applicable, rather than upon technical rules of procedure" (McMahon, supra, at 21).

The mandate of article 5051 and the practical elimination of the civil jury trial through the plenary review of facts on appeal align the procedural regime embodied in the 1960 Code with current judge-and-law-centered processes that apply in England and in continental practice. Given the disincentive to have trials by jury, the judge can take a more active and expert part in the proceeding. The relaxation of evidentiary rules in nonjury trials attributes greater discretion and authority to the judge and can give a greater prominence to written evidence. Whether the theoretical design of the Code is borne out in the reality of practice, however, and whether it has survived the process of legislative amendment are obviously other matters.

Recent experience suggests that the retention of vestiges of continental procedural law in the Code may, in fact, be a pyrrhic victory given the geopolitical pressures to conform with the national legal culture. Most, if not all, judges and attorneys in Louisiana have had a thorough pedagogical exposure to the adversarial ethic. Lawyers usually represent clients in both state and federal courts; litigation in federal court is conducted according to the usual common-law rules of procedure. The doctrine of "no review without manifest error" has lessened the impact of the plenary appellate review of facts. See *Arceneaux v. Domingue,* 365 So.2d 1330 (La. 1978) ("appellate review of facts is not completed by reading so much of the record as will reveal a reasonable factual basis for the finding of the trial court; there must be a further determination that the record establishes that the finding is not clearly wrong [manifestly erroneous]") (clarifying and redressing the appellate court construction of *Canter v. Koehring Co.,* 283 So.2d 716 [La. 1973] whose statement of the manifest error rule, 283 So.2d at 724, had been overlooked by the appellate courts). See also *Succession of Fields,* 222 La. 310, 62 So.2d 495 (1952) ("[A] judgment of the trial court on questions of fact will not be disturbed on appeal unless manifestly erroneous" 62 So.2d at 498); Maraist, *Civil Procedure,* 40 LA. L. REV. 761, 761-64 (1980).

Moreover, the considerable reference to precedent in judicial opinions attests to the strength of common-law reasoning in the Louisiana adjudicatory process. Legislative enactments that contravene the civilian methodology, the popular election of judges, the organization of courts according to the American common-law pattern, and the growing recourse to statutory law also are factors that diminish the presence of civilian procedure and dilute the judge-centered construct of justice.

Recent experience further indicates that the impact of the federal rules of civil procedure upon the content and basic orientation of the Code of Civil Procedure is growing. See LA. CODE CIV. PROC. (Supp. 1986). The federal model is increasingly being assimilated into discovery practice (see id.). Legislation enacted in 1983 has reinvigorated the importance of the civil trial by jury; apparently, the legislation aims to have only one procedure, the common-law rules, govern in both state and federal court (see id.). Although Louisiana still requires fact pleading, it has impliedly allied itself to the federal model by having liberal rules of amendment (see id.). The judicial practice of relying upon the mandate of article 5051 only in the absence of other, more specific provisions not only is an untoward construction, but also may extinguish—for all practical purposes—the reach of the article's civilian command.

As a general rule, Louisiana courts have emphasized the attorneys' adversarial responsibility to their clients and exhibited an inflexible attitude that requires the rigorous conformity to procedural dictates—an attitude characteristic of common-law courts. As a consequence, courts will rarely rescue a client from counsel's failure to abide by the requisites of procedure, preferring to have clients pursue their attorneys on professional negligence grounds. Finally, the single most important civilian aspect of Louisiana procedure—the plenary review of facts and law on appeal—although theoretically available, has been severely minimized by the appellate courts' lax view of their plenary review powers in cases involving a jury trial. Interview with Howard W. L'Enfant, Jr., Louisiana State University Law School, February 10, 1987.

Some may decry the contemporary state of adjectival law in Louisiana as cultural erosion or an inevitable abdication to the circumstances of geopolitical necessity. It may well be that Louisiana's attempt to accommodate diverse legal influences is approaching termination, that the common-law procedural model is being accepted and integrated, and that the original civil-law acquisitions will founder and gradually disappear. The vision of an intractable march toward the finality of a singular juridical identity, however, has little credibility in Louisiana's historical dynamic. The hallmark of Louisiana's legal culture has been its ability to blend contradistinctive legal traditions into a synthetic juridical amalgam. The dichotomous opposition between coexisting legal forces in mixed jurisdictions can literally tear the fabric of their identity asunder. The integrity, and in some measure the survival, of these legal systems are dependent upon the strength of their creative energies: their ability to reconcile contrasting tendencies into a cohesive systemic expression.

Viewing the evolution of adjectival law in Louisiana through the prism of the state's legal history, it seems that the procedural law has simply progressed to another cycle in its development. This same history provides some basis for believing that Louisiana's veritable juridical identity—its core legal personality—resides in a perpetual ebb and flow between opposing influences that is periodically characterized by stages of imbalance and equipoise. At any given time, the system may gravitate in one direction, repelling the other influence, or stabilize itself between the two influences. The current pull toward common-law procedure may then be merely an episode in a long and continuing historical dynamic. The fomentation between the American common-law culture and civil-law origins in matters of procedure places the identity of the legal culture into a state of flux. A stable procedural identity, such as the one that arguably characterizes the content of the 1960 Code, is reached when the governing rules establish an equilibrium between the competing models and also respond to the global adjudicatory needs of the system.

In any event, for adjudicatory processes dominated by the adversarial ethic and proffering a full right to civil trial by jury, the teaching of Louisiana's hybrid procedural culture coincides with the experience of other legal systems. Its history reveals that legal expertise and knowledge are the better means to achieving legally truthful adjudicatory determinations.

Appendix B. *Comparative Law Lessons and the Reformation of Adversarial Justice*

The relationship among society, legal systems, and adjudicatory processes bears a rough affinity to the psychodynamic development of the human personality and its relationship to the environments that form behavior. An individual's identity results in part from the psychological internalization of parental examples in childhood. In adult life, these internalized behavioral influences sometimes generate counterproductive psychic conflicts and create a need to reformulate personality dispositions based upon more apposite behavioral examples. In some respects, the adversarial ethic acts as the primary force of the American common-law adjudicatory personality and, in the setting of contemporary American society, it has become a pathology.

Certain features of judge-centered justice, in evidence in the civil-law tradition and in the history of the Louisiana procedural experience, provide general guidance about how the abusive aspects of the adversarial ethic might be eliminated or at least curtailed. A plan for reformulating adjudicatory processes impelled by the adversarial ethic should incorporate some of the principal features of civilian justice: the elimination or modification of the civil jury trial; the simplification of procedure and its subordination to substantive law; and the emphasis upon legal knowledge in reaching determinations.

Despite its democratic resonance, the institution of the jury places an excessive burden upon the civil adjudication of claims. Although they perform a necessary public law function in determining criminal culpability and safeguarding individual liberties from state encroachment, juries destabilize the process of civil litigation by their potential for unpredictable determinations. The jury's inexpert vision of justice not only fosters inconsistency, but also makes many of the intricate rules of procedure indispensable. The jury thereby further contributes to reinforcing the adversarial ethic's predominantly procedural view of justice.

Having a judge or a bench of judges perform the essential decision-making role in civil proceedings strengthens truth-seeking in adjudication. Decisions are grounded in the greater predictability and consistency of substantive knowledge. Although judges are not immune from making impressionistic judgments or being subject to irrational influences, the likelihood is that they, because of their professional training and expertise, are less likely than juries to fall prey to such influences. Having a standard of de novo review of facts and law on appeal would further lessen the possibility of aberrant or unfair results. Also, filling judicial positions through periodic popular elections might give the administration of justice a sufficiently democratic base while maintaining relative judicial independence.

Most important, the reliance upon a judge as the sole adjudicator in civil proceedings would obviate the need for rigorous procedural rules and minimize the opportunity for advocates to engage in theatrics and maneuvering. The chief drawback of the civil jury trial is not that it makes adversarial procedural rules necessary, but that, by its very composition and function, the jury fosters the adversarial defacement of the truth-seeking function of adjudication. A judge-centered process would be much less likely to tolerate or, in the event of some toleration, to be persuaded by the histrionic dramatization of facts or of legal questions. An attendant relaxation of procedural rules would allow for a greater emphasis upon substantive determinations. Although legal truth is inexorably tied to the adjudicatory process, having judge-centered features integrated into the American common-law adversarial process would give that process greater potential for achieving a fairness of result more consonant with how a just truth should be derived. By eliminating the conflict between the misplaced democratic value and the use of legal expertise, between privileging the appearance of truth and seeking truthful results, a modified adversarial personality could achieve more salutory dispute resolution ends.

The elimination of the civil jury trial would inevitably raise federal constitutional challenges. It would also require amending forty-eight state constitutions. A more moderate and graduated system of dispute resolution remedies, effecting less radical and problematic change, could be devised. State legislatures, for example, could limit the use of the civil jury trial to cases where they believe private disputes impinge upon questions of broad public concern — for example, claims relating to consumer fraud or professional negligence. Although somewhat surrepticious, legislation also might provide, as it does in Louisiana, for the plenary review of facts and law on appeal, thereby creating a significant practical disincentive to have recourse to the jury in the first instance.

Other proposals for change might focus more specifically upon modifying the jury's responsibility in the adjudicatory process. The civil jury could be maintained, but its function restricted exclusively to the determination of facts—in cases, for example, in which only circumstantial evidence exists. Once the jury determines where the factual probabilities lie, the court would then apply the law to the facts as determined by the jury. In yet other variations, juries could be composed only of individuals with a minimal amount of legal training, possibly leading to a class of professional jurors certified by the state. There could be mixed juries consisting of both professional and lay members. Judges might relinquish their usual passivity and join the jury in its deliberations either in a nonvoting supervisory capacity or as an actual participant voting in all cases or only in tie-breaking situations. These models obviously would require the elaboration of an entirely new set of procedural rules to define the role of the jury in the adjudicatory process.

Eliminating, significantly reducing, or totally redefining the civil jury process is at the very core of the quest for a more truthful process of American common-law adjudication. A judge-and-law-centered process, minimizing the reach of contentious procedural strictures, appears to be a better method by which to achieve a humanistic framework for dispute resolution. The dynamics of adversarial litigation disappoint the public trust invested in adjudicatory processes; that trust would be better served by reliance upon the guiding force of experience and knowledge, rather than a roll of the dice. Proposals for reforming the legal adjudicatory process should continue to be associated with the consideration of extrajudicial devices for dispute resolution. The experience with commercial and labor arbitration has been very favorable, and alternative remedies—such as mediation—although more recent in their contemporary role, have fared well in the resolution of family law disputes. The experience with such devices either could inform judicial adjudication and lead it to incorporate some of their more successful techniques or allow the alternative mechanism to assume under judicial supervision the dispute resolution function in those areas where it shows itself to be particularly effective.

As noted earlier, the truth of law and adjudication resides in the process and its operation—how they service the global dispute resolution needs of society. A truthful legal system, one that is at once necessary and conforms to the societal perception of fairness, proffers remedial mechanisms that respond to the particular characteristics of disputes. It produces determinations that are both workable and legitimate through a civilized and humanistic process that educates the disputing parties as well as finalizes their controversy.

For a more elaborate discussion of the use of nonlegal and non-adversarial dispute resolution mechanisms in the context of specific domestic conflicts, see ch. 5 at notes 31-82; and ch. 6 at notes 78-90.

For a discussion of the jury system, including defenses and criticisms, see P. DIPERNA, JURIES ON TRIAL: FACES OF AMERICAN JUSTICE (1984), reviewed in 84 MICH. L. REV. 1030 (1986); A. GINGER, JURY SELECTION IN CIVIL AND CRIMINAL TRIALS (2d ed. 1984); V. HANS & N. VIDMAR, JUDGING THE JURY (1985); R. HASTIE, S. PENROD, & N. PENNINGTON, INSIDE THE JURY (1983); H. KALVEN & H. ZEISEL, THE AMERICAN JURY (1971); L. MOORE, THE JURY, TOOL OF KINGS, PALLADIUM OF LIBERTY (1973); R. SIMON, ed., THE JURY SYSTEM IN AMERICA: A CRITICAL OVERVIEW (1975); TRIAL BY JURY — PRESERVE IT — DEFENSE RESEARCH INSTITUTE, INC. (1965); S. WISHMAN, ANATOMY OF A JURY: THE SYSTEM ON TRIAL (1986). See also H. WILCOX, FRAILTIES OF THE JURY (1985); Feikens, *The Civil Jury: An Endangered Species,* 20 U. MICH. J. L. REF. 789 (1987); Stephens, *Controlling the Civil Jury: Towards a Functional Model of Justification,* 76 KY. L. J. 81 (1987-88).

For an insightful discussion and suggestions regarding the modification of the civil jury process, see Alschuler, *Mediation With a Mugger: The Shortage of Adjudicative Services and the Need for a Two-Tier Trial System in Civil Cases,* 99 HARV. L. REV. 1808 (1986).

SECTION III. CHAPTER THREE
Appendix A. *Additional References on Terrorism and Extradition*

Hague Convention on the Suppression of Unlawful Seizure of Aircraft, Dec. 16, 1970, [1971] 2 U.S.T.. 1641, T.I.A.S. No. 7192, reprinted in 10 INT'L LEGAL MAT'LS 133 (1971); Montreal Convention for the Suppression of Unlawful Acts Against the Safety of Civil Aviation, Sept. 23, 1971, [1973] 1 U.S.T. 564, T.I.A.S. No. 7570, reprinted in 10 INT'L LEGAL MAT'LS 1151 (1973); United Nations Convention on the Prevention and Punishment of Crimes Against Internationally Protected Persons Including Diplomatic Agents, Dec. 14, 1973, G.A. Res. 3166, 28 U.N. GAOR, Supp. (No. 30), at 146, U.N. Doc. A/9030 (1974), reprinted in 68 AM. J. INT'L L. 388 (1974); European Convention on the Suppression of Terrorism, opened for signature, Jan. 27, 1977, EUROP. T.S. No. 90, reprinted in 15 INT'L LEGAL MAT'LS 1272 (1976).

These conventions attempt to deal with the problem of excluding terroristic acts from the purview of the political offense exception by listing specific offenses as extraditable crimes not subject to any exception. The European Convention on the Suppression of Terrorism follows the trend established by the other instruments — specifying that certain acts will be crimes under the domestic law of the signatory States and imposing upon these states a duty to prosecute or extradite perpetrators of terrorist acts. The European Convention contains a detailed list of paradigmatic terrorist crimes specifically exempted from the political offense exception. See European Convention, supra, arts. 1 & 2. Accord arts. 5 & 7. For a discussion of these conventions and problems posed by extradition and terrorist acts in the international community, see M. C. BASSIOUNI, ed., INTERNATIONAL TERRORISM AND POLITICAL CRIMES (1973); M. C. BASSIOUNI, ed., INTERNATIONAL CRIMINAL LAW (1986); M. C. BASSIOUNI, INTERNATIONAL EXTRADITION AND WORLD PUBLIC ORDER (1974); M.C. BASSIOUNI, INTERNATIONAL EXTRADITION IN UNITED STATES LAW AND PRACTICE (1983). On extradition theory and practice generally, see I. SHEARER, EXTRADITION IN INTERNATIONAL LAW (1971).

See also Blakesley, *A Conceptual Framework for Extradition and Jurisdiction over Extraterritorial Crimes,* [1984] UTAH L. REV. 685 (1984); Kane, *Prosecuting International Terrorists in United States Courts: Gaining the Jurisdictional Threshold,* 12 YALE J. INT'L L. 294 (1987); Koh, *Civil*

Remedies for Uncivil Wrongs: Combatting Terrorism Through Transnational Public Law Litigation, 22 TEX. INT'L L. J. 169 (1987); Symposium, *Terrorism and the Law: Protecting Americans Abroad,* 19 CONN. L. REV. 697 (1987).

Appendix B. Additional References on the Political Offense Exception

Classical treatments include: Bassiouni, *Ideologically Motivated Offenses and the Political Offense Exception in Extradition: A Proposed Juridical Standard for an Unruly Problem,* 19 DE PAUL L. REV. 217 (1969); Garcia-Mora, *Crimes Against Humanity and the Principle of Nonextradition of Political Offenders,* 62 MICH. L. REV. 927 (1964); Garcia-Mora, *The Nature of Political Offenses: A Knotty Problem of Extradition Law,* 48 VA. L. REV. 1226 (1962). Some of my writings in the area include: *The Political Offense Exception to Extradition and Transnational Terrorists: Old Doctrine Reformulated and New Norms Created,* 1 ASIL INT'L L.J. 1 (1977); *The Provisional Arrest and Subsequent Release of Abu Daoud by French Authorities: A Legal Critique,* 17 VA. J. INT'L L. 495 (1977); *Terrorist Acts: Crimes or Political Infractions? A Survey of Recent French Extradition Cases,* 3 HASTINGS INT'L & COMP. L. REV. 265 (1980); *The Political Offense Exception as Applied in French Cases Dealing with the Extradition of Terrorists: The Quest for an Appropriate Doctrinal Analysis Revisited,* in [1983] MICH. Y.B. INT'L LEGAL STUDIES 209 (1983).

For more recent articles, see Bannof & Pyle, *To Surrender Political Offenders: The Political Offense Exception to Extradition in United States Law,* 16 N.Y.U. J. INT'L L. & POL. 169 (1984); Blakesley, *The Evisceration of the Political Offense Exception to Extradition,* 15 DEN. J. INT'L L. & POL'Y 109 (1986); Comment, *Combatting International Terrorism: Limiting the Political Exception Doctrine in Order to Prevent "One Man's Terrorism from Becoming Another Man's Heroism,"* 31 VILL. L. REV. 1495 (1986); Comment, *The Political Offense Exception to Extradition: Protecting the Right of Rebellion in an Era of International Political Violence,* 66 OREGON L. REV. 405 (1987); Gilbert, *Terrorism and the Political Offence Exemption Reappraised,* 34 INT'L & COMP. L.Q. 695 (1985); Kellet, *Extradition: Concept of the Political Offense,* 8 LIVERPOOL L. REV. 1 (1986); Kulman, *Eliminating the Political Offense Exception for Violent Crimes: The Proposed United States—United Kingdom Supplementary Treaty,* 26 VA. J. INT'L L. 755 (1986); Larschan, *Extradition, the Political Offense Exception and Terrorism: An Overview of Three Principal Theories,* 4 B.U. INT'L L.J. 231 (1986); Molner, *Extradition: Limitation of the Political Offense Exception— Supplementary Treaty Concerning Extradition (U.S. —U.K.),* 27 HARV. INT'L L.J. 266 (1986);

Note, *Expediting Extraditing: The United States-United Kingdom Supplemental Extradition Treaty of 1986,* 10 LOY. L.A. INT'L & COMP. L. J. 135 (1988); Note, *Extradition in an Era of Terrorism: The Need to Abolish the Political Offense Exception,* 61 N.Y.U. L. REV. 654 (1986); Thompson, *The Evolution of the Political Offense Exception in an Age of Modern Political Violence,* 9 YALE J. WORLD PUB. ORD. 315 (1983); Sofaer, *The Political Offense Exception and Terrorism,* 15 DEN. J. INT'L L. & POL'Y 125 (1986). See also Note, *Extraterritorial Jurisdiction Over Acts of Terrorism Committed Abroad: Omnibus Diplomatic Security and Antiterrorism Act of 1986,* 72 CORNELL L. REV. 599 (1987).

Appendix C. *Additional References on the Hague Evidence Convention*

Hague Convention on the Taking of Evidence Abroad in Civil or Commercial Matters, opened for signature, Mar. 18, 1970, 23 U.S.T. 2555, T.I.A.S. No. 7444, 847 U.N.T.S. 231. For a comprehensive treatment of the Hague Evidence Convention, see *Hague Evidence Convention: A Practical Guide to the Convention, United States Case Law, Convention-Sponsored Review Commissions (1978 & 1985), and Responses of Other Signatory Nations: With Digest of Cases and Bibliography,* 16 GA. J. INT'L & COMP. L. 73 (1986). See also Betti, *Reconciling American and Civil Law Concerns in Taking Evidence Abroad: A Reevaluation of the Compromise from the Hague,* 10 ASILS INT'L L. J. 109 (1986); Collins, *The Hague Evidence Convention and Discovery: A Serious Misunderstanding?,* 35 INT'L & COMP. L.Q. 765 (1986); Comment, *Anschuetz, International Discovery American-Style, and the Hague Evidence Convention,* 19 N.Y.U. J. INT'L L. & POL. 87 (1986); Heck, *United States Misinterpretation of the Hague Evidence Convention,* 24 COLUM. J. TRANS. L. 231 (1986); McLean, *The Hague Evidence Convention: Its Impact on American Civil Procedure,* 9 LOYOLA (L.A.) INT'L & COMP. L.J. 17 (1986); Maier, *Extraterritorial Discovery: Cooperation, Coercion and the Hague Evidence Convention,* 19 VAND. J. TRANS. L. 239 (1986); Note, *Extraterritorial Discovery under the Hague Evidence Convention,* 31 VILL. L. REV. 253 (1986); Note, *In Re Anschuetz & Co. Gmbh (754 F.2d 602): A Critical Analysis,* 15 DEN. J. INT'L L. & POL'Y 135 (1986); Note, *The Evidence Convention: Supreme Law of the Land?,* [1984] WISC. INT'L L.J. 183 (1984); Note, *The Hague Evidence Convention: Determining Its Applicability Through Comity Analysis,* 38 SYRACUSE L. REV. 717 (1987); Note, *The Securities Acts and International Discovery: The Hague Evidence Convention After Anschuetz (754 F.2d 602) and Messerschmitt Bolkow Blohm (757 F.2d 729),* 12 SYRACUSE J. INT'L L. & COM. 600 (1986); Rogers,

On the Exclusivity of the Hague Evidence Convention, 21 TEX. INT'L L.J. 441 (1986); Sadoff, *The Hague Evidence Convention: Problems at Home of Obtaining Foreign Evidence,* 20 INT'L LAW. 659 (1986); Shemanski, *Obtaining Evidence in the Federal Republic of Germany: The Impact of the Hague Evidence Convention on German-American Judicial Cooperation,* 17 INT'L LAW. 465 (1983).

Appendix D. *Additional References on the Warsaw Convention*

On the Convention's conditions for liability, see, for example, Balzarini, *Embarking or Disembarking: A French Connection?,* 10 BRIEF 26(2)(1981); Cahn, *Saks: A Clarification of the Warsaw Convention Passenger Liability Standards,* 16 U. MIAMI INTER-AM. L. REV. 539 (1985); Johnson & Minch, *The Warsaw Convention Before the Supreme Court: Preserving the Integrity of the System,* 52 J. AIR L. & COM. 93 (1986); Judge & Schirott, *Heart Attack on Plane Not Considered "Accident,"* 132 CHICAGO DAILY L. BULL. at 3, col. 1 (Mar. 1986); Martin, *Intentional or Reckless Misconduct: From London to Bangkok and Back Again,* 8 ANN. AIR & SPACE L. 145 (1983); Note, *Air France v. Saks (105 S.Ct. 1338): The Applicability of the Warsaw Convention to a Passenger Injury Sustained During a Routine International Flight,* 11 N.C. J. INT'L L. & COM. REG. 157 (1986); Note, *Recovery for Mental Harm Under Article 17 of the Warsaw Convention: An Interpretation of Lesion Corporelle,* 8 HASTINGS INT'L & COMP. L. REV. 339 (1985); Note, *Up in the Air without a Ticket: Interpretation and Revision of the Warsaw Convention,* 6 FORDHAM INT'L L.J. 332 (1982-1983); Price, *Article 25 the Warsaw Convention Meaning of "Recklessly,"* 8 AIR L. 171 (1983); Reukema, *Article 17 of the Warsaw Convention: An Accident Is Required for Recovery,* 10 ANN. AIR & SPACE L. 191 (1985).

On the constitutional aspects of the Convention, see, for example, Comment, *Warsaw Convention Liability Limitations: Constitutional Issues,* 6 NW. J. INT'L L. & BUS. 896 (1984); Monts, *Due Process, Equal Protection and the Right to Travel: Can Article 22 of the Warsaw Convention Stand up to These Constitutional Foes?,* 49 J. AIR. L. & COM. 907 (1984); Rowe, *After Bali: Can the Warsaw Convention Be Proven a Taking Under the Fifth Amendment?,* 49 J. AIR. L. & COM. 947 (1984).

On the limits of liability and the use of the gold standard under the convention, see, for example, Achampong, *U.S. Courts and the Warsaw Convention: TWA v. Franklin Mint,* 20 J. WORLD TRADE L. 329 (1986); Barloco, *Article 22 of the Warsaw Convention: In a State of Limbo,* 8 AIR. L. 2 (1983); Comment, *Limitations on Air Carrier Liability: An Inadvertent*

Return to Common Law Principles, 48 J. AIR L. & COM. 111 (1982); Corrigan, *Air Cargo-Liability Limitations of the Warsaw Convention for Loss of Cargo Are (Unenforcable) Enforcable in the United States of America,* 9 AIR L. 184 (1984); Fisher, *The Gold Issue: The Supreme Court Upholds the Limitations on Liability Established by the Warsaw Convention,* 28 TRIAL LAW. GUIDE 471 (1985); Kean, *Warsaw Convention: Limitation of Liability,* J. BUS. L. 77 (1984); Kreindler, *Franklin Mint,* 191 N.Y.L. J. 1 (1984); Larsen, *New Work in UNCITRAL on Stable, Inflation Proof Liability Limits,* 48 J. AIR L. & COM. 665 (1983); Leigh, *Warsaw Convention: Conversion of Liability Limitations from Gold Standards to Dollars,* 77 AM. J. INT'L L. 320 (1983); Lyall, *Warsaw Relieved: Gold Reinstated, but—Application of Warsaw Convention to Air Transport to and from the United States,* 30 J. L. SOC. SCOTLAND 102(3) (1985); McGilchrist, *Limitation of Liability Under the Warsaw Convention: Further Developments in the U.S.: Carriage by Air,* LLOYD'S MAR. & COM. L.Q. 308 (1983); Note, *Aviation—Article 22 of the Warsaw Convention—Supreme Court Adopts a Purpose Approach to Enforce an Anachronistic Convention System,* 7 FORDHAM INT'L L.J. 592 (1983-1984); Note, *Aviation: Liability Limitations for Wrongful Death or Personal Injury—A Contemporary Analysis of the Warsaw System,* 10 BROOKLYN J. INT'L L. 381 (1984); Note, *International Liability Limitations Agreements—Republic Nat'l Bank of N.Y. v. Eastern Airlines, 815 F.2d 232 (2d Cir. 1987),* 53 J. AIR. L. & COM. 839 (1988); Note, *Limiting Air Carrier Liability Under the Warsaw Convention,* 11 SYRACUSE J. INT'L L. & COM. 651 (1984); Note, *Torts—Liability Limitations Under the Warsaw Convention—The Cargo Liability Limits of the Warsaw Convention Are Fully Enforceable at the Rate of $9.07 per Pound,* 50 J. AIR L. & COM. 155 (1984); Note, *Trans World Airlines, Inc. v. Franklin Mint: The Judiciary's Problematic Role in Treaty Interpretation,* 17 N.Y.U. J. INT'L L. & POL. 323 (1985); Reukema, *No New Deal on Liability Limits for International Flights,* 18 INT'L LAW. 983 (1984); Sehr, *Recent Developments in Aviation Case Law,* 53 J. AIR L. & COM. 85 (1987); Sheinfeld, *From Warsaw to Tenerife: A Chronological Analysis of the Liability Limitations Imposed Pursuant to the Warsaw Convention,* 45 J. AIR L. & COM. 653 (1980); Silets, *Something Special In the Air and on the Ground: The Potential for Unlimited Liability of International Air Carriers for Terrorist Attacks Under the Warsaw Convention and Its Revision,* 53 J. AIR. L. & COM. 321 (1987); Young, *Court Upholds Warsaw Convention Limits on Liability,* 70 A.B.A. J. 109 (1984).

On the various amendments to the Warsaw Convention, see, for example, Cohen, *Montreal Protocol: The Most Recent Attempt to Modify the Warsaw Convention,* 8 AIR. L. 146 (1983); Dubuc & Doctor, *Legislative Developments Affecting the Aviation Industry 1981-82,* 48 J. AIR. L. & COM. 263 (1983); Fitzgerald, *The Four Montreal Protocols to Amend the Warsaw*

Convention Regime Governing International Carriage by Air, 42 J. AIR L. & COM. 273 (1976); Kreindler, *Montreal Protocols: Moment of Truth,* 188 N.Y.L. J., at 1, col. 1 (Aug. 20, 1982); Kreindler, *Montreal Protocols Ready for Vote,* 189 N.Y.L. J., at 1, col. 1 (Mar. 7, 1983); Leich, *The Montreal Protocols to the Warsaw Convention on International Carriage by Air,* 76 AM. J. INT'L L. 412 (1982); Mankiewicz, *The 1971 Protocol of Guatemala City to Further Amend the 1929 Warsaw Convention,* 38 J. AIR L. & COM. 519 (1972); Tompkins, *The Montreal Protocols: What Happens Next?,* 12 BRIEF 26 (Aug. 1983).

SECTION IV. CHAPTER 4
Appendix A. *Federal Court Cases Espousing the Strong Policy on Arbitration*

The following list refers to other recent federal court cases endorsing the "strong [or emphatic] federal policy" supporting arbitration: Rush v. Oppenheimer & Co., Inc., 681 F.Supp. 1045, 1049 (S.D.N.Y. 1988); Osterneck v. Merrill Lynch, Pierce, Fenner & Smith, Inc., 841 F.2d 508, 511 (3d Cir. 1988); Conover v. Dean Witter Reynolds, Inc., 837 F.2d 867, 868 (9th Cir. 1988); Brick v. J. C. Bradford & Co., Inc., 677 F.Supp. 1251, 1253 (D.D.C. 1987); Gilmore v. Shearson/American Express, Inc., 668 F.Supp. 314, 321 (D.C.N.Y. 1987); Hurlbut v. Gantshar, 674 F.Supp. 385, 388 (D. Mass. 1987); Fraser v. Merrill Lynch, Pierce, Fenner & Smith, Inc., 817 F.2d 250, 253 (4th Cir. 1987); Hoffman v. Missouri Pac. R.R., 806 F.2d 800, 801 (8th Cir. 1986); Page v. Moseley, Hallgarten, Estabrook & Weeden, Inc., 806 F.2d 291, 293 (1st Cir. 1986); Letizia v. Prudential Bache Sec., Inc., 802 F.2d 1185, 1188 (9th Cir. 1986); Felkner v. Dean Witter Reynolds, Inc., 800 F.2d 1466, 1470 (9th Cir. 1986); John F. Harkins Co. v. Waldinger Corp., 796 F.2d 657, 664 (3d Cir. 1986); Eli Lilly & Co. v. Home Ins. Co., 794 F.2d 710, 719 n.21 1156, 1162 (5th Cir. 1986); Explo, Inc. v. Southern Natural Gas Co., 788 F.2d 1096, 1098 (5th Cir. 1986); Woodcrest Nursing Home v. Local 144, Hotel, Hosp., Nursing Home & Allied Services Union, 788 F.2d 894, 897-98 (2d Cir. 1986); Taylor v. Nelson, 788 F.2d 220, 223 (4th Cir. 1986); Valentin v. United States Postal Service, 787 F.2d 748, 750 (1st Cir. 1986); Int'l Union of Elevator Constructors v. Nat'l Elevator Indus., 772 F.2d 10, 13 (2d Cir. 1985); Local 703, Int'l Bhd. of Teamsters v. Kennicott Bros. Co., 771 F.2d 300, 302 (7th Cir. 1985); Sharon Steel Corp. v. Jewell Coal & Coke Co., 735 F.2d 775, 777 (3d Cir. 1984); City of Meridian v. Algernon Blair, Inc., 721 F.2d 525, 529 (5th Cir. 1983); Liskey v. Oppenheimer & Co., 717 F.2d 314, 319 (6th Cir. 1983); Kroog v. Mait, 712 F.2d 1148, 1151 (7th Cir. 1983); Zimmerman v. Continental Airlines, Inc., 712 F.2d 55, 57 (3d Cir. 1983); Ryder Truck Lines, Inc. v. Teamsters Freight Local Union No. 480, 705 F.2d 851, 856 n.7 (6th Cir. 1983); Federated Metals Corp. v. United Steelworkers of Am. 648 F.2d 856, 859 (3d Cir. 1981); Midwest Window Systems v. Amcor Indus., Inc., 630 F.2d 535, 536 (7th Cir. 1980); Chauffeurs, Teamsters and Helpers Local Union No. 878 v. Coca-Cola Bottling Co., 613 F.2d 716, 716-17 (8th Cir. 1980); Compania Chilena De Navegacion Interoceanica,

S.A. v. Norton, Lilly & Co., 652 F. Supp. 1512, 1514 (S.D.N.Y. 1987); Management Recruiters of Albany, Inc. v. Management Recruiters Int'l, Inc., 643 F. Supp. 750, 752 (N.D.N.Y. 1986); Levine v. Merrill Lynch, Pierce, Fenner & Smith, Inc., 639 F. Supp. 1391, 1397 (S.D.N.Y. 1986); Dow Chemical Pac. Ltd. v. Rascator Maritime, S.A., 640 F. Supp. 882, 884 (S.D.N.Y. 1986).

Appendix B *Defining the Concept of Private International Law*

A majority view holds that private international law or conflicts of law is part of municipal law. Distinct bodies of conflicts rules exist in various countries and may be as different from one another as other national legal provisions. These rules draw their authority from municipal sources; the resulting law is, therefore, municipal in character. A universalist trend — which views private international law as an evolving body of transnational commercial law — opposes the classical perspective. See E. LANGEN, TRANS-NATIONAL COMMERCIAL LAW 8-33 (1973); Schmitthoff, *International Business Law, a New Law Merchant,* in 2 CURRENT LAW AND SOCIAL PROBLEMS 129 (1961). The universalists argue that transnational law will gradually overcome the fragmentation of municipal legal systems. Although it has its source in municipal law, private international law — in the universalist perspective — is international in character. In order to devise a properly transnational law, municipal authorities need to engage in a comparative law synthesis that responds to the transnational character of international commercial dealings. See C. SCHMITTHOFF, COMMERCIAL LAW IN A CHANG-ING ECONOMIC CLIMATE 21 (2d ed. 1981)

According to the classical view, the primary function of private international law or conflicts of law is to designate an appropriate municipal law to govern the provisions of an international contract. Differing inter-pretations of the effect of party choice exist in the various municipal systems. Some national laws hold that, even when the parties have des-ignated an applicable law, the municipal jurisdiction must still invoke its choice-of-law rules to determine whether the agreement itself is valid. Unlimited party autonomy in this regard would allow private individuals to perform an essentially legal function. The more pervasive view is that express party choice controls; absent party selection, the proper law of the contract is the law of the country with which the contract has the closest connection. This view assumes that a transaction that touches upon the legal order of several countries will be more closely connected to one of them. The attempt to identify a contract's "center of gravity" proceeds from the territorial doctrine of localization. See DICEY AND MORRIS ON THE CONFLICT OF LAWS (J. Morris ed. 10th ed. 1980); P. NORTH, CHESHIRE'S AND NORTH PRIVATE INTERNATIONAL LAW (10th ed. 1979).

The American view parallels its English analogue described above, although it places less emphasis upon the role of party autonomy. See Cavers, *The Two Law Theories*, in THE CHOICE OF LAW: SELECTED ESSAYS (1933-1983), 4-7 (1985). For the most part, Anglo-American practice is firmly rooted in considerations of territoriality. See R. WEINTRAUB, COMMENTARY ON THE CONFLICT OF LAWS (3d ed. 1986); R. LEFLAR, AMERICAN CONFLICTS LAW (4th ed. 1986).

The universalist view argues that private international law has been transformed from a choice-of-law system to a set of substantive rules that regulate transnational dealings and activities. The transformations in the global community and the economic interdependence of states have rendered the concept of territoriality obsolete. Moreover, private international law — in its substantive sense — only gains its origins in national legal systems; it is a regime of legal governance that transcends the parochial boundaries of municipality. It regulates "delocalized" international contracts and evidences the emergence of a new "lex mercatoria." See Kegel, *The Crisis of Conflicts of Laws*, 112 REC. DES COURS (Hague Academy Lectures) 91 (1964-II). Although proponents of the universalist view of private international law have advanced different justifications for this "anational" law, they are still searching for an appropriate calculus by which to explain the complexity of factors that have transformed international legal and economic relationships. See generally W. FRIEDMANN, THE CHANGING STRUCTURE OF INTERNATIONAL LAW (1964). On the role of state contracts in this evolution, see Hyde, *Economic Development in General and Development Agreements*, 105 REC. DES COURS (Hague Academy Lecture) 267 (1962-II); LaLive, *Contracts Between a State or a State Agency and a Foreign Company*, 13 INT'L & COMP. L.Q. 987 (1964); Schmitthoff, *The Unification or Harmonisation of Law by Means of Standard Contracts and General Conditions*, 17 INT'L & COMP. L.Q. 551 (1968).

The universalist school further argues that neither municipal law nor international law provides a sufficient juridical basis for transnational economic relationships (particularly those between states and foreign corporations). Subjecting transnational commercial parties to domestic legal requirements and the territorial authority of municipal systems is both inappropriate and undesirable. A new legal order needs to be fashioned that takes new realities into account. According to Lord McNair, "the complexity of the modern world . . . compels the abandonment of any . . . facile dichotomy of law into national law and public international law."

McNair, *The General Principles of Law Recognized by Civilized Nations,* 33 BRIT. Y.B. INT'L L. 1 (1957). See also Schmitthoff, *Nature and Evolution of the Transnational Law of Commercial Transactions,* in 2 THE TRANS-NATIONAL LAW OF INTERNATIONAL COMMERCIAL TRANSACTIONS (STUDIES IN TRANSNATIONAL ECONOMIC LAW) 19 (N. Horn & C. Schmitthoff eds. 1982) ("This is the area in which a transnational law of international trade has developed and can be further evolved. This law is essentially founded on a parallelism of action in the various national legal systems, in an area in which . . . the sovereign national state is not essentially interested." Id. at 21). See generally Berman, *The Law of International Commerical Trans-actions (Lex Mercatoria),* 2 EMORY J. INT'L DISP. RES. 235 (1988); Goldman, *La "lex mercatoria" dans les contrats et l'arbitrage international: réalités et perspectives,* 106 J. DR. INT'L-CLUNET 475 (1979).

These views have been subjected to considerable criticism primarily because the effects of contracts are transposed from the established and well-defined realm of municipal law to allegedly vague general principles of law or other, equally indefinite, systems with inarticulate substantive norms and uncertain sources. See Mann, *The Proper Law of Contracts Concluded by International Persons,* 35 BRIT. Y.B. INT'L L. 35 (1959) ("Lord McNair . . . somewhat surprisingly considers the general principles as af-fording, in certain cases, 'the choice of a legal system,' and, indeed, de-scribes them as a 'system of law.' Yet it is hardly open to doubt that, unless they are equiparated to public international law, the general prin-ciples are not a legal system at all." Id. at 45); Mann, *State Contracts and State Responsibility,* 54 AM. J. INT'L L. 572 (1960); Mann, *Lex Facit Ar-bitrum,* in INTERNATIONAL ARBITRATION LIBER AMICORUM FOR MARTIN DOMKE 157 (P. Sanders ed. 1967) ("Although, where international aspects of some kind arise, it is not uncommon and, on the whole, harmless to speak, somewhat colloquially, of the international arbitration, the phrase is a misnomer. In the legal sense no international commercial arbitration exists. . . . Every arbitration is a national arbitration, that is to say, subject to a specific system of national law. . . . Every right or power a private person enjoys is inexorably conferred by or derived from a system of municipal law." Id. at 159-60); Mann, *England Rejects "Delocalised" Con-tracts and Arbitration,* 33 INT'L & COMP. L.Q. 193 (1984); Mann, *Lex Arbitri and Locus Arbitri (Great Britain),* 104 L.Q. REV. 348 (1988); Park, *The Lex Loci Arbitri and International Commercial Arbitration,* 32 INT'L & COMP. L.Q. 21 (1983) ("The paradox of a legal obligation independent of a legal order suggests Athena springing full-blown from the head of Zeus: a binding commitment, free from any municipal law, just appears." Id. at 26); Suratgar, *Contracts Between Governments and Foreign Nations,* 2 INDIAN J. INT'L L. 273 (1961) ("The major criticism of this [Lord McNair's] suggestion is that no such legal system exists and that it could have no connection with any definable society, and would not amount in positivist terms to a legal system at all." Id. at 311). See also Park, *National Law and Commercial Justice: Safeguarding Procedural Integrity in International Arbitration,* 63 TUL. L. REV. 647 (1989).

But see Paulsson, *Delocalisation of International Commercial Arbitration: When and Why It Matters,* 32 INT'L & COMP. L.Q. 53 (1983) ("What this critique misses is that the delocalised award is *not* thought to be independent of any legal order. Rather, the point is that a delocalised award may be accepted by the legal order of an enforcement jurisdiction although it is independent from the legal order of its country of origin." Id. at 57 [emphasis in the original]). See also Paulsson, *Arbitration Unbound: Award Detached from the Law of Its Country of Origin,* 30 INT'L & COMP. L.Q. 358 (1981).

Appendix C. *Progression in the Federal Courts' Attitude toward Arbitration*

Before the *McMahon* decision (see text ch. 4, at notes 116-150 supra), federal courts generally extended the *Wilko* holding barring arbitration in disputes involving the 1933 Securities Act to claims arising under the 1934 Securities Act. These courts have reasoned that, given the similarity between the non-waiver provisions of the acts (15 U.S.C. § 77 [n] and 15 U.S.C. § 78 cc [a]), the preclusion of pre-dispute arbitration agreements should apply in both types of claims. See *Merrill Lynch, Pierce, Fenner & Smith, Inc. v. Moore,* 590 F.2d 823 (10th Cir. 1978); *Weissbuch v. Merrill Lynch, Pierce, Fenner & Smith, Inc.,* 558 F.2d 831 (7th Cir. 1977); *Sibley v. Tandy Corp.,* 543 F.2d 540 (5th Cir. 1976); *AFP Imaging Corp. v. Ross,* 780 F.2d 202 (2d Cir. 1985); *Ayres v. Merrill Lynch, Pierce, Fenner & Smith, Inc.,* 538 F.2d 532 (3d Cir. 1976); *Fratt v. Robinson,* 203 F.2d 627 (9th Cir. 1953); *Belke v. Merrill Lynch, Pierce, Fenner & Smith, Inc.,* 693 F.2d 1023 (11th Cir. 1982).

The *Byrd* and *Mitsubishi* decisions cast serious doubt on the wisdom of this decisional law. See Comment, *Section 10(b) and Rule 10b-5 Federal Securities Law Claims the Need for the Uniform Disposition of the Arbitrability Issue,* 24 SAN DIEGO L. REV. 199 (1987); Comment, *The Case for Domestic Arbitration of Federal Securities Claims: Is the Wilko Doctrine Still Valid?,* 16 S.W. U. L. REV. 619 (1986); Note, *The Preclusive Effect of Arbitral Determinations in Subsequent Federal Securities Litigation,* 55 FORDHAM L. REV. 655 (1987). After *Byrd* and *Mitsubishi,* in fact, circuit courts split on the question of whether 1934 act claims are subject to arbitration. Those courts that had precedent on the issue maintained their previous decisions, that is, nonarbitrability. See *Conover v. Dean Witter Reynolds, Inc.,* 794 F.2d 520 (9th Cir. 1986); *Wolfe v. E.F. Hutton & Co.,* 800 F.2d 1032 (11th Cir. 1986); *Girard v. Drexel Burnham Lambert, Inc.,* 805 F.2d 607 (5th Cir. 1986). In contradistinction, the two circuit courts not constrained by precedent determined that 1934 act claims were arbitrable. See *Phillips v. Merrill Lynch, Pierce, Fenner & Smith,* 795 F.2d 1393 (8th Cir. 1986); *Page v. Moseley, Hallgarten, Estabrook & Weeden,* Fed. Sec. Law Rpt. (CCH) § 93,001 (1st Cir. 1986).

Moreover, expressly following the line of Supreme Court decisions from *Zapata* to *Scherk* and ending with *Mitsubishi,* a federal court ruling in an international case held that bankruptcy proceedings do not prevent the arbitration of a dispute between the bankrupt company and one of its suppliers. *Sonatrach v. Distrigas Corp.,* Civil Action No. 86-2014-Y (D. Mass. March 17, 1987). In overturning an earlier opinion by the bankruptcy court, the court reasoned that,

> In weighing the strong public policy favoring international arbitration with any countervailing potential harm to bankruptcy policy upon the present facts, this Court finds the scales weighted in favor of arbitration. As discussed earlier, no major bankruptcy issues will be implicated in valuing contract damages and the international arbitration panel requires no special expertise to accomplish their task. While international arbitration will require a temporary and limited incursion into the Bankruptcy Court's exclusive jurisdictional bailiwick, no bankruptcy policies will suffer adverse impact. Conversely, the very image of the United States in the international business community stands to be tarnished. It is important and necessary for the United States to hold its domiciliaries to their bargains and not allow them to escape their commercial obligations by ducking into statutory safe harbors. Rather, our country should take special pains to project those qualities of honesty and fairness which are essential parts of the traditional American character and be perceived as a fair and equal player in the global marketplace, particularly in our commercial relations with the underdeveloped world. Any additional time and expense required by the international arbitration process— which is only speculative at this point—will be overshadowed in importance by the virtues of having the parties abide by their commitments. Id. (footnotes omitted).

See 2 MEALEY'S INT'L ARB. REP. 226, 269 (Apr. 1987); Westbrook, *The Coming Encounter: International Arbitration and Bankruptcy,* 67 MINN. L. REV. 595 (1983).

Federal court decisions have continued apace in other areas. The Eighth Circuit recently decided, in *Arnulfo P. Sulit Inc. v. Dean Witter Reynolds, Inc.,* [1988] W.L. 50740 (1988), that ERISA claims (claims based upon the Employee Retirement Income Security Act) can be submitted to arbitration. The case involved an agreement between a customer and a stockbroker containing a standard arbitration clause. Referring to *McMahon,* the court held that the ERISA legislation did not require a judicial forum for the resolution of claims and that ERISA claims should not be treated any differently from securities or RICO claims. Accord *Steck v. Smith Barney, Harris Upham & Co.,* 661 F.Supp. 543 (1987) (federal district court in New Jersey held that federal age discrimination and other anti-discrimination claims override the FAA mandate). See also *Nicholson v. CPC Int'l Inc.,* 56 U.S.L.W. 2607 (1988). In a related case, *Cohen v. Wedbush, Noble, Cooke Inc.,* 841 F.2d 282 (1988), the Ninth Circuit held that margin account agreements containing a mandatory arbitration provision do not constitute contracts of adhesion. The court reasoned that arbitration agreements in such clauses are part of industry practice. Moreover, because the SEC has approved the applicable arbitral procedures as impartial, the court is bound by that determination.

In a similar but somewhat distinct vein, the Seventh Circuit ruled, in *Geldermann, Inc. v. Commodity Futures Trading Comm'n,* 836 F.2d 310 (1987), that the Commodity Exchange Act's provision for the mandatory submission by commodity brokers to customer-initiated arbitration does not violate the Article III right to a federal judicial forum. Congress created the Commodity Futures Trading Commission and empowered it to implement the act; the agency chose to compel arbitration as a means of dispute resolution.

Other federal court decisions have also supported the "emphatic federal policy" on arbitration. In *Lawrence v. Comprehensive Business Services Co.,* 833 F.2d 1159 (1987), the Fifth Circuit ruled that a franchisee seeking a judicial declaration that the franchise agreement is illegal and unenforceable must arbitrate that issue pursuant to the governing arbitration clause. In *Legion Insurance Co. v. Insurance General Agency, Inc.,* 822 F.2d 541 (1987), the Fifth Circuit also held that a full hearing was not required on a challenge to an arbitral award: "The statutory basis for overturning an arbitral tribunal are precisely and narrowly drawn to prohibit such complete de novo review of the substance of the award...." 822 F.2d at 543. In *Management & Technical Consultants, S.A. v. Parsons-Jurden Int'l Corp.,* 820 F.2d 1531 (1987), the Ninth Circuit held that a general arbitration agreement, which contains no limiting language, "logically includes not only the dispute, but the consequences flowing from it." 820 F.2d at 1535. The court broadly construed the scope of the arbitrator's jurisdiction in light of the federal policy favoring arbitration.

A number of federal court decisions, especially in the labor area, however, indicate a less than complete allegiance to the "emphatic federal policy." For example, in contrast to *Parsons-Jurden,* the Fourth Circuit ruled in *B & R Associates v. Dependable Insurance Co., Inc.,* 835 F.2d 526 (1987), that, in circumstances involving multiple claims and a broad arbitration clause, the trial judge, not the arbitrator, must decide which claims are to be submitted to arbitration. The question of whether to consolidate arbitral proceedings is also a matter of court authority. *Del E. Webb Construction v. Richardson Hospital Authority,* 823 F.2d 145 (5th Cir. 1987). The federal courts have also vacated awards for reasons of public policy. In *Stead Motors v. Automotive Machinists Lodge No. 1173,* 843 F.2d 357 (1988), the Ninth Circuit ruled that an arbitrator's reinstatement of a reckless auto mechanic showed a "manifest disregard" of state law on automobile safety and maintenance. The Eighth Circuit, in *Iowa Electric Light & Power Co. v. IBEW Local 204,* 834 F.2d 1424 (1988), reversed an award reinstating a nuclear power plant employee who was fired for intentionally violating a safety rule at the plant. Reinstatement violated "a well-defined and dominant national policy requiring strict adherence to nuclear safety rules." 834 F.2d at 1427. The public policy in question was "well-defined and dominant and ascertained by reference to the laws and legal precedent. . . ." (Citing *W. R. Grace & Co. v. Local Union 759, Int'l Union of the United Rubberworkers,* 461 U.S. 757 [1983].) See Comment, *Judicial Deference to Grievance Arbitration in the Private Sector: Saving Grace in the Search for a Well-Defined Public Policy Exception,* 42 U. MIAMI L. REV. 767 (1988); Meltzer, *After the Labor Arbitration Award: The Public Policy Defense,* 10 IND. REL. L. J. 241 (1988).

See also *S. D. Warren Co. v. Paperworkers Local 1069,* No. 87-1570, 1988 (First Circuit ruled that arbitrator ignored the plain language of a collective bargaining agreement by reinstating three workers fired for selling marijuana on company property even though she found they had committed the charged offenses; reinstatement did not violate public policy, but court ruled that, once arbitrator found that workers committed offenses, she had no discretion to reduce the penalty from discharge to suspension). However, in *U.S. Postal Service v. Letter Carriers,* 839 F.2d 146 (1988), the Third Circuit reversed the district court's decision overturning an arbitrator's award reinstating an unpromoted postal worker who shot at his supervisor's car. The appellate court held that the district court had clearly exceeded the scope of its reviewing authority. It had given too little deference to the arbitrator's fact-finding and interpretations that a "supercharged emotional atmosphere" caused the incident, which failed to meet the "just cause" standard required to dismiss the worker.

The United States Supreme Court's recent rulings in the area of labor arbitration have been in keeping with the Court's general objective of eliminating restrictions upon arbitration. In *U.S. Postal Service v. Nat'l*

Ass'n of Letter Carriers, 810 F.2d 1239 (D.D.C. 1987), the Court dismissed a writ of certiorari as improvidently granted. See 99 L. Ed. 2d 770 (1988). The lower court ruling, which upheld an arbitrator's reinstatement of an employee, stated that an arbitral award is reversible only if it violates established law or seeks to compel some unlawful action. More significantly, in *United Paperworkers Int'l Union, AFL-CIO v. Misco,* 98 L.Ed.2d 286 (1987), decided on December 1, 1987, the Court upheld an arbitrator's reinstatement of a worker fired for drug use. The Court held that it was inappropriate for a court to reanalyze the facts of the case; "improvident, even silly fact-finding" by the arbitrator was an insufficient basis for overturning the award. Also, the lower court had misapplied the public policy exception because its decision was based on "general considerations of supposed public interests" and not upon a "reference to the laws and legal precedents." 98 L.Ed. 2d at 302. According to the Court, the public policy exception does not allow courts to take over the arbitrator's adjudicatory role. See also *Gulfstream Aerospace Corp. v. Mayacamas Corp.,* 108 S. Ct. 1133 (1988) (Court overrules *Enelow-Ettelson* doctrine under which stay of action pending arbitration was subject to automatic appeal as an injunction).

Appendix D. *Punitive Damages in Arbitration*

Garrity v. Lyle Stuart, Inc., 40 N.Y.2d 354, 353 N.E.2d 831 (1976), is the controlling case in New York State. There, the court of appeals held that arbitrators could not award punitive damages even if the parties had authorized them to do so in their agreement because punitive damages are meant to punish parties and deter negative social conduct, not compensate disappointed contractants. Fearing an unwarranted intrusion upon public functions and state authority, the court held that,

> Punitive damages is a sanction reserved to the states, a public policy of such magnitude as to call for judicial intrusion to prevent its contravention. Since enforcement of an award of punitive damages as a purely private remedy would violate strong public policy, an arbitrator's award which imposes punitive damages should be vacated. (353 N.E.2d at 794).

The position of the federal courts on the question of the arbitral award of punitive damages is in striking contrast to the reasoning in *Garrity* and aligns itself with the general tenor and logic of the second trilogy, *Mitsubishi,* and *McMahon.* In *Willoughby Roofing & Supply v. Kajima International,* 598 F. Supp. 353 (N.D. Ala. 1984), the court found that the arbitrators had the authority to award punitive damages pursuant to a broad arbitral clause (allowing the arbitrators to entertain "all claims, disputes, and other matters in questions arising out of, or relating to, this agreement . . . or the breach thereof") and wide-ranging institutional rules ("The arbitrator may grant any remedy or relief which is just and equitable and within the terms of the agreement of the parties"). The court held, "only in the presence of 'clear and express exclusions' could it be said that the arbitrators lacked authority under the contract to consider the plaintiff's claims for punitive damages" (see 598 F. Supp. at 357). The holding reflects the view that the federal policy favoring arbitration (and its institutional and juridical autonomy) requires allowing arbitrators to fashion the remedies they deem appropriate in the particular case.

See also *Willis v. Shearson/American Express, Inc.,* 569 F.Supp. 821 (D.C. N.C. 1983) ("This court agrees that there is no public policy bar which prevents arbitrators from considering claims for punitive damages."); *Rodgers Builders, Inc. v. McQueen,* 76 N.C. App. 16, 331 S.E.2d 726 (N.C. App. 1985), cert. denied 315 N.C. 590, 341 S.E.2d 29 (1986) (state court agrees that claims for punitive damages are arbitrable); *Grissom v. Greener & Sumner Construction, Inc.,* 676 S.W.2d 709 (Tex. Ct. App. 1984) (upholding arbitrability of punitive damages where arbitration agreement expressly conferred authority on arbitrators to consider exemplary damages; further, such awards did not violate public policy in contractual disputes); *Baker v. Sadick,* 208 Cal. Rptr. 676 (Cal. S. Ct. 1984) (upholding validity of punitive damage awards in medical malpractice arbitration).

See generally Bedell, *Punitive Damages in Arbitration,* 21 J. MAR. L. REV. 21 (1987); Berg, *Punitive Damages: Are They Properly Awarded in Arbitration?,* 1 MEALEY'S INT'L ARB. REP. 248 (1986); Jones, *Punitive Damages in Arbitration in the USA,* 14 INT'L BUS. LAW. 188 (1986); Note, *Punitive Damages in Arbitration: The Search for a Workable Rule,* 63 CORNELL L. REV. 272 (1978); Note, *The Arbitrator's Power to Award Punitive Damages in International Contract Actions,* 19 N.Y.U. J. INT'L L. & POL. 203 (1986); Note, *The Award of Punitive Damages as a Public Policy Question—Garrity v. Lyle Stuart, Inc.,* 43 BROOKLYN L. REV. 546 (1976); Shell, *The Power to Punish: Authority of Arbitrators to Award Multiple Damages and Attorney's Fees,* 72 MASS. L. REV. 26 (1987); Stipanowich, *Punitive Damages in Arbitration: Garrity v. Lyle Stuart, Inc. Reconsidered,* 66 B.U. L. REV. 953 (1986).

A division of authority exists on this question in labor arbitration. See *Safeway Stores, Inc. v. International Assoc. of Machinists & Aerospace Workers,* 534 F.Supp. 638 (D.C. Md. 1982) (disallowing punitive damages); *Baltimore Regional Joint Board v. Webster Clothes, Inc.,* 596 F.2d 95 (4th Cir. 1979) (holding that arbitrator's award of punitive damages exceeded authority granted by collective bargaining agreement); *Sweeney v. Mor-*

ganroth, 451 F.Supp. 367 (S.D. N.Y. 1978) (upholding an arbitral award for "liquidated" damages, "recognizing the substantial leeway which must be granted an arbitrator in fashioning remedies, especially in labor-related disputes. . . ."); *Local 369, Bakery & Confectionary Workers International Union of America, AFL-CIO v. Cotton Baking Co., Inc.,* 514 F.2d 1235 (5th Cir. 1975) (allowing award of punitive damages as being within arbitrator's discretion). See also *Westmoreland Coal Co. v. United Mine Workers of America,* 550 F.Supp. 1044 (W.D. Va. 1982); *Westinghouse Electric Corp., Aerospace Div. v. International Brotherhood of Electrical Workers,* 561 F.2d 521 (4th Cir. 1977); *International Union of Operating Engineers v. Mid-Valley, Inc.,* 347 F. Supp. 1104 (D.C. Tex. 1972); *School Committee of New Bedford v. New Bedford Educators Assoc.,* 405 N.E. 2d 162 (1980); *U.S. Fidelity & Guaranty Co. v. DeFluiter,* 456 N.E. 2d 429 (1983); *Shaw v. Kuhnel & Assocs., Inc.,* 698 P.2d 880 (N.M. 1985); *Dean Witter Reynolds, Inc. v. McNally,* 835 F.2d 1378 (1988).

Appendix E. *Justice Stevens's Position on Arbitration*

The Court's current stance on arbitration is lodged, so it seems, in the general policy objective of improving the administration of justice by promoting the recourse to arbitration. Its intent appears to be to have arbitral adjudication act as a substitute for the judicial process, thereby reducing the volume of cases on federal court dockets. In pursuing this policy objective, the Court has minimized the importance of other, arguably equally important juridical values — such as federalism concerns and the interest in regulatory policy. Moreover, the Court has achieved its aim by responding to the legal questions engendered by the litigation through analytical reasoning that is so single-minded at times as to be transparently ill-conceived and tortuous.

In this setting, Justice Stevens's dissenting opinion in *Mitsubishi* was an enlightening counterpart to the majority's view of, and approach to, arbitration. The Stevens dissent was grounded in persuasive legal reasoning and in a realistic sense of the dimensions of the arbitral process. It also countered the majority's policy vision with a set of critical and opposing policy considerations: what are or should be the demands of international trade and business upon national processes? When should national interests be considered vital in this setting, and how are they to fare in the elaboration of a policy on international commerce? How can an effective balancing of priorities be achieved?

Stevens's reference to judicial restraint in *McMahon* no longer carries with it an implied understanding of the arbitral process or of its mission in the larger landscape of dispute resolution and public policy. Nor does it convey a persuasive opposing view of the policy underpinnings of the specifically legal questions ordinarily raised in the litigation on arbitration. In effect, it sounds a retreat to a refuge of doctrine likely to be inconsequential as a dissenting view.

Given the history of his opinions on arbitration, it may have been unrealistic to expect that Justice Stevens would become a voice of reasoned opposition to the Court's arbitration doctrine. Taken as a whole, the opinions contain a number of marked inconsistencies. Moreover, rather than reflect an elaborated concept of the systemic or institutional stature of arbitral adjudication, they reveal an assessment of the alternative process that is subordinated to the traditional legal issues that dominated the particular litigation.

For example, Justice Stevens, as a judge on the Seventh Circuit Court of Appeals, dissented in *Scherk v. Alberto-Culver Co.*, arguing that the arbitration agreement should be enforced (see 484 F.2d 611 [7th Cir. 1973]). According to then-Judge Stevens, although both statutes rendered "void any waiver by a plaintiff of defendant's obligation to comply with the statute," neither the 1933 Act nor the 1934 Act "expressly applies to the plaintiff's waiver of his right to sue in federal court." *Scherk,* 484 F.2d at 618 (Stevens, Cir. Judge, dissenting). *Wilko* was distinguishable from *Scherk* on the ground that *Wilko* involved actions contrary to the purpose of the statute, whereas *Scherk* was merely a disguised contract case. "In a case such as this, . . . I would interpret sec. 29(a) as meaning no more than it actually says, and respect what I regard as the stronger policy mandated by sec. 201 of the Federal Arbitration Act. . . ." (*Scherk,* 484 F.2d at 619).

While the tenor of the opinion appears to announce in an ironic way the type of reasoning that would eventually characterize the majority opinion in *Mitsubishi* and *McMahon,* Judge Stevens's logic was not adopted by the United States Supreme Court, which anchored its agreement with Stevens's conclusion in language relating to international comity and to the needs of international commerce (see Scherk, 94 S.Ct. at 2457). Justice Stevens later vehemently dissented against such reasoning in *Mitsubishi,* criticizing the majority opinion for subordinating the "national interests in a competitive economy" to "vague notions of international comity." *Mitsubishi,* 105 S.Ct. at 3361, 3369 (Stevens, J., dissenting). According to Stevens, a makeshift "vision of world unity" should not be allowed "to distort the importance of the selection of a prior forum for resolving this dispute" (105 S.Ct. at 3374).

Therefore, as a circuit judge, Justice Stevens argued that claims under the 1934 act should be submitted to arbitration, while in *McMahon,* as a Supreme Court justice, he dissents on the ground that such claims should not be arbitrable. Moreover, his strong opposition to the arbitrability of antitrust claims expressed in *Mitsubishi* is accompanied in *McMahon* by the silent approval of the submission of RICO claims to arbitration— even though civil RICO claims can be considered roughly equivalent to antitrust claims in terms of their importance to the public interest.

The dichotomy between Stevens's reasoning in *Scherk* and *McMahon* could be explained by reference to a belief in judicial restraint. Since and prior to his circuit court dissent in *Scherk*, the *Wilko* bar to the arbitrability of 1934 act claims has been upheld by a long line of courts. Even if Justice Stevens believes that the application of *Wilko* is mistaken, his conservative view on the exercise of judicial authority may have led him to conclude that the erroneous decisional law should be corrected by legislative, not judicial, action. Judicial restraint would further require that the justice's misgivings yield to overwhelming case precedent and to the congressional acquiescence in the non-arbitrability of such claims.

The conflict between the determination of the arbitrability of antitrust and RICO claims may be explained by Justice Stevens's long association and intimate acquaintance with antitrust law. Justice Stevens not only practiced antitrust law, but has also extensively taught and is an accomplished scholar in that area. Justice Stevens's affinity to the "Chicago School" of antitrust economics may have motivated the justice's view in *Mitsubishi* that "the public interest in free competitive markets" is too close to fundamental values and core regulatory interests to be implemented through private arbitral resolution. The anticompetitive restrictions allegedly imposed by Mitsubishi are the very type of actions that the antitrust laws were intended to guard against and prosecute.

According to Justice Stevens, RICO claims raise a very different set of considerations. Few RICO claims actually involve allegations of criminal conduct by mobsters. Civil RICO violations, like those allegedly involved in *McMahon*, are not essential claims in that they do not arise from organized crime's encroachment upon legitimate business. They are not, according to the Stevens's thinking, part of the primary concerns of the statutory framework. Moreover, there is no express statutory language evidencing a congressional intent to render such claims inarbitrable. Finally, there is no body of decisional law supporting the inarbitrability of civil RICO claims. Therefore, although the alleged violations in *Mitsubishi* were exactly the type of misconduct that the antitrust statutes were meant to prevent, the RICO violations alleged in *McMahon* cannot, realistically or analytically, be equated with the social evil that the RICO statute was intended to extinguish.

Taken in the context of the entirety of his opinions on arbitration, the Stevens dissent in *Mitsubishi*, then, does not so much reflect an insightful understanding of the institution of arbitral adjudication as such, but rather a studied concern for the role and integrity of antitrust regulation. As a whole, while the majority view in arbitration litigation focused upon the politics of judicial administration, Justice Stevens was preoccupied with either substantive juridical concerns or policies relating to the exercise of judicial authority. On either side of the equation, the Court, then, appears to have only a minimal regard for the integrity of arbitration itself.

For a discussion of Justice Stevens's judicial career and philosophy, see generally R. KAY, R. KHAYAT, J. ZIRKLE, A REFERENCE GUIDE TO THE UNITED STATES SUPREME COURT 329 (S. Elliott ed. 1986); 5 L. ORLAND, *John Paul Stevens,* in THE JUSTICES OF THE UNITED STATES SUPREME COURT OF THE UNITED STATES 149 (L. Friedman ed. 1978); *Tribute to John Paul Stevens,* 56 CHI.-KENT L. REV. 1 (1980); Riggs & McCarrey, *Justice Stevens and the Law of Antitrust,* 43 U. PITT. L. REV. 649 (1982). I am indebted to Craig E. Frosch for his research assistance in the writing of this appendix.

SECTION V. CHAPTER 6
Appendix A. *Selective Summary of Legislative Activity and Tort Reform Measures in Various States*

(source for data [summaries inclusive through January 1989]): 1 MEAL-EY'S LITIG. REP. NAT'L TORT REFORM Nos. 1-24 [1986-1987]; 2 MEAL-EY'S LITIG. REP. NAT'L TORT REFORM Nos. 1-24 [1987-1988]; 3 MEAL-EY'S INSURANCE ANTITRUST & TORT REFORM REP. Nos. 1-13 (1988-1989) [MEALEY'S].

This survey of the legislative activity in forty-eight states and the District of Columbia shows that the vast majority of state legislatures believe that there is some sort of crisis in tort litigation and a need to respond to it. Some states, like Connecticut, which had enacted early strong measures, however, are reconsidering the basic thrust of their legislative reforms. The most popular devices for curbing the would-be liability crisis include reinforcing the use of comparative negligence considerations; placing limitations on the dollar amount of recovery for noneconomic damages; limiting or disallowing the award of punitive damages and the application of joint and several liability; allowing the introduction of benefits from collateral sources; requiring itemized verdicts; redefining statutes of limitation; restricting attorney contingency fees; imposing sanctions for frivolous suits, defenses, or pleadings; encouraging structured settlements; allowing for periodic payments of future damages; and devising more stringent requirements for the qualification of witnesses as medical experts. Commonly, state legislation also requires or allows the arbitration or mediation of smaller civil claims or all medical malpractice claims. These "reforms" of the civil justice system usually are coupled with measures relating to insurance reporting requirements, rate changes, and cancellation or renewal policy practice.

ALABAMA. As a result of a task-force study, the Alabama state legislature passed a ten-bill tort reform package in 1987 that makes substantial changes in medical malpractice laws including a $250,000 ceiling on non-economic damage awards, a $1 million ceiling on general damage awards, a permissive structured payment system for future damage awards, and the abrogation of the collateral source rule and other evidentiary reforms

(H.B. 432). The legislation also places substantial restrictions on the award of punitive damages, sanctions frivolous suits, and provides for itemized verdicts and permissive periodic payments for future damage awards (H.B. 81). [1 MEALEY'S at 398, 2037-38, 2051.]

ALASKA. In June 1986, Alaska enacted the Limitations on Civil Liabilities Act (S.B. 377) that addresses issues affecting virtually all forms of civil liability. Among other provisions, the act limits noneconomic damage awards in all personal injury actions to $500,000 per claim, except for disfigurement or severe physical impairment (§ 9.17.010(a)); abolishes punitive damages except in circumstances in which the claim is supported by clear and convincing evidence (§ 9.17.020); prohibits recovery to convicted felons for personal injury or death substantially sustained as a result of commission of the felony (§ 9.17.030); requires itemized verdicts (§ 9.17.040); provides for proportional diminution of the award for compensatory damages based on the injured party's contributory fault (§ 9.17.060); allows introduction of evidence of compensation received from collateral sources with some limitations, the most notable being its inapplicability in medical malpractice actions (§ 9.17.070); and establishes a scheme for limitation of joint and several liability (§ 9.17.080(d)).

In April 1987, the state legislature enacted other measures placing a $100,000 cap on noneconomic damage awards and abolishing punitive damage awards in all cases but those in which there is convincing proof of fraud, malice, gross negligence, or reckless misconduct on the part of the defendant (S.B. 211, H.B. 7 & 88). The legislation also prohibits recovery of damages for injuries incurred during the commission of a felony; establishes permissive structured payments of future damages; grants tort immunity for certain classes of directors or officers in all cases in which no gross negligence occurred; permits the introduction of collateral source benefits; and establishes a restrictive joint and several liability formula. The November 1988 ballot included a provision for abolishing joint and several liability in favor of pure several liability. [1 MEALEY'S at 39, 388-89, 422-25, 1847-48; 3 MEALEY'S at 16-17 (Sept. 21, 1988).]

ARKANSAS. In addition to tort reforms proposed for the 1987 legislative session, a comprehensive insurance reform package was established (S.B. 509 and H.B. 1267). [1 MEALEY'S at 538, 1848, 1861-71.]

ARIZONA. Tort reform measures signed into law in early 1986 established penalties for filing frivolous suits (H.B. 2377) and restricted the liability of sellers of liquor (H.B. 2170). In addition, the legislature established joint underwriting associations for medical malpractice coverage

(H.B. 2418). The governor, however, vetoed five other tort reform measures that would have modified joint and several liability (H.B. 2013), allowed the introduction of collateral source benefits into evidence (H.B. 2163), limited attorney contingency fees (H.B. 2376), and allowed for itemized verdicts and structured settlements (S.B. 1378). He also vetoed medical malpractice insurance legislation (S.B. 1395) because it failed to abolish medical malpractice panels. The governor did sign into law new insurance regulations demanding increased disclosure for insurers writing property or casualty policies and requiring insurers to pay claims within thirty days after the provision of acceptable proof of loss. The new laws also guarantee medical malpractice insurance to qualified nurse-midwives and require arbitration in all cases of disputes up to $50,000 in value, although the court may waive the arbitration upon a showing of good cause and agreement by all parties.

In November 1986, voters defeated Proposition 103, a controversial tort reform package that would have allowed the legislature to enact laws providing for ceilings on noneconomic damage awards, structured settlements, and limits on attorney contingency fees. Evan Mecham, then the newly elected governor, signed into law legislation that abolished the doctrine of joint and several liability in all but exceptional circumstances and limited the award of punitive damages in all tort actions but those involving statutorily drunk drivers and those in which the victim was injured during the commission of a felony. The legislation also establishes medical malpractice review panels, provides immunity from civil liability to directors and officers of corporations who act in good faith (S.B. 1051), authorizes joint underwriting associations and risk-retention pools for non-profit corporations and organizations (S.B. 1094), and a comprehensive insurance reform act (S.B. 2034). In response, a consumer group proposed its own legislative agenda comprised of insurance reform measures. The fate of the consumer agenda remains to be determined. In July 1988, Governor Rose Mofford vetoed two medical malpractice bills which would have granted immunity to any physician during the delivery of a child if the mother did not receive prenatal care and which would have required periodic payments for medical malpractice awards in excess of $250,000. [1 MEALEY'S at 39, 159-62, 179-201, 391-92, 625, 823, 1537-39, 1624-26, 1911-13, 2034, 2073-85; 2 MEALEY'S at 915-16; 3 MEALEY'S at 3 (July 20, 1988).]

CALIFORNIA. California has been very active in pushing for insurance and tort law reform. On October 4, 1985, the California legislature passed Proposition 51 (The Multiple Defendants' Liability for Tort Damage Act), ending joint and several liability for noneconomic loss in tort cases, to which comparative fault principles are applied. The Fair Responsibility Act of 1986 led to the introduction of a variety of other tort reform measures. The act was subsequently challenged as unconstitutional (*Breit v. Los Angeles Superior Court,* No. B 021926). Its constitutionality in toxic tort and some products liability cases was eventually upheld. In addition, a number of California circuit courts are in major conflict over the retroactive application of the act. See, for example, *Russell v. Superior Court of Alameda County,* No. A0 35818 (Calif. 1st App. Dist.) (no retroactive application) and *Evangelatos v. Superior Court for Los Angeles County* and *Van Waters & Rogers v. The Superior Court for Los Angeles County*— Nos. B0 21968 and B0 22000 (Calif. 2d App. Dist.) (retroactively applied to pending cases). The California Supreme Court took the matter for consideration in the *Evangelatos* case and unanimously held that Proposition 51 was constitutional and, by a vote of 4 to 3, ruled that it did not apply retroactively.

In other litigation dealing specifically with medical malpractice, a California appellate court held that a doctor owes no duty of emergency care to a plaintiff and, therefore, is entitled to the immunity under the Good Samaritan laws. *Burciaga v. St. John's Hospital,* No. B017895 (Calif. 2d App. Dist.). Plaintiff alleged he suffered injuries during birth at the hospital. The defendant was a staff doctor; while visiting patients, he responded to an emergency call for a pediatrician. The court found that the physician did not have an existing duty to treat the plaintiff, and so acted as a volunteer and was shielded by the state's Good Samaritan law. Also, in *Cassandra Green v. Aram Franklin, M.D.,* No. B002436 (Calif. 2d App. Dist.), the court reversed a $5 million medical malpractice award upon finding that the trial court erroneously declared unconstitutional certain provisions of the Medical Injury Compensation Reform Act (MICRA), including the fixed-dollar limitation on noneconomic damages and periodic payments of future damages.

To date, the only tort reform legislatively adopted, in addition to Proposition 51, are five bills that add reporting requirements for insurers operating in the state. One act requires notice of cancellation or nonrenewal, and allows midterm cancellation only on specific grounds. Although no other legislation has been enacted, a report was issued in July 1986 by the Commission on California State Government Organization and Economy. The commission recommended seven tort reform and insurance regulation changes—including the establishment of a ceiling on noneconomic damages with a cost-of-living adjustment feature; stricter proof as the standard for awarding punitive damages; implementation of structured settlements for future damage awards in excess of $100,000; modification of the collateral source rule; and limitation of plaintiff's attorney

| 301

fees to one-third of amount recovered. As of early 1989, none of these recommendations had been implemented. In November 1988, the election ballot in California included five insurance reform initiatives. The insurance industry supported the measures which placed restrictions upon the current process of legal adjudication: Proposition 101 that placed limits on recoveries for bodily injury; Proposition 104 that proposed a no-fault system of auto insurance; and Proposition 106 that advocated a reduction of attorney contingency fees. The voters, however, endorsed Proposition 103, an anti-insurance industry measure that was supported by Ralph Nader. In *Calfarm Insurance Co v. Deukmejian,* the insurance industry asked the California Supreme Court to declare Proposition 103 unconstitutional because of its rollback and private corporation provisions and the standard it establishes for rate relief. The litigation and implementation of the legislation are pending. [1 MEALEY'S at 29-32, 107-18, 296-99, 374-78, 441-53, 526-29, 556-65, 611-12, 678-79, 707-25, 758, 1424-25, 1449-79, 1713-15, 1720-22, 1812-35, 1915-16, 1917-18, 1967-68, 1972-73, 1977, 2036-37; 2 MEALEY'S at 8-9, 11-13, 62, 68-70, 74-75, 108-28, 133, 136-39, 183-85, 207-08, 264-65, 279-81, 304-06, 330-31, 391-95, 444-60, 740, 798-99, 799-801, 910-12, 1336-38; 3 MEALEY'S at 17-18 (July 6, 1988), 11 (Aug. 3, 1988), 9 (Aug. 17, 1988), 14 (Sept. 7, 1988), 9 (Oct. 19, 1988), 6 (Nov. 2, 1988), 3 & 5 (Dec. 21, 1988), 3 (Jan. 4, 1989).]

COLORADO. The Colorado legislature has adopted several tort reform measures, including elimination of the collateral source rule (S.B. 67); limitation of noneconomic damage awards to $250,000 in nonexempt cases with a $500,000 ceiling (S.B. 67); imposition of a three-year statute of limitations applicable to most actions (S.B. 67) and the elimination of joint and several liability (S.B. 70); implementation of a formula tying punitive damages to actual damages (H.B. 1197); and a Good Samaritan law for paid volunteers (S.B. 76) and limitations in the liability of various classes of persons (S.B. 86, H.B. 1192, H.B. 1201, H.B. 1205). Insurance reforms have been instituted as well (H.B. 1193, 1204 and 1358). In May 1988, Governor Romer signed tort reform legislation which limits recoveries in medical malpractice actions to $1 million unless the plaintiff can prove more substantial costs or losses, limits noneconomic damages to $250,000, and requires periodic payments of awards in excess of $150,000 unless the court orders a lump sum payment. [1 MEALEY'S at 19-40, 154-55; 2 MEALEY'S at 11 (June 1, 1988).]

CONNECTICUT. Connecticut has enacted major reforms in its insurance laws (H.B. 5400) in addition to several tort reforms, including modification of joint and several liability; elimination of the collateral source rule; imposition of penalties for filing frivolous suits; permissive structured settlements providing periodic payments of noneconomic damage awards; and a sliding scale schedule of attorney's contingency fees. (H.B. 6134).

In 1986, Connecticut passed a comprehensive tort reform plan (Public Act. No. 86-338) that mandates a sliding scale for attorney contingency fees and allows itemization of damage awards and periodic payments as to certain future damages. In addition, the act abolishes joint and several liability and the last clear chance and assumption of the risk doctrines. It requires that awards be reduced by insurance and other benefits received. Since these reforms were enacted, however, the Connecticut legislature reevaluated the wisdom of some of the measures. A modified form of joint and several liability and the application of the collateral source rule were reinstituted (S.B. 1015). As of early 1989, the bills awaited the governor's signature. Insurance reform bills, granting the insurance commissioner greater rate review powers were also under consideration. (S.B. 116, H.B. 5292 and 5294). [1 MEALEY's at 40, 463-64, 481-86, 1442, 1971-72, 1993-2001.]

DELAWARE. The legislature enacted several insurance reforms, including an increase in required disclosure from insurers (H.B. 470). In addition, the liability of directors and stockholders of Delaware corporations was limited. [1 MEALEY's at 462-63.]

DISTRICT OF COLUMBIA. The Fair and Equitable Compensation for Injuries Act of 1987, introduced in February 1987, included provisions for a limitation of noneconomic damage awards to $350,000; slight modification of the rules regarding the application of joint and several liability; establishment of a comparative negligence system; increased proof requirements for the award of punitive damages; and other provisions. The reforms were to be applied only in personal injury, wrongful death, and property damage claims. [1 MEALEY's at 1444-45.]

FLORIDA. The Florida legislature enacted The Florida Tort Reform and Insurance Act of 1986. The act limits punitive damages to three times the compensatory damages award in all civil cases and provides that 60% of all punitive damage awards will be allotted to the Public Medical Assistance Trust Fund or to the state's General Reserve Fund. It also authorizes the forum court to order a settlement conference at least three weeks before the trial date; the conference to be attended by the attorneys who will conduct the trial, the parties, and persons with the authority to settle. The act also introduces other reforms including the abrogation of the collateral source rule; itemized jury verdicts; structured settlements in certain cases; penalties for unreasonable refusals to settle; modification of the doctrine of joint and several liability; allows courts to award reasonable attorney's fees in cases found to be frivolous; extends the Good Samaritan act immunity from civil liability to acts conducted inside a hospital or trauma center in response to a "code blue" emergency; and places increased reporting and other requirements on insurers operating in Florida.

Litigation by insurers challenging the constitutionality of the act have failed except with regard to those provisions requiring premium rebates. *American Ins. Ass'n v. State of Florida, Dept. of Insurance*, No. 86-2262 (Fla. App. 2d Cir.), 86-2272, 86-2362. Moreover, on April 23, 1987, the Florida Supreme Court, in *Smith v. State of Florida*, No. 69,551, upheld most sections of the act as they relate to tort reforms. Following a task-force study, the governor called a special session of the legislature to consider a comprehensive medical malpractice reform package which, among its features, imposes a ceiling on damages, and establishes arbitration procedures and a no-fault plan for recovery of birth-related neurological injuries (commonly called "the Virginia Plan"). The act creates the Division of Medical Quality Assurance within the state's Department of Professional Regulation (DPR), requires hospitals to appoint peer review panel members, and requires reporting of malpractice incidents to the DPR. [1 MEALEY'S at 3-11, 50-64, 58, 118-20, 152-53, 282-83, 413-21, 517-19, 576-602, 749-52, 766-87, 816, 911-12, 1101-02, 1414-20, 1905-08, 1925-41, 2124-26; 2 MEALEY'S at 3-4, 306-08, 398, 476-90, 1117-20, 1220-23; 3 MEALEY'S at 11 (July 6, 1988), 9 (Aug. 3, 1988), 16-17 (Sept. 21, 1988).]

GEORGIA. In 1986, the Georgia legislature enacted S.B. 384, which increased reporting requirements for insurers operating in the state, including providers of medical malpractice insurance. Information required annually includes a list of direct premiums on policies written and earned, net investment income realized, reserves available, actual claims made and expenses incurred, and net operating and underwriting gain or loss. Other bills passed require notice of termination or of increases in premium in excess of 15% by forty-five days before the date on which a policy lapses (H.B. 1503); authorize agreements among insurers, subject to the commissioner's approval, to apportion property and casualty insurance for individuals otherwise unable to obtain it (S.B. 553). Another bill provides sanctions that allow the award of attorney's fees and costs to a party against whom a frivolous suit is brought (H.B. 1146). H.B. 1268 would prevent insurers from cancelling or refusing to renew policies of automobile liability insurance for any reason other than those allowed by the commissioner of insurance.

304

In November 1986, the Governor's Tort Reform Advisory Committee recommended tort and medical malpractice reforms, increasing the power and funding of the State Board of Medical Examiners; granting immunity to all state hospital staffs, governing boards, and witnesses providing information regarding disciplinary matters; requiring the staff board to investigate physicians' records in other states or countries where they practiced before issuing a Georgia license; and requiring the state board to enforce rigidly the requirement that malpractice claims payments be reported to the state board. Other insurance reform matters were recommended for further study.

Proposals for tort reform include abolishing joint and several liability; requiring disclosure to the fact finder of collateral source benefits paid; amending the medical malpractice statute of limitations for minors' claims; establishing a ceiling on awards for punitive damages recoverable for nonintentional tort claims; requiring that affidavits by experts be filed in medical malpractice cases, setting forth each claim of negligence and the basis in fact for it; requiring that any insurance company writing medical malpractice coverage in the state make that coverage coextensive with the range of coverage afforded by fourteen other states; requiring structured payments of future medical expenses; and expanding the Good Samaritan Rule to apply to any noncompensated medical care, except in cases of gross negligence or willful and wanton conduct.

On March 17, 1987, the legislature passed the Tort Reform Act of 1987 and the Medical Malpractice Reform Act of 1987, but the Georgia ACLU filed suit against the measures, alleging their unconstitutionality because the details of the bills were worked out in closed session in violation of the state's open meeting law. The Georgia Supreme Court accepted the ACLU's challenge to the acts, although, on November 4, 1987, the court dismissed the ACLU's portion of the claim challenging the legislation on the ground that it violates House and Senate rules. *Am. Civil Liberties Union, Inc. v. Murphy,* No. D-40713. [1 MEALEY'S at 467-68, 759, 762-63, 798, 1018-19, 1081-90, 1108, 1130-40, 1319-20, 1635-36, 1696-1707, 1716-19, 1981-82; 2 MEALEY'S at 666, 707-09, 1292; 3 MEALEY'S at 13 (Oct. 5, 1988).]

HAWAII. The only reported legislation is a comprehensive tort and insurance reform package that provides for a 37% insurance rate roll back over three years; limits attorney's contingency fees through judicial review; imposes sanctions upon attorneys who file frivolous lawsuits or urge frivolous defenses; establishes a six-year statute of limitations for filing medical malpractice lawsuits for children over ten; repeals the collateral source rule; modifies joint and several liability for noneconomic damages in most cases; provides for periodic payments when an award exceeds the limitation of $375,000 for noneconomic damages; provides for mandatory, non-binding arbitration in cases with claims of $150,000 or less; and disallows recovery for emotional distress resulting exclusively from property damage. The state Supreme Court was ordered to adopt rules for implementation and administration of the program by January 1, 1987. The program applies to all civil tort actions. [1 MEALEY'S at 279-81, 324-338.]

IDAHO. In March 1987, the Idaho legislature passed tort reform measures that provide for periodic payments of future damages in certain cases; a $400,000 limitation on noneconomic damage awards; imposition of limits on punitive damages; reference to comparative fault to reduce awards; modification of the joint and several liability doctrine; allowing interest on rejected offers of settlements in certain instances; and sanctions for filing frivolous claims. Insurance reporting requirements also were increased. [1 MEALEY'S at 1851-53, 1872-79, 2040.]

ILLINOIS. In March 1986, the Illinois Supreme Court declared unconstitutional legislation requiring review of medical malpractice cases by a panel prior to trial. *Bernier v. Burns,* No. 62876, Agenda 36 (Mar. 1986, Ill. S.Ct.). The court, however, upheld other sections of the legislation: periodic payment of future damages; the collateral source rule that allows consideration of collateral source payments in some instances; the prohibition of punitive damages for medical or legal malpractice; and a sliding scale for attorney contingency fees.

In September 1986, the governor signed An Act in Relation to the Insurance Crisis. Among its many provisions are modification of conditions under which punitive damage awards can be made, and under which the doctrine of joint and several liability can be imposed. It changes the collateral source rule so that any medical benefits in excess of $25,000 are automatically deducted from the victim's award. Insurance companies are required to give sixty-day notice of nonrenewal or cancellation.

The governor called a special session in November 1986 to consider eleven other bills. [1 MEALEY'S at 26-28, 102-06, 150-51, 234-42, 389-91, 620-21, 818-19, 840-57.]

INDIANA. The Indiana legislature has enacted legislation that provides penalties for filing frivolous suits (S.B. 393) and modifies the collateral source rule (S.B. 394). A Good Samaritan law was enacted that applies to all volunteers unless the entity they assist has insurance that provides coverage for their acts or omissions (H.B. 1284). New reform measures were passed in August 1986, which create an insurance "pool" for political subdivisions (H.E.A. 1255). Senate Enrolled Act No. 398 allows sanctions for the filing of a frivolous claim or counterclaim. Senate Enrolled Act No. 394 eliminates the collateral source rule. [1 MEALEY's at 40, 393-94, 2131-32.]

IOWA. By June 1986, Iowa had passed legislation to establish review committees for medical malpractice claims. It also authorized structured settlements for medical malpractice claims (S.F. 2265) and the formation of insurance marketing assistance pools. On July 1, 1986, the governor signed S.F. 2265, enacting other tort reforms: establishing procedures that juries must follow in awarding punitive damages; modifying the liability of hosts in liquor liability cases; and disallowing claims against defendants who are not assemblers, designers, or manufacturers in strict liability cases based on defective design or manufacture. Other reforms include the establishment of a peer review panel for medical malpractice claims. Also, expert medical witnesses are defined as those whose medical qualifications relate directly to the medical problem at issue and the treatment in question.

The commission established to study liability insurance concerns issued a preliminary draft of its final report on December 15, 1986. It recommended that the Iowa Justice Department study alternative dispute resolution (ADR), make suggestions as to rule-making, legislation, funding, and personnel for alternative mechanisms, and study the possible impact of ADR reforms. The commission also recommended that contingency fee regulations not be imposed because contingency fee prohibition or restriction would not affect insurance availability and cost; that no action be taken on punitive damages or frivolous suits; that the legislature consider a statute of repose for licensed professionals; that the legislature enact a $200,000 limitation on the amount recoverable for noneconomic damages, require itemized verdicts, increase the use of structured settlements and judgments, and provide additional staff and funding for the Iowa Board of Medical Examiners

Three other bills passed the legislature, which establish stricter regulations of the insurance industry, mandate a formula for the award of pre-judgment interest, allow amounts paid through collateral sources into evidence, grant immunity to certain persons working for nonprofit organizations, and promulgate new standards for the award of punitive damages. (H.F. 506, S.F. 471 & 482). In May 1988, Governor Branstad vetoed legislation providing for a catastrophic injury fund for health care providers and hospitals, believing it was unwise to tax consumers for medical malpractice claims without taking action to solve these problems in another manner. [1 MEALEY's at 40, 386-88, 1222-27, 2039; 2 MEALEY's at 10 (June 1, 1988), 21 (May 4, 1988).]

KANSAS. Most legislative reform measures through June 1986 are in the area of medical malpractice. Total damage awards in medical malpractice suits are limited to $1 million; noneconomic damage awards are limited to $250,000. Juries in medical malpractice cases must itemize their verdicts. Further, H.B. 2661 allows for structured settlements. Other legislation establishes a health care stabilization fund to pay damages for personal injury or death arising out of malpractice claims subsequent to the time a provider qualifies for coverage. The fund is financed through surcharges and fees from the medical community. The fund has a $3 million cap on its potential payments for any one claim. The board of directors may terminate coverage for a health care provider who presents a material risk to the fund. The legislation also requires each medical care facility to establish and maintain an internal risk management program to analyze incidents of malpractice. It includes guidelines for reporting incidents of possible malpractice or impaired providers, and grants immunity to those who report or provide information in good faith about health care providers. Attorney's fees in medical malpractice cases must be approved by the judge.

Following the recommendations of the Kansas Citizens' Committee on Legal Liability, the governor signed into law three new tort-related measures in 1987, requiring itemized verdicts for all civil damage awards for personal injury claims, limiting the liability of directors, officers, and volunteers of nonprofit organizations, and limiting pain and suffering damage awards to the greater of $250,000 or the amount of economic losses, except in medical malpractice awards. On July 17, 1987, the Kansas Supreme Court held a law abrogating the collateral source rule to be unconstitutional as violative of the equal protection provisions of both the United States and Kansas constitutions. *Farley v. Engelker,* No. 59, 314. In subsequent litigation, the Kansas Supreme Court declared that caps on medical malpractice awards and annuity payments on future economic losses, provisions contained in the 1986 Kansas medical malpractice legislation, were unconstitutional. *Kansas Malpractice Victims Coalition v. Fletcher Bell,* No. 61. 945. (June 3, 1988).

Other bills pending in the 1987 session would allow periodic payments in personal injury awards without reduction to present value, allow judges to order separate trials to determine punitive damage awards in medical malpractice cases, impose a $250,000 ceiling on noneconomic damage awards in medical malpractice claims and limit the total amount recoverable to $1 million.

In 1988, Kansas Governor Michael Hayden signed into law Senate Bill No. 623, an insurance rate-making measure. The new law imposes requirements upon insurance companies which withdraw business from

Kansas and amends the rules pertaining to health care coverage. Moreover, insurance rates are not to be "excessive, inadequate, or unfairly discriminatory." The law also establishes the Kansas Health Care Stabilization Fund to cover health care providers for medical malpractice claims. The Governor also signed into law H.B. 2692 which reintroduces a $250,000 cap for noneconomic damages in medical malpractice actions and extends the cap limit to pain and suffering damages in all other liability actions. The Kansas Malpractice Victims Coalition challenged the new provision on the ground that it contravenes the Kansas Supreme Court's rulings in *Farley* and *Fletcher Bell* (above). Finally, the federal district court in Kansas certified to the Kansas Supreme Court the question of whether the $250,000 cap on noneconomic damages contained in the 1987 Kansas act is constitutional. *Douglas Samsel v. Wheeler Transport Services, Inc.*, No. 88-62983-S. [1 MEALEY'S at 40, 379-81, 410-12, 1102-05, 1141-98, 1853-54, 1974, 2027-29; 2 MEALEY'S at 205-06, 499-500, 1121-23, 1143-72, 1293-94; 3 MEALEY'S at 8 (July 6, 1988), 5 (Aug. 17, 1988), 12 (Dec. 21, 1988).]

KENTUCKY. The legislature has directed the Legislative Research Commission to appoint a task force to study and investigate insurance laws and regulations, the availability of insurance, the state's Department of Insurance, and the rate-making process. The task force, formed on July 1, 1987 and armed with subpoena powers, issued its recommendations in January 1988. Included in the recommendations are constitutional modifications to allow limitations to be imposed upon noneconomic damages, require more definite standards of conduct for the awarding of punitive damages, totally abolish joint and several liability, and impose sanctions for filing frivolous lawsuits. [1 MEALEY'S at 174; 2 MEALEY'S at 1009-13, 1040-92.]

LOUISIANA. Senate Bill 719 (Act No. 965) directs that all malpractice claims against the state be submitted to the Division of Administration, which will investigate claims, assemble the findings, and endeavor to settle the claim. If a claim is not settled, the act mandates submission of the claim to a medical review panel. Claimants have two years from the time of investigation to request a medical review panel. Use of the panel may be waived if both parties to the suit agree. House Bill 1932 (Act No. 574) prohibits risk pools and establishes liability trust funds set up primarily for the benefit of statewide hospital associations and nonprofit organizations. Finally, in June 1987, the Louisiana legislature enacted a modified and restrictive form of joint and several liability. In June 1988, Governor Roemer signed into law a product liability bill that significantly curtails the potential liability of product manufacturers. [1 MEALEY'S at 288-89; 2 MEALEY'S at 7; 3 MEALEY'S at 6 (July 6, 1988).]

MAINE. A Maine medical liability law (An Act Relating to Medical and Legal Professional Liability, Pub. L. ch. 804) provides for structured awards and limits contingency fees in medical malpractice cases. The new law places attorney contingency fees on a sliding scale and allows structured payments at the request of either party in medical malpractice cases that exceed $250,000. Any licensed health professional whose privileges are suspended must be reported to the appropriate board within sixty days. Fines are levied against insurers of the subject provider for the failure to report. The law also establishes panels to monitor mandatory pre-litigation screening.

The Commission to Examine Tort Litigation and Liability Insurance in Maine submitted a report in December 1987 that recommended no major changes in the tort system. The recommendation was based on a finding that tort reform legislation in other states had an extremely limited effect. One of the few changes recommended includes the development of an alternative dispute resolution system for civil claims.

A comprehensive worker's compensation bill was signed into law in November 1987; the law severely restricts the rights of injured employees and allows reduction of awards based on collateral sources, including social security payments. Lump-sum settlements are to be prorated on a monthly basis and deducted from disability retirement benefits, except when the settlement is for vocational rehabilitation, professional, or medical fees. Other reforms are included in the act.

The state's insurers have filed a class action suit seeking to find legislation directing them into an assigned risk pool to be unconstitutional (*Nat'l Council on Compensation Ins. v. Superintendent of Ins.*, No. KEN-87-223). [1 MEALEY'S at 41, 466-67; 2 MEALEY'S at 500-02, 745-48, 1131-33.]

MARYLAND. Senate Bill 558 provides that evidence of a defendant's financial means shall not be placed into evidence in a personal injury case, and caps noneconomic damages at $350,000. Itemized awards are required, and periodic payments are allowed in settlements. Additional requirements are mandated for insurers issuing liability insurance to health care providers. S.B. 600 grants immunity to officers of charitable organizations.

The Governor's Oversight Committee on Liability Insurance issued a report in January 1987 calling for tort reforms, including collateral source deductions and lowering the age at which the statute of limitations begins to run for minors with medical malpractice claims. In April 1987, legislation was enacted establishing a competitive rating system for workers' compensation insurance (H.B. 238), imposing new reporting requirements on general liability insurers (S.B. 236), and reforming medical malpractice laws

(S.B. 225 and 235). Also, in 1987, The Medical Injury Awards Modification and Remittitur Act (H.B. 1593) was passed, which requires mandatory arbitration of medical malpractice claims that had not reached trial. The Local Governments and Employees Tort Act was also passed, which limits the liability of local government employees (S.B. 237). As of early 1989, all these bills awaited the governor's signature. [1 MEALEY'S at 286, 1321-22, 1912-13.]

MASSACHUSETTS. A medical malpractice bill was signed into law in July 1986. It gives the insurance commission the power to adjust rates for changes in fixed and established medical malpractice insurance premiums. The law also establishes a medical malpractice bureau within the division of insurance to analyze and collect data and to advise the commissioner of insurance on requests for rate changes filed by joint underwriting associations. It authorizes the commissioner to make an assessment against the medical malpractice joint underwriting association to pay for the expenses of the bureau at a rate sufficient to produce $500,000 annually.

The act also provides that any licensed health care provider report denials, revocations, or restrictions placed on any board-qualified physician and the reasons for which such action was taken or resignation accepted. Section 9 of the act contains provisions for the suspension of a health care provider's privileges following review by a medical peer review committee. Such a provider is entitled to notice and a hearing. The proceedings of the medical peer review committee are to be confidential and immune from subpoena—although the original sources of the documents are not immune. All physicians registered in the commonwealth are required to renew their certificates of registration with the board at two-year intervals, and the board is authorized to require physicians to obtain malpractice insurance. The board is given investigative powers and the authority to revoke, suspend, or cancel a physician's certificate of registration.

In section 23, the act provides for a three-year statute of limitations for minors (from the date the cause of action accrues); for itemized jury verdicts in medical malpractice cases; and for the admission of collateral source payments, leading to a reduction in the award for amounts received, less premiums paid. Section 26 of the act limits awards for noneconomic damages in most medical malpractice cases to $500,000. Section 27 of the act mandates that attorney's fees be fair and reasonable and governed by a sliding scale; these limitations apply regardless of whether the recovery is obtained by settlement, arbitration, or judgment. Other provisions delineate requirements for rate increases, and provide for surcharges and credits for physicians within the system based on claims against them.

A task force appointed by the governor in March 1986 to study liability issues and recommend action concluded that liability insurance in Massachusetts failed to provide the coverage needed in several areas, including human service providers. Inadequate coverage was attributed to both unavailability and expense. Unavailability was found to be a particular problem in professional malpractice. Recommendations included changes in the insurance system and in the tort system. Suggestions included forming insurance pools, increasing reporting requirements, extending comparative fault principles to products liability cases, and modifying the current joint and several liability rule.

Other tort reforms under consideration include a plan of no-fault automobile insurance and a bill to make assumption of risk a complete defense in products liability cases. The latter bill also establishes that proof of a warning on a product would serve as a presumption that a plaintiff assumed the risk (H.B. 3676). Still another bill would allow the state-of-the-art defense in products liability cases (H.B. 2133). H.B. 1524 provides for sanctions in the amount of the opposing party's attorney's fees if a subsequently rendered trial court award does not match or exceed a settlement offer. Finally, H.B. 1354 proposes to abolish joint and several liability, reinstate the assumption of the risk defense, and provide for treble attorney's fees if a frivolous suit or defense is brought. [1 MEALEY'S at 285-86, 339-57, 1322-24, 1357-84; 2 MEALEY'S at 1347-49.]

MICHIGAN. Michigan enacted Public Act No. 173 (H.B. No. 5209) in July 1986 to revise insurance laws. The law imposes increased reporting requirements on insurers in the state and broadens the insurance commissioner's authority. Insurers are required to establish a merit-rating system for commercial liability rates, although such a rating plan for medical malpractice insurance may provide for a premium surcharge based upon the filing of an action against the insured (subject to certain limitations). The commissioner will prescribe the rating classifications for use by medical malpractice insurers after consultations with representatives of that group and physicians. The act also allows for the establishment of a limited liability pool by business and professional groups. All insurers of board-licensed physicians must report all malpractice claims made and the status of each claim to the commissioner.

The Michigan House of Representatives received a commissioned report by Casualty Actuaries, Inc. in November 1986, which concludes that the insurance industry, and not tort laws, is responsible for exorbitant premiums in liability insurance. The report documented the profitability of commercial liability insurance in Michigan, and compared rates in Michigan to those in other states, reviewed the potential impact of suggested legislation, and included recommendations for increased insurance availability and enforceability.

Legislation affecting medical malpractice claims, personal injury claims, and regulation of the insurance industry includes the following bills: H.B. 4676 requires medical facilities with medical staff to report to the appropriate licensing board and to the Department of Health any disciplinary action taken against a member of its medical staff. H.B. 5154 limits noneconomic damages in some less serious medical malpractice cases to $225,000. It also requires the trier of fact to itemize damages and plaintiffs with medical malpractice claims to file affidavits swearing that a written opinion from a licensed health care provider has stated that the claim or defense has merit, or the claim must be bonded for costs. Further, the act requires that pretrial mediation be implemented in all medical malpractice cases, regardless of the dollar amount of the claim. H.B. 5154 requires mediation in all other civil actions in which $10,000 or more is in controversy. In addition, the act makes the following changes applicable to all personal injury claims: collateral source evidence is admissible, joint and several liability is modified, and itemized judgments are required in cases in which judgment for future damages exceeds $250,000 gross at present value. House Bill 4231 proposes to respond to insurance concerns by requiring more stringent regulation of municipal pools created in the 1986 legislation.

In 1987, a task force was formed to study a possible modification of the state's products liability laws. Proposals include modification or repeal of the doctrine of joint and several liability, imposition of ceilings on noneconomic damage awards, abrogation of the collateral source rule, imposition of sliding scale fees in contingency fee cases, and other reforms.

In 1988, identical legislation was introduced in the state house and senate, proposing a number of tort reforms. The legislation seeks to require "clear and convincing" proof in products liability cases and provides that state of the art and governmental standards are defenses in such cases. The legislation also increases standards for qualifying as an expert witness; places a ceiling on noneconomic damages; limits contingency fees; imposes sanctions for filing frivolous claims; provides for itemized verdicts; and abrogates joint and several liability in proximate cause cases. [1 MEALEY'S at 385, 427-40, 1007-09, 1032-61, 1641-42; 2 MEALEY'S at 1294, 1346-47, 1406-11.]

MINNESOTA. Minnesota enacted several tort reforms in a single measure, including a $400,000 limitation on recovery for intangible losses; reduction of awards based on payment from collateral benefits; and sanctions for filing frivolous suits (H.F. 1950). S.F. 1612 allows the state's temporary joint underwriting association to issue medical malpractice insurance to hospitals and nursing homes.

A bill was passed in July 1986 enacting a comprehensive insurance and tort reform package. It requires that each insurer operating in the state file an annual report to show its national underwriting in various areas. The statute of limitations is extended in medical malpractice suits under certain circumstances. Collateral sources of payment may now be introduced. Itemized verdicts are mandatory, and joint and several liability is modified.

On November 17, 1987, a district court judge declared a statutory formula for discounting future damage awards violative of due process and a denial of a victim's right to full and fair compensation for injuries (*Ashton v. Group Health Plan, Inc.*, No. 473431). On December 16, 1987, a Minnesota appellate court held that the state's $100,000 limit of liability, applicable to state governmental units, is inclusive of interest and court costs (*Lienhard v. Minnesota*, No. C8-87-1002). An appeal was made to the state supreme court. [1 MEALEY'S at 41, 157-59, 201-34; 2 MEALEY'S at 797-98, 838-41, 1002-03, 1108-14.]

MISSISSIPPI. In August 1986, the state insurance board suspended all but "emergency" rate increases until January 1987, pending a study of insurance industry practices and rates. At that time, the Mississippi Senate Judiciary Committee heard testimony from a variety of groups, including the insurance industry, regarding the alleged insurance crisis and tort law. More than 150 insurance-related bills and a tort reform package have been introduced in the legislature. On February 9, 1987, the Mississippi Senate passed legislation that would establish a competitive rating law requiring increased disclosures by insurers and instituting a prior approval rate filing system.

The United States Supreme Court is reviewing the constitutionality of a statute passed by the Mississippi state legislature that provides sanctions for filing a frivolous appeal. The case involves an allegation of bad faith against an insurer brought by a Mississippi man who was denied benefits after he lost his leg in an accident-triggered disease. The award included $1.6 million in punitive damages against the insurer (*Bankers Life & Casualty Co. v. Crenshaw*, No. 85-1765 Miss. S.Ct.). [1 MEALEY'S at 461-62, 532-37, 681-82, 1107-08, 1318-19, 1539-41, 1651; 2 MEALEY'S at 795-97, 842-902.]

MISSOURI. As of July 1, 1986, Missouri had passed legislation limiting the award of noneconomic damages in medical malpractice suits to $350,000, requiring certain doctors to carry medical malpractice insurance, and also requiring the reporting of disciplinary actions taken by hospitals against doctors (S.B. 663). In June 1986, the governor signed into law legislation providing pooled liability insurance to public entities from a specially created fund (H.B. 1435 and 1461). A report from the Missouri Task Force on Liability Insurance concluded that both the insurance industry and civil justice system are to blame for the insurance crisis. The panel recommended changes in both insurance regulation and in the civil justice system. On March 11, 1987, the legislature passed an extensive insurance and tort reform package, based on task force recommendations. The insurance reforms include increased surplus line and capitalization regulation, increased cancellation notification periods, and a flex-rating system. The bill contained twelve substantive and procedural changes in tort law, including certain restrictions on products liability law (aimed at benefitting sellers), instituting comparative fault in products liability cases, slight modification of the collateral source rule, modification of the process for awarding punitive damages (so as to require a two-stage trial), as well as modification of the doctrine of joint and several liability when the victim is at least partially at fault. Ad damnum clauses are abolished completely. [1 MEALEY'S at 41, 167-68, 256-59, 1227-29, 1637-39, 1652-80.]

MONTANA. House Bill 16 establishes an insurance assistance plan to aid in resolving insurance availability problems in the state. It provides that if insurance remains unavailable through a voluntary plan, then a joint underwriting association, consisting of insurance carriers, will be established. A second new law created an interim study committee to evaluate insurance availability and affordability and issue a report at the next session.

Montana voters passed Ballot Initiative 30, clearing the way for legislatively enacted tort reform, the product of an attempt to circumvent court decisions declaring certain tort reforms unconstitutional. The initiative changed the Montana constitution to expand the power of the legislature to limit, modify, or abolish damages and responsibility for damages in civil suits. In May 1987, the State Supreme Court, however, struck down Ballot Initiative 30 because the language of the bill did not match that submitted to voters, as well as for another procedural irregularity.

Following voter passage of Ballot Initiative 30, the Governor's Council on Economic Development issued a preliminary report proposing eight tort reforms, including limitations on punitive damage awards at $5 million, to be decided by judges, not juries; limitations of attorney contingency fees to 40% of the award; and rules to enforce vigorously penalties for filing frivolous suits. In addition, the council recommended modification of the joint and several liability doctrine and the collateral source rule. Bills were introduced in the Montana legislature proposing changes in judges' ethical requirements (to require that judges report attorneys guilty of error to the state bar association), the payment of future damages, attorney's fees, the liability of employees of nonprofit organizations, and the insurance rating system. None of the bills had yet been passed as of early 1989.

In April 1987, the governor signed five tort reform bills into law that limit the liability of corporate officers, directors, and volunteers running rodeos for nonprofit organizations (H.B. 219); modify the doctrine of joint and several liability (several liability granted to a defendant who is 50% liable, or less) (S.B. 51); expand products liability legislation to implement strict liability (S.B. 380); and prohibit recovery in contract claims for emotional or mental damages, unless physical injury was also sustained by the victim (H.B. 167). [1 MEALEY'S at 41, 162-63, 821-22, 1230-31, 1443, 1975, 2126-27, 2206-14; 2 MEALEY'S at 9-11.]

NEW HAMPSHIRE. Legislation was enacted which, among its features, abolishes punitive damages (H.B. 513); imposes an $850,000 limitation on awards for noneconomic damages; imposes penalties for filing frivolous suits or defenses; empowers judges to review contingency fees in certain circumstances; and limits the operation of joint and several liability of municipalities. Attorneys are required to offer clients the option of paying fees on either a contingency fee basis or an hourly rate. Legislation modifies the comparative fault doctrine and imposes more stringent requirements for cancellation or nonrenewal of insurance policies. H.B. 513-FN also requires itemized verdicts, which are to be entered in judgment according to the rules of joint and several liability; it further provides that all claims for contribution may be resolved by arbitration in accordance with the rules of the American Arbitration Association. Further, the act abolishes awards for punitive damages and alters the plaintiff's burden of proof by requiring expert testimony — even in actions in which the plaintiff claims that a medical care provider failed to supply adequate information to obtain the informed consent of the injured party. The act limits recovery for noneconomic loss to $875,000 and establishes a Commission on Tort Law and Insurance Availability to study and make recommendations on tort law and insurance availability. [1 MEALEY'S at 41, 155-57, 260-65.]

NEW JERSEY. The New Jersey Senate passed seven tort reform measures in December 1986 that were sent to the state's Assembly Insurance Committee for consideration. Among other provisions, they modify joint and several liability (S.B. 2703); provide for structured verdicts when future damages exceed $200,000 (S.B. 2706); impose a $500,000 limitation on noneconomic damage awards (S.B. 2707); eliminate the collateral source rule (S.B. 2708); and construct an arbitration system for cases involving awards of $20,000 or less (S.B. 2709). Legislation designed to lower automobile insurance rates is under senate consideration. In return for a reduction in premiums, the bill would limit pain and suffering lawsuits to those actions involving "death, serious impairment of bodily function, or permanent and serious disfigurement."

In July 1987, the legislature passed a bill instituting reforms in products liability. The New Jersey American Trial Lawyers Association [ATLA] filed suit seeking to set the bill aside on grounds of its unconstitutionality. *In the Matter of the Assoc. of Trial Lawyers of America, New Jersey and Chapter 197 of the Laws of 1987*, No. AM-1450-87T2F, M-5689-87, N.J. Sup. Ct. App. Div. The bill sets both substantive and procedural limits on products liability actions and prohibits punitive damage awards unless such awards accompany compensatory damage awards. In December 1987, three tort reform bills were signed into law that modify the doctrine of joint and several liability when the defendant is a municipal government or a voluntary association and reduces awards by the amount received from collateral sources. In September 1988, Governor Kean signed into law a new no-fault auto insurance bill which will reduce premium rates for most drivers. [1 MEALEY'S at 171-73, 294-96, 1014, 1916-17; 2 MEALEY'S at 396-98, 744-1008, 1036-39, 1125-26, 1139-43; 3 MEALEY'S at 25 (Sept. 7, 1988), 5 (Sept. 21, 1988), 15 (Oct. 5, 1988).]

NEW MEXICO. A November 24, 1986, report by the New Mexico Interim Legislative Workmen's Compensation Committee on Liability Insurance and Tort Law Reform found that the insurance crisis in the state was not related to either the amount or quality of tort litigation. New Mexico enacted a Medical Malpractice Act in 1976 that limits liability to $500,000 per accident for nonmedical damages. The act also instituted a three-year statute of limitations that runs from the date of the subject incident, not the date of discovery. The report also noted that the New Mexico Supreme Court had abolished joint and several liability and instituted comparative negligence so that liability would be assessed in proportion to fault. Looking to the experience in other states, the report stated that there had been no concomitant reduction in insurance rates. Therefore, the report recommended no changes in the tort system, but did suggest several liability insurance reforms, including the creation of an independent Department of Insurance with a mandate to review and approve or reject rate increases. In April 1987, New Mexico enacted laws regarding rate-making legislation and reinstituting joint and several liability in certain classes of cases. [1 MEALEY'S at 1021-22, 1062-66, 1854-56, 1894-1902, 1913, 1962-63.]

NEW YORK. A bill signed into law on June 28, 1986, adopted a variety of reforms. The stated goal of the legislation is to make insurance more available and affordable, provide secure rates, and mandate increased disclosure by insurance companies. Among its many features, it provides for the establishment of joint underwriting associations in a variety of areas, including professional liability insurance, and increases the power of the superintendent of insurance to control rates and cancellations, as well as the renewal of policies. Further, it imposes sanctions for filing frivolous claims and counterclaims, and modifies the collateral source rule.

Senate Bill 9470, relating to medical malpractice, was passed on June 19, 1986. The Medical Malpractice Act empowers the superintendent of insurance to establish medical malpractice insurance rates, reduces lost earnings awards by assessing the effect of income taxes on lost wages, and institutes a system for establishing a claims-made policies program. The act authorizes and sets guidelines for medical malpractice insurance panels to be used by health maintenance organizations and establishes a system of arbitration in certain circumstances. However, disciplinary standards for medical professionals were increased. Assembly Bill 10664, passed at approximately the same time, demands new forms of disclosure for medical malpractice claims, modifies the rule of joint and several liability in certain circumstances, and requires juries to itemize verdicts. The bill allows periodic payments of future damages in verdicts exceeding $250,000. However, the bill extends the statute of limitations to three years from the date of discovery of injury, or the date an injured party should have discovered a latent disease or injury.

On September 9, 1986, the Department of Insurance issued new regulations enacting a flex-rating system in order to promote stability and predictability of insurance rate changes in problem markets involving vital coverages (including professional liability). Three insurance trade associations, six insurance companies, and two policyholders sued to have certain portions of the New York State Medical Malpractice Reform Act of 1986 declared unconstitutional. *Alliance of American Insurers v. Cuomo,* No. 87-Civ.-0169 (S.D.N.Y.). The plaintiffs claim violations of their Fifth and Fourteenth Amendment rights and contend that sections 40 and 80 of Chapter 266 deprive them of due process of law and constitute a taking of private property without just compensation (because the act prohibits medical malpractice insurers from seeking rehabilitation or liquidation for three years after insolvency occurs).

Legislation that would allow certain defenses, modify joint and several liability in order to restrict it to defendants found to be over 50% liable, and codify the defense of assumption of the risk in products liability cases was introduced in the legislature in 1988 (S. 6279).

In June 1988, Governor Cuomo signed into law Senate Bill 9065.

318

The law places new reporting requirements on medical malpractice insurers, establishes a medical malpractice liability pool, and creates a fund to supplement rates that may prove to be inadequate. The law also modifies medical malpractice procedures and laws relating to the designation of expert medical witnesses and the appeal of medical malpractice judgments. It makes pre-trial conferences mandatory in medical malpractice suits. [1 MEALEY'S at 32-33, 164-65, 243-55, 384, 606-07, 641-58, 1314, 1407-15, 1425-26, 1909-11; 2 MEALEY'S at 1131, 1172-76; 3 MEALEY'S at 7 (Aug. 3, 1988), 18 (Sept. 21, 1988), 10 (Dec. 21, 1988).]

NEVADA. A joint legislative commission studying medical malpractice insurance in Nevada issued a comprehensive report in late 1986 calling for extensive tort reforms and some changes in the state insurance system. Recommendations include modifying joint and several liability; granting immunity to independent contractors providing medical services to the Nevada prison system; requiring physicians to carry at least $500,000 in medical malpractice insurance or provide proof that they have such an amount available to them (insurance commissioner may, however, waive this requirement if coverage is unavailable or unaffordable); requiring insurance companies to inform the Board of Medical Examiners of policy cancellations; empowering the Board of Medical Examiners to examine the curriculum of foreign medical schools attended by license applicants; and allowing periodic payments in certain cases, at the discretion of the judge. [1 MEALEY'S at 1023.]

NORTH CAROLINA. A law was passed in July 1986 to revise and improve the regulation of commercial property and liability insurance rates and to increase reporting requirements placed on insurers (S.B. 873). The bill amends insurance laws by increasing the regulatory powers of the insurance commissioner as they relate to policy rates and cancellation of policies.

As of October 1987, the state legislature has reinstated the Medical Malpractice Reporting Act, which imposes annual reporting requirements upon insurers doing business in the state—including claims pending, settlements paid, amount of reserves and other information. The law also authorizes the commissioner of insurance to study medical malpractice claims brought in the state. [1 MEALEY'S at 284-85, 312-24; 2 MEALEY'S at 612, 643-52.]

NORTH DAKOTA. In the 1987 session, the North Dakota legislature enacted sweeping changes in the state's civil justice system. House Bill No. 1571 modifies comparative fault provisions, barring plaintiff recovery if plaintiff fault exceeds defendant fault, and otherwise reduces awards by the amount of plaintiff fault. Upon motion of a party, the court can direct the jury to itemize its damage verdict. Joint and several liability is reduced to several liability, unless defendants acted in concert. Other provisions direct the trier of fact to make separate findings on past and future economic and noneconomic damages; allow a modified collateral source rule; establish specific pleading requirements for claimants seeking noneconomic damages; and allow courts to reduce awards and to provide for periodic payments if a plaintiff will need medical care for more than two years in the future. [1 MEALEY'S at 626-27, 1324-25, 1725-26.]

OHIO. A major tort and insurance reform package passed by the Ohio House on September 4, 1986, would modify joint and several liability, limit the award of punitive damages, abrogate the collateral source rule, authorize periodic payments of future damage awards, penalize those who file frivolous suits, require a sixty-day notice of nonrenewal by insurers, increase insurance reporting requirements, expand the powers of the superintendent of insurance, and create a Joint Insurance/Civil Justice Reform Review Committee. In March 1987, the senate passed an amended version of the bill which the governor did not approve of and vetoed.

The Ohio legislature later promulgated legislation affecting medical malpractice claims that was signed into law on June 20, 1987. The act imposes a one-year statute of limitations and a four-year statute of repose for medical, dental, optometric, and chiropractic claims; allows for periodic payments of future damage awards in excess of $200,000; prohibits plaintiffs seeking more than $25,000 from specifying the amount sought; permits nonbinding arbitration; eliminates mandatory arbitration for medical claims; and grants civil immunity to volunteers of charitable, nonprofit hospitals. The Joint Select Committee on Insurance/Civil Justice Reform Review will monitor the effects of the new law. [1 MEALEY'S at 166-67, 273-76, 468-69, 529, 618, 1011, 1095-96, 1544-47; 2 MEALEY'S at 131, 387-91, 494.]

OKLAHOMA. Statewide tort reform was enacted on June 24, 1986, in the form of Senate Bill No. 488. The bill limits punitive damages, prohibits property and casualty insurers doing business in the state from engaging in unfair trade practices, and imposes increased reporting requirements on insurers in the state. A comprehensive rate-making and filing insurance reform bill passed in the House in May 1987, and went to a Joint Committee (S.B. 340). In May 1987, the governor signed into law tort reform measures that change the statute of limitations for minors with medical malpractice claims, establish sanctions for filing frivolous pleadings, and establish medical malpractice review panels.

Oklahoma's Select Committee on Insurance Rates and Tort Claims proposed the establishment of limitations on noneconomic damage awards (except in claims for bodily disfigurement); periodic payments in cases awarding more than $200,000—at the discretion of the courts; modification of the collateral source rule and statutes of limitations for products liability cases; limitations of interest on judgments (to the average United States treasury bill rate of the previous year); and establishing the defense of contributory negligence, as well as other reform measures. Insurance reforms have been recommended, and a flex-rating scheme has been put into law. [1 MEALEY'S at 24-26, 97-101, 373-74, 400-09, 520-22, 617-18, 680, 761-62, 1423-24, 1715-16, 1726-28, 1982-83, 2132; 2 MEALEY'S at 912-14.]

OREGON. The Oregon Task Force recommended a variety of changes in tort law and insurance reforms that were proposed as legislation. Senate Bill 323, a controversial proposal, would overhaul the tort system as it pertains to punitive damage awards, narrowly defining conduct warranting the award of such damages. It would limit noneconomic damage awards to $500,000 and allow the introduction of collateral sources into evidence. It would also modify joint and several liability so that those less than 20% at fault are severally, but not jointly, liable, and require juries to itemize verdicts about both percentages of fault and amounts awarded. It calls for the commissioner of insurance to establish a market assistance plan and increases reporting requirements for most forms of insurance. It would also prohibit midterm policy cancellations and cancellation of policies without proper justification. Senate Bill 324 would institute increased filing requirements for insurers and increase the commissioner's power to control rates. It also asks the state to set up a Department of Insurance. Senate Bill 325 would change court procedures regarding crossclaims, counterclaims, and discovery.

On June 27, 1987, the Oregon legislature enacted legislation that adopts most of the task-force recommendations. It also establishes criminal activity of the claimant as a defense to a tort claim, imposes a state version of Rule 11 (to be imposed against attorneys who file frivolous pleadings), and requires that an attorney's contingency fee contract be made in writing. [1 MEALEY'S at 300-03, 1232-36, 1325-29, 1728-29; 2 MEALEY'S 4-7, 19-43.]

PENNSYLVANIA. On October 1, 1986, the Pennsylvania House of Representatives passed an insurance investment bill calling for several insurance regulation reforms (H.B. 934). The bill increases reporting requirements on insurers regarding their loss experience by claims areas. It proposes a liability underwriting services plan to service commercial and public entity commercial liability policyholders and the creation of a standby joint underwriting association for general liability insurance coverage. It increases the insurance commissioner's powers of review and restricts carrier withdrawal by implementing its own withdrawal system.

The House Insurance Committee issued a report recommending tort reform measures, including the imposition of penalties against attorneys for filing frivolous suits and defenses, limitations on the award of punitive damages, and the encouragement of structured settlements. These bills have not yet gone before the Pennsylvania Senate. The reforms were included in a twelve-point tort reform proposed by the governor. Corporate officers are immune from liability in most circumstances. Other proposed reforms include a shift of the initial review of tort claims from judicial to administrative proceedings subject to a right of appeal for a trial in the common pleas court. The Pennsylvania Supreme Court has held legislation limiting recovery against political subdivisions of the state unconstitutional (*Smith v. City of Philadelphia,* Nos. 70, 71 and 74, App. Doc. 1984, Pa. S. Ct.).

In August 1988, a number of tort reform measures were introduced in the Pennsylvania state legislature to overcome the legislative stalemate occasioned by the inaction of the House Judiciary Committee. The seven bills provide penalties for filing frivolous suits, modify the collateral source rule, amend joint and several liability, reduce jury awards to present worth, alter the standard for awarding punitive damages, and call for changes in the product liability and medical malpractice laws. [1 MEALEY'S at 168-70, 623-25, 675-76, 684-85, 698-704, 1014, 1630; 3 MEALEY'S at 15 (Sept. 21, 1988).]

RHODE ISLAND. The Rhode Island legislature enacted a new medical malpractice law that took effect in October 1986. It was passed in response to the financial drain recently experienced by the Medical Malpractice Joint Underwriting Association of Rhode Island. The law imposes increased reporting requirements on medical malpractice carriers, including sharply detailed annual reports to be submitted to the medical licensing board. The law also requires the insurers to report lawsuits against health care professionals. Section 2 establishes a merit-rating plan, based on claims filed, to determine appropriate rates; it freezes rates through June 30, 1987. Section 3 requires all licensed health care providers to be covered by professional liability insurance. Section 4 creates a special legislative commission to study the rate structure, deficit, and the method of charging health and dental care providers (by the medical malpractice joint underwriting association and other medical and dental malpractice insurers in the state), and their effect on health care costs in Rhode Island.

Section 5 limits expert witnesses in medical malpractice cases to those health care providers qualified as experts in the particular field about which they are testifying. Section 6 imposes sanctions for frivolous lawsuits in the malpractice area. Section 7 allows the admission of collateral source evidence for the purpose of reducing awards in medical malpractice actions. Section 8 allows for 12% interest on jury verdicts, and section 9 compels parties to consider periodic payments for awards in excess of $100,000. Section 10 provides for expedited trials in medical malpractice cases by granting docket priority.

Section 11 provides immunity from suit to the director of health care and board members; it also protects any person reporting to, giving testimony to, or communicating with the board of health, a peer review organization, or any supervisory personnel concerning unprofessional conduct, incompetence, or negligence — as long as the report is made in good faith. Section 12 provides privileges and immunities for peer review activities. Both the proceedings and the records are immune from discovery, although restrictions or requirements imposed on physicians for "professional conduct" are subject to discovery and admissible in proceedings against the health care provider, physician, or health care facility.

In 1987, the governor introduced a package of nine tort law proposals to the legislature which, among others, includes provisions to allow collateral source benefits into evidence; abrogate joint liability for noneconomic damages; mandate a conference to consider periodic payments for awards of $150,000 or more; impose sanctions for the filing of frivolous suits, pleadings, and motions; allocate 90% of all punitive damage awards to the state; require itemized verdicts; disallow ad damnum clauses; and limit the liability of certain volunteers and public bodies. [1 MEALEY'S at 458-60, 486-92, 763, 1729-30; 2 MEALEY'S at 1000-01, 1099-1103.]

SOUTH CAROLINA. South Carolina enacted major tort reforms in 1986. These include enactment of a restricted three-year statute of limitations, the elimination of both the collateral source rule and the joint and several liability doctrine, and imposition of a limitation of $250,000 on the amount recoverable for noneconomic damages. Reforms also include limits on punitive damage awards. In March 1988, a comprehensive tort reform proposal (H. B. 2610) was passed by the House and the Senate Judiciary Committee in the legislature; the proposal includes a restriction on punitive damage awards — limited to those cases in which a compensatory damage claim is awarded, as well as revised statutes of limitations (three years) in ordinary tort and medical malpractice cases with an exception for minors alleging a medical malpractice claim. In addition, the act limits the circumstances under which a manufacturer can be held liable to a consumer, and it calls for contribution among joint tortfeasors. [1 MEALEY'S at 287-88, 1642-43; 2 MEALEY'S at 1233-34.]

SOUTH DAKOTA. The 1986 legislature enacted measures limiting the award of punitive damages to instances in which proof of willful and malicious conduct is made (S.B. 280), and limiting medical malpractice awards to $1 million (S.B. 282). On March 17, 1987, the governor signed into law six new tort reform measures (modifying the doctrine of joint and several liability, limiting the liability of directors of profit and nonprofit corporations, and empowering cities, counties, and school boards to form risk-sharing pools). [1 MEALEY'S at 42, 1719-20.]

TENNESSEE. House Bill 1582, enacted in 1986, with some exceptions, prohibits cancellation and nonrenewal of commercial liability policies. Another act grants civil immunity to directors of certain nonprofit organizations, electrical cooperatives, and membership corporations, as well as to certain governmental entities. The Governor's Task Force on Tort Liability Insurance Reform issued a report in December 1986. Concluding that expanded tort liability has resulted in an insurance "crisis," the panel recommended tort reform proposals that include the imposition of limitations on the amounts recoverable for noneconomic damages; abolition of the doctrine of joint and several liability except in those circumstances in which subrogation rights exist in favor of the payer, and of the collateral source rule, as well as of the award of punitive damages. It also recommends that expert witnesses in medical malpractice cases practice in Tennessee, and that physician witnesses be in the active practice of medicine in the same field as the defendant. In addition, the panel recommended that trials be conducted on a one-day, one-trial system, and that occupational exemptions for prospective jurors be abolished. The panel also recommended several insurance reforms. Five panel members dissented from the conclusions, feeling that those conclusions are groundless and detrimental to consumers. [1 MEALEY'S at 42, 1236-39.]

TEXAS. The Texas Joint Committee Report on Liability Insurance and Tort Law Procedure, released on January 22, 1987, called for a balanced package of insurance and tort law reforms. The tort law reforms include the imposition of limitations on the amounts recoverable for noneconomic damages; abolition of the collateral source rule; imposition of limitations on the amount of attorney's contingency fees; abolishes the joint and several liability doctrine; institutes a periodic payment system for the payment of personal injury judgments in excess of $100,000; and allows sanctions for filing frivolous claims. The recommended insurance reforms are mandatory reporting of any physician misconduct constituting grounds for denial or revocation of a medical license, and requiring mandatory reporting by licensed physicians of any sanctions taken against them. It also recommended extending a grant of immunity to any health care provider who charges another health care provider with incompetent professional behavior (based on reasonable evidence).

On June 3, 1987, the governor signed into law a comprehensive tort reform package that includes the imposition of more rigid standards for insurance reporting, sanctions for filing frivolous claims, establishment of a Division of Consumer Protection in the State Board of Insurance, institution of a comparative fault provision, limitations on the award of punitive damages and on government liability, formulae for establishing pre-judgment interest, and establishment of risk-management pools. In May 1988, the Texas Supreme Court held that the statutory cap on medical malpractice legislation, set at $500,000 and enacted by the Texas legislature in 1987, was unconstitutional because it failed to guarantee plaintiffs' right to legal remedies. *Richard Lucas v. U.S. of America*, No. C-6181. [1 MEALEY's at 173, 1435-41, 1629-30, 1984-86, 2035, 2128-31, 2140-2203; 2 MEALEY's at 12 (May 18, 1988).]

UTAH. In 1986, the legislature repealed joint and several liability (S.B. 64), established limitations on the amount recoverable for noneconomic damages to $100,000/$300,000, established a two-year statute of limitations in this area (S.B. 182), and enacted a law limiting recovery in medical malpractice claims to $250,000 (S.B. 155). Insurance reforms were also instituted. [1 MEALEY's at 42.]

VIRGINIA. The Virginia State Corporate Commission issued an order on September 10, 1986, authorizing the formation of a joint underwriting association as a nonexclusive source of medical malpractice liability insurance for physicians and surgeons. Virginia circuit courts have found unconstitutional the state's medical malpractice law placing a $1 million limitation on awards. One case involved a child suffering from cerebral palsy, quadraplegia, and blindness as a result of the attending physician's refusal to be monitored. As a consequence, the physician was not present when an emergency arose during the child's birth. *Boyd v. Bulala*, No. 83-0557-A-C (W.D. Va. Charlottesville Div.). In another case, the attending obstetrician failed to disclose the presence of abnormal cells revealed by a pap smear. *Williams v. Van Der Woude* No. 70286 (Cir. Ct. Fairfax Cty.). Both judges concluded that the limitation interfered with the victims' right to a jury trial by mandating the amount of judgment that could be awarded. [1 MEALEY's at 683, 739-40, 907-08, 989-1004, 1019-21, 1108-09, 1208, 1240-54, 1428-34, 1508-30, 1639-41.]

VERMONT. Vermont has instituted a package of insurance reforms, including a law allowing the formation of joint underwriting associations (H.B. 657, Act. No. 265). The act sets notice requirements for the cancellation of insurance policies.

Pending H.B. 660 calls for a finding of actual malice or fraud as a condition precedent to an award of punitive damages; it requires itemized verdicts, and periodic payments of awards over $100,000; it would modify joint and several liability and the collateral source rule; and it requires mandatory arbitration of claims over $50,000. [1 MEALEY'S at 286-87; 2 MEALEY'S at 1235.]

WASHINGTON. Senate Bill No. 4630 limits attorney's fees and noneconomic damage awards; it modifies joint and several liability; and it changes the statute of limitations in medical malpractice suits to three years from the date of the act or one year from the time the patient knew, or should have known, of the cause of the injury. The Washington State Trial Lawyer's Association (WSTCA) challenged the constitutionality of the bill on the ground that it violates due process and equal protection. WSTCA argued that the act places arbitrary limitations on noneconomic damage awards, thereby denying claimants due process and equal protection by taking away valuable property rights. There is no report on the outcome of this litigation.

A Washington Supreme Court judge has issued a preliminary ruling that the act, which went into effect in August 1986, is unconstitutional because, in limiting awards for noneconomic damages in tort claims, a victim's right to a jury trial and guarantees of equal protection are violated (*Foster v. Fibreboard Corp.*, No. 87-2-05629-5). In September 1986, another court held that the statutory abolition of the doctrine of joint and several liability does not apply to asbestos litigation because asbestos is a hazardous substance. The court, however, upheld the constitutionality of the statutory ceiling on noneconomic damages. (*Sofie v. Fibreboard Corp.*, No. 87-2-000107-6.) The question of the constitutionality of the statutory ceiling on noneconomic damages is now before the Washington Supreme Court. *Austin Sofie v. Fibreboard Corp.*, No. 54610-0.

In addition, a state-created panel directed to study the 1986 Tort Reform Act has recommended numerous amendments, including a repeal of the limitation on recovery of noneconomic damages. In May 1987, the governor signed into law a modification of certain provisions of the Tort Reform Act of 1986; the amendments liberalize the act. [1 MEALEY'S at 18-20, 90-96, 1541-44, 2133; 2 MEALEY'S at 400-01, 460-470, 494, 662-65, 681-91; 3 MEALEY'S at 18 (Sept. 7, 1988), 9 (Sept. 21, 1988), 10 & 6 (Oct. 5, 1988), 7 (Oct. 19, 1988).]

WEST VIRGINIA. An emergency amendment to the West Virginia Medical Malpractice Act modifies joint and several liability for malpractice suits and limits the amount recoverable for noneconomic damages (H.B. 149). It also gives the insurance commissioner increased review powers, imposes more extensive reporting requirements on insurance companies, and imposes fines on insurers who fail to comply. The West Virginia Medical Malpractice Act establishes a Board of Medicine, provides for disciplining of medical personnel, sets rate-making procedures for medical malpractice insurance and procedures to review rates, specifies pretrial procedures, limits recovery for noneconomic losses to $1 million, and sets standards for expert testimony on the standard of care. [1 MEALEY'S at 11-17, 78-89, 368, 1329-31, 2136-37.]

WISCONSIN. New tort reforms were enacted at a 1986 special session of the legislature, setting a $1 million limitation on recovery of noneconomic damages in medical malpractice actions, limiting attorney's fees by establishing a sliding scale for contingency fees, and mandating itemized verdicts. The measures also authorize risk-sharing pools for liability coverage of both the public and private sectors. Act 340 requires a hospital to notify the medical examining board (created by the act) if a licensed staff member loses staff privileges for thirty days or more as a result of a peer investigation. Among many other features, the act provides immunity to censuring bodies and peer review committees acting in good faith, and establishes a mandatory pre-litigation mediation system. A request for mediation may also be filed in conjunction with a court action. The legislation also provides for the appointment of the mediation panel and establishes a mediation procedure.

Legislation was under consideration that includes implementation of a comparative negligence rule, allows the introduction of collateral source payments for the purpose of deducting them from damage awards, regulates attorney's contingency fees, modifies the application of the rule of joint and several liability, limits awards of punitive damages, and establishes a $250,000 limitation on all noneconomic damage awards. [1 MEALEY'S at 42, 289-90, 358-68; 2 MEALEY'S at 612-13, 643-52.]

WYOMING. As of July 1986, the Wyoming legislature, which has been very active in tort reform, had passed acts to modify standards of care used to determine medical malpractice (H.B. 12), impose sanctions on those who file frivolous lawsuits (H.B. 14), define unfair insurance claims (H.B. 15), grant immunity to certain government officials for errors of omission (H.R. 39), establish pretrial screening panels for medical malpractice suits (H.B. 40), repeal the joint and several liability doctrine (S.F.

17), and prohibit mid-term cancellation of insurance policies in certain circumstances (S.F. 69). [1 MEALEY'S at 42.]

Index

Note on the Author

THOMAS E. CARBONNEAU is a graduate of Bowdoin College; he studied French literature in Paris and at l'Université de Tours. As a former Rhodes Scholar, the author holds degrees from Oxford University; he was in residence at St. John's College. His legal education and interest in comparative and international law began at the University of Virginia, where he earned a J.D., and continued at Columbia University, where he earned an LL.M. and a J.S.D. degree, the latter for a dissertation on international commercial arbitration. His interest in alternative dispute resolution arose from his work on international arbitration and the study of social and individual values in literary texts. The author is professor of law and deputy director of the Eason-Weinmann Center for Comparative Law at Tulane University School of Law in New Orleans.

CABONNEAU